FOR DUMMIES®

The fun and easy way™ to travel!

U.S.A.

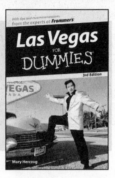

Also available:

Alaska For Dummies
Arizona For Dummies
Boston For Dummies
California For Dummies
Chicago For Dummies
Colorado & the Rockies For Dummies
Florida For Dummies
Los Angeles & Disneyland For Dummies
Maui For Dummies
National Parks of the American West For Dummies

New Orleans For Dummies
New York City For Dummies
San Francisco For Dummies
Seattle & the Olympic Peninsula For Dummies
Washington, D.C. For Dummies
RV Vacations For Dummies
Walt Disney World & Orlando For Dummies

EUROPE

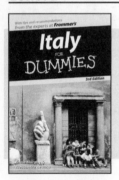

Also available:

England For Dummies
Europe For Dummies
Germany For Dummies
Ireland For Dummies
London For Dummies

Paris For Dummies
Scotland For Dummies
Spain For Dummies

OTHER DESTINATIONS

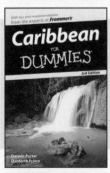

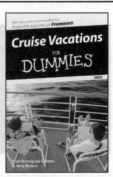

Also available:

Bahamas For Dummies
Cancun & the Yucatan For Dummies
Costa Rica For Dummies
Mexico's Beach Resorts For Dummies
Montreal & Quebec City For Dummies
Vancouver & Victoria For Dummies

Available wherever books are sold.
Go to www.dummies.com or call 1-877-762-2974 to order direct.

19.99

Rome For Dummies,
2nd Edition

Cheat Sheet

St. Peter's Basilica

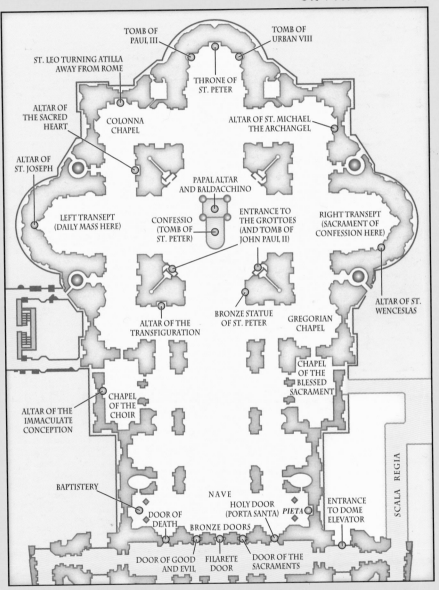

TOMB OF
PAUL III

TOMB OF
URBAN VIII

ST. LEO TURNING ATILLA
AWAY FROM ROME

THRONE OF
ST. PETER

ALTAR OF
THE SACRED
HEART

COLONNA
CHAPEL

ALTAR OF ST. MICHAEL
THE ARCHANGEL

ALTAR OF
ST. JOSEPH

PAPAL ALTAR
AND BALDACCHINO

LEFT TRANSEPT
(DAILY MASS HERE)

CONFESSIO
(TOMB OF
ST. PETER)

ENTRANCE TO
THE GROTTOES
(AND TOMB OF
JOHN PAUL II)

RIGHT TRANSEPT
(SACRAMENT OF
CONFESSION HERE)

ALTAR OF ST.
WENCESLAS

ALTAR OF THE
TRANSFIGURATION

BRONZE STATUE
OF ST. PETER

GREGORIAN
CHAPEL

CHAPEL
OF THE
BLESSED
SACRAMENT

ALTAR OF THE
IMMACULATE
CONCEPTION

CHAPEL
OF THE
CHOIR

SCALA REGIA

BAPTISTERY

NAVE

HOLY DOOR
(PORTA SANTA)

PIETA

ENTRANCE
TO DOME
ELEVATOR

DOOR OF
DEATH

BRONZE DOORS

DOOR OF GOOD
AND EVIL

FILARETE
DOOR

DOOR OF THE
SACRAMENTS

The Sistine Chapel Ceiling

Brazen Serpent	Prophet Jonah	Punishment of Haman
Libyan Sibyl	Separation of Light from Darkness	Prophet Jeremiah
	Creation of the sun, moon and planets	
Prophet Daniel	Separation of Land from Sea	Persian Sibyl
	Creation of Adam	
Cumaean Sibyl	Creation of Eve	Prophet Ezekiel
	Original Sin and Banishment from the Garden of Eden	
Prophet Isaiah	Sacrifice of Noah	Libyan Sibyl
	The Flood	
Delphic Sibyl	Drunkenness of Noah	Prophet Joel
Judith and Holofernes	Prophet Zechariah	David and Goliath

Rome
FOR
DUMMIES®
2ND EDITION

by Bruce Murphy and Alessandra de Rosa

Wiley Publishing, Inc.

Rome For Dummies®, 2nd Edition

Published by
Wiley Publishing, Inc.
111 River St.
Hoboken, NJ 07030-5774
www.wiley.com

914.5632

MUR

WILEY

About the Authors

Bruce Murphy has lived and worked in New York City, Boston, Chicago, Dublin, Rome, and Sicily. His work has appeared in magazines ranging from *Cruising World* to *Critical Inquiry.* In addition to guidebooks, he has published fiction, poetry, and criticism, most recently the *Encyclopedia of Murder and Mystery* (St. Martin's Press).

Alessandra de Rosa was born in Rome and has lived and worked in Rome, Paris, and New York City. She did her first cross-Europe trip at age 2, from Rome to London by car. She has continued in that line ever since, exploring three out of five continents so far. Her beloved Italy remains her preferred destination and is where she lives part-time.

Authors' Acknowledgments

Thank you to our wonderful development editors, Alexia Travaglini and Marie Morris, who have helped us make this book better.

Publisher's Acknowledgments

We're proud of this book; please send us your comments through our Dummies online registration form located at www.dummies.com/register/.

Some of the people who helped bring this book to market include the following:

Editorial

Editors: Marie Morris with Alexia Travaglini, Development Editors; Jana M. Stefanciosa, Production Editor

Copy Editor: Cara Buitron

Cartographer: Roberta Stockwell

Senior Photo Editor: Richard Fox

Cover Photos: Front cover: ©Travelpix Ltd/Getty Images, Back cover: © Wilmar Photography / Alamy

Cartoons: Rich Tennant (www.the5thwave.com)

Composition Services

Project Coordinator: Katherine Key

Layout and Graphics: Carl Byers, Joyce Haughey, Laura Pence

Proofreaders: Caitie Kelly, Sossity R. Smith

Indexer: Slivoskey Indexing Services

Publishing and Editorial for Consumer Dummies

Diane Graves Steele, Vice President and Publisher, Consumer Dummies

Joyce Pepple, Acquisitions Director, Consumer Dummies

Kristin A. Cocks, Product Development Director, Consumer Dummies

Michael Spring, Vice President and Publisher, Travel

Kelly Regan, Editorial Director, Travel

Publishing for Technology Dummies

Andy Cummings, Vice President and Publisher, Dummies Technology/General User

Composition Services

Gerry Fahey, Vice President of Production Services

Debbie Stailey, Director of Composition Services

Contents at a Glance

Maps at a Glance

Table of Contents

Introduction

• •

*R*ome, the Eternal City, the capital of the ancient Roman Empire and of the modern Italian state, is a city with many faces and myriad charms. Its history is epic — the city vanquished Carthage and was itself sacked by barbarians, saw the birth and development of the Catholic Church, suffered fascism and World War II — and is written in its monuments and ruins. Rome is also one of the most beautiful cities in the world, and more tourist friendly than ever. With its noise, traffic, and meandering streets, Rome can be bewildering. But you'll find Romans warm, welcoming, and ready to help ease you into *la dolce vita,* particularly if you learn a few key words and phrases in Italian (we list some of them throughout this book and especially in Chapter 17 and Appendix B).

About This Book

Whether you're a first-timer or making a repeat visit to see sights you missed the on first go-round, *Rome For Dummies* is designed to give you all the information you need to help you make savvy, informed decisions about your trip, while also guiding you to the discovery of known and lesser-known facets of this exciting city.

You'll be able to use this guide as a reference book to look up exactly what you need at the time you need it. No need to read the entire thing from cover to cover — you can just dive in at any point. No need, either, to remember what you read: There are plenty of easy-to-find flags for quickly locating the bit of info you want.

Some people spend more time planning their trip than they do taking it. We know your time is valuable, so here, we happily do the work to help ease you into a memorable Roman holiday. Unlike some travel guides that read more like phone books, listing everything and anything, this book cuts to the chase. We've done the legwork for you, offering our expertise and not-so-humble opinions to help you make the right choices for your trip.

Please be advised that travel information is subject to change at any time — and that this is especially true of prices. We therefore suggest that you write or call ahead for confirmation when making your travel plans. The authors, editors, and publisher cannot be held responsible for the experiences of readers while traveling. Your safety is important to us, however, so we encourage you to stay alert and be aware of your surroundings. Keep a close eye on cameras, purses, and wallets, all favorite targets of thieves and pickpockets.

Conventions Used in This Book

The structure of this book is nonlinear: You can open it at any point and delve into the subject at hand. We use icons to guide you toward particular kinds of tips and advice (see "Icons Used in This Book," later in this introduction).

We include lists of hotels, restaurants, and attractions, and for each we give you our frank evaluation. We divide the hotels into two categories: our personal favorites and excellent choices that don't quite make our preferred list but still get our hearty seal of approval. Don't be shy about considering these "runner-up" hotels if you're unable to get a room at one of our favorites, or if your preferences differ from ours.

We use these abbreviations for commonly used credit cards in our hotel and restaurant reviews:

AE: American Express

DC: Diners Club

MC: MasterCard

V: Visa

Note that Discover is not listed. The Discover Card is unknown in Italy, so carrying one or more of the big three — American Express, Visa, and MasterCard — is a good idea.

We also include some general pricing information to help you as you decide where to unpack your bags or dine. We use a system of dollar signs to show a range of costs for one night in a hotel (the price refers to a double-occupancy room) or a full meal at a restaurant — including a pasta or appetizer, a *secondo* (main course or entree), a side dish, and a dessert (but no beverages). Note that within the restaurant listing info, we give you the price range for main courses, or *secondi*. See Chapter 9 for a detailed chart telling you exactly what to expect in each hotel category. Here is a table to help you decipher the dollar signs:

Cost	Hotel	Restaurant
$	140€ ($182) or less	35€ ($46) or less
$$	141€–230€ ($183–$299)	36€–50€ ($47–$65)
$$$	231€–350€ ($300–$455)	51€–65€ ($66–$85)
$$$$	351€–450€ ($456–$585)	66€ ($86) and up
$$$$$	more than 450€ ($585)	

Follow the bouncing euro

Only a few years ago, the euro was worth about 90¢. Now it has bounced back strongly, to around $1.30. That 40¢ swing can make a huge difference. The 100€-per-night hotel that seemed like a bargain at $90 a few years ago now costs $130 (if you can still find it; for more about price changes and increases, see Chapter 4).

Prices are given in euros, with the U.S. dollar conversion; the exchange rate used is 1€ = $1.30. Although we give you definite prices, establishments sometimes change prices without notice. Also, in some cases a price goes down but because of exchange fluctuations, the cost goes up. (See the "Follow the bouncing euro" sidebar for more on euro exchange rates.)

Another thing you'll find accompanying each listing is contact information. Web sites are listed whenever possible. As for telephone numbers, don't be surprised if you see ☎ 06-93021877 near ☎ 06-290831. The number of digits in Italian phone numbers is not standardized. Area codes can have two, three, or four digits; the rest of the number may have as few as four or as many as eight digits.

For hotels, restaurants, and attractions that are plotted on a map, a page reference appears in the listing information. If an establishment is outside the city or in an out-of-the-way area, it may not be mapped.

Foolish Assumptions

We've made some assumptions about you and what your needs may be as a traveler. Here's what we assume about you:

- ✔ You may be an experienced traveler who hasn't had much time to explore Rome and wants expert advice when you finally do get a chance to enjoy the Eternal City.

- ✔ You may be an inexperienced traveler looking for guidance when determining whether to take a trip to Rome and how to plan for it.

- ✔ You're not looking for a book that provides all the information available or that lists every hotel, restaurant, or attraction. Instead, you're looking for a book that focuses on the places that will give you the best or most memorable experience in Rome.

If you fit any of these criteria, *Rome For Dummies* gives you the information you're looking for!

How This Book Is Organized

The book has six parts plus two appendixes. Each can be read independently if you want to zero in on a particular area or issue.

Part I: Introducing Rome

This is where you find in-depth information about Rome. It begins with our rundown of the best of Rome in Chapter 1; continues in Chapter 2 with Rome's history, culture, people, architecture, and cuisine; and ends in Chapter 3 with climate information and a calendar of special events.

Part II: Planning Your Trip to Rome

Here, we guide you through trip planning: budgeting (Chapter 4), deciding on escorted and package tours, and choosing whether you want to make the travel arrangements yourself or work through an agent (Chapter 5). We include Web sites throughout the section (and, indeed, the entire book), because that's where you often can find the best deals. We also address the special concerns of travelers with mobility issues, families, seniors, and gays and lesbians (Chapter 6). Finally, we give you tips on all the other necessary details, from getting your passport to thinking about your health (Chapter 7).

Part III: Settling into Rome

Rome may be eternal, but it's far from dead. Here, we give you all the logistical info on how to get around this bustling city and where to find additional information (Chapter 8), as well as the lowdown on hotels (Chapter 9) and restaurants (Chapter 10).

Part IV: Exploring Rome

This section provides our selection of what, for us, are the best features and attractions of Rome (Chapter 11), its best shops and markets (Chapter 12), and a choice of guided tours and itineraries through its maze of ancient and modern treasures (Chapter 13). We also include side trips to great destinations on the outskirts of Rome (Chapter 14).

Part V: Living It Up after Dark: Rome's Nightlife

Here is where we give you tips on where to find the entertainment that best suits your mood, from classical concerts and opera (Chapter 15) to bars, pubs, and discos (Chapter 16).

Part VI: The Part of Tens

The Part of Tens allows us to squeeze in some extra stuff — Italian expressions worth knowing (Chapter 17), our favorite Italian artists (Chapter 18), and ideas for special souvenirs (Chapter 19) — that we believe will complement your vacation and make your trip complete.

In the back of this book, we've included two appendixes. The first — your Quick Concierge — contains lots of handy information you may need when traveling in Rome. It includes phone numbers and addresses of emergency personnel and area hospitals and pharmacies, lists of local newspapers and magazines, protocols for sending mail or finding taxis, and more. Check out this appendix when searching for answers to lots of little questions that may come up as you travel. You can find the Quick Concierge easily because it's printed on yellow paper.

Appendix B contains a glossary of Italian words that will earn you warm appreciation from the locals.

Icons Used in This Book

We use icons throughout this book as signposts and flags for facts and information of a particular nature or interest. Following are the six types of icons we use:

 Keep an eye out for the Bargain Alert icon as you seek out money-saving tips and great deals.

 Best of the Best highlights the best Rome has to offer in all categories: hotels, restaurants, attractions, activities, shopping, and nightlife.

 Watch for the Heads Up icon to identify annoying or potentially danger-ous situations such as tourist traps, unsafe neighborhoods, rip-offs, and other things to beware.

 Look to the Kid Friendly icon for attractions, hotels, restaurants, and activities that are particularly hospitable to children or people traveling with kids. When the icon appears with a restaurant listing, it means that high chairs and _mezza porzione_ (half portions) are available, and we spell out what other special attention the establishment provides. When we use the icon with a hotel listing, it means that the hotel can provide a crib or an extra bed or two (or the hotel has triples and quads). It also means that the hotel might offer babysitting and other amenities suit-able for children, such as a garden, swimming pool, or play area.

 The Plan Ahead icon draws your attention to details or plans that you should take care of before you leave home.

 Find useful advice on things to do and ways to schedule your time when you see the Tip icon.

Where to Go from Here

Now you can dig in wherever you want. Chapter 1 highlights the best of Rome, from museums to hotels to intangibles (experiences you might not want to miss). If you already have an itinerary in mind, you can jump ahead to the ins and outs of finding a flight and making a budget; or you can browse through sights and attractions you may want to visit. And if you've already visited Rome once or a score of times, you're sure to find something here you haven't seen before.

Part I
Introducing Rome

The 5th Wave   By Rich Tennant

"I insisted they learn some Italian. I couldn't stand the idea of standing in front of the Trevi Fountain and hearing, 'gosh', 'wow', and 'far out.'"

In this part . . .

Here's where we give you a taste of Rome, offering up highlights without weighing you down with details. (Don't worry: We fill in all the blanks in the remainder of the book — we promise!)

Chapter 1 gives you the lowdown on the city's best bets, from ancient ruins and awe-inspiring churches to fantastic hotels and delicious restaurants; you can use this as a reservoir of suggestions when planning your trip. Chapter 2 delves into the city's rich history, culture, and architecture; tempts your taste buds with a discussion of Roman cuisine; and suggests interesting books and films about this most historic of cities. In Chapter 3, we describe the best seasons for visiting Rome and give you a calendar of the most important festivals and events, a number of which are attractions all on their own and may provide the focus for your trip.

Chapter 1

Discovering the Best of Rome

In This Chapter

▶ From picture galleries to ruins

▶ From frescoes to gelato

▶ From smart dining to picnic fare

▶ From hotels to nightclubs

*P*eople visit Rome for all sorts of reasons. Art lovers flock to its great museums, the faithful make pilgrimages to St. Peter's Basilica and the Vatican, and others come to soak up Italy's culture and atmosphere (or just the sun). In *Rome For Dummies,* we give you our opinions on the best Rome has to offer. In this chapter, we list our very favorites. Throughout the rest of this book, the Best of the Best icon marks the places listed in this chapter.

The Best Museums

Rome boasts numerous museums, some vast and famous, others small and catering to specialized audiences. Here is our short list of the not-to-be-missed museums that contain internationally renowned masterpieces and other mind-boggling beauties.

  ✔ The **Vatican Museums** top our list, for the monumental size of their collections and amazing number of masterpieces. They include dozens of rooms dedicated to Renaissance painting and sculpture, as well as a fantastic Egyptian section, an impressive ancient Roman collection, and ethnological art from all over the world. The museums are also home to the Sistine Chapel (mentioned in the next section). See Chapter 11.

  ✔ The **Borghese Gallery** isn't very big, but it is a triumph of Renaissance beauty. Caravaggio paintings and Bernini sculptures are only a few of its many treasures. See Chapter 11.

✔ The **National Roman Museum in Palazzo Massimo alle Terme** is a huge museum completely dedicated to ancient Roman art. It contains hundreds of artifacts unearthed during the excavation of archaeological sites in Rome and the surrounding areas, including a superb collection of sculptures and some breathtakingly beautiful Roman frescoes. See Chapter 11.

✔ The **National Etruscan Museum of Villa Giulia** holds a wonderful collection dedicated to the Etruscans, the mysterious predecessors of the Romans. This is a unique treasure trove of Etruscan artifacts and jewelry. See Chapter 11.

The Best Churches

Among Rome's hundreds of churches, we considered not only the architecture and the importance of the artwork inside, but also the individual charm and personality of each. Here are our top picks.

✔ **St. Peter's Basilica** is the most famous church in a city filled with magnificent churches. Its majestic colonnade and soaring dome are a symbol of Rome as well as of the Catholic Church; treasures inside include Michelangelo's *Pietà*. See Chapter 11.

✔ **Santa Maria sopra Minerva,** the city's only Gothic church, is filled with artistic delights such as Michelangelo's sculpture *Cristo Portacroce*. See Chapter 11.

✔ The **Sistine Chapel** contains the most famous artwork in all of Italy. After the *Mona Lisa,* the ceiling of the chapel is probably the most famous single piece of art in the world. Decorated with Michelangelo's frescoes, it is accessible from the Vatican Museums. Don't forget your binoculars. See Chapter 11.

✔ The little chapel of **San Zenone in Santa Prassede** will take your breath away. It is one of the oldest churches in Rome and completely covered with gilded mosaics. See Chapter 11.

✔ The church of **Santa Maria in Trastevere** is a splendid example of Medieval and Byzantine art, which is rare in Rome after the general baroque overhaul. It is also an excellent excuse to visit Trastevere, a delightful neighborhood. See Chapter 11.

The Best Ruins

On your visit to the site of the world's largest collection of ancient Roman archaeological remains, deciding which places to visit can be a trying affair. Here's a list of our favorite and most atmospheric sites.

- The majestic and austere **Colosseum,** where the Romans watched "sports" (as in fights to the death) and chariot races, is Rome's most famous ruin and an impressive work of architecture. See Chapter 11.

- The **Roman Forum** and the nearby **Palatine Hill,** containing the remains of temples, public buildings, villas, and triumphal arches, will take you back in time. They are particularly evocative on romantic Roman nights. See Chapter 11.

- The Appian Way, the first road built by the ancient Romans, has been transformed into the **Appian Way Archaeological Park,** which you can visit on foot or by bicycle. Along the way are the remains of tombs and villas that make the trip well worth the exercise. See Chapter 11.

- The **Caracalla Baths** were among the largest in Rome and are still an impressive sight. They also stage opera performances during the summer. See Chapters 11 and 15.

- The **Villa Adriana** near Tivoli, outside Rome, is more than just a villa. It is a huge complex of buildings, gardens, reflecting pools, and theaters built by the Emperor Hadrian in the second century A.D. In the mountains above Rome where Hadrian and a few hundred friends could get away from it all, the villa remains an atmospheric retreat. See Chapter 14.

The Best Hotels

We picked our favorite luxury hotels as well as our preferred moderately priced and inexpensive accommodations.

- **Hotel Hassler** tops our list as the hotel with the best service among Rome's many wonderful luxury lodgings. Its location on top of the Spanish Steps also makes it a unique place to stay. See Chapter 9.

- Presidents and stars stay at the **Hotel de Russie,** positively one of the most elegant and classiest hotels in the world. Contemporary design and exquisite good taste are coupled with the classic beauty of its architecture. See Chapter 9.

- The **Albergo Santa Chiara** is one of the oldest hotels in Rome and our favorite in the middle price range. The beauty of the palace and the quality of the service make it a great value. See Chapter 9.

- The **Hotel Arenula** is the best of Rome's budget hotels for service, quality of furnishings, and location. See Chapter 9.

The Best Restaurants

Here is a short list of our favorite restaurants in Rome. We love many more than those we describe here, and you'll find the ones we left behind in Chapter 10.

- ✔ For fantastic views over the Eternal City, with wonderful food to match, try **La Pergola.** A meal at this elegant restaurant will be one of your most romantic experiences in Rome. See Chapter 10.

- ✔ For a truly Roman outing — vetted by Alessandra, a Rome native — nothing can beat **Checchino dal 1887,** a historical restaurant in Monte Testaccio. See Chapter 10.

- ✔ The best *enoteca* (restaurant winery) in town is **Enoteca Capranica.** Not only will you love the food, the wine, and the atmosphere, but you'll also get to enter one of the most charming Roman palaces in the historic center. See Chapter 16.

The Best Buys in Rome

Shopping in Rome is great fun and a perfect excuse to stroll the labyrinthine streets. You can also find some unique treasures, including some great souvenirs.

- ✔ Select a pair of **socks fit for a cardinal** — or any other religious item you might think of — from one of the shops in the center of Rome. The vendors showcase a variety of items, from apparel to artwork. See Chapter 12.

- ✔ Give yourself the pleasure of a handmade piece of **gold jewelry.** The ancient tradition of goldsmithing is alive and well in Rome, and you'll find craftspeople working in a variety of styles, from reproductions of ancient classics to contemporary designs. See Chapter 12.

- ✔ An **antique print** makes a wonderful gift — for yourself or a loved one. This craft has been a Roman tradition since the Renaissance. See Chapter 12.

- ✔ Get a **picture of the pope** from the huge collection at the Vatican gift shop. See Chapter 11.

- ✔ Take your pick of **fashion accessories** — scarves, leather gloves, handbags, wallets, watches, sunglasses — from the many local designers. See Chapter 12.

The Best Daytime and Nighttime Outings

In our opinion, you shouldn't leave Rome without taking part in at least a few of the following adventures.

✔ Go for a **river cruise along the Tiber.** The Compagnia di Navigazione Ponte San Angelo organizes both romantic dinner cruises and day excursions, including a great one to Ostia Antica. See Chapter 11.

✔ Take a walk by moonlight near the church of **Santa Maria in Aracoeli** and up to the **Capitoline Museums** on **Piazza del Campidoglio** for a unique view over the Forum. See Chapter 11.

✔ Book tickets for an **opera performance** at the Caracalla Baths, the summer location of the Teatro dell'Opera. See Chapter 15.

✔ Enjoy a concert or a dance performance at the **Parco della Musica,** the city's recently opened state-of-the-art performing arts center. See Chapter 15.

✔ Have a drink at one of Rome's historical cafes, the best being the **Caffè Greco** in Via Condotti, near the Spanish Steps. It still has its original 19th-century furnishings and decoration. See Chapter 16.

Chapter 2

Digging Deeper into Rome

. . . .

In This Chapter

▶ Understanding Rome, past and present

▶ Exploring 2,500 years of great architecture

▶ Discovering the great artists of the Roman Renaissance

▶ Savoring Rome's culture and cuisine

▶ Reading more about Rome

. . . .

*U*nder the Roman Empire, all roads really did lead to Rome, which was the cosmopolitan heart of the ancient Roman civilization. In spite of passionate attempts by other Italian cities — Milan, Florence, Venice, Naples — to steal her role, Rome remains the focus of Italian civilization and culture. For thousands of years, artists have been coming to Rome to study and work; visitors to see the grandiose monuments; and pilgrims to visit the many Christian and Catholic holy places.

The artists and scholars who were drawn to Rome during the Renaissance left their contribution in churches, buildings, and public squares. The young aristocrats who came from all over Europe and the United States in the 19th century flocked here to absorb the classical world and admire Renaissance art in a rite of passage known as the Grand Tour (the months-long European excursion enjoyed by the rich and satirized by Mark Twain in *The Innocents Abroad*). Rome was maybe the single most important stop then, and it remains so today.

Here we draw a quick picture of the most striking cultural features of this historically and culturally rich city.

History 101: The Main Events

As legend has it, Rome was founded by Romulus, also known as Romolo, one of two semigod twins (the other was Remus, or Remo) born to Mars and the daughter of a local king, Rea Silvia. After narrowly escaping death — they were saved by a wolf who nursed them — the twins grew up and set about establishing a new town. After a dispute, Romolo took over and marked the borders on the ground. The date was April 21, 753 B.C. The city grew to be a beacon of civilization, absorbing and borrowing any good features from other cultures it encountered (or conquered), and creating a set of rules, principles, and laws that are still the bedrock of modern Western values and institutions.

Rome started as a collection of shepherds' huts, a small town populated by the local Italic tribe. These people were descended from the Villanova tribes, which had settled in the region of Rome around 1,000 B.C. on the Palatino (Palatine Hill). The town was deeply influenced by the **Etruscans,** a people famed for their seafaring, gold and metal work, and trading. The Etruscans probably came from Asia Minor, but they established themselves in Tuscany and then expanded southward. They gave Rome its name, drained the swamps, built sewers, and introduced writing. At that time, Rome had kings, and the chasing out of the last king coincided with the loss of the Etruscans' influence. Weakened by their struggles with the Greeks, who were colonizing southern Italy, the Etruscans lost their power over Rome near the beginning of the fifth century B.C.

The **Roman Republic** was founded in 509 B.C., when the last of Rome's kings was overthrown. The republic was headed by two consuls and the senate, all controlled by the upper or *patrician* (aristocratic) class. The *plebeians* (the working class) later had their own council and were represented by tribunes. It took hundreds of years for Rome to gain control over the Italian peninsula; in the meantime, it suffered many reverses, including the destruction of the city by the Gauls in 390 B.C.

Gradually, Rome established military supremacy. The Romans have been called the "Prussians of the ancient world," for their militarism. They first showed their might in decades of bloody war against the city of Carthage, whose empire spread across North Africa and into Spain. Known as the Punic Wars, these conflicts began in 264 B.C. It took the Carthagian general Hannibal six months to make his famous march over the Alps to attack the Romans from behind in 218 B.C., marking the start of the Second Punic War. Hannibal's army inflicted crushing defeats on the Roman armies, but the Punic Wars eventually ended with the Romans erasing Carthage from the map in 146 B.C. The door was then open for Rome to spread its influence across the Mediterranean. It ruled its provinces through governors and allowed subject countries to retain local government and customs — though betrayal of Rome was brutally avenged. The republic became fantastically rich, and Hellenic and Eastern art, wealth, and cultural influences flowed into Rome. Recent archaeological finds have shown a Roman presence as far away as the borders of China.

The end of the Roman Republic and the beginning of the **Roman Empire** arrived largely through the antagonism of two great generals, **Pompey** and **Julius Caesar.** Caesar became a tyrant after his defeat of Pompey. Following Caesar's murder on March 15, 44 B.C. (the Ides of March), civil war ensued. The victor, Caesar's grandnephew and adopted son, Octavian, became the first emperor, **Caesar Augustus.** His reign turned Rome into a glowing marble city the likes of which the world had never seen, signaling the beginning of the two centuries of peace that allowed the empire to reach its highest point. Not all was well in Rome, though, and a string of mostly debauched and even insane rulers took power: **Tiberius, Caligula, Claudius,** and **Nero.** Thanks to Robert Graves's historical novel *I, Claudius* (and the television miniseries based on the book), Claudius is popularly considered a partial exception even though his third wife, Nero's mother, was also his niece, and he had 40 senators put to death during his reign — by no means a model of enlightened statesmanship. And then there was **Nero,** whose very name is a synonym for cruelty: He had his own mother put to death in A.D. 59 and was suspected of having ordered the terrible fires that destroyed large parts of the city in A.D. 64.

Order returned in the second century, when Rome enjoyed a string of "good" emperors who brought stable succession and civility — instead of madness and corruption — to the state. They were **Nerva, Trajan, Hadrian, Antoninus Pius,** and the emperor philosopher **Marcus Aurelius.** With the ascension of Marcus's 19-year-old son **Commodus** (the villain of the hugely popular but fictionalized film *Gladiator*), the empire was again headed for trouble. The corrupt and arrogant Commodus even had the senate recognize him as divine. With his assassination in A.D. 192, the empire plunged once more into chaos.

At its height, the empire extended from the Caspian Sea to Scotland. However, a chaotic period of war, plague, barbarian invasions, and inflation spelled the beginning of the bitter end for Rome. When **Emperor Constantine** converted to Christianity and founded Constantinople in A.D. 330, Rome's wealth shifted east. The western empire began to crumble under barbarian pressure: The **Goths** sacked Rome in A.D. 410; the Huns came next under **Attila;** and the **Vandals** of North Africa followed. In A.D. 476, the German chief Odoacer deposed the western Roman emperor, in effect signaling the end of Roman rule over the city. The once-invincible Roman Empire had lost much territory and shrunk to its eastern part, where it continued to rule from Constantinople (until 1453, when it fell to the Ottoman Empire).

Almost 80 years passed before Rome was reconquered by the Byzantines of the Roman Oriental Empire at the end of a long and destructive war against the Goths. The city had suffered terrible destruction, and its population had dwindled from over 2 million at the height of the Roman Empire to about 35,000. After the church's right to have a political state was recognized and the Vatican state was established under the aegis of the Franks, Rome reverted to a small provincial town. The French king **Charlemagne** had the pope crown him emperor in A.D. 800, hoping to revive the western Roman Empire. He instead ended up founding the **Holy Roman Empire.**

This historical oddity profoundly affected Roman politics during the Middle Ages and Renaissance. The German emperor was elected by the German princes, but only the pope could crown him Holy Roman

The Roman Empire at a glance

1500 B.C. Bronze Age peoples settle the site of Rome.

c. 753 B.C. Rome is officially founded.

c. 509 B.C. The last of the Roman kings is overthrown, and the Republic is born.

264 B.C. The Punic Wars with Carthage begin.

216 B.C. In the worst defeat in Roman history, more than 50,000 Romans fall at the battle of Cannae against Hannibal's smaller force.

146 B.C. Carthage is destroyed, and all human habitation of the site is forbidden.

44 B.C. Julius Caesar is assassinated.

31 B.C. Octavian (Augustus) defeats Mark Antony and Cleopatra at the battle of Actium. He reigns as emperor for the next 40 years.

27 B.C.– *Pax Romana* (Roman peace) prevails, from the ascension of Augustus to
A.D.180 the death of Marcus Aurelius. There is plenty of war during the *pax,* but Rome brings the whole Mediterranean world under its administrative control.

27 B.C. Marcus Agrippa, friend of Augustus, builds the Pantheon.

A.D. 64 Great Fire of Rome, blamed by history on Nero (and by Nero on Christians), devastates the city.

A.D. 69 A power struggle follows Nero's death, and Rome has four emperors in one year.

A.D. 79 Pompeii and Herculaneum are destroyed.

A.D. 80 The Colosseum is completed.

A.D. 98 Ascension of Trajan, the second of the so-called "good" emperors.

A.D. 148 Rome celebrates its 900th anniversary.

A.D. 161 The reign of the humanistic Marcus Aurelius begins.

A.D. 395 Emperor Constantine builds Constantinople. The empire splits into eastern and western factions.

A.D. 410 The Visigoths sack Rome.

A.D. 441 The Romans fall behind in their payments to Attila the Hun, who begins his attacks on the empire.

A.D. 455 The Vandals sack Rome.

A.D. 476 Western emperor Julius Nepos is executed, and the German warrior Odoacer is proclaimed king, effectively ending Roman rule over the western part of the Empire. Roman rule continues over the Eastern Empire, which resists the attacks.

A.D. 1453 Constantinople falls to the hands of the Ottoman Empire. This marks the end of the Roman Empire.

From the Byzantines to modern Rome

A.D. 552   Narsete, the general of Justinian and emperor in Constantinople, occupies Rome after the long war against the Goths. The Byzantine domination of Rome begins, together with the slow rise of the temporal power of the church.

A.D. 756   In the famous "donation of Pepin," the Carolingian ruler Pepin III (predecessor of Charlemagne) recognizes the papacy's right to its own state and territory, in exchange for being crowned king by the pope. The Vatican State has formally begun.

A.D. 800   Charlemagne is crowned emperor in St. Peter's Basilica by Pope Leo III.

1084   Robert Guiscard, the Norman, overcomes the resistance of the city after a three-year siege.

1309   The popes, with Clement V, move to Avignon, France, at the urging of the French crown. They will not be back until 1377, when Gregory XI returns to Rome.

1526   First reliable census: Rome has 55,000 inhabitants.

1527   The sack of Rome by Holy Roman Emperor Charles V.

1600   The pope and Rome's most important families start lavishing artwork on the Eternal City: New churches and palaces and great redecorations of existing buildings are undertaken.

1798   Rome is occupied by the French, who proclaim a "Jacobite" Roman republic.

1800   The census calculates the city's population at 150,000.

1815   Pope Pio VII is restored after the fall of Napoleon.

1849   Mazzini and Garibaldi proclaim a new Roman Republic, but the French help the pope regain his power over the city.

1870   Rome is occupied by Victor Emanuel II's troops; it will be proclaimed capital of the kingdom in 1871.

1881   A new census counts the city's population at 273,952. Twenty years later, in 1901, the population reaches 422,411 inhabitants.

1922   After the "march on Rome," Benito Mussolini obtains from the king the right to form a new government. He will rapidly transform it into a dictatorship.

1929   The Vatican signs the Lateran Pacts, agreeing to relinquish all of Rome except its churches and the territory of the Vatican.

1943   Rome, occupied by the Germans in spite of the resistance of Italian troops, is later heavily bombed by the Allies.

1944	The Allies liberate Rome on June 4.
1961	Rome reaches over 2 million inhabitants, returning to ancient levels.
1995	In preparation for the millennium celebrations and the Papal Jubilee, a great campaign of restorations, reorganizations, and renovations begins.

Emperor. For the next 1,000 years, the pope became a key element in the struggle for power among the Holy Roman Emperor (who was German), Spain, and France (aspiring to the imperial crown). In spite of the troubles that such a system brought to Rome — the city was under siege between 1081 and 1084, before being won by the Normans — the papacy grew stronger and richer, becoming a leading force in Italy. The popes, usually from the leading families in Rome, attracted the best artists from all over Italy and Europe to decorate the city's ever-increasing number of religious and secular buildings. They gave great influence to the artistic side of the **Renaissance** — the rediscovery of classical learning and culture — as they sought to make their city and its churches more and more splendid, with works of art and architectural masterpieces.

But in many ways, Rome was very backward. Unfortunately, the popes were not very interested in commerce, and they imposed a reactionary and stultifying rule that killed the economy and stopped the city's development, making them quite unpopular. This state of affairs lasted for hundreds of years. Rome was also caught up in international politics and war, as well as in the struggle for power in Europe between the Germans and the French. The German troops of the Holy Roman Emperor Charles V sacked the holy city on May 6, 1527, one of Rome's darkest days. Peace was restored in 1529, and the popes kept control over the city until the 19th century.

When the *Risorgimento* (resurgence) movement, which envisioned a unified Italy, started developing, Rome was the designated capital for the united country, and local patriots started working toward that aim. In 1848, when revolution swept Europe, Romans seemed to have a somewhat sympathetic ruler in Pius IX, who granted many concessions. However, after a democratic republic was declared the following year, Pius fled. He entreated France, Austria, Spain, and the Kingdom of Naples to help him regain his temporal power. The Romans could not defeat several great empires at once, and papal rule was restored.

In fact, Rome was the last piece of the Italian puzzle to fall to the nationalist movement, because the pope continued to receive help from the French. In 1870, almost ten years after the unification of the rest of Italy, Rome was finally wrested from papal–French control and made into the capital of the Italian kingdom — the parliamentary monarchy of the Savoy house — thus completing the unification.

After **World War I,** discontent and economic depression helped **Mussolini** rise to power in Rome and in the rest of the country. One of his first actions was to reach an agreement with the Vatican, the issue of whose political role had continued to divide the people of Rome ever since the unification of Italy in 1870. With the Lateran Pacts of 1929, the pope agreed to a much-reduced state, and Rome relinquished the territory of the Vatican while recognizing the pope's authority on church ground. Mussolini's imperialist adventures abroad were matched by repression at home, and his alliance with the Nazis was disastrous. Italians turned against him in 1943, and his puppet government was overthrown. Under the king's rule, Italy continued in **World War II** on the Allied side while suffering under German occupation. Rome was bombed repeatedly during the occupation and suffered much destruction. The Allies liberated the city on June 4, 1944, two days before D-day.

After the war, Rome voted against the monarchy and was established as the capital of the new Italian republic. Economic recovery was slow, but Rome emerged from the process as a thriving modern city and seat of the Italian government on the one hand, and an ancient archaeological site badly in need of preservation on the other. This contrast created tension between modernization and preservation of the city's unique historical endowment that persists to this day. (Rome has been building its subway system for over a century but still has only two lines because of the innumerable archaeological treasures hidden underground.) Traffic — a Roman problem since antiquity — continues to top the list of local priorities, together with the management of the massive influx of illegal immigrants and refugees that has been a factor since the 1990s.

Architecture: From Ruins to Rococo

Rome offers an almost complete compendium of architectural styles — ancient Roman, Romanesque, medieval, Gothic, Renaissance, baroque, rococo, neoclassical, modern, and so on. Roman architecture was deeply influenced by Greek culture, as can be seen in column-capital styles around the city.

- ✔ The **Doric** style is most easily spotted in the simple rectilinear capitals at the tops of columns.

- ✔ The **Ionic** capital resembles a scroll.

- ✔ The **Corinthian** is the most ornate capital, decorated with a profusion of leaves.

The **Colosseum** demonstrates all three styles, or *orders.* Roman architects added enormously to their Greek heritage with the invention of the **arch** and the vault. The dome of the **Pantheon** is the apogee of such art, a model that has been copied over the centuries, not least by Michelangelo for the cupola in **St. Peter's Basilica.**

Of the country's Christian-era churches, the earliest to be found are in the **Romanesque** style, which, as its name suggests, drew inspiration from Roman architecture and particularly the use of the rounded arch. These churches have thick walls and massive piers that support the superstructure of the building, as well as bell towers with arched openings. The Romanesque style has an appealing simplicity (especially in comparison with some gaudy later developments in church architecture), which you can admire in many churches in Rome, including **Santa Maria in Trastevere.**

With the **Gothic** style, lines become longer and arches pointed, giving a feeling of soaring toward the sky. Rome's only card-carrying Gothic church, **Santa Maria sopra Minerva,** is a less obvious version of the style, much restored (and, alas, mutilated) over the centuries.

With the **Renaissance** style, ancient architecture is rediscovered, and proportion and balance are stressed. The classical orders have a comeback, with the Doric in the first story of the building, the Ionic in the middle, and the Corinthian at the top. Michelangelo's **Palazzo Farnese** in Rome is a classic example of the Renaissance style.

Eventually, the Renaissance style evolved into the more elaborate **baroque.** The sweeping colonnade in front of St. Peter's, designed by Bernini, is considered baroque. Rome went through a huge face-lift during the baroque period, when popes and all the important families in the city poured money into new palaces and churches and lavish decorations. If baroque was an elaboration of the Renaissance style, **rococo** — the addition of all sorts of baubles and flourishes to the underlying structure — was overkill. Perhaps the best word to describe rococo is *busy.* With its twisting columns and encrusting of gold, Bernini's ***baldacchino*** (baldachin, or canopy) inside St. Peter's shows the baroque starting to get out of hand.

A Taste of Rome: Eating Locally

As in the rest of Italy, meals (and restaurant menus) are divided among *primi* (first courses), ***secondi*** (second courses), and ***contorni*** (side dishes). The distinction is mostly a matter of presentation: In the U.S., all the components typically arrive together in one dish, while Italians serve them one at a time. Proportions are also different, with meat or fish representing a smaller part of the meal than in the U.S. ***Antipasti*** (appetizers) are an option to open the meal — and allow time for preparation of the main courses — while *dolci* (sweets) or *gelato* (ice cream) are alternatives to fruit or cheese to end the meal.

Roman cuisine is just one style of Italian cuisine, with a number of local characteristics that make it unique. You'll find many of the staples of Italian food — all kinds of pasta, plenty of veggies, olive oil, fresh herbs — but also a lot of specific and traditional ingredients and preparations that you won't find elsewhere in Italy. The leitmotif of Roman cuisine is simplicity, with dishes based on few and fresh ingredients. Traditional Roman cuisine is based on pasta, fresh seasonal vegetables, seafood, and meat — especially organ meat and smaller animals such as pork, chicken, rabbit, lamb, and goat. Preparations are usually simple and flavorful, and a number of "established" dishes remain great favorites with the locals.

Traditional Roman cuisine is always cooked with olive oil, not butter and cream — although, of course, you'll find those in dishes from other Italian regions (the north in particular). Parmesan cheese (the best being *Parmigiano Reggiano,* the original from Reggio, which makes the commercial stuff taste like sawdust) is widely used. You'll find savory *Pecorino Romano* grated on traditional pasta dishes; it is the local sheep cheese from the Roman countryside and has a sharp, distinctive flavor. Vegetarian dishes are common both as main dishes (pasta dishes and *secondi*) and as side dishes and salads.

A little oddity in traditional restaurants and trattorie is that each day of the week is traditionally associated with a few specialties. For example, Thursday is the day for gnocchi, and Friday is the day for *seppie coi piselli* and *baccalà* (see "Secondo," later in this chapter). The underlying reason is that many of these dishes require lengthy preparations, and because in the best restaurants everything is strictly homemade, these operations are performed only once a week. Be adventurous, and try the local specialties when you can.

Antipasto

The tradition of antipasto is relatively recent and refers to the "munchies" brought out to while away the time before the real meal is served. We aren't talking about a bowl of peanuts or potato chips, either. In everyday meals at home, the appetizer is a pasta dish or *risotto,* but on special occasions, a large spread precedes the *primo.* With current concern about carbs, many will choose to have antipasto instead of a starchy *primo.*

Traditional Roman antipasti usually include a choice of the best local cured meats — salami, ham, and sausages from the area around Rome — and some of the best specialties from the rest of Italy, such as the incomparable *prosciutto di Parma* (air-cured ham) and *lardo di Colonnata* (a cholesterol-free lard cured in marble vats). Other typical appetizers include *insalata di mare* (sliced octopus seasoned with olive oil, vinegar, and herbs), olives, and *carciofini* (pickled artichokes). In *pizzeria* restaurants, you may also be offered *bruschetta* (slices of toasted peasant-style bread dressed with olive oil, garlic, and sometimes tomatoes), *supplì* (egg-shaped balls of seasoned rice filled with cheese and deep fried), *olive Ascolane* (large green olives filled with meat and cheese, battered and deep fried), or *fiori di zucca* (zucchini flowers filled with cheese and anchovy and deep fried).

Primo

This is the first course of a traditional meal, but nowadays, many will make a meal out of it, maybe accompanied by a *contorno* (see description later in this section).

Pasta occupies an important place in Roman cuisine: you'll find spaghetti, penne, tagliatelle, and innumerable varieties of fresh and stuffed pasta. The most traditional dishes are spaghetti *con le vongole* (with clams, no tomato), bucatini or rigatoni *all'amatriciana* (a spicy tomato sauce with lard and onions served with pecorino cheese), and pasta *all'arrabbiata* (tomato and lots of hot red pepper). Another delicious traditional pasta seasoning is *gricia* (lard, onions, and pecorino). Among the fresh filled pasta, the best are *ravioli* filled with ricotta and spinach, *agnolotti* (filled with meat), and *cannelloni* (large rolls of fresh pasta filled with meat or fish, and baked with tomato sauce and cheese). Tradition dictates that fresh filled pasta is usually reserved for special days — Sunday and holidays — but it's always on offer for the visitor. Another kind of fresh pasta is potato *gnocchi* (dumplings, usually in a tomato-based sauce), a beloved local specialty traditionally served on Thursday.

Although less traditional, at least one kind of *risotto,* a typical dish of somewhat sticky and very tasty seasoned Italian rice, appears on most menus. In seafood restaurants, you'll find risotto *alla pescatora* (with fresh shellfish and a bit of tomato); in other restaurants, you'll find seasonal vegetable-based risotto — with artichokes, asparagus, or radicchio, among others. Soups include the traditional *minestrone* (a thick vegetable and bean soup) and *pasta e ceci* (a thick savory soup of pasta and chickpeas, usually served on Thursday).

Secondo

This is the second course of the meal and consists of meat or fish. Tradition holds that Romans eat fish on Tuesday and Friday, meat on other days. Vegetarian dishes are always acceptable. Although few Romans still observe these traditions at home, they are more than happy that Roman trattorie do, and you'll find them gaily eating the traditional daily specials — so much so that if you arrive too late, the specials will be gone.

Although most trattorie offer fish every day, Tuesday and Friday bring a greater variety of seafood dishes, especially traditional ones such as *seppie coi piselli* (cuttlefish stewed with peas) and *baccalà* (salted cod prepared in a stew with potatoes). Among the best traditional meat dishes are the *abbacchio arrosto* (young lamb roasted with herbs), *scottadito* (literally "finger burning" — thin grilled lamb cutlets), and *saltimbocca alla romana* (literally "jump in your mouth Roman style" — thin slices of veal or beef rolled with ham and sage and sautéed with a bit of wine). For the more adventurous, there are *trippa alla romana* (tripe Roman style, stewed with a light tomato sauce) and *coda alla vaccinara* (oxtail stew).

Contorno and salad

When you order a *secondo* in a restaurant, it will come without a side dish; you'll have to order that separately. That's convenient for vegetarians, who always have a choice of fresh vegetables. Cooked greens are very common; you'll always find a choice of *cicoria* (dandelions), spinach, or *bieda* (Swiss chard), prepared *all'agro* (seasoned with oil and lemon juice) or *ripassati* (sautéed with garlic and hot pepper). Other traditional *contorni* are *patate arrosto* (roasted potatoes, deliciously prepared with fresh herbs), *patate fritte* (french fries), and *fagiolini* (green beans — but beware; they are well cooked and seasoned with olive oil and lemon juice). January through March is the season for the unique *carciofi Romani* (wonderful artichokes you can eat in their entirety — no spines, woody leaves, or barbs inside to contend with).

You'll also always find salad, usually a simple affair of plain lettuce, but sometimes more elaborate, with sliced carrots, fennel, and tomatoes. A special salad that's very common in the summer (lots of people with their swimsuit size in mind order it as a main course) is the *Caprese,* made of fresh mozzarella, tomatoes, and basil; sometimes it incorporates the famous *mozzarella di bufala* (buffalo mozzarella), imported from nearby Campania. All these salads are served unseasoned, with olive oil and vinegar or lemon on the side.

Last but not least is *puntarelle,* our favorite local fresh green. It's a specialty in early spring in Rome. This salad is made from the hearts of the *cicoria* plant, which are sliced and seasoned with garlic, anchovy, and olive oil.

Dolci and dessert

At lunch, most working people end their meal with a piece of fresh fruit or cheese (usually, local *pecorino*). Rome is not particularly famous for its sweets, but that doesn't mean your sweet tooth will go unsatisfied — not by a long shot.

Among the most common desserts are *creme caramel* and the traditional *crostata* (tart) in two main versions: *crostata alla marmellata* (tart with homemade jam) and *crostata della nonna* (tart filled with pastry cream and pine nuts). Other desserts include *bignè alla crema* (puff-pastry balls filled with cream, covered with dark chocolate, and served with whipped cream) and *tiramisù* (layers of mascarpone cheese and espresso-soaked ladyfingers).

You'll also always find ice cream (gelato), but it will rarely be homemade in a restaurant, and you're definitely better off waiting and having your ice cream at a proper ice cream parlor. There, you'll also find *granita* (frozen coffee or lemon ice), which is very refreshing and low in calories (unless you add real whipped cream to your coffee *granita,* which is delicious). The main attraction, gelato, comes in a variety of fruit and cream flavors (see Chapter 10); one of our favorites is *zabaglione* (a cream made with sugar, egg yolks, and Marsala wine, similar in taste to eggnog).

The etiquette of drinking

Don't expect to order a martini before dinner in a local *trattoria* — in many restaurants, and more particularly in *trattorie, osterie,* and *pizzerie,* you are unlikely to find a full bar, because drinking liquor before dinner is not very common. Indeed, an *aperitivo* is always served with tidbits to eat, and in restaurants you won't see a waiter bring out wine before putting some food, or at least bread, on the table. More formal and internationally oriented restaurants will have an "American bar," Italian for full bar. There you'll be able to ask for a scotch and water and not be rewarded with a perplexed stare. Elsewhere, follow the "when in Rome" rule: Have an *aperitivo* at a bar, follow with wine over dinner, and have a grappa (clear brandy) or *amaro* (60- to 80-proof bitter drink, made with herbs) *after* your meal.

Wine

The best-known Roman wines come from the nearby Castelli Romani (hill towns east of the city; see Chapter 14). Among these, the white varieties — such as *Frascati* — are especially good, very dry, and treacherously refreshing. Other excellent wines come from the region of Viterbo, near Tarquinia and the Lago di Vico (see Chapter 14), such as the famous *Est, Est, Est!* and the dessert muscat wine *Aleatico di Gradoli.*

Word to the Wise: The Local Language

Italian is Rome's primary language; if you know it a bit, or if your ear is particularly good, you'll notice that in Rome people speak differently than in other parts of Italy. Roman is the local dialect, a very colorful lingo that has given life to a rich heritage of poetry — Trilussa is the most famous poet writing in the Roman dialect — and popular sayings, often full of a witty philosophy, that are sometimes quite untranslatable.

The other language you can resort to is sign language. Actually, other Italians make fun of Romans for using their hands so much. In Rome, your hands talk — both to emphasize your words and to convey further meaning. If you don't speak any Italian, many Romans will go out of their way to try to understand you and help you out, and signs will be of great help. See the glossary of Italian words in Appendix B for some key words and phrases. Also see Chapter 17, where we list what we deem are the ten most useful Italian expressions to know before your trip. If you're more adventurous, devote some time to *Italian For Dummies,* by Francesca Romana Onofri and Karen Antje Möller (Wiley), and become a pro.

Background Check: Recommended Books and Movies

Rome has been the subject or the background of innumerable works, both of fiction and nonfiction. We have excluded guidebooks from the suggestions in this section — you'll find those recommended in Appendix A. Whether you want to bone up on history or be entertained by sights of the Eternal City, here are a few surefire choices.

True stories

The following nonfiction favorites not only will expand your knowledge of Rome, but also will be pure reading pleasure.

- ✔ **Polybius** was a Greek hostage in Rome for 16 years in the second century B.C., during which he wrote his *Histories* (reprinted by Regnery/Gateway as *Polybius on Roman Imperialism* and by Penguin as *The Rise of the Roman Empire*) to explain "by what means and under what kind of constitution, almost the whole inhabited world was conquered and brought under the dominion of the single city of Rome, and that, too, within a period of not quite fifty-three years" (219–167 B.C.).

- ✔ The Roman historian **Tacitus** is one of our primary sources of information — and lurid stories — about the early emperors, including Augustus, Tiberius, Caligula, and Nero. His *Annals* have been published in the Penguin Classics series as *The Annals of Imperial Rome* and reprinted many times since.

- ✔ If you read 25 pages a day, it'll take you only about four months to get through **Edward Gibbon's** *History of the Decline and Fall of the Roman Empire* (begun in 1776), a monument of English prose in several volumes. (You can find a less monumental Penguin abridged version in paperback.)

- ✔ **Johann Wolfgang von Goethe** was the first great modern literary visitor to Italy, and his wonderful *Italian Journey* (1816) contains a few great pages on Rome as it was at the time of his visit.

- ✔ Shortly following Goethe, **Stendhal** — the author of *The Red and the Black* and *The Charterhouse of Parma* — visited Rome and fell deeply in love with the city. You can read his impressions in *Three Italian Chronicles* (1826–1829).

Art history

When you visit Rome, you will see art, and in particular Renaissance art, everywhere you look. Here are a few books to help you brush up on the subject of Roman art:

✔ Italian **Giorgio Vasari** was a painter, architect, and (literally) Renaissance man. His *Lives of the Most Eminent Painters and Sculptors* (1550; expanded in 1568) has been criticized for inaccuracy but is full of interesting information about the great painters of the Renaissance. The Oxford edition (1998) is one of the many abridgements in translation of this huge work.

✔ **Benvenuto Cellini's** famous *Autobiography* (1728) presents a vivid picture of Cellini's time in Renaissance Florence and Rome.

✔ **Karl Ludwig Gallwitz's** *Handbook of Italian Renaissance Painters* (1999) gives you an at-a-glance guide to 1,200 Italian painters; it also has some nice reproductions, brief essays on the major schools of painting, and some weird charts that show who influenced whom. You may want to peruse it before you go, if you're really into art — it's softcover and not very thick, so you may even want to bring it along.

Works of fiction

A good novel is often one of the best ways to acquaint yourself with a place, allowing you to immerse yourself in its culture. Our choices include excellent books on both modern and ancient Rome.

✔ **Alberto Moravia,** one of the great Italian writers of the 20th century, wrote many novels and short stories but none as famous as *The Conformist* (1951), a study of the Fascist personality. He also wrote two novels about Rome and Romans: *Roman Tales* (1954) and *The Woman of Rome* (1949).

✔ **Robert Graves** wrote two novels — *I, Claudius* (1934) and its sequel, *Claudius the God* (1935) — about the best of Augustus's Claudian successors. Although they're works of fiction, they're a highly entertaining way to learn about the glory and decadence of Imperial Rome.

✔ **Henry James's** great novel *The Portrait of a Lady* (1881) unveils the heart of Rome as seen by a young American woman in the 19th century. (See the next section for info about the movie.)

✔ Polish writer **Henryk Sienkiewicz** won the Nobel Prize in 1905 largely on the strength of his monumental *Quo Vadis?* (1896), set in Rome during the time of Nero and concerning the relationship between a Christian woman and a Roman soldier.

✔ **Carlo Emilio Gadda's** novel *That Horrible Mess in Via Merulana* (1954) is a wonderful Italian thriller; it was also adapted on the screen in Pietro Germi's film *The Facts of Murder* (1959).

The moving image

Rome has been the subject or the setting of several hit films over the years. Of course, Roman and Italian directors have used Rome as the background for many of their masterpieces. Fellini created one of the most famous Italian films of all time, *La Dolce Vita* (1960), and his beloved Rome figures in many of his other movies, including *The Nights of Cabiria* (1957), a touching story showing unusual views of the city. Vittorio De Sica got his second Oscar with *The Bicycle Thief* (1948) and kept going with *Umberto D.* (1952) and *Yesterday Today and Tomorrow* (1963). Rossellini's *Open City* (1945) is another masterpiece, as is Pasolini's *Mamma Roma* (1962). Bernardo Bertolucci gained fame with *The Conformist* (1970), an adaptation of Moravia's novel (see the preceding section), and used Rome in some of his other great movies, such as the psychological *Luna* (1979) and the dramatic *Besieged* (1998).

International directors have also loved the city, beginning with the many movies that re-created the grandeur of Imperial Rome: William Wyler's *Ben-Hur* (1959); Mervyn LeRoy's *Quo Vadis* (1951); Joseph L. Mankiewicz's *Cleopatra* (1963); Anthony Mann's *The Fall of the Roman Empire* (1964); and *Spartacus* (1960), the Oscar-winning Kirk Douglas movie about a slave revolt in ancient Rome (Spartacus's story actually took place in Capua). It was a precursor to Ridley Scott's *Gladiator* (2000), which also gives a visceral feel for the brutal side of the empire. Also treading the paths of ancient Rome is Julie Taymor, in her *Titus* (1999), an adaptation of Shakespeare's *Titus Andronicus.*

Innumerable movies, both oldies and recent successes, have been set in Rome. William Wyler's *Roman Holiday* (1953), the Gregory Peck–Audrey Hepburn romance, is said to have caused a surge in tourism. Jean Negulesco's *Three Coins in the Fountain* (1954) was a great hit, followed by Vincent Minnelli's *Two Weeks in Another Town* (1962) and Jean-Luc Goddard's *Contempt* (1963). More recently, Rome has appeared in cameos in an increasing number of movies: from Peter Greenaway's *Belly of an Architect* (1987) to Michael Lehmann's madcap art-theft caper *Hudson Hawk* (1990). Rome even turns up in Gus Van Sant's *My Own Private Idaho* (1991), as well as in Norman Jewison's *Only You* (1996), Anthony Minghella's *The Talented Mr. Ripley* (1999), and the final scene of Neil Labute's *Nurse Betty* (2000). Rome was used more extensively in Jane Campion's *The Portrait of a Lady* (1996), based on Henry James's novel.

Chapter 3

Deciding When to Go

*R*ome has met the challenge of the new millennium: Longer open hours, Web sites, information hotlines, cumulative tickets, air-conditioning, shuttle services, and so on. More than ever, tourists are welcome in the Eternal City, and the added benefit of the euro makes things a lot easier for visitors used to dollars or pounds — no more 3,500-lire ice cream cones or shoes costing a cool quarter-million.

Rome, though, is also a metropolis, with cultural and logistic quirks that can make your visit more or less pleasant, depending on when you go. Here, we give you tips to plan what we hope will be your best trip ever.

Revealing the Secrets of the Seasons

Rome has a warm, dry climate with well-defined seasons. Winters are mild, and what Romans call "bitter cold," is around 30°F (–4°C), which rarely happens during the day. In summer, the weather is hot, maybe not as humid as it gets in, say, Washington, D.C., but still rather unpleasant, particularly if you're sensitive to heat. Also, many attractions are out-doors, where you can't resort to air conditioning (which, by the way, more times than not will not work as well in your hotel room as at home).

We really don't recommend coming in August: It is crowded with tourists and lines, and unbearably hot. All the locals have gone out of town, including shop and restaurant owners who often take at least two weeks off in August, if not the entire month. July isn't much better temperature wise, but at least most restaurants and shops are open.

Check the average temperatures in Table 3-1 before you plan your trip. Most of the rain usually falls in the late fall and winter (it rarely snows in Rome — maybe once every ten years), with November usually being rainiest. Heavy and brief thunderstorms are common, not only during the fall and winter, but also in the spring and summer (particularly in Aug), and the occasional rainy day — rarely more than two in a row — can happen all year around but particularly from fall to spring.

Table 3-1 Average Temperatures and Precipitation in Rome

	Jan	Feb	Mar	Apr	May	June	July	Aug	Sep	Oct	Nov	Dec
High (°C/°F)	12/ 53	13/ 55	15/ 59	18/ 65	23/ 73	27/ 81	30/ 87	30/ 87	27/ 80	22/ 71	16/ 61	13/ 55
Low (°C/°F)	3/ 37	4/ 38	5/ 41	8/ 46	11/ 52	14/ 58	17/ 63	18/ 64	15/ 59	11/ 51	7/ 44	4/ 39
Rainfall (cm/in.)	10.3/ 4	9.8/ 4	6.8/ 3	6.5/ 3	4.8/ 3	3.4/ 1	2.3/ 1	3.3/ 1	6.8/ 3	9.4/ 4	13/ 5	11.1/ 4

The once well-defined **high season** for tourism has become somewhat variable. As more and more people travel to Italy at all times, the off season is shrinking. Currently, hotels in Rome consider high season mid-March to June, September to mid-October, and December 24 to January 6. Low season is July and August, as well as January and February. The rest of the year is shoulder season, during which the application of higher rates depends on the hotel. As a general guideline, high season starts earlier and lasts longer for smaller and cheaper hotels (which tend to fill faster). The reverse is true for more expensive hotels.

Here are what we consider to be the pros and cons for traveling in each season.

April through June

In our opinion, spring and early summer are the most pleasant time to visit Rome:

✔ Temperatures are moderate, and the weather is mild, making it a pleasure to walk through the city both during the day and at night.

✔ Limited rainfall allows you to get out and enjoy the outdoor activities — without worrying about excess heat and sunstroke.

But keep in mind:

✔ Everybody knows this is a great season — including hotels and airlines, which jack up their prices. Make your reservations as early as possible, particularly for small, highly desirable hotels.

✔ Around Easter time, vast numbers of Catholic pilgrims and large groups of *very* noisy schoolchildren from all around the world descend on Rome. Plan your museum visits carefully, and definitely make reservations.

✔ May 1 is Labor Day in Italy, and all workers in Rome have the day off, including waiters, shopkeepers, and bus drivers. Everything shuts down, even public transportation.

July and August

Summertime is when most people take their vacations, and there are many upsides:

✔ The weather is beautiful, and outdoor life — especially in the sweet evenings — is at its max.

✔ You can get discount rates in most hotels.

✔ There is little traffic because residents tend to escape to the seashore, especially on weekends.

On the other hand, it may also be the worst time to come to Rome:

✔ Airfares are high.

✔ You can expect long lines for major attractions, because many tourists visit.

✔ The heat can make things quite uncomfortable — temperatures during the day often soar into the 90s, and Roman ruins turn into ovens (also, Rome is still mostly non-air-conditioned).

✔ Many shops and restaurants close during August, most definitely on August 15, the Italian holiday of Ferragosto.

September and October

Next to spring, fall is our favorite time to travel to Italy:

✔ The weather is still fairly mild and pleasant.

✔ With school back in session, crowds are relatively sparse.

On the other hand:

✔ Hotel prices are high.

✔ You have to watch for the rain, which typically starts falling in October.

November through March

More and more vacationers are reaping the benefits of traveling to Italy in the winter; if you can put up with rain and occasional cold spells, this is an excellent time for traveling to Rome:

✔ The relatively mild weather keeps the city pleasant for touring. Rain is at its heaviest in November and December but is usually manageable, with brief heavy rainfall followed by periods of calm.

✔ You can enjoy your visit more, because there are fewer crowds at the prime attractions, and you often receive better and more attentive service.

✔ Except for the Christmas–New Year's period, airfares and hotel rates are at their lowest.

✔ On a rainy day in November, we once found the Pantheon almost *empty.*

But keep in mind:

✔ Although average temperatures are mild, and cold spells tend to be short, it can get quite chilly. Depending on how resistant you are to colder temperatures, you may not be able to enjoy some of the outdoor attractions.

✔ Traffic is at its worst because most people take their cars to go to work and shopping when it gets nippy; correspondingly, air- and noise-pollution levels rise.

Perusing a Calendar of Events

Rome has many events worth planning a holiday around. Alternatively, you can use the following calendar to *avoid* big events and their attendant crowds.

Most Christian holidays — not just Christmas and Easter, but also saints' days and **Tutti Santi (All Saints' Day,** Nov 1) — are marked by some kind of celebration and often by processions and special foods.

January

Celebrate the **new year** with your children in **Piazza del Popolo,** and watch the clowns, acrobats, papier-mâché masks, and other fun attractions. Contact the tourist info line for a schedule of events at ☎ **06-36004399.** January 1.

The religious holiday **Epifania (Feast of the Epiphany)** takes a secular turn in Rome, and children receive special gifts — more than on Christmas. The open-air fair in Piazza Navona, selling toys and gifts, stays open until the wee hours of the morning. January 6.

February

In Rome, as everywhere else in Italy, **Carnevale** swallows up the week before Ash Wednesday, culminating on Fat Tuesday or *Martedi Grasso.* During this former pagan rite of the coming of spring, people — especially children — dress up in costumes and participate in masked parties. Everyone celebrates Carnevale, at least by eating *frappe* (thin slices of crunchy fried dough with powdered sugar) and *castagnole* (deep-fried balls of dough, often filled with custard). In Rome, you can find concerts and organized events, as well as lots of people parading around the city (particularly along Via Veneto) in costume on Fat Tuesday evening. Call the tourist office at ☎ **06-4889991** or check www.comune.roma.it for details. Tuesday before Ash Wednesday.

March and April

Every year, more than 40 directors from over 25 countries participate in **RIFF,** the **Roma Independent Film Festival (**☎ **06-45425050;** www.riff.it). One week in March or April.

Rome's Marathon (www.maratonadiroma.it) takes place along a scenic route passing by the Colosseum. Though not as famous as its New York counterpart, it is nonetheless a high-profile competition among international athletes and a wonderful event. Around March 20.

On **Venerdì Santo (Good Friday),** the Catholic rite of the procession of the Stations of the Cross *(Via Crucis)* is presented in most Roman churches, sometimes as a reenactment with costumes. The Vatican's procession takes place at night, led by the pope, between the Colosseum and Palatine Hill. Friday before Easter Sunday.

The pope gives his traditional **Benedizione Pasquale (Easter Benediction)** in Piazza San Pietro. Easter Sunday, between the end of March and mid-April.

During the **Mostra delle Azalee (Exhibition of Azaleas),** more than 700 azalea plants are exhibited on the Spanish Steps to celebrate the beginning of spring. Concerts take place in Trinità dei Monti at the head of the steps. Call ☎ **06-4889991** for more information. Mid-April through July, weather permitting.

Tradition has it that Romulus founded Rome — by tracing its original limits on the ground — on April 21 in the year 753 B.C. The day, **Rome's Birthday (Natale di Roma),** is still warmly celebrated in Rome with a series of cultural events. Contact the tourist info line at ☎ **06-36004399** for more information. April 21.

Via Margutta turns into an open-air gallery for the **Cento Pittori Via Margutta** (see November listing). Five days in April/May.

May

For **Labor Day (Festa del Lavoro),** everything shuts down except in Piazza San Giovanni, where the holiday is celebrated with a great pop-music festival (check the tourist info line for a program of events at ☎ **06-36004399**). May 1.

Rome's **Concorso Ippico Internazionale di Roma (International Horse Show)** attracts the best riders and mounts from all over the world to Villa Borghese's beautiful Piazza di Siena. You can buy tickets at the gate. For details, contact the Piazza di Siena ticket agent at ☎ **06-6383818** or visit www.piazzadisiena.com. Late May.

June and July

The **Estate Romana (Roman Summer)** is a multifarious festival with an extremely rich program of concerts, theater, special exhibits, and shows for every audience, featuring a huge number of events from sport to art and culture throughout Rome. Performances held inside Roman ruins are particularly dramatic. See Chapters 15 and 16 for details (☎ **06-4889991** or www.estateromana.comune.roma.it for a schedule of events) Mid-June through early September.

One offshoot of the **Estate Romana** festival is the **Villa Celimontana Jazz** (Via della Navicella; ☎ **06-77208423;** www.villacelimontana jazz.com), which mounts jazz concerts by international and national musicians in the picturesque setting of the Villa Celimontana park. June through August.

Another is **Gay Village** (☎ **340-5423008;** www.gayvillage.it), a small town of tolerance and culture, where gay and straight people mingle to enjoy dining, music, and a variety of artistic performances for all age groups. Late June to early September.

August

The pagan holiday of **Ferragosto** — and the religious holy day of the Assumption — celebrates the culmination of the summer. Romans vacation on the seashore and in the mountains. Most businesses are closed, so call ahead to make sure your destination is open. August 15.

September

La Notte Bianca — White Night, in English — is a magic night of entertainment, cultural events, and shows scheduled throughout the city and throughout the night. The first edition was in 2003, and the event has grown ever since. Check the Web site (www.lanottebianca.it) for a calendar of events in English. First or second Saturday in September.

The **Romaeuropa Festival** (☎ **800-795525;** www2.romaeuropa.net) is a cultural extravaganza, presenting the best innovative and experimental European dance, music, and theater performances. It celebrated its 20th season in 2005, and its success continues unabated. End of September to end of November.

October

The **Festa di San Francesco d'Assisi (Feast of St. Francis of Assisi),** a celebration for the patron saint of Italy, is observed with processions, special masses, and other religious events. October 4.

With concerts scheduled in all of Rome's basilicas, the **International Festival of Sacred Music and Art** (☎ **06-6869187;** Fax 06-6873300; www.festivalmusicaeartesacra.net) was born in 2002 and offers a unique opportunity to all lovers of classical and sacred music. Second week in October.

November

One hundred artists are selected for the **Cento Pittori Via Margutta** exhibit (www.centopittoriviamargutta.it), which turns scenic Via Margutta into an open-air gallery twice a year (another edition takes place in April/May). Five days in November.

Over 30 years down the road, the **Rome Jazz Festival** (www.romajazz festival.it) continues to attract the big Italian and international names. Concerts take place in various venues throughout Rome (another edition falls during the Estate Romana festival in June and July; see listing earlier in this calendar). Ten days in November.

December

For the **Feast of the Immaculate Conception,** Roman firefighters decorate the statue of the Madonna on the column of Piazza Trinità dei Monti, at the top of the Spanish Steps, with flowers. Believers and the pope himself visit the statue throughout the day to offer flowers to the Virgin. December 8.

For Rome's **Crèche Exhibit,** more than 50 nativity scenes are displayed in the Villa Giulia, and many others are on view in churches around the city. Particularly nice are the ones in the Basilica di Santa Maria Maggiore, Santa Maria d'Aracoeli (see Chapter 11), Santa Maria del Popolo (Piazza del Popolo 12; ☎ 06-3610487), and Chiesa del Gesù (Piazza del Gesù, off Via del Plebiscito; ☎ 06-6795131). Don't miss the life-size nativity scene in front of St. Peter's, either. Three weeks leading up to Christmas.

Piazza Navona becomes the seat of the **Mercatino di Natale (Christmas Market),** with toys and candy sellers. The market starts three weeks before Christmas and stays open all night on its last day, January 5, the eve of Epiphany. Beginning of December through January 6 at dawn.

If you don't mind crowds or getting up early, you can witness the pope giving a special **Christmas Blessing** to Rome and the world from St. Peter's Square at noon on Christmas Day. For a chance of being *in* the square, you should get there by 9 a.m. December 25.

Romans love **New Year's Eve,** and partying reaches its climax at midnight, when the city explodes with fireworks. The Vatican puts on its own fiery show, and there's an organized concert–cum–fireworks show in Piazza del Popolo, but everybody gets into the act, shooting fireworks from every window and roof. By tradition, fireworks are accompanied by the symbolic throwing away of something old to mark the end of the old year. Although the tradition has been outlawed, some people still get carried away, so watch out for falling UFOs if you take a stroll shortly after midnight! December 31.

Part II
Planning Your Trip to Rome

The 5th Wave   By Rich Tennant

" And how shall I book your flight to Italy – First Class, Coach, or Medieval?"

In this part . . .

*I*t's time to delve into the nitty-gritty of trip planning: all those details that are necessary to make your vacation as perfect as possible. We give you some tips on budgeting — how to save a few euro here and there — and tell you what to expect in terms of banks and currency exchange. We also lay out the different ways you can get to Rome, including various travel packages, and offer suggestions on buying travel insurance, staying healthy, and staying in contact with those who didn't get to make the trip. And, so everyone has a good time, we also offer advice to those people who have special travel needs or interests — travelers with disabilities, families, seniors, and gays and lesbians.

Chapter 4

Managing Your Money

● ●

In This Chapter

▶ Devising a realistic budget
▶ Determining travel, lodging, and dining expenses
▶ Remembering the extras: Shopping and entertainment
▶ Saving money

● ●

*W*hen it comes to planning a vacation budget, you usually deal with two different numbers: what you'd *like* to spend and what you *can* spend. In this chapter, we give you some pointers to help you decide where to trim the incidentals and splurge on the things that really matter to you, so that you can design a terrific vacation without breaking the bank.

Planning Your Budget

Rome's level of services has increased to match the highest international standards. Unfortunately, prices have followed suit, and the cost of living has more than doubled since the introduction in 2002 of the euro, the unit of currency that replaced the old *lire*. You get more in hotels and restaurant, but you pay more as well. On the good side, many public services, including state museums and attractions, have maintained — or even reduced — their prices, while offering a lot more than before. We figure there are six major elements that eat up your vacation budget: transportation, lodging, dining, sightseeing, shopping, and nightlife. Knowledge is key, and we want to share with you our hard-earned experience with each of these. With the euro flying higher against the dollar, how well you plan certain elements can make or break your budget.

The following sections provide more tips and consideration that emerge as you plan your budget. Table 4-1 gives you a sampling of costs that you may encounter on your trip. Oh, yes, and don't forget taxes — under some circumstances, you may be eligible for a refund (see Chapter 12).

Table 4-1	What Things Cost in Rome
Item	*Cost*
A metro or city bus ride	1€ ($1.30)
Can of soda	1€–2€ ($1.30–$2.60)
Pay-phone call	0.20€ (26¢)
Movie ticket	8€–12€ ($10–$16)
Caffè lungo (American-style espresso)	1€ ($1.30)
Cappuccino (or something similar)	1.20€ ($1.60)
Ticket to the Borghese Gallery (including reservation)	8.50€ ($11)
Gasoline	1.40€ ($1.82) per liter = 5.60€ ($7.28) per gallon
Average hotel room	230€ ($299)
Liter of house wine in a restaurant	10€ ($13)
Individual pizza in a pizzeria	8€–12€ ($10–$16)
First-class letter to United States (or any overseas country)	0.85€ ($1.11)

Transportation

Airfare is one of the biggest components of your budget. Keeping it low gives you a sort of cushion for the rest of your expenses. The actual cost depends on when you travel, but booking in advance helps, too — the cheaper seats are the first to go. If you wait until mid-June to reserve a flight to Rome for July, you'll be lucky to pay $1,200, if you can find a seat at all. Book ahead, and you may save $300 or $400; that's money you can put toward a shopping splurge or a more comfortable hotel. Wait for the off-season, and you may find tickets for half that much or even less. Make sure that you check out our money-saving tips before buying an airline ticket (see Chapter 5).

Getting around Rome after you're there is inexpensive — for example, a three-day public transportation pass is only 11€ ($14). Out-of-town trips are cheap, too, if you use public transportation. You have to budget more if you're planning to take a tour, hire a limousine, or rent a car — a rather expensive proposition in Rome.

Keep in mind that in Rome you absolutely don't need a car, and if you arrive there with one, you have to keep it garaged during your entire stay — and pay for that. Rome has too many roads and drivers for you to want to deal with, plus it bans nonresidents from driving in *il centro*

(the historic center), which is the part of the city where most attractions lie. Also, organized thieves steal cars and from cars, and you don't want the risk. If you feel you need a car for a day trip, rent one for the occasion, by all means, but expect to pay a minimum of 70€ ($91) per day for an economy car and about $7 per gallon for gas.

Lodging

Lodging is another big-ticket item. Accommodations are so expensive in Rome that the price of a medium-range hotel elsewhere covers only a budget hotel or a hostel here. Even in the off-season, you won't be able to spend much less than around $150 a night, and that is if you're willing to forgo amenities and put up with a certain amount of inconvenience (less central location, tiny room, and so on). In the high season, you should plan on spending at least $200 to have minimum comfort (see Chapter 9 for a lowdown on what to expect from your hotel room in Rome). Of course cheaper options exist, and you can save a lot of money if you don't mind smaller private facilities and a simpler room. But there, too, it all depends on how much you want to compromise. You don't want to make it so difficult for yourself that it will spoil your entire vacation. Here again, booking in advance will let you get the best deals. As an added advantage, if you book all your hotels in advance, you'll know that piece of the budget before you leave.

Prices also vary depending on which area of Rome you choose. Figure that 150€ ($195) pays for a decent double room with a private bathroom somewhere in Rome, but 230€ ($299) gets you a nice room in the historic center. From 350€ ($455) and up, you're in the luxury range, probably close to the most famous attractions. Of course, the amounts that these estimates represent in dollars constantly vary, according to current exchange rates.

 You can save money if you skip the breakfast your hotel serves, unless it's included with your room rate (which we indicate in our reviews in Chapter 9). Breakfast is worth paying for only at the more expensive hotels ($$$ and above), where you find a buffet with a variety of foods, usually including eggs, sausage, cheese, cold cuts, yogurt, fruit, and cereal. This kind of breakfast may run about 20€ ($26), so you have to decide if what you get is worth the money.

In all the hotel reviews in this guide, we supply the *rack rate,* which, in Rome, is the highest rate the hotel will charge you (at the peak of high season and when the hotel is completely full). You should be able to do better than that in most cases. See Chapter 9 for a table indicating what the $ symbols ($–$$$$$) mean.

Dining

Your expenses will vary with your style: What you spend will depend on what and how you eat. Possibilities in Rome are endless and, on the whole, very satisfactory: You'll find cheap eateries, gourmet haunts, and everything in between, all serving excellent food. You also have the option of buying your own food (for snacks and picnics, for example) and the choice is always large, ranging from small vendors to open-air markets to supermarkets. Prices depend on the elegance or trendiness of the place you choose and on the food you order. Drinks excluded, expect to spend about 40€ ($52) per person for a full dinner in Rome in a middle-range restaurant, and 25€ ($33) in a less formal one, such as a *pizzeria* or *osteria.* For a truly special meal in one of the top restaurants, expect to spend an average of 65€ ($85) per person for a meat dinner and as much as 85€ ($111) for a fish meal. Prices for food on the go are much lower: you can spend as little as 5€ to 8€ ($6–$9.60) in a *rosticceria* or *pizza a taglio* place. In most restaurants, prices are not significantly different at lunch or dinner, but some restaurants serve more elaborate dishes — with accordingly higher prices — only at dinner, or offer a lunch prix-fixe, which is a deal.

In the listings in Chapter 9 we give you the price range of *secondi;* these meat or fish dishes are the most expensive on the menu. Side dishes are priced separately, and you may be content with just a *primo* (a less expensive pasta dish; see Chapter 2 for more on the structure of a meal in Italy). Most restaurants impose a basic **table-and-bread charge,** called *pane e coperto,* of about 2€ to 4€ ($2.60–$5.20). Tipping isn't a big extra in Rome, because prices usually include service, and you need only leave a small token of appreciation. Check for the words *servizio incluso* (service included) on the menu; if they aren't there, expect to pay a full gratuity of 15 percent. Just as with the hotels, we use a dollar-sign system to designate the prices of restaurants; these refer to a complete meal. See Chapter 10 for a table indicating what the $ symbols ($–$$$$) mean.

Sightseeing

Museums and other attractions charge anywhere from 2€ to 12€ ($2.60–$16) for admission. Most churches are free (avoid visiting during mass unless you're attending the service, however). Frankly, sightseeing isn't an area where you can save a lot of money, and you'll probably be sorry if you try. On the other hand, entrance fees for most attractions aren't that expensive (with some notable exceptions), so your budget won't be stretched to its limits by daily sightseeing expenditures.

In Chapter 11, we describe special combination discount tickets and cards, which can represent a great savings.

Age-based discounts are available based on reciprocity between countries. Therefore, senior and children discounts aren't available to Americans but are available to British visitors and other residents of European Union (EU) countries.

You can calculate a large percentage of this item of your budget before leaving if you make advance reservations; they are offered for most museums and attractions (see Chapter 11).

> # Don't sit to sip
>
> Be aware that any time you sit down in a *caffè* or bar in Italy, things cost more. Coffee at an outside table in Piazza del Popolo or Piazza Navona, for example, may cost the same as lunch elsewhere. Most Italians stand at the bar while they have a coffee or a beer.

Shopping

Shopping is the one expenditure that is totally within your control: You can shop 'til you drop, spending hundreds or even thousands of dollars, or you can limit yourself to window shopping. In Chapter 12, we give you our recommendations for the best shops and items each neighborhood offers. Rome is famous for its artwork, design, and crafts — antique prints, handmade paper, plaster works, pottery, leather, gold, and lace, among many other fine wares. And the city isn't half bad for Italian fashion — besides the local designers, Valentino, Versace, Dolce & Gabbana, and Armani are a few of the world-famous Italian firms located in Rome.

Depending on exchange rates, you may actually save by buying Italian goods in Rome. More important, though, being in Rome gives you a chance to buy things that simply aren't available back home. Use your trip as a chance to pick up that special something you have an irresistible craving for — maybe a print of the Pantheon, a handmade golden necklace, a Gucci handbag, or even a nice used Ferrari (just kidding). Remember to plan in your budget enough shopping money for the kind of goods you think you may want to buy, and remember also that you can get back the value-added tax (known in Italy as IVA) for large purchases (see Chapter 12).

Nightlife

Visiting the opera, going out for a drink, listening to music in a jazz club, and dancing the night away can make your time in Rome that much more memorable. You can spend big bucks in this department, or you can cut costs by enjoying those serendipitous little things that are free or nearly so, such as people-watching on a beautiful floodlit piazza or ordering a coffee or drink in a classic *caffè* and soaking in the atmosphere.

Ticket prices for performances can vary a good deal, from 10€ ($13) for a concert at a small venue to 130€ ($169) for the best seat at the opera. Nightclubs in Rome are about as expensive as those anywhere else, but you may be able to avoid a cover charge by sitting or standing at the bar rather than taking a table, or by arriving before a certain hour. If you happen to be in Rome during a public holiday or festival, you may enjoy abundant free entertainment, much of it in the streets.

Cutting Costs — but Not the Fun

Don't feel like taking out a second mortgage on your house so you can afford a vacation to Rome? Well, you know the saying: "When in Rome. . . ." Start thinking like a Roman. Romans have relatively less disposable income than Americans; the more closely you mirror the way they live and move about town, the cheaper your trip will be — and the closer you'll get to the Romans themselves. Staying in a huge hotel designed for foreign tourists with all the fixings will cost you a lot, as will the luxury of renting a big car. Tack on a few five-star-restaurant experiences, and your budget flies out the window.

Instead, try to live for a week without your own private bathroom. Make big, healthy sandwiches from the delicious stuff you buy in a market. Pass on the postcards, trinkets, and other things that you pick up just to say that you've been to Rome — you may even save enough for a splurge here and there.

But remember that sometimes, paying more makes sense. For example, if you're facing sightseeing overload and are dead tired, you may not want to endure an hour-long bus ride to your hotel on the other side of town. Take a cab instead. And why not grab a bite to eat in the more expensive cafe near your hotel rather than deal with crossing town to an extra-cheap restaurant? Also watch out for areas where you simply shouldn't make cuts: Not seeing the Vatican Museums and Sistine Chapel, the Colosseum, the Borghese Gallery, or some other major attraction just because of the cost would be a tragedy. We'd rather skip lunch and take the opportunity to go to one of these must-sees twice. Who knows when you'll be back this way again?

 Throughout this book, we use the Bargain Alert icon to identify money-saving tips and great deals. Here are some additional cost-cutting strategies.

- ✔ **Go off season.** If you can travel at nonpeak times (Nov–Mar, with the exception of the Christmas–New Year's holidays), you can find airfares and hotel prices as much as 30 percent less than during peak months.

- ✔ **Travel on off-peak days of the week.** Airfares vary depending not only on the time of the year but also on the day of the week. International flights tend to be cheaper midweek. When you inquire about airfares, ask whether you can obtain a cheaper rate by flying on a different day. (See Chapter 5 for more tips on getting a good fare.)

- ✔ **Try a package tour.** For popular destinations such as Rome, you can book airfare, hotel, ground transportation, and even some sightseeing by making just one call to a travel agent or packager, and you may pay a lot less than if you tried to put the trip together yourself. But always work out the prices that you'd pay otherwise, just to double-check. See the section on package tours in Chapter 5 for specific suggestions.

✔ **Pack light.** Packing light enables you to carry your own bags and not worry about finding a porter (don't forget to tip yourself). Likewise, if you're carrying only one or two bags, you can take a bus or a train rather than a cab from the airport, saving yourself quite a few more euro.

✔ **Reserve a room with a refrigerator and coffeemaker.** You don't have to slave over a hot stove to cut a few costs; most hotels have minifridges, and some have coffeemakers. Buying supplies for breakfast will save you money — and probably calories.

✔ **Book a hotel in a less glamorous location.** In Rome, you'll find that the edge of the historic center is just as convenient as a more central location and may offer great bargains. You may need to do only a little more walking or deal with a short commute. Don't overdo it, though: If you pick a hotel too far out of the way, you'll waste hours of precious time in transportation, and you may well ruin your trip. The key is always to stay only a short distance from the attractions you want to visit. See Chapter 9 for more hotel information.

✔ **Have a picnic.** You can put together some delicious and inexpensive meals at a Roman grocery store, and then enjoy your feast in a garden or park.

✔ **Use public transportation.** In Rome, using the local bus system may be a little complicated at times, but it's also a great way to see the city the way locals do.

✔ **Walk a lot.** A good pair of walking shoes can save you money in taxis and other transportation expenses. As a bonus, you'll get to know your destination more intimately as you explore at a slower pace. Rome's historic center is quite large, but you'll want to visit it in sections, so that you can actually walk almost anywhere you need to go for that part of the day.

✔ **Skip the souvenirs.** Your photographs and your memories can be the best mementos of your trip. If you're concerned about money, you can do without the T-shirts, key chains, salt and pepper shakers, and other trinkets.

Handling Money

You're the best judge of how much cash you feel comfortable carrying or what alternative form of currency is your favorite. Consider, though, that the only type of payment that won't be quite as available to you away from home is your personal checkbook.

Making sense of the euro

Italy's currency, the *euro* (the plural is also *euro,* and it's abbreviated as € in this guide), was introduced in 2002 in Italy and in 11 other European countries. You can use the same currency in Austria, Belgium, Cyprus, Finland, France, Germany, Greece, Ireland, Italy, Luxembourg, Malta, the Netherlands, Portugal, Slovenia, and Spain.

The transformation to the euro has made things much easier for Americans because 1€ exchanges in a range nearer $1 (the exchange rate used in this book is 1€ = $1.30; we round off all dollar values above $10). Many Web sites present the latest exchange rates; our favorite is www.xe.com, where you can get up-to-date (and historical) comparisons between the euro and your currency, whether it is the U.S. or Canadian dollar, the British pound, or something else. At press time, the British pound exchanged at £1 = 1.51€. These were the rates of exchange used to calculate the values in Table 4-2.

Table 4-2		Foreign Currencies vs. the U.S. Dollar			
Euro €	*U.S. $*	*U.K. £*	*Euro* €	*U.S. $*	*U.K. £*
1.00	1.30	0.66	75.00	97.50	49.50
2.00	2.60	1.32	100.00	130.00	66.00
3.00	3.90	1.98	125.00	162.50	82.50
4.00	5.20	2.64	150.00	195.00	99.00
5.00	6.50	3.30	175.00	227.50	115.50
6.00	7.80	3.96	200.00	260.00	132.00
7.00	9.10	4.62	225.00	292.50	148.50
8.00	10.40	5.28	250.00	325.00	165.00
9.00	11.70	5.94	275.00	316.25	181.50
10.00	13.00	6.60	300.00	390.00	198.00
15.00	19.50	9.90	350.00	455.00	231.00
20.00	26.00	13.20	400.00	520.00	264.00
25.00	32.50	16.50	500.00	650.00	330.00
50.00	65.00	33.00	1000.00	1300.00	660.00

Note that in the word *euro,* Italians pronounce all three vowels, so it's *ay-ou-roh,* not *yurr-oh.*

The euro look

Paper bills come in 5€, 10€, 20€, 50€, 100€, 200€, and 500€ denominations. All bills are brightly colored and in a different shade for each denomination. In addition, the higher the value of the bill, the larger the size of the bill. A 50€ bill is bigger than a dollar bill, and even the smaller denominations are taller than U.S. dollars; if you have a bunch, you'll find stuffing them in your wallet a bit difficult. Remember that shops are always short of change, and breaking those large bills to buy a soft drink is sometimes difficult. Think ahead, and try to have a supply of 10€ bills with you.

Coins come in 1€ and 2€ (both thin and brass-colored); 10-cent, 20-cent, and 50-cent (all brass colored); and 1-cent, 2-cent, and 5-cent (all copper-colored) denominations.

For more information and pictures of the currency, check the Web site of the **European Union** (http://europa.eu.int/euro) or the **European Central Bank** (www.ecb.int).

Don't be surprised to see different country names on euro bills and coins: One face is the European side, common to each of the 15 participating countries, and the reverse is the national side, where each country prints its own design. All are valid and accepted in each of the countries.

From the U.S. standpoint, since the introduction of the euro, Italian prices have increased, and quite a lot. This is due to the loss of value suffered by the U.S. dollar on international currency markets. For instance, at press time, the dollar buys fewer euro than it could two years ago. By the time you read this, the two currencies may be closer to parity — but then again, maybe not. It's all the more important, then, to plan ahead and get the best deals you can.

You can exchange money at the airport in Rome, where you'll also find automated teller machines (ATMs), as well as at banks and exchange bureaus in town. These usually display multilingual signs (CHANGE/CAMBIO/WECHSEL). Rates may vary to some degree. For example, some bureaus advertise "no fee" but then give you a lower rate. Arriving in Rome with a small supply of euro, at least enough to pay for a cab to your hotel, is a good idea in case the ATMs at the airport don't work or the lines are unbearably long.

Using ATMs and carrying cash

The easiest and best way to get cash away from home is from an ATM. Look at the back of your bank card to see which network you're on, then call or check online for ATM locations at your destination. The **Cirrus** network (☎ 800-424-7787; www.mastercard.com) is the most common international network in Rome. **PLUS** (☎ 800-843-7587; www.visa.com) is less common. The Banca Nazionale del Lavoro (BNL) is one bank that does offer PLUS in its ATMs; another sure bet is the Italian Post Offices' ATMs.

Before leaving for Rome, make sure that you check the daily withdrawal limit for your ATM card, and ask whether you need a new personal identification number (PIN). You need a four-digit PIN for Europe, so if you currently have a six-digit PIN, you must get a new one before you go. Also, if your PIN is a word, make sure you know how it translates into numbers, because some ATM keypads in Italy display only numbers.

Many banks impose a fee every time your card is used at a different bank's ATM, and that fee can be higher for international transactions (up to $5 or more) than for domestic ones (where they're rarely more than $3). On top of this, the bank from which you withdraw cash may charge its own fee. For international withdrawal fees, ask your bank.

In Rome, ATMs are never far away, so you can walk around with 100€ ($130) in your wallet, and you should be set to dine and pay your museum admissions (but not your hotel bill). Before going off on a driving tour of the countryside, however, make sure that you have a good stock of cash in your wallet; banks and ATMs are rarer outside big cities, and lots of small businesses don't accept credit cards.

If you have linked checking and savings accounts and you're in the habit of moving relatively small amounts of money from savings to checking as you need it, beware: Italian ATMs won't show you the transfer-between-accounts option, and they won't allow you to withdraw money directly from your savings account. If your checking account runs dry, you must call or write your bank to move money from savings to checking. (We did so, and our bank charged us $30. Ouch!)

Charging ahead with credit cards

Credit cards are a safe way to carry money. They also provide a convenient record of all your expenses, and they generally offer relatively good exchange rates. You can also make cash advances against your credit cards at banks or ATMs, as long as you know your PIN. If you've forgotten yours, or didn't even know you had one, call the number on the back of your credit card, and ask the bank to send it to you. It usually takes five to seven business days, though some banks will provide the number over the phone if you tell them your mother's maiden name or some other personal information.

Keep in mind that when you use your credit card abroad, most banks assess a 2 percent fee above the 1 percent fee charged by Visa, MasterCard, or American Express for currency conversion on credit charges. But credit cards still may be the smart way to go when you factor in such things as exorbitant ATM fees and higher traveler's check exchange rates (and service fees).

Some credit card companies recommend that you notify them of any upcoming trip abroad so that they don't become suspicious when the card is used numerous times in a foreign destination and block your charges. Even if you don't call your credit card company in advance, you can always call the card's toll-free emergency number if a charge is refused — a good reason to carry the phone number with you. But perhaps the most important lesson here is to carry more than one card with you on your trip; a card may not work for any number of reasons, so having a backup is the smart way to go.

Toting traveler's checks

These days, traveler's checks are less necessary because 24-hour ATMs allow you to withdraw small amounts of cash as needed. However, keep in mind that you'll likely be charged an ATM withdrawal fee if the bank is not your own (in Rome, it won't be), so if you're withdrawing money every day, you may be better off with traveler's checks — as long as you don't mind showing identification every time you want to cash one. Traveler's checks are widely accepted in Rome, especially at large tourist stores and at hotels.

You can get traveler's checks at almost any bank. **American Express** offers denominations of $20, $50, $100, $500, and (for cardholders only) $1,000. You'll pay a service charge ranging from 1 percent to 4 percent. You can also get American Express traveler's checks over the phone by calling ☎ **800-221-7282;** AMEX gold and platinum cardholders who use this number are exempt from the 1 percent fee.

Visa offers traveler's checks at Citibank locations nationwide and at several other banks. The service charge ranges between 1.5 percent and 2 percent; checks come in denominations of $20, $50, $100, $500, and $1,000. Call ☎ **800-732-1322** for information. AAA members can obtain Visa checks without a fee at most AAA offices or by calling ☎ **866-339-3378. MasterCard** also offers traveler's checks. Call ☎ **800-223-9920** for a location near you.

 If you choose to carry traveler's checks, be sure to keep a record of their serial numbers separate from your checks, in case they're stolen or lost. You'll get a refund faster if you know the numbers.

Dealing with a Lost or Stolen Wallet

Being on vacation is a blissful time of distraction and discovery. Unfortunately, that makes tourists ripe targets for pickpockets. In Italy, violent crime is rare; most wallets that are stolen are lost to pickpockets, not muggers.

If you discover that your wallet has been lost or stolen, contact all of your credit card companies right away. You'll also want to file a report at the nearest police precinct. Your credit card company or insurer may require a police-report number or record of the loss. Most credit card companies have emergency toll-free numbers to call if your card is lost or stolen; they may be able to wire you a cash advance immediately or deliver an emergency credit card in a day or two. Call the following emergency numbers:

- ✔ **American Express** (☎ **06-72282** or 06-72900347 in Rome; 1-336-393-1111 collect in the United States; www.americanexpress.com)

- ✔ **Diners Club** (☎ **800-864064** toll-free within Italy; www.diners club.com)

- ✔ **MasterCard** (☎ **800-870866** toll-free within Italy; www.mastercard. com)

- ✔ **Visa** (☎ **800-819014** toll-free within Italy; www.visaeurope.com).

If you need emergency cash over the weekend, when banks and American Express offices are closed, you can have money wired to you through Western Union (☎ **800-325-6000;** www.westernunion.com).

Identity theft and fraud are potential complications of losing your wallet, especially if you've lost your driver's license or passport along with your cash and credit cards. Notify the major credit-reporting bureaus immediately; placing a fraud alert on your records may protect you against liability for criminal activity. The three major U.S. credit-reporting agencies are **Equifax** (☎ **800-766-0008;** www.equifax.com), **Experian** (☎ **888-397-3742;** www.experian.com), and **TransUnion** (☎ **800-680-7289;** www.transunion.com). Finally, if you've lost all forms of photo ID, call your airline and explain the situation; it may allow you to board the plane if you have a copy of your passport or birth certificate and a copy of the police report you've filed.

Watch your purse, wallet, briefcase, or backpack in any public place. And when walking on the streets, keep your purse on the side away from traffic, so a thief on a motor scooter can't speed by and grab it from you. Better yet, carry your money, credit cards, and passport in an interior pocket, where pickpockets won't be able to snatch them.

Chapter 5

Getting to Rome

● ●

In This Chapter

▶ Checking out the major airlines flying into Rome
▶ Getting to Rome by train, ship, bus, or car
▶ Sorting out packages and escorted tours

● ●

Rome is the capital of Italy and extremely well connected to other major cities around the world. You'll find direct flights to Rome from a great number of destinations. Most visitors fly to Rome, and you can also arrive by train from within Europe, by cruise ship, or (although we don't recommend it) by car. This chapter outlines all the ways and means you have to make getting to Rome a snap.

Flying to Rome

If you live near a major city, flying to Rome may be as easy as flying to another destination in your own country, but it won't be cheaper. Italy is farther from the U.S. than England or France, and airfares are significantly higher. A round-trip ticket during peak times can run between $800 and $2,000, depending on where you start and how far in advance you book your flight. Of course, with the cutthroat competition among airlines, you may be able to lock in a much better deal, especially if you book well in advance and have a flexible itinerary.

Finding out which airlines fly there

Rome is one of Italy's gateways (the other is Milan), to which you can fly nonstop from North America and other continents; you can also find lots of flights to Rome connecting through other European cities.

In general, European airlines offer the most legroom on intercontinental flights, and U.S. airlines the least, though things are slowly getting more uniform. **Alitalia** (☎ **800-223-5730** in the U.S.; 800-361-8336 in Canada; 020-8814-7700 in the U.K.; 8-8306-8411 in Australia; or 06-2222 in Italy; www.alitalia.it), the Italian national airline, offers direct flights to Rome from most major destinations in the world; it also offers connecting flights to every destination in Italy by way of Rome or Milan. Daily direct flights originate in a number of U.S. cities, including New York and Boston, as well as Toronto and Montreal. Service on Alitalia is excellent, with decent space even in economy class, and you'll be pampered with good food and wine.

From the United States, check **American Airlines** (☎ 800-433-7300; www. aa.com), **Delta** (☎ 800-241-4141; www.delta.com), **United** (☎ 800-538-2929; www.united.com), **US Airways** (☎ 800-428-4322; www.usairways. com), **Continental** (☎ 800-525-0280; www.continental.com), and **Northwest/KLM** (☎ 800-447-4747; www.nwa.com), which offer direct nonstop flights to Rome or Milan, at least during peak season. **Air Canada** (☎ 888-247-2262; www.aircanada.com) flies direct from Toronto to Rome.

From Australia, **Qantas** (☎ 13-13-13; www.qantas.com) offers direct flights daily from Melbourne to Rome, and several days a week from Sydney.

From Britain, you'll find direct flights to a number of Italian cities on **Alitalia** (☎ 020-8814-7700; www.alitalia.it) and **British Airways** (☎ 0845-773-3377 in the U.K.; www.britishairways.com). Other options include **Ryanair** (☎ 0871-246-0000; www.ryanair.com) and **EasyJet** (☎ 0871-244-2366 [10p per minute]; www.easyjet.com), which fill the old no-frills or discount airline slot.

On any day of the week, you can get a connecting flight through a major European capital with a European national carrier, such as **British Airways** (☎ 800-247-297; www.britishairways.com), **Air France** (☎ 800-237-2747; www.airfrance.com), **KLM** (☎ 800-374-7747; www. klm.nl), and **Lufthansa** (☎ 800-645-3880; www.lufthansa-usa.com).

Getting the best deal on your airfare

Business travelers who need the flexibility to buy their tickets at the last minute and change their itineraries at a moment's notice — and who want to get home before the weekend — pay (or at least their companies pay) the premium rate, known as the *full fare*. But you can often qualify for the least expensive price, several hundred — or even thousands — of dollars less than the full fare, if you purchase well in advance.

Keep in mind that the lowest fares are often nonrefundable, require advance purchase and a certain length of stay, have date-of-travel restrictions, and carry penalties for changing dates of travel.

The high season for flying to Rome is long and getting longer, and snagging low fares is increasingly difficult; at certain times, you may be lucky just to get on any plane heading for Italy. But fear not: You don't have to pay top dollar. Here are some tips on scoring the best airfare:

✔ **Book in advance and be flexible.** Fares can vary by hundreds of dollars, depending on how far in advance you book, day of the week, and the season. Airlines offer only a limited number of seats for each rate, and the cheapest go fast. Passengers who can book far in advance (21 days at least), who can stay over Saturday night, or who are willing to travel on Tuesday, Wednesday, or Thursday will pay a fraction of the full fare. If your schedule is flexible, say so — ask if you can secure a cheaper fare by staying an extra day, by flying midweek, or by flying at less busy hours.

✔ **Shop around for specials.** Airlines periodically hold sales, which tend to take place in seasons of low travel volume; for Rome, that means the dead of winter. As you plan your vacation, keep your eyes open for these sales advertised in newspapers and online. If you already hold a ticket when a sale breaks, exchanging your ticket, which usually incurs a $100 to $150 charge, may pay off.

✔ **Consider nondirect flights.** To encourage travelers to choose a nondirect route, round-trip rates are often handsomely discounted, and connections often involve just an hour or two of layover.

✔ **Join frequent-flier clubs.** Accruing miles on one program is best, so you can rack up free flights and achieve elite status faster. But opening as many accounts as possible makes sense. It's free, and you get the best choice of seats, faster response to phone inquiries, and prompter service if your luggage is stolen, if your flight is canceled or delayed, or if you want to change your seat.

You can also check *consolidators,* also known as *bucket shops.* Start by looking in Sunday newspaper travel sections; U.S. travelers should focus on the *New York Times, Los Angeles Times,* and *Miami Herald.* Several reliable consolidators are worldwide and available on the Net. **STA Travel** (☎ 800-781-4040; www.statravel.com), the world's leader in student travel, offers good fares for travelers of all ages. **ELTExpress** (☎ 800-TRAV-800; www.flights.com) started in Europe and has excellent fares worldwide. **Flights.com** also has "local" Web sites in 12 countries. FlyCheap, an industry leader, has become **Lowestfare.com** (www.lowestfare.com) and is owned by Priceline (see information later in this chapter). **Air Tickets Direct** (☎ 800-778-3447; www.airtickets direct.com) is based in Montreal.

Bucket shop tickets are usually nonrefundable or carry stiff cancellation penalties, often as high as 50 percent to 75 percent of the ticket price, and some put you on charter airlines with questionable safety records.

Booking your flight online

The "big three" online travel agencies, **Expedia** (www.expedia.com), **Travelocity** (www.travelocity.com), and **Orbitz** (www.orbitz.com) sell most of the air tickets bought on the Internet. (Canadian travelers should try www.expedia.ca and www.travelocity.ca; U.K. residents can go for expedia.co.uk and opodo.co.uk.) Each has different deals with the airlines and may offer different fares on the same flights, so shopping around is wise. Expedia and Travelocity will also send you an **e-mail notification** when a cheap fare becomes available to your favorite destination. Of the smaller ones, **SideStep** (www.sidestep.com) receives good reviews from users; it's a meta-search site (which finds low fares and then directs you to airline and hotel Web sites for booking).

Great **last-minute deals** are available through free weekly e-mail services provided directly by the airlines. Most of these deals are announced on Tuesday or Wednesday and must be purchased online. Most are valid only for travel that weekend, but some can be booked weeks or months in advance. Sign up for weekly e-mail alerts at airline Web sites or check mega-sites that compile comprehensive lists of last-minute specials, such as **Smarter Living** (smarterliving.com). For last-minute trips, www.lastminute.com often has better deals than the major-label sites.

If you're willing to give up some control over the details, use an *opaque fare service* such as **Priceline** (www.priceline.com) or **Hotwire** (www.hotwire.com). Both offer rock-bottom prices in exchange for travel on a "mystery airline" at a mysterious time of day, often with a mysterious change of planes. The airlines are major, well-known carriers — and the possibility of being sent hither and yon en route to Italy is remote. But your chances of getting a 6 a.m. or 11 p.m. flight are pretty high. For example, Hotwire has a "no red eye" check-off, but be aware that in its system, a 6 a.m. flight for which you have to be at the airport two hours in advance (it's hardly worth putting on your jammies, is it?) is *not* considered a red eye. Hotwire tells you prices before you buy; Priceline usually has better deals than Hotwire, but you have to play the "name our price" game — and with each try, you have to change something besides your bid. If you have fixed travel dates, make a realistic bid to start, or you'll have to change them or look elsewhere. Another Priceline option is **Lowestfare.com** (www.lowestfare.com), on which you don't have bid.

Arriving by Other Means

You may be adding Rome to a larger European vacation, or perhaps you live in Britain or Ireland. Although usually it will be cheaper and faster to fly, you do have other ways to get to Italy.

✔ **Train:** Railroads in Europe offer cheap, reliable, fast, and frequent service. Convenient overnight trains with sleeping cars connect Rome to most European capitals. High-speed TGV trains through Torino and Milan also connect Paris to Rome. **Trenitalia,** the Italian national train service (☎ 892021; www.trenitalia.it), offers excellent deals on rail passes for both Europe and Italy. **Eurailpass** grants unlimited first-class rail travel within most of continental Europe and comes in several versions for both adults and younger travelers; for example, an adult 15-day pass costs $588, and the three-month option is $1,654. The pass also includes discounts on certain bus and ferry routes. You can buy passes directly at any major European train stations; in advance from travel agents or rail agents in major cities such as New York, Montreal, and Los Angeles; and through **Rail Europe** (☎ 877-272-RAIL from the U.S.; www.raileurope.com).

✔ **Ship and Ferry:** Arriving by boat has not lost any of its charm in our frantic modern world, and if you have the time to visit Europe by cruise ship, we recommend the experience. Two harbors, Fiumicino and Civitavecchia, serve Rome. Most cruise ships and many ferries from destinations around the Mediterranean arrive in Civitavecchia, about one hour north of Rome and easy to reach by frequent train and bus service, as well as car service. A number of ferry companies (such as the lines to Sardinia) serve Fiumicino, a 35-minute ride from Rome by metropolitan train or car service.

✔ **Bus: Eurolines** (☎ **0990-143-219**; www.eurolines.com) is the leading operator of scheduled coach services across Europe. Service to Rome departs from London's Victoria Coach Station.

✔ **Car:** We don't recommend driving, even if it may appear tempting. It is expensive (you have to factor in gasoline at over $7 a gallon and highways tolls), exhausting, and *long* — Rome lies at about 500 miles from the Italian border. If you have the time and stamina, though, Rome is at the intersection of all major highways from the Italian border (thanks to the ancient Romans, who designed the main road network still in use today): All roads really do lead to Rome. Make sure you get a good map (the Italian Touring Club's are the best, followed by Michelin's).

Joining an Escorted Tour

You may be one of the many people who love escorted tours: The tour company takes care of all the details — from the itinerary to the meals, hotels, and attractions tickets and reservations — and your group leader smoothes over the occasional bumps along the road. The company tells you what to expect each day, you know what your vacation will cost up front, and you don't get many surprises. Fans of escorted tours know that they can take you to the maximum number of sights in the minimum amount of time with the least hassle. We give you some tips in this section on how to choose the escorted tour that best fits your needs.

 If you decide to take an escorted tour, we strongly recommend buying travel insurance, especially if the tour operator asks to you pay up front. It's wise to buy travel insurance through an independent agency. (Read more about the ins and outs of travel insurance in Chapter 7.)

When choosing an escorted tour, find out whether you must put down a deposit and when final payment is due, then ask a few simple questions.

✔ **What is the cancellation policy?** Can the operator cancel the trip if it doesn't get enough people? How late can you cancel? Do you get a refund if you cancel? If the company cancels?

✔ **How jam-packed is the schedule?** Do tour organizers try to fit 25 hours into a 24-hour day, or is there ample time for relaxing and shopping? Some escorted tours schedule every minute from 7 a.m. to 6 or 7 p.m.; if that sounds like a grind, they are not for you.

✔ **How big is the group?** The smaller the group, the less time you spend waiting for people to get on and off the bus. Tour operators may be evasive about this, because they may not know the exact size of the group until everybody has made reservations, but they should be able to give you a rough estimate.

✔ **Is there a minimum group size?** Some tours have a minimum group size, and the operator may cancel the tour if it doesn't book enough people. If a quota exists, find out what it is and how close the tour you're interested in is to reaching it.

✔ **What is included?** Don't assume anything. You may have to pay to get yourself to and from the airport. A box lunch may be included in an excursion, but drinks may be extra. How much flexibility do you have? Can you opt out of certain activities, or does the bus leave once a day, with no exceptions? Are all your meals planned in advance? Can you choose your entree at dinner, or does everybody get the same chicken cutlet?

Many international companies specialize in escorted tours to Rome. Here is brief list of the most reliable operators.

✔ **Italiatours.com** (www.italiatour.com) is part of the Alitalia Group; it offers a variety of low-cost tours. This is the only tour operator with a desk right at the Fiumicino airport in Rome and native expertise, and it offers very competitive prices.

✔ **Perillo Tours,** 577 Chestnut Ridge Rd., Woodcliff Lake, NJ 07675-9888 (☎ **800-431-1515** or 201-307-1234; www.perillotours.com), has been in business for more than half a century. Its diverse itineraries range from 8 to 15 days. Optional excursions are offered (at an extra charge) to allow you to customize your tour somewhat. Perillo tries to cover all the bases; it even has a package to help you get married in Rome.

✔ **Globus+Cosmos Tours** (☎ **800-338-7092;** www.globusandcosmos.com) offers first-class escorted coach tours lasting 8 to 16 days.

✔ **Insight Vacations** (☎ **800-582-8380;** www.insightvacations.com) books superior first-class, fully escorted motor-coach tours.

✔ **Central Holidays** (☎ **800-935-5000;** www.centralholidays.com) offers several levels of fully escorted tours — and levels of "escort" — in addition to packages.

✔ For luxurious tours of Italy, check out **Abercrombie & Kent,** 1520 Kensington Rd., Oak Brook, IL 60523 (☎ **800-554-7016;** www.abercrombiekent.com; London address: Sloan Square House, Holbein Place, London SW1W 8NS; ☎ **020-7730-9600**).

You can also choose from an increasing number of tours addressing special interests such as archeology or cuisine. **La Dolce Vita Wine**

Tours (☎ 888-746-0022; www.dolcetours.com) focuses on wine; **PaginediGusto** (☎ 0461-829964; fax: 0461-429756; www.paginedi gusto.com) organizes gastronomic and culinary tours in Italy, including one focusing on the Eternal City. Good resource Web sites for specialty tours and travels are the **Specialty Travel Index** (www.specialty travel.com), which offers a comprehensive selection of tours; **ShawGuides** (www.shawguides.com), with links to many offerings, ranging from archaeological programs to tours for opera fans; and **InfoHub Specialty Travel Guide** (www.infohub.com).

Choosing a Package Tour

Package tours — airfare-plus-hotel bundles that may include excursions or activities — are a smart way to visit Rome. In many cases, a package including airfare, hotel, and transportation to and from the airport costs less than the hotel alone would if you booked it yourself. That's because tour operators buy packages in bulk and resell them to the public. Package tours can vary widely. Some offer a better class of hotels than others; others provide the same hotels for lower prices. Some use scheduled airlines; others sell charters. In some packages, your choice of accommodations and travel days may be limited.

To find package tours, check out the travel section of your local Sunday newspaper or the ads in the back of travel magazines such as *Travel & Leisure, National Geographic Traveler,* and *Condé Nast Traveler.* **Liberty Travel** (☎ 888-271-1584 to find the store nearest you; www.liberty-travel.com), one of the biggest packagers in the Northeastern United States, usually has a full-page ad in Sunday papers.

Another good source of package deals is the airlines themselves. Most major airlines offer air/land packages, including **American Airlines Vacations** (☎ 800-321-2121; www.aavacations.com), **Delta Vacations** (☎ 800-221-6666; www.deltavacations.com), **Continental Airlines Vacations** (☎ 800-301-3800; www.coolvacations.com), **US Airways Vacations** (☎ 800-455-0123 or 800-422-3861; www.usairwaysvacations.com), and **United Vacations** (☎ 888-854-3899; www.unitedvacations.com).

Several big **online travel agencies** — Expedia, Travelocity, Orbitz, Site59, and Lastminute.com — also do a brisk business in packages. If you're unsure about a packager's pedigree, check with the Better Business Bureau in company's home city, or visit **www.bbb.org**. If a packager won't tell you where it's based, don't fly with it.

The **escorted tour** operators discussed earlier also offer packages. For example, **Italiatours.com** (☎ 800-845-3365; fax 212-765-2183; www. italiatour.com) specializes in packages for travelers who ride from one destination to another by train or rental car. Another recommended packager is **Kemwel** (☎ 800-678-0678; www.kemwel.com).

Chapter 6

Catering to Special Travel Needs or Interests

● ●

In This Chapter
▶ Traveling with kids
▶ Making the most of senior advantages
▶ Rising to the challenge: Travelers with disabilities
▶ Finding gay and lesbian communities and special events

● ●

*E*very traveler is a special traveler, but bringing kids along or trying to find wheelchair-accessible accommodations and attractions requires extra care and thought. Seniors may be interested in special programs and activities; gays and lesbians may wonder how friendly and welcoming Rome will be. We consider these issues in this chapter.

Traveling with the Brood: Advice for Families

 You may think that Rome, a large and congested capital city, is a difficult destination for kids. True, parks are few in the historic center, and kid-specific entertainment and services are rare or nonexistent. But if you follow our suggestions and avoid some common pitfalls, you may find Rome your favorite urban destination ever.

In Italy, kids do everything with the family. The downside is that you'll have a hard time finding places to park your offspring; the upside is that your kids will be welcome virtually anywhere. Restaurants will do what they can to accommodate youngsters, even preparing simple dishes that are not on the menu. Bars (which are more like cafes), bakeries, and other food shops will offer your cute little one a sliver of pizza, a sweet, or a piece of candy just to get a smile in return. Hotels will provide you with a cot or extra bed for your child, and most have rooms (often duplexes or suites) geared for families. These units, which accommodate four or even five, book up quickly, especially in high season.

The key to a fun visit is planning. First, try to schedule your trip during the fair season. Rome never experiences bitter cold, but it always has a couple of weeks in winter (usually in January) that are particularly cold and wet. Most important, skip the sultry days of midsummer, especially if you come from a colder climate. July and August may prove unbearable for young tourists, unless you keep to the locals' schedule: out between 8 and 11 a.m., indoors in the cool until 5 or 5:30 p.m., and then out again until evening falls and beyond. Planning for a siesta in the afternoon is not a bad idea at all. To make all this easier, choose accommodations in the heart of Rome's historic center. Being able to walk to and from all major attractions offers unlimited advantages.

Another important tip: Children of all ages hate to wait in lines, particularly to see something they are only marginally interested in. Strictly follow our tips to avoid lines and crowds (see individual entries in Chapter 11), and keep your timetable light: only one big attraction per day, or two or three small ones.

Also, involve your children in the planning, letting them choose the main attraction whenever possible. As your second attraction for the day, always schedule something your kids will enjoy or have chosen themselves. Also, splurge on *Rome Past and Present,* a book with plastic overlays, showing the ruins as they looked in Roman times (see Chapter 11). Ruins are not the only option: Children are usually very sensitive to beauty (often surprising their parents), and many sights in Rome are so beautiful that even the youngest will be impressed. St. Peter's Basilica, for example, is an experience you can certainly share.

Throughout this book, we have marked the attractions that usually get kids' approval with the Kids icon.

Always schedule an age-appropriate fun break during the day: a stop at the Pincio Gardens merry-go-round, Villa Borghese Park (carry a baseball, tennis ball, or Frisbee), or, for younger kids, the gardens behind the Golden House of Nero (see Chapter 11).

Last but not least, Rome is the home of the world's best ice cream and pizza. Pizza parlors (see Chapter 10) — both eat-in and take-out — are ubiquitous and make an excellent (and reasonably priced) dining choice for a family. High-quality ice cream is available on almost every corner and makes a perfect break for tired young visitors and their parents, especially in the warmer months (see Chapter 10). We suggest you make a midafternoon ice cream break a central point of your planning. Schedule your break for around 4:30 or 5 p.m.; few restaurants serve dinner before 7:30 p.m.

Meal planning is another area that requires attention when you are traveling with kids. Renting an apartment with a kitchen is the best option if you have very young or finicky kids; if you have to rely on restaurants, you need to adjust to later eating hours. Restaurants open around 12:30 p.m. for lunch and 7:30 p.m. or later for dinner; only take-out places and tourist joints serve food earlier.

Baby changing may be a problem. You'll find changing tables only in modern museums and airports. Bathrooms in larger hotels and large nicer restaurants may have a table or flat surface you can use, but sometimes you may have to settle for using your stroller. If you find yourself in difficulty, always ask a local.

If you're sightseeing with a stroller, prepare yourself for a crash course in cobblestone street navigation. It's not easy, especially with badly parked cars everywhere and mopeds zooming through, but it is feasible. Kids less than 1m (39 in.) tall travel free on urban public transportation, but avoid public transportation at rush hours (about 8:15–9:30 a.m. and 5–7:30 p.m.), particularly in summer: Children hate to be crushed and uncomfortable. Definitely splurge on taxis.

If these tips are not enough, here are some additional resources.

- ✔ **Family Travel Forum** (www.familytravelforum.com) is a comprehensive Web site that offers customized trip planning.

- ✔ **Family Travel Network** (www.familytravelnetwork.com) is an award-winning site that offers travel features, deals, and tips.

- ✔ **Traveling Internationally with Your Kids** (www.travelwithyour kids.com) is another comprehensive Web site that offers customized trip planning.

- ✔ **Family Travel Files** (www.thefamilytravelfiles.com) offers an online magazine and a directory of off-the-beaten-path tours and tour operators for families.

- ✔ *How to Take Great Trips with Your Kids* (The Harvard Common Press) is full of good general advice that can apply to travel anywhere.

- ✔ *Family Travel Times* (☎ 888-822-4FTT or 212-477-5524; www.familytraveltimes.com) is published six times a year and includes a weekly call-in service for subscribers. Subscriptions are $39 per year.

Making Age Work for You: Tips for Seniors

In general, Romans accord older people a great deal of respect, probably because of the Roman embrace of extended family as well as the culture and nature of the Italian language (polite forms of address are to be used when speaking with someone who is older than you). Therefore, you're unlikely to encounter ageism.

Members of **AARP,** 601 E St. NW, Washington, DC 20049 (☎ **888-687-2277** or 202-434-2277; www.aarp.org), get discounts on international chain hotels, airfares, and car rentals. AARP offers members a wide range of benefits, including *AARP: The Magazine* and a monthly newsletter. Anyone over 50 can join.

Being a senior entitles you to some terrific travel bargains. Many reliable agencies and organizations target the 50-plus market and offer trips to Rome. **Elderhostel** (☎ 877-426-8056; www.elderhostel.org) arranges study programs for those ages 55 and over (and a spouse or companion of any age) in the United States and in more than 80 countries around the world. Most courses last five to seven days in the United States (two to four weeks abroad), and many include airfare, accommodations at university dormitories or modest inns, meals, and tuition. **ElderTreks** (☎ 800-741-7956; www.eldertreks.com) offers small-group tours to off-the-beaten-path or adventure-travel locations, restricted to travelers 50 and older.

Recommended publications offering travel resources and discounts for seniors include the quarterly magazine *Travel 50 & Beyond* (www.travel50andbeyond.com); *Travel Unlimited: Uncommon Adventures for the Mature Traveler* (Avalon); *101 Tips for Mature Travelers,* available from Grand Circle Travel (☎ 800-221-2610 or 617/350-7500; www.gct.com); *The 50+ Traveler's Guidebook* (St. Martin's Press); and *Unbelievably Good Deals and Great Adventures That You Absolutely Can't Get Unless You're Over 50* (McGraw-Hill).

 Senior discounts on admission at theaters, museums, and public transportation are subject to reciprocity between countries. Because the United States and Italy don't have a bilateral agreement (you discount us, and we'll discount you), Americans aren't eligible for senior discounts in Italy. (The same rule applies to the under-17 discount.) All discounts apply if you are a citizen of a European Union country.

Accessing Rome: Advice for Travelers with Disabilities

Most disabilities shouldn't stop anybody from traveling, and more options and resources are available than ever before. Rome is working to make its treasures more accessible, but it's a slow process.

Although Italy may not be as advanced as some other countries in its accessibility, Rome, as the capital, is more in step with the times than other destinations. But keep in mind that the age of the housing stock and the difficulty of retrofitting medieval buildings with elevators or ramps pose serious limits. Some major buildings and institutions have been converted; others have not been or cannot be adapted. Calling ahead is always best. When a special entrance for visitors with disabilities exists, you'll often need to arrange to have an attendant meet you there. Public transportation reserves spaces for the disabled, and the Roman transportation authority has kneeling busses that make getting in and out quite easy. Some train stations and bus lines, though, can prove difficult, even impossible, if you're in a wheelchair. Major towns have special grooves on the sidewalks to help the visually impaired with street crossing, and a number of street lights have sound signals.

You can avoid some problems by joining a tour that caters specifically to your needs. Many travel agencies offer customized tours and itineraries for travelers with disabilities. **Flying Wheels Travel** (☎ 507-451-5005; www.flyingwheelstravel.com) offers escorted tours and cruises that emphasize sports and private tours in minivans with lifts. **Access-Able Travel Source** (☎ 303-232-2979; www.access-able.com) offers extensive access information and advice for traveling around the world with disabilities. **Accessible Journeys** (☎ 800-846-4537 or 610-521-0339; www.disabilitytravel.com) caters to wheelchair travelers and their families and friends.

Organizations that offer assistance to disabled travelers include **MossRehab Hospital** (www.mossresourcenet.org), which provides a library of accessible-travel resources online, and **SATH, the Society for Accessible Travel and Hospitality** (☎ 212-447-7284; www.sath.org; annual membership fees: $45 adults, $30 seniors and students), which offers a wealth of travel resources for people with all types of disabilities, and informed recommendations on destinations, access guides, travel agents, tour operators, vehicle rentals, and companion services. The **American Foundation for the Blind** (☎ 800-232-5463; www.afb.org) provides information on traveling with Seeing Eye dogs.

For more information, check out the quarterly magazine *Emerging Horizons* ($14.95 per year, $19.95 outside the U.S.; www.emerging horizons.com), and *Open World Magazine,* published by SATH (see above; subscription: $13 per year, $21 outside the U.S.).

Following the Rainbow: Resources for Gay and Lesbian Travelers

Rome is a very tolerant city in a fairly tolerant country, and violent displays such as gay bashing are quite unheard of. However, as in the United States, an active gay and lesbian movement is trying to raise public consciousness about prejudice and discrimination.

Rome has an active gay life; check out the local branch of **ARCI-Gay/ARCI-Lesbica** (www.arcigay.it/roma), the country's leading gay organization. Its Web site has an English-language version. The Eternal City can boast of having held the first-ever World Pride event in Italy in July 2000, to coincide with the Jubilee celebrations. During the summer, coinciding with the **Estate Romana** festival, the town-within-a-town known as **Gay Village** (www.gayvillage.it) lets gay and straight mingle while enjoying a variety of cultural events (see Chapters 15 and 16).

The **International Gay & Lesbian Travel Association (IGLTA; ☎ 800-448-8550** or 954-776-2626; www.traveliglta.com) is the trade association for the gay and lesbian travel industry and offers an online directory of gay- and lesbian-friendly travel businesses; go to its Web site and click "Members."

Chapter 7

Taking Care of the Remaining Details

*E*ven if you have a destination, an itinerary, and a ticket in hand, you aren't going anywhere until you get a passport. You also need to figure out whether you need a rental car, whether to get traveler's insurance, and how you want to stay in touch with the folks back home. In this chapter, we help you tie up all the loose ends.

Getting a Passport

A valid passport is the only legal form of identification accepted around the world. You can't cross an international border without it. Getting a passport is easy, but the process takes some time. For an up-to-date, country-by-country listing of passport requirements around the world, visit the Foreign Entry Requirement Web page of the U.S. Department of State at http://travel.state.gov/foreignentryreqs.html.

Applying for a U.S. passport

If you're applying for a first-time passport, follow these steps:

1. Complete a **passport application** in person at a U.S. passport office; a federal, state, or probate court; or a major post office (you can download the form online; see below).

2. Present a **certified birth certificate** as proof of citizenship. (Bringing along your driver's license, state or military ID, or social security card is also a good idea.)

3. Submit **two identical passport-size photos,** measuring 2 × 2 inches. You often find businesses that take these photos near a passport office. *Note:* You can't use a strip from a vending machine.

4. Pay a **fee.** For people 16 and over, a passport is valid for ten years and costs $85. For those 15 and under, a passport is valid for five years and costs $70.

Allow plenty of time before your trip to apply for a passport; processing normally takes three weeks but can take longer during busy periods (especially spring).

If you already have a passport in your current name that was issued within the past 15 years (and you were over age 16 when it was issued), you can renew the passport by mail for $55.

Whether you're applying in person or by mail, you can download passport applications from the U.S. Department of State Web site at http://travel.state.gov, where you can also get general information and find your regional passport office; alternatively, call the **National Passport Information Center** (☎ 877-487-2778 for automated information, or ☎ 202-647-0518).

Losing your passport may be worse than losing your money. Why? Because a passport shows (and proves to authorities) that you are you. Safeguard your passport in an inconspicuous, inaccessible place such as a money belt. Always carry a photocopy of your passport with you, in a separate pocket or purse. If you lose your passport, visit the nearest consulate of your native country as soon as possible for a replacement.

Applying for other passports

Australians can visit a local post office or passport office, call the **Australia Passport Information Service** (☎ 131-232 toll-free from Australia), or visit www.passports.gov.au for details on how and where to apply.

Canadians can pick up applications at passport offices throughout Canada, at post offices, or from the central **Passport Office, Department of Foreign Affairs and International Trade,** Ottawa, ON K1A 0G3 (☎ 800-567-6868; www.ppt.gc.ca). Applications must be accompanied by two identical passport-sized photographs and proof of Canadian citizenship. Processing takes five to ten days if you apply in person, or about three weeks by mail.

New Zealanders can pick up a passport application at any New Zealand Passports Office or download it from the Web site. Contact the **Passports Office** (☎ 0800-225-050 in New Zealand or 04-474-8100; www.passports. govt.nz) for more information.

United Kingdom residents can pick up applications for a standard ten-year passport (five-year passport for children under 16) at passport offices, major post offices, or a travel agency. For information, contact the **United Kingdom Passport Service** (☎ **0870-521-0410;** www.ips. gov.uk).

 When you get your passport photos taken, ask for six to eight total photos if you plan to apply for an International Driving Permit and an international student or teacher ID, which may entitle you to discounts at museums. Take the extra photos with you. You may need one for random reasons on the road, and if — heaven forbid — you ever lose your passport, you can use them for a replacement request.

Renting a Car — Not!

Rome's historic district is closed to nonresident traffic, and its narrow streets can be a nightmare to negotiate. If you must drive, it is imperative that you get a good map marking the driving direction for each street (they are for sale at tobacconists and newsstands as you approach Rome). Then you'll have to find parking, an almost impossible proposition. In all likelihood, you'll end up parking your vehicle in a garage (expect to pay 18€–36€/$23–$47 per day if you have a deal through your hotel, more otherwise) and using public transportation and taxis, which is the best way to go (see Chapter 8).

Playing It Safe with Travel and Medical Insurance

Three kinds of travel insurance are available: trip-cancellation insurance, medical insurance, and lost luggage insurance. The cost varies widely, but expect to pay between 5 percent and 8 percent of the price of the vacation. Here is our advice on all three.

✔ **Trip-cancellation insurance** helps you get your money back if you have to back out of a trip or go home early, or if your travel supplier goes bankrupt. Permissible reasons for cancellation can range from sickness to natural disasters to the Department of State's declaring your destination unsafe for travel, but not vague fears caused by airplane crashes and the like. If you are worried about flying, check out **"Travel Guard Alerts,"** a list of companies considered high-risk by Travel Guard International (www.travelguard. com). Protect yourself further by paying for the insurance with a credit card — by law, consumers can get their money back on goods and services not received if they report the loss within 60 days after the charge appears on their statement.

✔ Most health plans (including Medicare and Medicaid) do not provide coverage for travel overseas, and the ones that do often require you to pay for services up front and reimburse you only after you return home. Even if your plan does cover overseas treatment, most out-of-country hospitals make you pay your bills up front, then send you a refund only after you've returned home and filed the necessary paperwork with your insurance company. As a safety net, you may want to buy travel medical insurance; try **MEDEX Assistance** (☎ 410-453-6300; www.medexassist.com) or **Travel Assistance International** (☎ 800-821-2828; www.travelassistance.com; for general information on services, call the company's Worldwide Assistance Services, Inc., at ☎ 800-777-8710).

✔ **Lost luggage insurance** is not necessary for most travelers. On international flights (including U.S. portions of international trips), baggage coverage is limited to approximately $9.07 per pound, up to approximately $635 per checked bag. If you plan to check items more valuable than the standard liability, see if your valuables are covered by your homeowner's policy, get baggage insurance as part of your comprehensive travel-insurance package, or buy Travel Guard's "BagTrak" product. Don't buy insurance at the airport, where it's usually overpriced. Be sure to take any valuables or irreplaceable items with you in your carry-on luggage, because many valuables (including books, money, and electronics) aren't covered by airline policies.

If your luggage is lost, immediately file a lost-luggage claim at the airport, detailing the luggage contents. For most airlines, you must report delayed, damaged, or lost baggage within four hours of arrival. The airlines are required to deliver luggage, once found, directly to your house or destination free of charge.

For more information, contact one of the following recommended insurers: **AccessAmerica** (☎ 866-807-3982; www.accessamerica.com); **Travel Guard International** (☎ 800-826-4919; www.travelguard.com); **Travel Insured International** (☎ 800-243-3174; www.travelinsured.com); and **Travelex Insurance Services** (☎ 888-457-4602; www.travelex-insurance.com).

Staying Healthy When You Travel

Talk to your doctor before leaving if you have a serious or chronic illness. For conditions such as epilepsy, diabetes, or heart problems, wear a **MedicAlert identification tag** (☎ 888-633-4298; www.medicalert.org), which immediately alerts doctors to your condition and gives them access to your records through MedicAlert's 24-hour hotline. Contact the **International Association for Medical Assistance to Travelers** (☎ 716-754-4883 or, in Canada, 416-652-0137; www.iamat.org) for tips on travel and health concerns in the countries you're visiting and lists of English-speaking doctors. The United States **Centers for Disease Control and Prevention** (☎ 800-311-3435; www.cdc.gov) provides up-to-date information on health hazards by region or country and offers tips on food safety.

If you get sick in Rome, ask the concierge at your hotel to recommend a local doctor — even his or her own, if necessary. If you can't locate a doctor, try contacting your embassy or consulate; they maintain lists of English-speaking doctors. For an emergency, dial ☎ **113** for the police: They can call an ambulance or help you in many ways. If your situation is life-threatening, call ☎ **118** for an ambulance; or rush to the *pronto soccorso* (emergency department) at the local hospital.

Under the Italian national health-care system, you're eligible only for free *emergency* care. If you're admitted to a hospital as an inpatient, even through the emergency department, you're required to pay (unless you're a resident of the European Economic Area and are eligible for health insurance coverage). You're also required to pay for follow-up care. For the names, addresses, and phone numbers of hospitals offering 24-hour emergency care, see the "Fast Facts" section in Appendix A.

Staying Connected by Cellphone or E-Mail

If you're from England or another European country, you're in luck: Your phone works in Italy. If you're from another continent, things are a little complicated. The three letters that define much of the world's **wireless capabilities** are GSM (Global System for Mobiles), a big, seamless network that makes for easy cross-border cellphone use throughout Europe and dozens of other countries worldwide. In the U.S., T-Mobile and AT&T use this quasi-universal system; in Canada, Microcell and some Rogers customers are GSM. All Europeans and most Australians use GSM.

If your cellphone is on a GSM system and you have a world-capable multiband phone (such as many Sony Ericsson, Motorola, or Samsung models), you can make and receive calls across much of the globe. Just call your wireless operator and ask for "international roaming" to be activated on your account. Unfortunately, per-minute charges can be high — usually $1 to $1.50 in Western Europe.

That's why it's important to buy an "unlocked" world phone from the get-go. Many cellphone operators sell "locked" phones that restrict you from using any removable computer memory phone chip card (called a **SIM card**) other than the ones they supply. Having an unlocked phone allows you to install a cheap, prepaid SIM card (found at a local retailer) in your destination country. (Show your phone to the salesperson; not all phones work on all networks.) You'll get a local phone number — and much, much lower calling rates. Getting an already locked phone unlocked can be a complicated process, but it can be done; just call your cellular operator and say you'll be going abroad for several months and want to use the phone with a local provider.

For many, **renting** a phone is a good idea. You can rent from any number of overseas sites, including kiosks at airports and at car-rental agencies, but we suggest making arrangements before you leave home. That way you can give loved ones and business associates your new number, make sure the phone works, and take the phone wherever you go — especially helpful for overseas trips through several countries. Phone rental isn't cheap. You'll usually pay $40 to $50 per week, plus airtime fees of at least $1 a minute. In Europe, local rental companies often offer free incoming calls within their home country, which can save you big bucks. Two good wireless rental companies are **InTouch USA** (☎ 800-872-7626; www.intouchglobal.com) and **RoadPost** (☎ 888-290-1606 or 905-272-5665; www.roadpost.com). Provide your itinerary, and the company will tell you what wireless products you need. InTouch will also, for free, advise you on whether your existing phone will work overseas; simply call ☎ 703-222-7161 between 9 a.m. and 4 p.m. Eastern time, or go to http://intouchglobal.com/travel.htm.

 In Italy, you don't have to look for a place to rent a phone; you can make the phone come to you. **Rentacell** (☎ 877-736-8355 in the U.S.; 39-02-8633-7799 in Italy; www.rentacell.com) will deliver a phone anywhere, free. You can also pick it up in the U.S. before you leave. Incoming calls are free. **Easyline** (☎ 800-010-600 in Italy) also delivers phones free.

Accessing the Internet away from home

Travelers have any number of ways to check their e-mail and access the Internet. Using your PDA (personal digital assistant) or electronic organizer will give you the most flexibility, but Internet points are so widespread nowadays that you really don't need to carry a laptop. You'll find that most hotels — medium range and up — offer at least an Internet point. Some offer Wi-Fi everywhere in the hotel, others Internet connection through the TV in each room. Often this service is free; some lodgings charge a small fee. Check with your hotel. Avoid **hotel business centers** unless you're willing to pay exorbitant rates.

Rome also has a great number of **cybercafes.** Although there's no definitive directory, two places to start looking are www.cybercaptive.com and www.cybercafe.com (but be aware that their listings are not comprehensive). The concierge at your hotel will direct you to the closest Internet point.

Most major airports now have **Internet kiosks** scattered throughout their gates. Fiumicino airport has them; they give you basic Web access for a per-minute fee that's usually higher than cybercafe prices. The kiosks' clunkiness and high prices mean they should be avoided whenever possible.

To retrieve your e-mail, ask your **Internet Service Provider (ISP)** if it has a Web-based interface tied to your existing e-mail account. If it doesn't, you can use the free **mail2web** service (www.mail2web.com) to view and reply to your home e-mail. For more flexibility, you may want to open a free, Web-based e-mail account such as **Yahoo! Mail** (http://mail.yahoo.com), **Gmail** (http://mail.google.com), or Microsoft's **Hotmail** (www.hotmail.com). Your home ISP may be able to forward your e-mail to the Web-based account automatically.

If you need access to files on your office computer, look into a service called **GoToMyPC** (www.gotomypc.com). It provides a Web-based interface and allows you to manipulate a distant PC from anywhere — even a cybercafe — provided your "target" PC is on and has an always-on connection to the Internet. The service offers top-quality security, but if you're worried about hackers, use your own laptop rather than a cybercafe computer to access the GoToMyPC system.

If you are bringing your own computer, you'll find that most top hotels in Rome offer free **Wi-Fi** connection. (To locate free hot spots, check www. personaltelco.net/index.cgi/WirelessCommunities.) Most laptops have built-in Wi-Fi capability. Mac owners have their own networking technology, Apple AirPort. For those with older computers, a **Wi-Fi card** (around $50) can be plugged into your laptop. If you don't want to bum a connection, you can sign up for wireless access much as you do cellphone service. **T-Mobile Hotspot** (http://hotspot.t-mobile.com) serves up wireless connections at more than 1,000 Starbucks coffee shops nationwide. **Boingo** (www.boingo.com) and **Wayport** (www. wayport.com) have set up networks in airports and high-class hotel lobbies. IPass providers (see below) also give you access to a few hundred hotel lobby wireless setups. The companies' pricing policies can be byzantine, with a variety of monthly, per-connection, and per-minute plans, but in general you pay around $30 a month for limited access — and as more and more companies jump on the wireless bandwagon, prices are likely to get even more competitive.

In addition, major ISPs have **local access numbers** around the world, allowing you to go online by placing a local call. Check your ISP's Web site or call its toll-free number and ask how you can use your current account away from home, and how much it will cost. If you're traveling outside the reach of your ISP, the **iPass** network has dial-up numbers in most of the world's countries. You'll have to sign up with an iPass provider, which will then tell you how to set up your computer for your destination(s). For a list of iPass providers, go to www.ipass.com and click on "Individual Purchase." One solid provider is **i2roam** (www.i2roam.com; ☎ **866-811-6209** or 920-235-0475).

Wherever you go, bring a **connection kit** of the right power and phone adapters, a phone cord, and an Ethernet network cable — or find out whether your hotel supplies them to guests. For information on the electric current in Rome, see the "Fast Facts" section in Appendix A.

Keeping Up with Airline Security

With the federalization of airport security, security procedures at U.S. airports are more stable and consistent than ever. Generally, you'll be fine if you arrive at the airport **one hour** before a domestic flight and **two hours** before an international flight; if you show up late, tell an airline employee and she may whisk you to the front of the line.

Bring a **current, government-issued photo ID** such as a driver's license or passport. Keep your ID at the ready to show at check-in, the security checkpoint, and sometimes even the gate. (Children under 18 do not need government-issued photo IDs for domestic flights, but they do for international flights to most countries, including Italy.)

In 2003, the Transportation Security Administration (TSA) phased out **gate check-in** at all U.S. airports. And **E-tickets** have made paper tickets nearly obsolete. Passengers with E-tickets can beat the ticket-counter lines by using airport **electronic kiosks** or even **online check-in** from their home computers. If you're using a kiosk at the airport, bring the credit card you used to book the ticket or your frequent-flier card. Print out your boarding pass from the kiosk and simply proceed to the security checkpoint with your pass and a photo ID. If you're checking bags or looking to snag an exit-row seat, you will be able to do so using most airline kiosks. Even the smaller airlines are employing the kiosk system, but always call your airline to make sure these alternatives are available. **Curbside check-in** is also a good way to avoid lines, although a few airlines still ban it; call before you go.

Security checkpoint lines remain unpredictable. If you have trouble standing for long periods of time, tell an airline employee; the airline will provide a wheelchair. Speed up security by **not wearing metal objects** such as big belt buckles. If you've got metallic body parts, a note from your doctor can prevent a long chat with the security screeners. Keep in mind that only **ticketed passengers** are allowed past security, except for folks escorting disabled passengers or children.

Federalization has stabilized **what you can carry on** and **what you can't.** The general rule is that sharp things are out, nail clippers are okay, and liquids and gels in quantities greater than 3 ounces are a no-no. Bring solid food in your carry-on rather than checking it; explosive-detection machines used on checked luggage have been known to mistake food (especially chocolate, for some reason) for bombs. Travelers in the U.S. are allowed one carry-on bag, plus a "personal item" such as a purse, briefcase, or laptop bag. Carry-on hoarders can stuff all sorts of things into a laptop bag; as long as it has a laptop in it, it's still considered a personal item. For the current list of restricted items; check the TSA's Web site (www.tsa.gov/public/index.jsp).

Advance reservations

 Because of the long lines at busy times, many museums and attractions in Rome offer advance ticketing. You can make reservations before you leave home (and avoid a wait of up to three hours at the local ticket booth). Check under each listing in Chapter 11 for the procedure. We definitely recommend you make reservations for the **Vatican Museums and Sistine chapel** (booking a tour) and the **Borghese Gallery.**

Part III
Settling into Rome

The 5th Wave   By Rich Tennant

"I appreciate that our room looks out onto several Baroque fountains, but I had to get up 6 times last night to go to the bathroom."

In this part . . .

This is where we provide all the logistical information you'll need to make your way around the city, find a comfortable bed, and eat a delicious meal.

In Chapter 8, we give you a few tips about Rome's airports and other entry points, and how to get from there to your accommodations. We also provide a detailed description of the city's neighborhoods and suggest the best ways to get around in Rome. In Chapter 9, we recommend our favorite Roman hotels — in a number of price categories and locations — and offer tips for reserving the best room at the best rate. In Chapter 10, we tell you what to expect from Roman restaurants and offer extensive reviews of our favorite choices, as well as provide handy lists of restaurants by neighborhood, price, and cuisine. And because you'll need some snacks to keep you going between meals, we give you the scoop on snacks such as pizza and gelato.

Chapter 8

Arriving and Getting Oriented

In This Chapter

▶ Arriving in Rome
▶ Acquainting yourself with the neighborhoods
▶ Finding information after you arrive
▶ Getting from place to place

*A*rriving in a foreign city is always a challenge, and although Rome isn't one of the largest cities in the world, it is large enough to be confusing, and the narrow, winding streets of the historic center are a maze, even for Romans! In this chapter, we give you all the information you need to negotiate the Eternal City like a native.

Navigating Your Way through Passport Control and Customs

To enter Italy, you need a passport. Because Italy is part of the group of European countries that have unified their passport and Customs procedures under the Schengen agreement, your passport is checked as soon as you enter European or Italian territory, whichever comes first. If you've already landed in a European country that is part of the Schengen area, chances are that you won't need to show your passport again — only spot checks are performed at the Italian border. If Rome is your first port of call in Europe, you'll have to line up for passport control; often, you'll find two lines: one for European Union citizens and one for everyone else. If everything is okay with your passport, you'll be allowed in — but don't expect your passport to be stamped.

While you're on Italian soil, you're required to have your passport with you at all times, and you can be asked to produce it at any time to prove your identity and your legal status. All hotels will ask to see your passport when you check in. Carry your passport in a safe place on your person (such as a document pouch worn under your clothes), or leave the original in the safe at your hotel and carry a photocopy.

Items for personal use enter duty free up to 175€ ($210) for each adult and 90€ ($108) for each child under 15. In addition, adults can import a maximum of 200 cigarettes (50 cigars), 1 liter (slightly more than 1 quart) of liquor or 2 liters of wine, 50 grams of perfume, 500 grams (1 pound) of coffee, and 100 grams (3 ounces) of tea; children are allowed only perfume. Also, you cannot bring currency in excess of 10,329€ ($12,395 at press time, subject to the fluctuating conversion rate). See Appendix A for Customs regulations regarding what you can bring home. You can find more information at the Italian Customs Web site (www.agenziadogane.it).

Making Your Way to Your Hotel

It's still true that all roads lead to Rome, but nowadays, so do all planes, trains, coaches, and even ferries.

Arriving by plane

Rome's main airport, Leonardo da Vinci, is in **Fiumicino,** and this is where you're likely to land if you come by plane. Charter flights and some European companies serve the smaller airport of **Ciampino.**

If you arrive at Fiumicino airport

Though it's officially named after Leonardo, everybody refers to this airport as Fiumicino (☎ **06-65951;** www.adr.it), after the nearby town. The airport is compact and very well organized (but ever expanding), with three terminals connected by a long corridor: Terminal A handles domestic travel; Terminal B handles domestic and Schengen European Community flights (that is, internal flights to the EC countries that have signed a special agreement to waive Customs controls); and Terminal C manages all other international flights. If you're flying direct from a U.S. airport, Terminal C is your likely point of entry. Terminal C is connected to a newer set of gates by a cool monorail.

Don't be concerned if you see police officers with submachine guns walking around — it's routine procedure, and one to be glad of. Be aware, though, that the security forces at Fiumicino have terrorists in mind, not common thieves. You still have to watch your belongings like a hawk, and don't leave anything precious in your checked luggage.

After exiting passport control and Customs, you enter the main concourse, a long hall that connects all three terminals. There you'll find ATMs (one per terminal) as well as 24-hour currency exchange machines and a *cambio* (change) office, open from 8:30 a.m. to 7:30 p.m. and located just outside Customs in the international arrivals area.

If you're using traveler's checks, you may want to change them at the *cambio* office — its rates are usually the best in town.

The airport terminal has a very good **tourist information desk** (☎ 06-65956074) that provides information on Rome at one end and on the rest of Italy at the other. Nearby is a help desk that arranges **last-minute hotel reservations** but doesn't cover all hotels in Rome. **Public transportation** — including **taxis** and car-rental shuttle buses — is outside the terminal along the sidewalk; the **train** station is on the second floor of a building attached to the international terminal by an overpass.

Fiumicino lies about 30km (18 miles) from Rome and is well connected by highway, train, shuttle, and bus. The easiest way to get to your hotel is by taking a **taxi.** The line forms on the curb just outside the terminals and is marked by a sign; taxis are white and have a meter. The Municipality of Rome recently introduced a flat rate from Fiumicino Airport; the fare is 40€ ($52) for the 50-minute ride (well over an hour at rush hour) to any destination in the historic center and vicinity. Unfortunately, the Municipality of Fiumicino imposes a flat rate of 60€ ($78) — the difference is justified because the Fiumicino-licensed taxis cannot pick up passengers in Rome to bring back and must make the return trip empty. At press time this annoying local quirk (passengers cannot choose a taxi in the line) was being discussed; we hope a solution will be found before you arrive in Rome, because otherwise you'll have to accept your lot and be prepared to shell out the extra money.

Although they have almost disappeared, beware of gypsy cab drivers who approach you as you exit the arrival gate. They don't have meters and charge a lot more than the regulated cab rates.

Taking the **train-shuttle** into Rome is equally simple — and a lot faster during rush hour. If you have a lot of luggage, you can hire help at the baggage-claim area for 2€ ($2.60) per item; the attendant will take your bags to the train. The railroad terminal is connected to the air terminal through a corridor on the second floor outside arrivals (follow the sign marked TRENI). The best train is the **Leonardo Express,** a 35-minute shuttle ride to **Termini** (Rome's central rail station), which runs daily every 30 minutes from 6:37 a.m. to 11:37 p.m. and costs 9.50€ ($12). There also is a cheaper local commuter train (look for a train with final destination Orte or Fara Sabina), which makes various stops along the way and within Rome but doesn't stop at Termini. It takes about 40 minutes, depending on your stop, and runs every 15 minutes Monday through Saturday and every 30 minutes on Sunday. The fare is about 5€ ($6.50). Get off at **Roma Ostiense** if your hotel is in the area of the Aventino or the Colosseum; **Roma Trastevere** for Trastevere, San Pietro, or Prati; or **Roma Tiburtina** for the Porta Pia or Villa Borghese area. The booth in the terminal sells tickets for both trains. Remember to stamp your ticket at one of the small yellow validation boxes before you board the train.

If you are planning to take the commuter train and will use public transportation in Rome, consider buying a day pass (see "Getting Around Rome," later in this chapter) at the tobacconist in the railroad terminal. Use it to get from the airport to Rome because the ride is included (the Leonardo Express is not included).

Whichever train you take, a taxi stand is located immediately outside the train stations upon your arrival. You can also take public transportation. Ranks of buses, with signs indicating their numbers and routes, stop in front of the train station; the subway is underneath the station.

Finally, you can take a **bus shuttle** into Rome. **Terravision** (☎ 06-79494572; www.terravision.it) runs a shuttle to Termini station and to Tiburtina station, with stops at a few major hotels. It costs 9€ ($12), 5€ ($6.50) for children ages 2 to 12.

Note: We do not recommend renting a car at the airport and driving it into Rome. See Chapter 7 for additional information.

If you arrive at Ciampino airport

A number of international charter flights and some companies that mainly serve Europe use **Ciampino** (☎ 06-794941 or 06-79340297), 16km (10 miles) from the center of Rome. The airport has few services; it's almost like an American civil-aviation airport.

Taxis are by far the easiest way to get to town from Ciampino. The flat rate is 40€ ($52) for the 45-minute trip. You can also take a **shuttle bus; Terravision** (☎ 06-79494572; www.terravision.it) schedules service in concert with Ryanair flights, and **Schiaffini** runs a shuttle coinciding with EasyJet flights. Both take you to Termini station for 8€ ($10); tickets are sold at the Hotel Royal Santina and at the Hotel Stromboli on Via Marsala, just across from the Termini train station.

Arriving by ship

If you're coming by sea, your ocean liner will dock in the harbor of **Civitavecchia** (about 80 km/50 miles north of Rome). There, you can catch one of the frequent coaches and trains to Rome's Termini or Tiburtina station. Trains leave every about 20 minutes for the hour-long ride to Rome, with direct coaches departing every hour.

You can call a taxi from either the harbor or the train station; dial ☎ 0766-26121 or 0766-24251, should none be available at the taxi stand. You can also arrange for limousine service from the harbor. The best no-frills service is **Rome Shuttle Limousine** (☎ 348-5141804 or 06-61969084; www.romeshuttlelimousine.com); it offers Civitavecchia-to-Rome transfer for 110€ ($143) for a maximum of four people. **Best Limos in Rome** (☎ 338-4289389; www.bestlimosinrome.com) is an English-speaking company based in Rome that specializes in seaport services. Another good company is **Romalimo** (☎ 800-999669 or 06-5414663; www.romalimo.com).

By train

Rome is a major railroad hub, offering service to every domestic and international destination. Italy's **Trenitalia** train service (☎ 892021; www.trenitalia.it) is excellent: cheap, reliable, and frequent. No fewer than six railway stations are in the center of Rome. The central and largest is **Termini** (☎ 800-431784), and the second-busiest is **Tiburtina.** Trains usually stop at one or the other.

At Termini station, public toilets and luggage checks are at either end of the platform area. Exits near platforms 1 and 22 lead to the main concourse, a long commercial gallery with a bar to the north and a pharmacy to the south; in between are many newsstands, a tobacconist, a travel agency, ATMs, and a *cambio* office, as well as information booths. One floor below you'll find a mall complete with a large bookstore, supermarket, cosmetics store, shoe-repair shop, and ATMs; here also is the entrance to the subway (see "Getting Around Rome," later in this chapter). Continuing in a straight line across the gallery above, you reach the main hall, where train tickets are sold at the windows and at automatic machines. You can exit to the street at either end of the gallery (where you'll find small taxi stands), or from the main hall, opening onto Piazza dei Cinquecento, the largest bus terminal in Rome. The main taxi stand is just outside the main hall near the metro sign on the right. For some mysterious reason, the line forms at the end farthest from the train station exit, so depending on how many people are waiting, you may have to walk a bit (see rates and the gypsy cab warning earlier in this chapter).

Figuring Out the Neighborhoods

Rome started outgrowing its ancient Roman and medieval walls (some of which are still standing in places) only in the 20th century, but it has seen immense urban sprawl over the past two decades. From the older central body, arms of new development have formed along the main roads heading out of the city, and lately, modern developments have filled the space in between. As a result, Rome is quite large — it is Italy's largest city. The city is divided by the river **Tevere** (Tiber), which meanders southward, leaving about a third of the city on its western bank and the rest on its eastern bank.

On the eastern bank of the Tevere is the political, cultural, commercial, and tourist heart of the city. About three millennia of consecutive layers of urban development have created a confused layout of streets, with tiny medieval roads crossed by larger and more recent avenues. At the east end on **Piazza dei Cinquecento** is Termini — Rome's main train station and major public transportation hub. Branching out of Piazza dei Cinquecento is **Via Cavour,** heading toward the Colosseum. From the connected Piazza della Repubblica departs **Via Barberini,** which leads into Via Veneto and Via del Tritone; and **Via Nazionale,** which descends to Piazza Venezia and continues — as Via del Plebiscito, then Corso Vittorio Emanuele II — all the way to the River Tiber, and as Via della Conciliazione across it to St. Peter's and the Vatican. The major cross streets at Piazza Venezia are **Via del Corso** and **Via dei Fori Imperiali,** joining Piazza del Popolo at one end, and the Colosseum at the other.

Rome Orientation

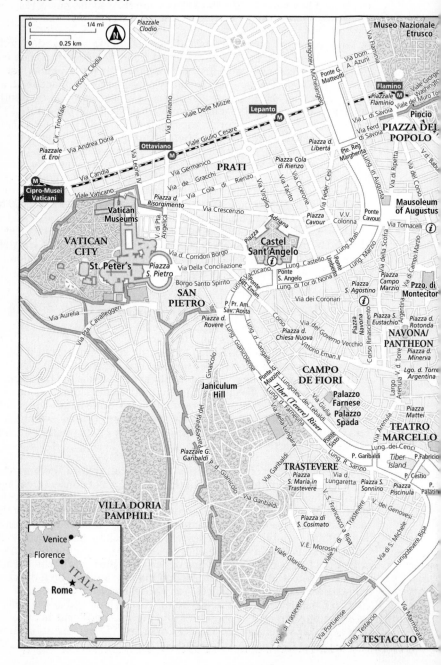

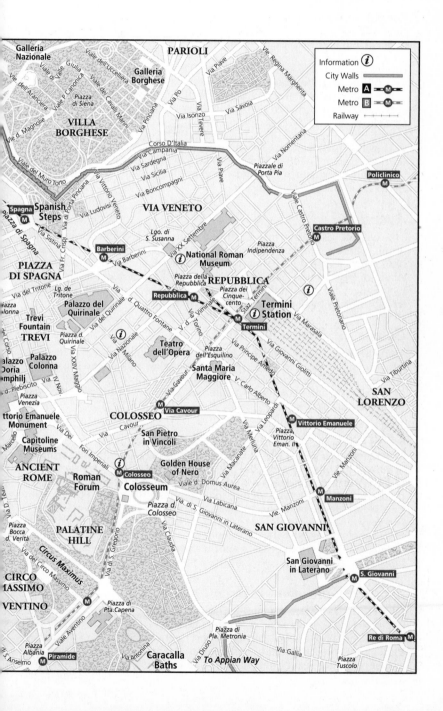

Beyond the Colosseum starts **Via Appia,** the first highway created by the ancient Romans. A section of it has been transformed into an archaeological and natural park (see Chapter 12).

On the western bank of the Tevere you'll find the **Janiculum hill** overlooking the neighborhood of **Trastevere,** as well as the **Vatican,** whose major feature is **St. Peter's Basilica.** North of the Vatican is the largish area called **Prati,** crossed by the busy **Via Cola di Rienzo** and **Via Ottaviano.**

We have divided the historic center of Rome into several smaller neighborhoods; all are desirable places to stay, with lively nightlife, restaurants, and cafes nearby. The neighborhoods are identified on the "Rome Orientation" map in this chapter.

Aventino

This elegant residential neighborhood is one of the original seven hills of Rome, where a number of monasteries were built in the Middle Ages. It has known very little urban development since, and today, it's a unique island of quiet, where small restaurants and a few hotels are surrounded by greenery and peaceful streets. It is well connected through public transportation to all other destinations in Rome.

Campo de' Fiori

Along the left bank of the Tiber, this authentic neighborhood is mostly residential but is made very lively by the market square and the connected commercial strip of **Via dei Giubbonari.** Here, you'll find plenty of restaurants and an active nightlife. Among the attractions is the beautiful **Palazzo Farnese.**

Colosseo

The Colosseum was at the heart of ancient Rome, and the area around it is a romantic mix of residential buildings and ruins. The Colosseo is home to the most illustrious monuments of ancient Rome, including the **Palatino;** the **Roman Forum;** the **Campidoglio;** and, of course, the **Colosseum** itself. To the north, in an area sloping up along Via Cavour, is a very authentic residential neighborhood. Although not elegant, it is experiencing new life with the opening of trendy restaurants, small hotels, and bars. To the east is another small, typically Roman neighborhood, with a few hotels and some nice neighborhood restaurants.

Navona/Pantheon

On the southwestern side of the **Corso,** this lively neighborhood is a mix of elegant Renaissance and medieval buildings, including the beautiful palaces that house the government and the two chambers of the Italian Parliament (the **Parlamento** and **Senato**). Many hotels occupy this area, and several nice restaurants and bars can be found along **Via del**

Governo Vecchio. Some of Rome's best antiques shops line the **Via dei Coronari.** Graced by two of Rome's greatest attractions — **Piazza Navona** and the **Pantheon** — at its heart, this is one of the most desirable areas to stay; its popularity means that you have to put up with crowds, especially in summer.

Piazza del Popolo

Squeezed between the old city walls and the river, around one of the most beautiful squares in Rome, this lively neighborhood has a lot of trendy new restaurants and bars in the area extending west of the **Corso.**

Piazza di Spagna

On the east side of the **Corso,** this former residential neighborhood has been almost completely taken over by the fashion and tourist industries. It is the best shopping neighborhood in Rome, home to all the great names of Italian couture, plus a lot of other tony shops. It has many hotels, including some of the city's best. The shopping streets get a bit deserted at night, and if you're seeking some nightlife, you have to edge toward **Fontana di Trevi** or cross over the Corso.

Prati

This residential neighborhood on the western bank of the Tiber takes its name from the fields *(prati)* that survived here through the end of the 19th century. It stretches north of the Vatican along the river. Reflecting its late-19th-century origin, the tree-lined streets are wide and straight. The area is pleasant and only a bridge away from Piazza del Popolo; it has a relatively active, if subdued, nightlife, with restaurants, jazz clubs, and an important shopping area along **Via Cola di Rienzo.**

Repubblica

Piazza della Repubblica is a gorgeous square created over what was the main hall of Diocletian's thermal baths, a few steps west of Piazza dei Cinquecento and the Termini train station. The areas along Via Cernaia on one side of the square and Via Nazionale on the other are lively during the day because of the numerous shops and offices, but not particularly happening at night, when it turns into a quiet residential neighborhood with a few hotels and restaurants. Very convenient to most of Rome's attractions and very well connected by public transportation, this is a good alternative to the more glamorous and pricey areas nearby.

San Pietro

On the western bank of the Tiber, this area is mainly occupied by the walled city of the **Vatican** (seat of the Holy See and site of the Vatican Museums and the Sistine Chapel). It is dominated, of course, by the grandiose **St. Peter's Basilica** and **Castel Sant'Angelo.** Flanking the basilica are two ancient and picturesque residential neighborhoods that are home to a few hotels and restaurants.

Teatro Marcello

This area covers what is still commonly referred to as the Ghetto, the old Jewish neighborhood at the edge of ancient Rome. It is among the most authentic of the historical neighborhoods and remains very residential. Some nice restaurants are tucked away in its small streets, along with pubs, local shops, and a few archaeological treasures.

Trastevere

Located on the western bank of the Tiber at the foot of the **Gianicolo** hill, this neighborhood is just across the river from the Aventino. Literally "on the other side of the Tiber," this was the traditional (and rather seedy) residence of poorer artisans and workers during ancient Roman times. Its character was preserved during the Middle Ages and the Renaissance, and to some extent up to the last century. In recent times, though, it has been largely transformed into an artsy, cultured neighborhood, famous for its restaurants, street life, and nightlife, appealing to younger and not-so-young Romans and visitors.

Trevi

On the east side of the **Corso,** this neighborhood slopes up the Quirinale hill with the magnificent Renaissance presidential (formerly papal) residence as its centerpiece. Aside from the tourist hubbub around its famous fountain — always surrounded by a sea of humanity — it's a relatively unspoiled neighborhood with many small restaurants and shops.

Via Veneto

Made famous by Fellini as the heart of *La Dolce Vita,* this elegant street is lined by famous hotels and a few upscale stores. The environs are very quiet at night; they have a number of nice hotels in the side streets but relatively few restaurants and nightspots. Well connected by public transportation, the areas behind the glitzy strip of Via Veneto are actually a good alternative to the glamorous and expensive areas nearby, especially if you go toward **Via XX Settembre** (at the southeastern edge of this neighborhood).

Finding Information after You Arrive

The Visitor Centre, Via Parigi 5, off Piazza della Repubblica (☎ 06-488991; www.romaturismo.it; Mon–Sat 9 a.m.–7 p.m.), offers plenty of literature on Rome and on side trips from the city, plus a free map and a monthly calendar of events. You'll also find a tourist information desk at the international arrivals section of Terminal B at Fiumicino Airport (☎ 06-65956074; daily 8 a.m.–7 p.m.). Tourist info points dot the city near major attractions (daily 9 a.m.–6 p.m.).

✔ **Castel Sant'Angelo,** Piazza Pia, west of the Castel Sant'Angelo (☎ 06-68809707; Metro: Ottaviano–San Pietro)

- **Largo Goldoni,** Via del Corso at Via dei Condotti (☎ 06-68136061; Metro: Piazza di Spagna)

- **Piazza delle Cinque Lune,** off Piazza Navona to the north (☎ 06-68809240; Minibus: 116)

- **Fori Imperiali,** Piazza Tempio della Pace on Via dei Fori Imperiali (☎ 06-69924307; Metro: Colosseo)

- **Santa Maria Maggiore,** Via dell'Olmata, on the southeastern side of the church (☎ 06-4740955; Metro: Termini)

- **Stazione Termini,** Piazza dei Cinquecento, in front of the railroad station (☎ 06-47825194; Metro: Termini)

- **Stazione Termini,** inside the gallery (☎ 06-48906300; Metro: Termini)

- **Trastevere,** Piazza Sonnino (☎ 06-58333457; Tram: 8)

- **San Giovanni,** Piazza San Giovanni in Laterano (☎ 06-77203535; Metro: San Giovanni)

- **Fontana di Trevi,** Via Minghetti, off Via del Corso (☎ 06-6782988; Minibus: 117, 119)

- **Palazzo delle Esposizioni,** Via Nazionale (☎ 06-47824525; Bus: 64)

Staff members at the info points in and near Termini station are usually the most overwhelmed; elsewhere, you'll find people more available to assist you.

The **Holy See** maintains its own tourist office. It is in Piazza San Pietro (☎ 06-69884466; Mon–Sat 8:30 a.m.–6 p.m.), just left of the entrance to St. Peter's Basilica. The office has information on the Vatican and on its tourist attractions and religious events. You may also make reservations for a visit to the Vatican gardens or fill out the form to participate in a papal audience — but we recommend that you make a reservation before you leave home (see "How to Attend a Papal Audience" in Chapter 11 for more information).

Getting Around Rome

Rome's historic hills are no myth: They are real — and sometimes even steep. The one myth is that there are only seven of them. Rome may look flat on a map, but it's very hilly. You'll soon understand why locals use mopeds (or cars, unfortunately) and public transportation, and why you see so few bicycles around. Remember also that the city is thousands of years old, meaning that much of it isn't designed for any mode of conveyance other than the human foot. There are times, however, when you'll welcome public transportation. Taxis, for example, are a great convenience when crossing large sections of the city.

Rome's Metropolitana (Subway)

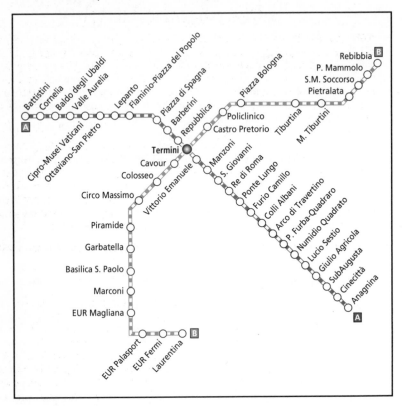

By subway (metro)

Although the Metropolitana, or metro for short, has only two lines (work has just started on the third line, which is not close to completion), it is the best way to get around because the underground routes don't suffer from the terrible city traffic. In addition, the routes stay the same — unlike the city bus system, which is under constant reorganization. **Line A Battistini–Anagnina** and **Line B Laurentina–Rebibbia** cross at Termini station. A big red *M* marks all metro entrances. The metro runs Sunday through Friday from 5:30 a.m. to 11:30 p.m. and Saturday from 5:30 a.m. to 12:30 a.m.

The Colosseum, Circus Maximus, and Cavour stops on Line B don't offer full elevator/lift service and aren't accessible to travelers with disabilities. (For tips for travelers with disabilities, see Chapter 6.)

Getting a ticket to ride

ATAC (☎ **800-431784** or 06-46952027; www.atac.roma.it), Rome's transport authority, runs all public transportation in the city. The same ticket is valid for all services. You need to buy tickets **before boarding** (although a few bus lines have on-board vending machines, do not count on finding one), and you must **stamp** them upon boarding or they aren't valid. On subway and trains, the stamping machines — little yellow boxes — are at the entrance gates; on buses and trams, they're on board. A regular *biglietto* (ticket) for the bus or metro is valid for 75 minutes and costs 1€ ($1.30). Within the 75 minutes of validity, you can take as many buses and trams as you want, but only one subway ride. You can also get a day pass, or **BIG**, which costs 4€ ($5); a three-day ticket, or **BTI**, for 11€ ($14); or a weekly pass, or **CIS**, for 16€ ($21). All passes give you unlimited rides on bus, metro, and urban trains. You can buy tickets and passes at metro ticket booths, the ATAC bus information booth in front of Stazione Termini (near Platform C), from vending machines at some major bus stops, and at many bars, tobacconists (look for a TABACCHI sign or a white *T* on a black background), and newsstands. The Roma Pass (see Chapter 11) includes a public transportation pass.

By bus and tram

Rome's bus system is large and under continuous improvement, yet the city's ancient layout resists modernization, so things don't always go smoothly. Buses are very crowded at rush hour, and traffic jams are endemic. Still, buses remain excellent resources because they go absolutely everywhere in Rome. The diminutive **electric buses** (**116** and **116T** from the Gianicolo hill to Villa Borghese; **117** from Piazza del Popolo to San Giovanni in Laterano; **118** from Piazzale Ostiense to Appia Antica; and **119** from Piazza del Popolo to Largo Argentina) are the only vehicles allowed on the tiny, narrow streets of the historic heart of the city. Among the other bus lines, those that you are most likely to use are the **23** (Prati to Aventino), **62** (Castel Sant'Angelo to Repubblica), **64** (Termini to Vatican), **87** (Prati to Colosseum), **492** (Tiburtina railroad station to Vatican Museums), and **910** (Termini to Villa Borghese). Rome also has a few tram lines; they aren't as spectacular as the cable cars in San Francisco, but they're fun to ride. A line we like a lot is the **3,** which passes by the Basilica di San Giovanni and the Colosseum. Another line that you're likely to use is number **8,** from Largo Argentina to Trastevere. Most buses run daily from 5:30 a.m. to 12:30 a.m., but some stop at 8.30 p.m. A few night lines are marked with an *N* for *notturno* (night); they usually run every hour, leaving the ends of the line on the hour.

On foot

Walking is by far the best way to experience Rome, because you see the most as you wander the curving streets that merge, narrow to almost

Rome's Most Useful Public Transportation

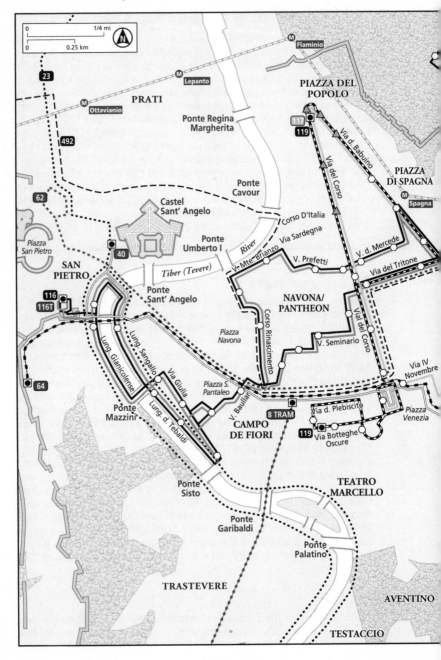

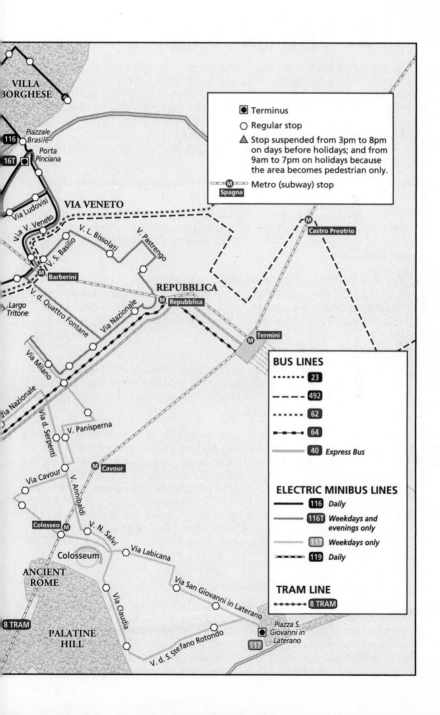

Taxi fares in Rome

The meter starts at 2.33€ ($3). It adds 1.29€ ($1.70) for every kilometer (⅔ mile) if you're moving at up to 20kmph (12 mph), and for every 85.3m (280 ft.) if you are going faster; this rate decreases within the urban limits (G.R.A. highway) to 0.78€ ($1) for every kilometer (⅔ mile) if you're moving at up to 20kmph (12 mph); for every 141m (462 feet) if you are going faster; and for every 19.2 seconds if you're stuck in traffic. At night (10 p.m.–7 a.m.) you'll have to pay a surcharge of 2.58€ ($3.40); on Sundays and holidays, it's 1.03€ ($1.30). The luggage supplement is 1.04€ ($1.30) for each bag larger than 35 × 25 × 50cm (14 × 9.8 × 20 inches).

---

shoulder width, change names, and meander among beautiful old buildings. Wear very comfortable shoes, and be ready to switch to another form of transportation — which will usually be handy — should you get tired.

To enjoy Rome's delightful labyrinth, you need a good map. The free tourist-office map is quite good, but it doesn't have a *stradario* (street directory), which is essential for locating addresses. You can buy a detailed map with a *stradario* at any newsstand and many bookstores.

By taxi

Taxi rates are reasonable, but the fare can add up during busy times of day when you're stuck in traffic. They're a great resource for getting to your hotel from the train station and traveling around at night after the buses and metro stop running.

Taxis don't cruise the streets, as in most U.S. cities; they return to taxi stands and wait for a call. That means you usually cannot hail a taxi on the street unless you happen to find one returning to a stand. You'll find many taxi stands, especially near major landmarks, including **Piazza Barberini** (at the foot of Via Veneto), **Piazza San Silvestro,** and **Piazza SS. Apostoli** (both not far from the Trevi Fountain). You can identify taxi stands by a smallish telephone on a pole marked TAXI. If you're starting from a place with a phone — a hotel or restaurant, say — asking the staff to call a taxi for you is easiest. For a **24-hour radio taxi,** call ☎ 06-88177, 06-6645, or 06-4994.

By motor scooter (motorino)

Most Romans travel on mopeds, or so it seems when you're on a street corner waiting for the signal to turn green. If you have some two-wheel experience — Rome is most definitely *not* the place to learn how to operate a scooter — the best spot to rent a *motorino* is **Treno e Scooter (TeS)** on Via Marsala, just outside Termini station by the taxi stand and metro entrance (☎ **06-48905823**). TeS gives you a 10 percent discount if you've traveled by train that day. The scooters are very good quality, and the prices (for example, 52€/$68 for the weekend) include insurance, taxes, and a free map; TeS also rents bicycles. To get there, take the metro to Termini. **Rent a Scooter Borgo,** Via delle Grazie 2, off Via di Porta Angelica, on the right side of the Vatican (☎ **06-6877239;** Metro: Ottaviano), and **New Scooter,** Via Quattro Novembre 96, up from Piazza Venezia (☎ **06-6790300;** Bus: 64), are also good options. You can get a complete list from one of the tourist information points.

Riding a scooter can be dangerous in Rome's busiest areas. Accidents are increasingly common, and scooters are pretty flimsy compared with cars. However, it's a great way to travel on Sundays and holidays, when car and bus traffic is light, or to explore quiet neighborhoods.

Chapter 9

Checking In at Rome's Best Hotels

In This Chapter

▶ Finding the best rates
▶ Booking the best room
▶ Selecting the best hotel
▶ Locating hotels by neighborhood and price

*T*ravelers may gladly experiment with new tastes and flavors for their food, but when it comes to sleeping, they want familiar creature comforts. Sometimes even the slightest variation from what they are used to will lead to sleepless nights. In this chapter, we share with you not only our list of favorite hotels, but also our best tips on what to expect, how to tackle the inevitable cultural differences, and how to choose among a wide and, in some cases, unfamiliar variety of lodging possibilities.

Knowing Your Roman Hotels: What to Expect

Destination of some 20 million tourists every year and with literally thousands of years of hospitality experience, Rome offers a huge choice of accommodations, not only in numbers but also in type and quality. Some hotels have been in business for several centuries; others are brand new. Some are family-run; others belong to international chains. Some are mom-and-pop places; others are the haunts of jet setters. You'll find anything from very basic to supremely elegant, and from great value to rip-off.

The hotel industry in Rome has made enormous progress toward standardization and upgrading older and historical lodgings to bring them in line with the expectations of international travelers. Persistent cultural differences, which are hard to iron out, become more and more apparent as you go down the luxury scale. Your room in a top five-star hotel in Rome will be basically the same, except in its décor, as another top five-star hotel room elsewhere in the world. You'll have space, top-notch service, and state-of-the-art amenities, plus, of course, Italian style and design in every single detail.

Rome's "architectural barriers"

Steps are ubiquitous in Roman hotels and may be particularly difficult to tackle when you are loaded with luggage. The street level of Renaissance and baroque *palazzi* was not a living floor (imagine the stench), and the main stairwell usually started from an internal alcove or courtyard well away from the road. Even in the most expensive hotels, a short flight of steps to reach the lobby from the street is common, and the elevator often lies another few steps along. Some hotels provide ramps for wheelchair accessibility, but that is far from the rule, particularly because space is so tight. Elevators have commonly been constructed inside the stairwell enclosed by the staircases — the only space available — which is why they often can't be accessed from curbside and why, in smaller hotels, they are minuscule. If steps are a problem for you, make sure you inquire about how many you must negotiate to reach the lobby and the elevator before you make your reservation.

Some things are hard to come by in Rome, whatever the price: a pretty view, lots of light, quiet nights, and plenty of space. Because medieval and Renaissance buildings were not designed with our modern lifestyle in mind, rooms tend to be smaller than you may expect. Also, the medieval and Renaissance streets in the historic district are narrow, and buildings were built literally on top of each other, with only darkish inner courtyards in between in the best of cases. Having a view is rare, and a real treat when you can have it without street noise. Most hotels may have one or two rooms with a decent view, if at all. If this feature is important to you, you will have to search far and wide and be ready to pay for it. Brightness is a similar issue: it isn't very common, though it is easier to come by than a view. We specify which hotels have brighter rooms than others, but of course, much depends on the room you are allotted. Again, if this is important to you, you will have to make some compromises, either on location or price. Similarly, if you want quiet, you'll have to pay more or give up being in the heart of the historic district, especially in summer, when street life becomes ubiquitous. Space, by contrast, is easier to come by: You only need to pay for it.

One interesting feature of Roman hotels is that as you go down in price, rooms become less standardized. Within the same hotel *and* the same price range — something we fail to understand — some rooms are great while others are dumps. In our experience, hotels usually give out their worst rooms only when they are overbooked, but we have seen some haphazard room allotment in our years on the road. Space is usually the first thing to go. Bathrooms are especially tiny — before they were added, relatively recently, it used to be common to have shared bathrooms in hotels. Elevators are rare and often broom-closet-size — or totally absent, in the cheaper hotels — and often start from one level above street level. Floors are a consideration, too: marble, tiles, and hardwood used to be more common than carpeting, but in cheaper hotels we feel that it is better to stay away from carpeting, because it is difficult to clean and is replaced less often than in upscale places. Just remember to bring your slippers in the cooler months if you don't want to get cold feet! More expensive hotels usually provide slippers, but then usually you have carpeting there as well.

Then there are amenities: Some that are commonplace in the United States — big ice machines, for instance — are virtually unknown in Italy. Of course, you can always step out of your hotel and sit on the terrace of a nearby cafe to have that iced drink. Other amenities, such as air-conditioning and satellite TV, are now more the rule than the exception, although you may have to pay extra in smaller and cheaper hotels (we spell this out in our write-ups). By the way, regular TVs are standard except in the cheapest accommodations, but they don't offer English-language programs. Then again, you didn't go to Italy to watch TV, did you? Window soundproofing is commonplace — and in the older *palazzo,* the thickness of the old walls helps protect you from noisy neighbors and the roar of traffic. Street noise is a problem that sound-proofed windows cannot eliminate if you like to sleep with your window open, though. If that is the case, ask for an inner room when you do your booking. Hair dryers are routine only in pricier lodgings, but you can ask and most often obtain one from the desk in cheaper accommodations. Irons are rarely offered, but you can ask for laundry or ironing service at most hotels, even in the lower price ranges. All hotel lobbies and break-fast rooms are smoke free by law, but smoking is allowed in private rooms; make sure to specify whether you want a smoke-free room when you make your reservation.

Children's amenities deserve special mention: They are basically nonex-istent. The hotels we mark with our Kid Friendly icon have proven par-ticularly ready to accommodate the special needs of those with small children, or they just have a favorable set-up (with family or connected rooms, for instance). See Chapter 6 for more on this subject. All hotels should be able to provide you with a cot or extra bed upon request; make sure you ask when you make your reservation.

Local breakfast is different from our American one: Romans will have croissants, toast and jam, cereal, and fruit along with their coffee or tea, and this is the "continental" breakfast usually included in your room rate. Although an increasing number of middle-range hotels offer a buffet break-fast with yogurt, cheese, and cold cuts, only the most expensive hotels routinely serve eggs and hot dishes. In some hotels you can order — and pay extra for — eggs and bacon if they aren't on the spread; make sure you ask when you make your reservation, if this is important to you.

One last thing: Remember that most hotels in Rome are private busi-nesses, usually family operations (even if they belong to a group, it is usually only a hotel association that fixes standards or simply allows some economies of scale when purchasing supplies). As a result, man-agement takes a lot of pride in its product and will be eager to make your stay comfortable. Just mention your difficulties; it is our experience that management will try to accommodate your request, if it's at all possible.

Finding the Best Room at the Best Rate

Prices have risen sharply in recent years. The weak dollar and poor exchange rate haven't helped. Rome is a capital city, and capital cities the world over are expensive. Also, you cannot count on off-season rates anymore: Off season in Rome has shrunk to a few weeks in January, February, August, and November (see Chapter 3 for more on seasons). The rest of the time you will find it difficult to get a decent room without paying through the nose. The best moderately priced hotels in the historic district sell out fast (sometimes they are booked as far as a year ahead). The best way to get a good deal is to plan in advance.

Finding the best rate

The **rack rate** is the maximum rate a hotel can charge for a room. That's the rate you get if you walk in off the street at the peak of high season and ask for a room for the night when the hotel is almost full. You see these rates printed on the fire/emergency-exit diagrams posted on the back of your hotel-room door. Chains are happy to charge you the rack rate, but you can almost always do better. Perhaps the best way to avoid paying the rack rate is surprisingly simple: Just ask for a cheaper or discounted rate. You may be pleasantly surprised. Also, a travel agent may be able to negotiate a better price than you can get by yourself — but usually only with hotels that belong to a chain. (That's because the hotel often gives the agent a discount in exchange for steering his or her business toward that hotel.) Exploring package tours, which offer both airfare and hotel at a discount, is also worthwhile. (See Chapter 5 for more on this.)

With hotel chains, reserving a room through the central reservation toll-free number may result in a lower rate than calling the hotel directly. On the other hand, the central reservation number may not know about discounted rates for special events at specific locations. Your best bet is to call both the local number and the toll-free number, and see which one gives you a better deal.

On the other hand, in Rome, where most middle-range hotels don't belong to chains, you'll rarely be charged the rack rate. As a general rule, private hotels in Rome will give you their lowest price when you make your reservation directly instead of through an agent or a booking service. This is because room rates change with the season and with occupancy: If a hotel is half-empty, you'll likely get a better rate than if it has only one room available — but the rates management agrees on with agents are based on seasons, not occupancy, and therefore tend to be higher. Also, the hotel has to factor in the agent's fee, which is then reported on your room rate. Hence, booking directly — often through the hotel's Web site — is a good option in Rome.

Also, keep an eye out for specials: Most hotels in Rome offer deals for special events, such as Easter, the big retail sales in January, or major art exhibitions (see Chapter 3 for a calendar of events). They may also offer a special rate for a two- or three-night stay and sometimes a weekend rate. Always ask if there are any specials when you make your reservation. Also, always check the hotel's Web site — it often offers special Internet deals (see "Surfing the Web for hotel deals," later in this chapter).

Finally, if you're Irish or British, be sure to mention membership in any automobile clubs, which may have reciprocity with Automobil Club d'Italia or the Touring Club Italiano; you may get a 10 percent discount. Frequent-flier programs with Alitalia and some other European carriers also may get you some points. Unfortunately, U.S. associations such as AARP and AAA usually have nothing to do with private Italian businesses. Some international chains do offer discounts for these associations, so be sure to know if your hotel belongs to a chain.

Surfing the Web for hotel deals

Shopping online for hotels is generally done one of two ways: through the hotel's own Web site or through an independent booking agency (or a fare-service agency such as Priceline.com). Booking through the **hotel's own Web site** is definitely the way to go in Rome for private establishments: Many offer special online rates, while some also offer significant discounts for advance booking, provided that you also pay in advance. Another method is to narrow your options through one of the Internet agencies listed later in this section and then check the Web site of the hotel you selected directly. You'll often find that you can do better on the hotel's site — the hotel doesn't have to pay any agency fees.

Internet hotel agencies in mind-boggling numbers compete for the business of millions of consumers surfing for accommodations around the world. This competitiveness can be a boon to consumers who have the patience and time to shop and compare the online sites for good deals — but shop you must, because prices can vary considerably from site to site. And keep in mind that hotels at the top of a site's listings may be there for no other reason than that they paid money to get the placement. Among the many sites for Rome, we recommend **Venere Net** (www.venere.com), which is very comprehensive and user friendly, as well as **Roma Hotels** (www.roma-hotels.com), and the **Cooperativa Il Sogno** (www.romeguide.it), both comprehensive and the latter with good descriptions of the hotels (with pictures).

We don't particularly recommend intercontinental agencies, which tend to list only a few hotels in Rome. Yet you can always try your luck with **hoteldiscount!com** (www.180096hotel.com/cgi-bin/pickcity), **Late Rooms.com** (www.it.laterooms.com), and of course **Expedia, Travelocity,** and, in the opaque Web site category, **Priceline** and **Hotwire.**

For both Priceline and Hotwire, you pay up front, and the fee is nonrefundable. *Note:* Some hotels don't provide loyalty-program credits or points or other frequent-stay amenities when you book a room through opaque online services.

 If you book your room through one of these online services, always **get a confirmation number,** and **make a printout** of any online booking transaction in case your reservation is lost. Actually, after you've reserved your rooms, it doesn't hurt to contact your hotel directly and request a confirmation via fax or e-mail to eliminate the chance of your arriving at a hotel that has no record of your reservation. Make sure that you bring the confirmation fax or e-mail with you to Italy.

Reserving the best room

First and foremost, make your reservations well ahead of time, especially if you decide to stay in a small hotel: The best rooms are the first to go.

 After you make your reservation, asking one or two more pointed questions can go a long way toward making sure you get the best room in the house. The trick of asking for a corner room doesn't always work in Rome (usually, corner rooms are larger, quieter, and have more windows and light than standard rooms, without necessarily costing more, but in Rome's historical buildings, corner rooms may actually be smaller and darker). It is best to ask directly for what you need the most: quiet (away from the main road and the elevator), light (with more windows), the most spacious bathroom, and so on. Consider that to have it all you may need to move to a higher price range. Always ask if the hotel is renovating; if it is, book elsewhere, or request a room away from the renovation work. Inquire, too, about the location of restaurants and bars in the hotel or outside — all sources of annoying noise. And if you aren't happy with your room when you arrive, talk to the front desk. If the hotel has another room, it should be happy to accommodate you, within reason.

Finding Alternative Accommodations: Apartments and Convents

Rome offers several accommodations options beyond hotels. If you plan to stay for a week or more, you may want to consider renting an apartment. Another option is to stay at one of the many convents and other religious houses that rent rooms; they do allow couples, but the rooms, though not quite monastic cells, don't offer many frills. In this book, we don't list religious houses that accept guests, because they usually have curfews (10 or 11 p.m., sometimes even earlier), and we don't think that you want to deal with that, especially if your trip is relatively short. If you're interested, however, the **Cooperativa Il Sogno** (www.romeguide.it) is probably your best resource.

If you want to rent an apartment, consult an organization that specializes in such arrangements. **Vacation Rentals by Owner** (www.vrbo.com) lists hundreds of homes for rent. Each English-language listing contains pictures, prices, and descriptions of the area where the house or apartment is located. Usually, you deal directly with the owner, so you may save considerably over the rate a broker would charge for the same property.

B&Bs are also an option, but don't expect romantic getaways: In Rome, a B&B is often just a one-room operation in somebody's home where you also get breakfast. Most of the Italy-based Internet agencies maintain apartment and B&B listings (see the section "Surfing the Web for hotel deals," earlier in this chapter). Other agencies to try are **Hideaways International** (767 Islington St., Portsmouth, NH 03801; ☎ **800-843-4433**; www.hideaways.com), **At Home Abroad** (405 E. 56th St., Suite 6H, New York, NY 10022; ☎ **212-421-9165**), and **Rentals in Italy** (700 East Main St., Ventura, CA 93001; ☎ **800-726-6702** or 805-641-1650; www.rent villas.com).

Arriving without a Reservation

If you arrive without a room reservation, your best option is to stop at the hotel desk at the airport or in Termini station. Either will usually be able to help you find something, but don't expect great deals; those have all been booked far in advance, and cancellations are rare. Be prepared to find room only in the most expensive hotels or outside the historic center, particularly at the height of the tourist season.

Rome's Best Hotels

Following are our picks for our favorite hotels in Rome. We did not have room for a full review of every one, so we list a few as runner-up options — but they also have our full seal of approval. In selecting our favorite hotels, we use cleanliness, comfort, and the most amenities at the best prices as essential criteria. All the hotels we list in this section are conveniently located in the center of Rome, have private bathrooms, and offer basic amenities. We always specify in the description if a hotel has no elevator, satellite TV, or air-conditioning. In addition to giving you exact prices, we use a system of dollar signs ($) to show a range of costs for hotels (see Table 9-1). The dollar signs correspond to rack rates (nondiscounted, standard rates) for a double room. If the hotel offers triples, quads, or suites, we also give rack rates for those. To help you further with the selection, we've created quick-reference indexes at the end of this chapter that list all the hotels by neighborhood and by price category.

Table 9-1	Key to Hotel Dollar Signs	
Dollar Sign(s)	**Price Range**	**What to Expect**
$	140€ ($182) or less	No frills; dignified, simple room in a family-run budget hotel housed in an old building. Room and bathroom tend to be small, television is not necessarily provided, and you may have to pay extra for air-conditioning. Breakfast is minimal. These hotels may not accept credit cards and may not have elevators.
$$	141€–230€ ($183–$299)	Pleasantly furnished, medium-to-small-size guest room with air-conditioning in a middle-range hotel. Bathrooms tend to be small in hotels in the historic district; both rooms and bathrooms tend to be more modern and spacious in less centrally located hotels. Breakfast is often served buffet-style and may include yogurt, cheese, and cold cuts.
$$$	231€–350€ ($300–$455)	Stylishly furnished room in a superior hotel with some amenities. Both room and bathroom are good-size, maybe even luxurious, in the hotels located farther from the historic district. Service is good, public spaces pleasant. Rates usually include a buffet breakfast, which may offer eggs.
$$$$	351€–450€ ($456–$585)	Stylish, spacious, elegantly furnished room in a superior hotel with good amenities in a highly desirable location. Bathrooms are often luxurious. Service is excellent, public spaces are pleasant and airy, and the copious buffet breakfast usually includes eggs.
$$$$$	451€ ($586) and up	Lavishly decorated, spacious room with a separate sitting area and a large, state-of-the-art bathroom in deluxe hotel accommodations. Usually in a historic building, such as an aristocratic *palazzo,* in one of the most desirable locations in Rome. Guest rooms are decorated with antique or designer furnishings, fine materials, and top-quality linens and bedding. Public spaces are grand, staff is attentive and professional, and you get top amenities, from gyms and spas to gardens with pools. Rates usually include American-style breakfast.

Rome Accommodations

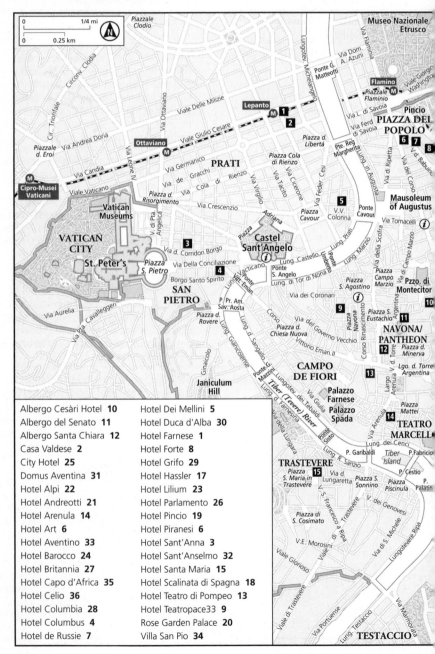

Albergo Cesàri Hotel **10**	Hotel Dei Mellini **5**
Albergo del Senato **11**	Hotel Duca d'Alba **30**
Albergo Santa Chiara **12**	Hotel Farnese **1**
Casa Valdese **2**	Hotel Forte **8**
City Hotel **25**	Hotel Grifo **29**
Domus Aventina **31**	Hotel Hassler **17**
Hotel Alpi **22**	Hotel Lilium **23**
Hotel Andreotti **21**	Hotel Parlamento **26**
Hotel Arenula **14**	Hotel Pincio **19**
Hotel Art **6**	Hotel Piranesi **6**
Hotel Aventino **33**	Hotel Sant'Anna **3**
Hotel Barocco **24**	Hotel Sant'Anselmo **32**
Hotel Britannia **27**	Hotel Santa Maria **15**
Hotel Capo d'Africa **35**	Hotel Scalinata di Spagna **18**
Hotel Celio **36**	Hotel Teatro di Pompeo **13**
Hotel Columbia **28**	Hotel Teatropace33 **9**
Hotel Columbus **4**	Rose Garden Palace **20**
Hotel de Russie **7**	Villa San Pio **34**

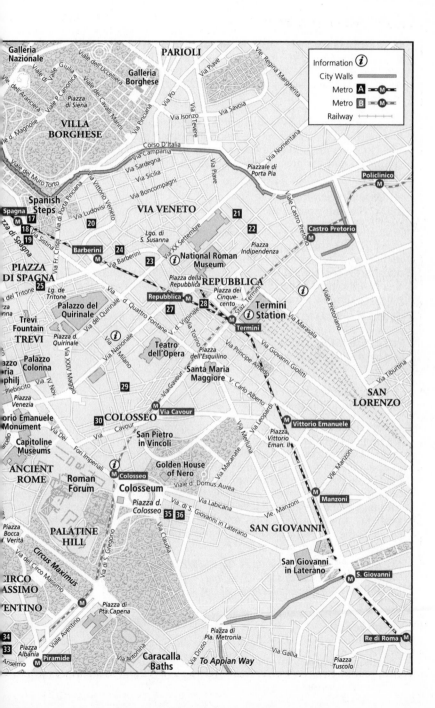

A note about parking: Very few hotels in Rome have their own garage or parking lot (when they do, we say so). Most often, they have an agreement with a nearby facility (usually a narrow-entrance underground garage). If you plan to bring a car — which we enthusiastically discourage (see Chapter 7) — ask your hotel for the rates when you book your room, and expect to pay 18€ to 36€ ($23–$47) per day, depending on location and car size.

In addition to our selections below, we also recommend some of the international chains. Over the years, they have purchased a number of highly desirable Roman hotels, such as the St. Regis Grand (a Starwood property) and various Best Westerns.

Albergo del Senato
$$$$ Navona/Pantheon

This elegant hotel occupies an ideal location across from the Pantheon. Guest rooms are spacious — the suites are palatial — and beautifully furnished, with antiques and quality reproductions, marble-topped tables, and hardwood floors. The marble bathrooms are huge (for Rome) and nicely appointed. The terrace has a spectacular view and is perfect for enjoying Rome's sunsets. The building is wired for Wi-Fi.

See map p. 98. Piazza della Rotonda 73. ☎ *06-6784343. Fax: 06-69940297.* www. albergodelsenato.it. *Bus: 60, 175, 492 to the Corso; 116 to Pantheon. Rack rates: 365€ ($438) double; 410€ ($492) triple; 440€ ($528) quad; suites 475€ ($570) and up. AE, DC, MC, V.*

Albergo Santa Chiara
$$$ Navona/Pantheon

Operated since 1838 by the Corteggiani family, this hotel offers great value. It's named after St. Clare, St. Francis's spiritual sister, who lived her last years in a room in this building. (That room has been transformed into a chapel, which you can visit.) The hotel is only a few steps from the Pantheon, with most attractions within easy reach. The service is usually attentive, and employees are ready to answer all your needs. The guest rooms are all different; some feature beamed ceilings, some are large, and some are small. Our favorites are the three garret suites with private terraces. Some rooms have hardwood and others carpeted floors; bathrooms are decent size and new.

See map p. 98. Via Santa Chiara 21. ☎ *06-6872979. Fax: 06-6873144.* www.albergo santachiara.com. *Bus: 40, 62, 63, and 64. Rack rates: 280€ ($364) double; 550€ ($715) suite. Rates include buffet breakfast. AE, DC, MC, V.*

Casa Valdese
$ Prati

Located on the Vatican side of the river, near Castel Sant'Angelo and the shopping district of Cola di Rienzo, this small hotel is a good deal. The name "Valdese" refers to the Protestant organization of Swiss origin that manages the hotel, which reflects the society's philosophy in its simple but spotlessly clean and pleasant rooms. The very moderate prices and the excellent location — basically across the river from Piazza del Popolo — are other pluses. The hotel can also provide half-board (breakfast and dinner) on request for 22€ ($29) per person per meal.

See map p. 98. Via A. Farnese 18, off Via Cola di Rienzo. ☎ *06-3218222. Fax: 06-3211843.* www.casavaldeseroma.it. *Metro: Lepanto. Via Farnese is the first right as you walk toward the river on Via Giulio Cesare. Rack rates: 119€ ($155) double; 163€ ($212) triple; and 194€ ($252) quad. Rates include breakfast. AE, V.*

City Hotel
$$ Piazza di Spagna/Via Veneto

This hotel is a good find. Located on the third floor of a nice *palazzo* (with an elevator from street level), it offers comfortable, well-appointed rooms, with classic furnishings and decent-size marble and tile bathrooms, all at moderate prices. Nice woodwork and bright spaces add to the atmosphere. The furnishings are tasteful and the service excellent. It also has the great advantage of a perfect location, within walking distance of the Spanish Steps and the Trevi Fountain, and it is very well connected to public transportation — a rare advantage in the historic district.

See map p. 98. Via Due Macelli 97. ☎ *06-6784037. Fax: 06-6797972. Metro: Barberini; then take the fifth right as you walk downhill on Via del Tritone: 230€ ($299) double; 250€ ($325) junior suite. Rates include buffet breakfast. AE, DC, MC, V.*

Grand Hotel Parco dei Principi
$$$$$ Villa Borghese

Abutting Villa Borghese, this luxurious hotel offers the best service in Rome and — if you can afford it — the best accommodations for families with young kids, particularly in the busy season. The swimming pool, the garden, and the proximity of the Villa Borghese Park and its various attractions (including the Borghese Gallery and the zoo) make it heaven for the younger set and their parents. The rooms are palatial (some are wheelchair accessible), with spacious marble-clad bathrooms and Wi-Fi. The excellent restaurants and room service on the premises are good options for meal planning. You'll be away from the action and crowds of the historic center, which will not suit everybody (you'll need to travel by taxi or cross the park on foot). On the good side, you'll have beautiful views from the hotel's terrace, quiet nights (oh, so rare in Rome), and easy parking (just unthinkable). Always check for Web specials, which may include the swimming pool and parking (which otherwise cost, respectively, 60€/$78 and 25€/$33).

Via G. Frescobaldi 5. ☎ *06-854421. Fax: 06-8551758.* www.parcodeiprincipi. com. *Bus: 910. Rack rates: 550€–620€ double ($715–$806). Rates include buffet breakfast. AE, DC, MC, V.*

Hotel Alpi
$$ Repubblica

Housed in a Liberty-style (Italian Art Nouveau) building, this family-run hotel offers quiet accommodations in a somewhat less glamorous area of the historic district, well served by public transportation and walking distance to many attractions and Termini train station. Guest rooms are medium-size with hardwood or carpeted floors and nicely appointed marble bathrooms (not huge, but not tiny either). Some are furnished in classic and others in contemporary style; we prefer the latter, but it is a matter of taste. Service is attentive and friendly, and children get some extra small attentions in the room. The hotel's kitchen is available for in-room dining. There is Wi-Fi in public spaces.

See map p. 98. Via Castelfidardo 84a, off Piazza Indipendenza. ☎ *06-4441235. Fax 06-4441257.* www.hotelalpi.com. *Bus: 492. Metro: Termini, then walk right on Via Solferino to Piazza Indipendenza. Rack rates: 165€–185€ double ($228–$241). Rates include buffet breakfast. AE, DC, MC, V.*

Hotel Arenula
$ Campo de' Fiori

We feel this is the best budget hotel in Rome: It offers spacious, well-appointed and spotlessly clean guest rooms in one of our favorite locations in the historic center, only steps from Campo de' Fiori, within easy reach of shopping, nightlife, and attractions. The drawback is that there is no elevator, and the hotel starts on the second floor (a pretty spiral marble staircase leads to the reception area). Guest rooms are simply furnished but bright and tasteful, with basic amenities and decent-size bathrooms and showers.

See map p. 98. Via Santa Maria de' Calderari 47, off Via Arenula. ☎ *06-6879454. Fax: 06-6896188.* www.hotelarenula.com. *Bus: 64, 70, 170, 492, 40 to Largo Argentina. Walk south on Via Arenula, and take the fourth street on your left. Rack rates: 125€ double ($163). Rates include buffet breakfast. AE, DC, MC, V.*

Hotel Art
$$$$ Piazza di Spagna

A postmodern creation in one of the most desirable areas of Rome, Hotel Art is worth a visit even if you don't get a room. Just go for a drink at the bar — created in the columned and frescoed chapel of a palace — to see the hall and the court, with its crystal staircase and designer-contemporary furnishings. Striking features illustrate the artistic "eclecticism" on which the hotel prides itself: public spaces and rooms are color coordinated down to the stationery, one color per floor, while the furniture is made of fine hardwoods. With the feel of boutique hotels you find in all the great cities of the world, it accents comfort, service, and, of course, style. Check the Web site for Internet specials. The hotel is wheelchair accessible.

See map p. 98. Via Margutta 56, next to Via del Babuino. ☎ *06-328711. Fax: 06-36003995.* www.hotelart.it. *Metro: Piazza di Spagna. Walk on Via del Babuino;*

take the first right and then the first left. Rack rates: 429€–495€ ($558–$644) double; 1,229€ ($1,598) suite. Rates include buffet breakfast. AE, DC, MC, V.

Hotel Britannia
$$$ Repubblica

This pleasant, elegant hotel enjoys a good location in the historic center and is convenient to most attractions and well served by public transportation. Guest rooms are not huge but are smartly appointed with neoclassic or modern furnishings and carpeted floors; some rooms have private terraces equipped with table and chairs, while some have vaulted ceilings and other architectural details. Each marble bathroom holds a tanning lamp. The daily fresh fruit basket and welcome drink are good touches from a professionally friendly and highly available staff.

See map p. 98. Via Napoli 64, off Via Nazionale. ☎ **06-4883153.** *Fax: 06-4882343.* www . hotelbritannia.it. *Metro: Repubblica. Walk 2 blocks on Via Nazionale, and turn left. Rack rates: 240€ ($312) double. Rates include buffet breakfast. AE, DC. MC, V.*

Hotel Capo d'Africa
$$$$ Colosseo

This elegant modern hotel is located on an atmospheric street between the Colosseum and San Giovanni, close to the Forum but not at the heart of the historic district. Under the same ownership as the Hotel Dei Mellini (see review later in this chapter) and known for its excellent service, the Capo d'Africa offers comfortable, spacious rooms furnished in a warm, modern-ethnic style, some with hardwood and other carpeted floors. The marble bathrooms are good size and nicely fitted. The hotel also offers some suites and wheelchair-accessible rooms. Don't miss the roof terrace and its splendid views.

See map p. 98. Via Capo d'Africa 54. ☎ **06-772801.** *Fax: 06-77280801.* www.hotel capodafrica.com. *Metro: Colosseo. Walk southeast across Piazza del Colosseo to Via Capo d'Africa. Rack rates: 360€–400€ ($468–$520) double; suites 500€ ($650) and up. Rates include buffet breakfast. AE, DC, MC, V.*

Hotel Columbia
$$ Repubblica

This refined hotel offers excellent value; it's in a somewhat less glamorous area of the historic district, yet convenient to a number of attractions and well connected by public transportation. The family that has managed the property since 1900 is proud of the quality of its service. Guest rooms are spacious and bright, many with beamed ceilings, some with arched windows or Murano chandeliers. All rooms are individually furnished with modern beds and antiques or quality reproductions. Bathrooms are good size and modern. The hotel also has a pleasant roof garden with a bar, where breakfast is served.

See map p. 98. Via Viminale 15. ☎ **06-4744289.** *Fax: 06-4740209.* www.hotel columbia.com. *Metro: Line A to Repubblica; then walk toward Termini station.*

Rack rates: 168€–235€ ($218–$306) double; 275€–327€ ($358–$425) suite. Rates include buffet breakfast. AE, DC, MC, V.

Hotel Dei Mellini
$$$ Prati

Within walking distance of Piazza del Popolo (across the bridge) and Castel Sant'Angelo, and convenient to public transportation, this hotel earns our vote with sophisticated atmosphere that doesn't cost an arm and leg. We also like its relaxing internal garden and the public areas decorated with contemporary art. Guest rooms are large and elegantly furnished in modern-classic style; some have private terraces. The good-size bathrooms are pleasingly arranged and marble-clad. Children up to age 12 stay free in their parent's room.

See map p. 98. Via Muzio Clementi 81, off Via Colonna. ☎ *06-324771. Fax: 06-32477801.* www.hotelmellini.com. *Bus: 30, 70, 81, 87, 186, 492 to Via Colonna. Rack rates: 350€ ($455) double; 450€–550€ ($585–$715) suite. AE, DC, MC, V.*

Hotel Farnese
$$$ Prati

Tucked behind Castel Sant'Angelo in a quiet neighborhood only steps from one of Rome's best shopping streets — Via Cola di Rienzo — and within walking distance of the Vatican and Piazza del Popolo (across the Tiber), this hospitable hotel occupies a 1906 patrician *palazzo,* which has been completely renovated. Quiet and off the tourist path, it is elegantly decorated. The guest rooms are spacious — the largest are geared for families — with stylish hardwood floors and classic furnishings. The bathrooms are particularly nice, clad in marble and tile, spacious (for Rome), and with new modern fixtures. The hotel also has a roof garden.

See map p. 98. Via Alessandro Farnese 30. ☎ *06-3212553. Fax: 06-3215129.* www. hotelfarnese.com. *Metro: Line A to Lepanto; then walk northeast on Via degli Scipioni to Via Farnese. Rack rates: 300€–370€ ($390–$481) double. Rates include buffet breakfast. AE, MC, V.*

Hotel Hassler
$$$$$ Piazza di Spagna

If money is no object, this luxury hotel, with its fantastic location up the Spanish Steps and its sophisticated elegance, is the place to be in Rome. The basic double rooms are not as opulent and spacious as the deluxe doubles, which are basically junior suites, but you enjoy the same top amenities (including a state-of-the-art health center), and most have a relaxing view over the inner garden. Bathrooms are wonderful, marble-clad retreats. The hotel also offers bicycles to take to nearby Villa Borghese, terraces where you can take in the view, and a number of bars and restaurants, including the recently opened **Imago,** serving creative Italian fare on the roof, with Rome at your feet.

See map p. 98. Piazza Trinità dei Monti 6. ☎ **06-699340.** *Fax: 06-6789991.* www.hotel hasslerroma.com. *Metro: Barberini; then take Via Sistina downhill to your right and walk all the way to the end. Rack rates: 580€–810€ ($754–$1,053) double. Rates include buffet breakfast. AE, MC, V.*

Hotel Lilium
$$ **Via Veneto/Repubblica**

This hotel defines refined and cheap. It's a great addition for budget travelers, offering a convenient, if not glamorous, location and bright, welcoming accommodations. The smallish guest rooms are individually decorated with wooden furniture and charming hand-painted floral motifs. The best rooms have small, delightful private balconies and spacious bathrooms. The hotel also offers 24-hour free Internet connection.

See map p. 98. Via XX Settembre 58a. ☎ **06-4741133.** *Fax 06-23328387.* www.lilium hotel.it. *Metro: Repubblica. Walk right on Via Cernaia, take the first left on Via Pastrengo and turn right on Via XX Settembre. Rack rates: 190€–220€ ($247–$286) double. Rates include breakfast. AE, DC, MC, V.*

Hotel Parlamento
$$ **Navona/Pantheon**

Located right in the heart of Renaissance Rome, only steps from Piazza di Spagna, the Trevi Fountain, and the Pantheon, this hotel on the third and fourth floors of a 15th-century building offers great accommodations at excellent prices (off-season prices can be half the rack rate). Rooms are bright and spacious, with tiled floors and large beds. Some of the comfortable bathrooms have tubs. Weather permitting, breakfast is served on the pleasant roof terrace. Guests have free Internet access, but air-conditioning costs extra (12€/$16) per day; book when you reserve.

See map p. 98. Via delle Convertite 5, off Piazza San Silvestro. ☎ */fax:* **06-69921000.** www.hotelparlamento.it. *Bus: 492 or 116 to Piazza San Silvestro. Rack rates: 170€ ($221) double. Rates include breakfast. MC, V.*

Hotel Pincio
$$ **Piazza di Spagna**

A splendid location and moderate prices are the key characteristics of this small family-run hotel, situated on the second floor (no elevator for the first level) of a historic building within walking distance of the Spanish Steps. Service is kind and attentive, and a 24-hour Internet point is available. The basic guest rooms and bathrooms are decent size and pleasantly appointed, with tiled floors and simple, good-quality wood furnishings. The rooftop terrace, where breakfast is served, is delightful.

See map p. 98. Via Capo Le Case 50. ☎ **06-6790758.** *Fax 06-6791233.* www.hotel pincio.com. *Bus: 62, 63, 116, 492. Rack rates: 195€ ($254) double. Rates include buffet breakfast. MC, V.*

Hotel Santa Maria
$$ Trastevere

This small hotel occupies a block of low buildings surrounding a romantic courtyard lined by a portico. Most of the guest rooms are on the first floor and open directly on the courtyard (there's one garret suite on the second floor). Rooms are cozy and welcoming, with terracotta-tiled floors, white-washed walls, and dark-wood furniture. They can be a bit dark on rainy days because all natural light comes from the portico. The courtyard is a pleasant place to take breakfast on a sunny morning. In the afternoon and early evening, guests can have a glass of wine from the wine bar. The suites are on two levels and are designed for families with children (up to six beds).

See map p. 98. Vicolo del Piede 2, off Piazza Santa Maria in Trastevere. ☎ *06-5894626. Fax: 06-5894815.* www.htlsantamaria.com. *Tram: 8 to Piazza Sonnino. Take Via della Lungaretta to Piazza Santa Maria in Trastevere; cross the square, and turn right. Rack rates: 210€ ($273) double; 250€ ($325) triple; suites 280€ ($364) and up. Rates include buffet breakfast. AE, MC, V.*

Hotel Sant'Anna
$$ San Pietro

We love this hotel: it is a great find in this price range. Located in a charming, authentic neighborhood a stone's throw from the Vatican, it is in a 16th-century building with an inner courtyard where breakfast is served in nice weather. The rooms are large and have elegant modern furnishings, carpeting, and good-size marble bathrooms; a number of rooms have coffered ceilings. The vaulted breakfast room has bright fresco decorations. The hotel is accessible to wheelchairs and allows pets.

See map p. 98. Via Borgo Pio 133. ☎ *06-68801602. Fax: 06-68308717.* www.hotel santanna.com. *Bus: 62 to Borgo Sant'Angelo. Take Via Mascherino, and turn right on Via Borgo Pio. Rack rates: 220€ ($286) double. Rates include buffet breakfast. AE, DC, MC, V.*

Hotel Scalinata di Spagna
$$$ Piazza di Spagna

This is a charming small hotel just above the Spanish Steps near the elegant Hotel Hassler (there is a public elevator from Piazza di Spagna if you're too tired to negotiate the tourist-clogged environs). The guest rooms are smallish but cheery and nicely appointed in classic style; some have exposed beams, and two have a private small terrace; most are carpeted. The marble bathrooms are fair-size but not large by any means. The suites are two connected rooms designed for families. The pleasant roof garden offers a nice spot to unwind in the good season. Wi-Fi in the rooms and an Internet point in the lobby are freely available to guests. The welcome fruit basket is a nice touch.

See map p. 98. Piazza Trinità dei Monti 17. ☎ *06-6793006. Fax: 06-69940598.* www. hotelscalinata.com. *Metro: Line A to Spagna; then up the Spanish Steps (or elevator). Rack rates: 230€–390€ ($299–$507) double; 470€ ($611) suite. Rates include buffet breakfast. AE, MC, V.*

Hotel Teatro di Pompeo
$$ Campo de' Fiori

Located in the lively, historic neighborhood near Campo de' Fiori, this is a good budget choice with plenty of charm. The name refers to the ancient Roman theater, dating from 55 B.C., that lies beneath the hotel; some of its structure is visible in the breakfast room. The rest of the building is much newer — that is, from the 15th century — as you see by the beamed ceilings in some rooms. The rooms are spacious for this ancient area of Rome, and the white plaster walls, hardwood floors, and simple furnishings give it an old-fashioned charm. The tiled bathrooms are not large but have new fixtures. We do not recommend the three rooms in the nearby annex, which are small and located on the third floor with no elevator.

See map p. 98. Largo del Pallaro 8. ☎ *06-68300170. Fax: 06-68805531.* www.hotel teatrodipompeo.it. *Bus: 64 to Sant'Andrea della Valle; then walk east on Via dei Chiavari, and turn right. Rack rates: 205€ ($267) double. Rates include buffet breakfast. AE, DC, MC, V.*

Hotel Teatropace33
$$ Navona/Pantheon

We like this hotel's romantic location — hidden in a narrow street behind Piazza Navona — and atmospheric lodgings. It's in a 17th-century *palazzo*, with a grand baroque marble staircase to the main lobby (the only way up, but hotel personnel will help with your bags), 10-foot-thick walls, and charming rooftop terrace. Guest rooms, furnished with personality, have hardwood floors, quality furniture, plenty of wooden ceiling beams, and good-sized marble bathrooms. Every room has Internet access and a tea/coffee kettle.

See map p. 98. Via del Teatro Pace 33, 1 block west of Piazza Navona. ☎ *06-6879075. Fax: 06-68192364.* www.hotelteatropace.com. *Bus: 64 to Corso Vittorio Emanuele. Rack rates: F235€ double ($306); 335€ ($436) junior suite. Rates include buffet breakfast. AE, DC, MC, V.*

Rose Garden Palace
$$$$ Via Veneto

This is one of our favorite hotels in the exclusive area around Via Veneto, housed in a Liberty-style (Italian Art Nouveau) building from the beginning of the 20th century. The eponymous rose garden is a lovely inner retreat that's perfect for a private moment of relaxation. Charm isn't the only thing you'll find here, however; the top-notch amenities include a fitness center with a small swimming pool and gym. The marble bathrooms have both showers and bathtubs; the rooms themselves are large; and the entire hotel is furnished with very sleek yet inviting modern décor in wood and fine materials. The American buffet breakfast is great.

See map p. 98. Via Boncompagni 19. ☎ *06-421741. Fax: 06-4815608.* www.rose gardenpalace.com. *Bus: 116 to Via Boncompagni; then walk north 1 block. Rack rates: 385€–440€ ($501–$572) double; 539€ ($701) suite. Rates include buffet breakfast. AE, DC, MC, V.*

Villa San Pio

$$$ Aventino

This is the best of a consortium of three beautifully located family-run hotels on the Aventino, each with its own personality, and all recommended. The San Pio is in a peaceful spot, surrounded by a private garden, yet only steps from attractions and transportation. Guest rooms are large and elegantly decorated, with period furniture and delicate frescoes and moldings on the walls. Good-size marble bathrooms add to the value. If this hotel is full, an employee will suggest that you reserve at one of the nearby sister hotels: **Hotel Sant'Anselmo,** Piazza Sant'Anselmo 2; and **Hotel Aventino,** Via San Domenico 10 (same Web site and phone).

See map p. 98. Via Santa Melania 19. ☎ *06-5745231. Fax: 06-5741112.* www.aventino hotels.com. *Tram: 3 to Piazza Albania; then take Via di Sant'Anselmo, and turn right. Metro: Circo Massimo; walk up Viale Aventino to Piazza Albania, and follow directions for Tram. Metro: Piramide. Rack rates: 240€ ($312) double. Rates include breakfast. AE, DC, MC, V.*

Runner-Up Accommodations

Albergo Cesàri Hotel

$$ Navona/Pantheon A family-run historic hotel with renovated guest rooms (some with modern furnishings; others with quality reproduction beds and armoires), in a fantastic location. For families or small groups, inquire about the triple and quad rooms. *See map p. 98. Via di Pietra 89a.* ☎ *06-6749701.* www.albergocesari.it.

Domus Aventina

$$ Aventino We are partial to the Aventino, a pleasant island of grace and quiet in an otherwise bustling city. We see it as a perfect night-time retreat. This hotel offers largish (only a few are small) and pleasant rooms, simply decorated with good-quality wooden furniture and carpeting. Some of them open on the garden, but they are a bit dark. Bathrooms are not large but are well appointed. *See map p. 98. Via Santa Prisca 11/b.* ☎ *06-5746135.* www.hoteldomusaventina.com.

Hotel Andreotti

$$ Repubblica This hotel is within walking distance of many attractions and convenient to public transportation. Its location, in a somewhat less glamorous area of the historic district, justifies its rates, but then, you are farther from the action. Guest rooms are largish and comfortable, each differently furnished but all in classic and somewhat flamboyant style, and bathrooms are good-sized and modern; some rooms have ceilings decorated with original moldings. The courteous service is a plus. *See map p. 98. Via Castelfidardo 55, at the corner of Via Cernaia.* ☎ *06-4441006.* www.hotel andreotti.it.

Hotel Barocco

$$$ **Via Veneto**   Right off Piazza Barberini, this charming small hotel offers tastefully furnished guest rooms, in dark woods and fine fabrics, with marble bathrooms; some rooms have a balcony or a terrace. The refined ambience is pleasant without being stuffy. *See map p. 98. Via della Purificazione 4, off Piazza Barberini.* ☎ *06-4872001.* www.hotelbarocco.com.

Hotel Celio

$$$ **Colosseo**   This small hotel is a real jewel of decoration, housed in an 1870 building just steps from the Colosseum. The smallish guest rooms are individually decorated in Renaissance and ancient Roman style, with mosaic floors and frescoed walls. Bathrooms are small but nicely done in marble and mosaics. The small roof terrace, where breakfast is served in good weather, enjoys gorgeous views over ancient Rome — as do the three private terraces of the Pompeian suite. *See map p. 98. Via dei Santissimi Quattro 35/c.* ☎ *06-70495333.* www.hotelcelio.com.

Hotel Columbus

$$$ **San Pietro**   Housed in the 15th-century Palazzo della Rovere, literally steps away from St. Peter's Square (the Della Rovere were an important aristocratic family linked to the Vatican), this is a unique hotel. Decorated with frescoes (some by Pinturicchio) and preserving the feeling of a dignified aristocrat's palace, it offers large and commodious rooms, some of which are a bit tired. The service is particularly kind and attentive. **La Veranda** restaurant (see Chapter 10) opens on the large and delightful inner garden courtyard. The hotel is accessible to travelers with disabilities. *See map p. 98. Via della Conciliazione 33.* ☎ *06-6865435.* www.hotelcolumbus.net.

Hotel de Russie

$$$$$ **Piazza di Spagna**   Making the lists of the world's top hotels ever since it opened in 2000, the de Russie is one of the most elegant place to stay in Rome, along with the Hotel Hassler (see earlier in this chapter). The location, service, and accommodations are superb. If you stay here, you'll follow the steps of the rich and famous — Bill and Chelsea Clinton, among others. Housed in a beautiful *palazzo* enclosing a delightful terrace garden, the hotel is furnished in extremely tasteful and classy contemporary Italian style, and guest rooms have all kinds of amenities. You'll also find a spa with sauna, gym, and swimming pool. The restaurant on the premises, **Le Jardin du Russie** (see Chapter 10), gets excellent reviews. *See map p. 98. Via del Babuino 9.* ☎ *06-328881.* www.hotelderussie.it.

Hotel Duca d'Alba

$$ **Colosseo**   This hotel occupies a good location, basically equidistant from the Colosseum, Forum, Santa Maria Maggiore, and Piazza Venezia, at the heart of a lively neighborhood with lots of small restaurants and pubs. Guest rooms aren't large, but all are nicely decorated in contemporary style, mostly with carpeted floors. Bathrooms are small, but nicely done in marble. The buffet breakfast is one of the best in this price range, including

continental choices as well as eggs and bacon. *See map p. 98. Via Leonina 14.* ☎ *06-484471.* www.hotelducadalba.com.

Hotel Forte

$$ **Piazza di Spagna** The Forte is often booked solid; it's a good find if accommodations at moderate prices in the most glamorous street of the historic center are important to you. Guest rooms vary in size (some are really tiny), but all are pleasantly decorated, with quality wooden furniture in streamlined classic style; most have carpeted floors. Bathrooms are small but functional. Wi-Fi is free. *See map p. 98. Via Margutta 16.* ☎ *06-3207625.* www.hotelforte.com.

Hotel Grifo

$$ **Colosseo** Centrally located in the lively neighborhood between the Colosseum and Piazza Venezia, this hotel is convenient to attractions and nightlife. Guest rooms are on the large side for this price range; they're bright, with white walls, and simply appointed with modern wood furniture. The roof garden is a plus. *See map p. 98. Via del Boschetto 144.* ☎ *06-4871395.* www.hotelgrifo.com.

Hotel Piranesi

$$$ **Piazza di Spagna** If you cannot stay at the Hotel de Russie (above), this is a more affordable option across the street, offering top service and high-quality amenities, including a gym with sauna. Housed in Palazzo Nainer, a *hotel particulier* redone by the architect Giuseppe Valadier (the man behind Piazza del Popolo and the Pincio Gardens) at the beginning of the 19th century, it is an atmospheric hotel. Guest rooms are not large, but they're elegantly appointed, with pleasing hardwood floors and stylish furnishings; a number of them have private balconies. Bathrooms are decent size, and nicely done in marble and tiles. *Via del Babuino 196.* ☎ *06-328041.* www.hotelpiranesi.com.

Index of Accommodations by Neighborhood

Hotel Piranesi ($$$)
Hotel Scalinata di Spagna ($$$)

Prati

Casa Valdese ($)
Hotel Dei Mellini ($$$)
Hotel Farnese ($$$)

Repubblica

Hotel Alpi ($$)
Hotel Andreotti ($$)
Hotel Britannia ($$$)
Hotel Columbia ($$)
Hotel Lilium ($$)

San Pietro

Hotel Columbus ($$$)
Hotel Sant'Anna ($$)

Trastevere

Hotel Santa Maria ($$)

Via Veneto

City Hotel ($$)
Hotel Barocco ($$$)
Hotel Lilium ($$)
Rose Garden Palace ($$$$)

Villa Borghese

Grand Hotel Parco dei Principi
($$$$$)

Index of Accommodations by Price

$

Casa Valdese (Prati)
Hotel Arenula (Campo de' Fiori)

$$

Albergo Cesàri Hotel
(Navona/Pantheon)
City Hotel (Piazza di Spagna/Via
Veneto)
Domus Aventina (Aventino)
Hotel Alpi (Repubblica)
Hotel Andreotti (Repubblica)
Hotel Columbia (Repubblica)
Hotel Duca d'Alba (Colosseo)
Hotel Forte (Piazza di Spagna)
Hotel Grifo (Colosseo)
Hotel Lilium (Via Veneto/Repubblica)
Hotel Parlamento (Navona/Pantheon)
Hotel Pincio (Piazza di Spagna)
Hotel Santa Maria (Trastevere)
Hotel Sant'Anna (San Pietro)
Hotel Teatro di Pompeo (Campo
de' Fiori)
Hotel Teatropace33
(Navona/Pantheon)

$$$

Albergo del Senato
(Navona/Pantheon)
Albergo Santa Chiara
(Navona/Pantheon)
Hotel Barocco (Via Veneto)
Hotel Britannia (Repubblica)
Hotel Celio (Colosseo)
Hotel Columbus (San Pietro)
Hotel Dei Mellini (Prati)
Hotel Farnese (Prati)
Hotel Piranesi (Piazza di Spagna)
Hotel Scalinata di Spagna (Piazza di
Spagna)
Villa San Pio (Aventino)

$$$$

Hotel Art (Piazza di Spagna)
Hotel Capo d'Africa (Colosseo)
Rose Garden Palace (Via Veneto)

$$$$$

Grand Hotel Parco dei Principi (Villa
Borghese)
Hotel de Russie (Piazza di Spagna)
Hotel Hassler (Piazza di Spagna)

Chapter 10

Dining and Snacking in Rome

• •

In This Chapter

▶ Discovering Rome's dining scene

▶ Tasting the best of Roman foods

▶ Seating yourself at Rome's best restaurants

▶ Having memorable dining experiences

▶ Finding the best quick snack

• •

*I*t used to be said that there wasn't a really good restaurant in Rome, but things have changed, and the capital now counts among its many treasures some of the best restaurants in the country.

Getting the Dish on the Local Scene

Rome's dining scene has gone a long way in just over a decade. Once home to a number of good but down-to-earth little *trattorie* offering traditional local food, interspersed with a few stuffy formal restaurants serving mediocre fare, the city now boasts hundreds of trendy eateries, elegant restaurants, and welcoming joints of all descriptions, including non-Italian spots. *Osterie, trattorie,* and *pizzerie* that specialize in traditional fare have multiplied even as they've become more careful about food quality (see Chapter 2 for more on Roman specialties and cuisine). The chefs at many traditional restaurants are purists, looking far and wide for the best ingredients and techniques. Those serving innovative cuisine have followed the same route, and, in general, you'll notice respect for ingredients' quality everywhere. Also, as hotel dining has become fashionable, more top hotels have hired world-renowned chefs, making previously nondescript restaurants into real winners.

Restaurants crowd the historic center, with the highest concentration in the area around Campo de' Fiori, in Trastevere, and in the Navona/ Pantheon and Trevi areas, in that order. A steady flow of locals — from government offices and the numerous businesses in these areas, but also from everywhere else in Rome — feeds constant renewal and ensures good quality. Feel free to try one of the small restaurants in these neighborhoods even if we don't specifically recommend it: It would be impossible to list all the good places in Rome. Just follow your nose. In addition, some areas have emerged recently — in residential neighborhoods such as Parioli, along Viale Liegi, and the little streets off Via Nomentana, near Porta Pia. Experimenting with new restaurants in these neighborhoods is always tricky: You certainly won't have a bad meal, but it may not be the best the city can offer.

Dining hours are later than in the United States. Romans sit down to dinner between 8:30 and 10:30 p.m.; lunch is between 1 and 3 p.m. A few restaurants in the historic district open around noon for lunch and 7:30 p.m. for dinner to accommodate tourists. Many pubs also open earlier. **Smoking is illegal in public places,** but it's allowed in separate rooms in restaurants that provide them. The price of each dish often includes a 10 percent to 15 percent charge for *servizio* (service) — if it's not specified on the menu, it is not included — but an extra 5 percent to 10 percent is expected for good service.

If you're visiting in the summer, remember that Roman men tend to dress in what may look rather formal to American eyes (no shorts, and rarely jeans), even during the day. A man in shorts and a tank top may not be able to have lunch except in the most informal eateries. Shorts and tank tops (except really stylish and elegant ones) are not a good choice for women, either, but they may pass more easily.

Trimming the Fat from Your Budget

Thanks to Rome's dining boom, it's getting easier and easier to find nice restaurants — but harder and harder to find really cheap ones that serve high-quality food. However, a good meal in Rome remains very affordable, and you don't need to make big sacrifices to save a little.

A common strategy is to have a bite on the go at a bar or *rosticceria* for lunch (see "Dining and Snacking on the Go," later in this chapter) and save your money for dinner. If you really want to save money, be prepared to stand — bars apply a surcharge for sitting at a table *(al tavolo)* rather than eating at the counter *(al banco)* — or take your food to a bench in a public garden; in that case you can even buy your food at an *alimentari* (a grocery store). In restaurants, you can easily spend less by having fewer courses. The classic Roman meal includes appetizer, pasta, *secondo* (meat or fish), *contorno* (salad, vegetables, or potatoes), and dessert, with copious wine and an espresso to finish, but this kind of meal — usually stretching for a couple of hours — is only for special occasions and weekends. For lunch or a light dinner, most Romans eat a *secondo* with a *contorno,* or even just a pasta dish with a *contorno,* or a pizza (round; individual size).

Another thing to watch is drinks. A bottle of wine will considerably increase your bill, but most restaurants offer *vino della casa,* sold by volume (minimum *un quarto* — a quarter liter, or about 9 ounces), and many have a few choices by the glass. What may surprise you is that wine is often less expensive than soft drinks. If you're a group or a family, agree on one kind of soda and ask for a large bottle (liter size) — it's much cheaper than individual cans. Most *pizzerie* serve family-size bottles of beer as well as soda. Cocktails are basically unknown except at the most fashionable bars.

Rome's Best Restaurants

We have reviewed what we feel are the best restaurants in Rome. Of course, there are many more than we have room for here, but these are our favorites, and we hope they'll be yours. Each listing is marked with dollar signs to give an idea of the cost of a full meal, including a pasta dish or appetizer, a *secondo* (main course or entree), a side dish, and dessert. Beverages are not included. Within the listings, the numbers we give you are the price range for main courses, listed as *secondi,* and first courses (*antipasto* or *primo*) are usually equally expensive or cheaper.

Here is a table explaining what the dollar signs translate to in cost:

Cost	***Restaurant***
$	35€ ($46) or less
$$	36€–50€ ($47–$65)
$$$	51€–65€ ($66–$85)
$$$$	66€ ($86) and up

At the end of this chapter, you'll find indexes of all the restaurants we recommend: by location, by cuisine, and by price. See the "Rome Dining and Snacking" map in this chapter for the locations of all eateries we review in this chapter.

HEADS UP

Italy recently instituted one of Europe's toughest laws against smoking in public places. All restaurants and bars come under the ruling except those with ventilated smoking rooms. Smokers face steep fines if caught lighting up. Only 10 percent of restaurants have separate smoking areas.

A little remark on **service:** In Rome, good service is unobtrusive. That may sound good, but it means that although nobody will rush you, you'll need to let the staff know when you want the menu, when you are ready to order, when you are ready for your second course, and so on. In the best restaurants, just raising your eyes summons your server in the wink of an eye; elsewhere you'll have to raise your hand.

Alberto Ciarla
$$$$ Trastevere ROMAN/FISH

A favorite with locals — both gourmets looking for creative dishes and fans of traditional Roman cuisine — this restaurant has only one drawback: price. The quality, though, is outstanding. The chef claims he invented the *crudo* ("raw" — as in raw fish), and he keeps researching new flavors while respecting traditional dishes. The ever-changing menu may list *millefoglie con mousse di dentice in salsa al vino bianco* (napoleon with local fish mousse in white wine sauce) and classic *zuppa di fagioli e frutti di mare* (bean and seafood stew) revisited by the chef. The tasting menus are a good way to explore: They range from Roman tradition (50€/$64) to the chef's grand cuisine (84€/$110).

See map p. 116. Piazza San Cosimato 40. ☎ *06-5818668.* www.albertociarla. com. *Reservations recommended. Tram: 8. Secondi: 18€–31€ ($23–$40). AE, DC, MC, V. Open: Mon–Sat 8:30 p.m.–12:30 a.m. Closed ten days in Jan and ten days in Aug.*

Angelino ai Fori
$$ Colosseo ROMAN/FISH/PIZZA

A local favorite, this stronghold of Roman cuisine may look like a tourist trap because of its perfect location across from the Forum, but it is actually an authentic traditional restaurant. We definitely recommend the *bucatini all'amatriciana, saltimbocca alla Romana* (sautéed veal with ham and sage), and — when on the menu — *pollo alla Romana* (chicken stewed with red and yellow peppers). Fish dishes vary with market offerings (check the display by the entrance door). The terrace is a great plus in good weather, but service may get slow.

See map p. 116. Largo Corrado Ricci 40. ☎ *06-6791121. Reservations recommended. Metro: Colosseo. Secondi: 7€–18€ ($9–$23). AE, DC, MC, V. Open: Wed–Mon noon–3:15 p.m. and 7–11 p.m. Closed Jan.*

Arcangelo
$$$ Prati ROMAN/CREATIVE ITALIAN/FISH

The chefs here are among those who've taken to the trend of enlivening Roman cuisine with new combinations that Grandma never imagined. Their experiments are subtle and delicious, and options include more traditional offerings, too. The *maccheroni all'amatriciana* (pasta in a spicy tomato and bacon sauce) is excellent, but so are the less usual *spaghetti aglio olio e mazzancolle* (spaghetti with garlic, olive oil, and local prawns), *tonno arrosto con melanzane* (baked tuna with eggplant), and *anatra in salsa di frutta secca* (duck in dried fruit sauce).

See map p. 116. Via G.G. Belli 59, off Via Cicerone, 1 block from Piazza Cavour. ☎ *06-3210992. Reservations recommended. Bus: 30, 70, 81. Secondi: 13€–21€ ($17–$27). AE, DC, V. Open: Mon–Sat 12:30–3 p.m. and 7:30–10:30 p.m. Closed Aug.*

Rome Dining and Snacking

Al Forno della Soffitta 1 **52**
Al Forno della Soffitta 2 **50**
Alberto Ciarla **45**
Angelino ai Fori **73**
Arcangelo **7**
Baffetto **30**
Baires **29**
Birreria Viennese **59**
Bistrot d'Hubert **54**
Bolognese **11**
Caffè Sant'Eustachio **26**
Cantina Tirolese **5**
Capricci Siciliani **20**

Charly's Saucière **76**
Checco er Carettiere **44**
Da Benito e Gilberto **3**
Da Giggetto **38**
Da Maciste al Salario **49**
Dante Taberna de' Gracchi **6**
Ditirambo **32**
Doozo **68**
Eau Vive **28**
Er Faciolaro **25**
Fattoria la Parrina **22**
Filetti di Baccalà **35**
Forno Food e Cafe **19**
Gelateria alla Scala **41**
Gelateria Cecere **66**
Gelateria dei Gracchi **3**
Gino **18**
Giolitti **24**
Girarrosto Fiorentino **55**
Grappolo d'Oro **33**
Grillpoint **51**
Gusto **14**
Hamasei **61**
Hasekura **70**
Hostaria da Nerone **74**
Il Convivio Troiani **21**
Il Drappo **31**

Il Gelato **26**
Il Gelatone **71**
Il Guru **69**
Il Matriciano **2**
Il Regno di Napoli **53**
Il Tempio del Buongustaio **1**
Imago **58**
Ivo **46**
Jaipur **47**
L'Antico Forno **67**
La Veranda **4**

Le Jardin du Russie **12**
Macondo **8**
Matricianella **16**
Mirabelle **57**
Naturist Club CMI **60**
Ninfa **56**
Olympus **63**
Opera **17**
Oriental Express **64**
Osteria Ponte Sisto **40**
Ouzerie **48**
Pica **36**
Pizza **15**
Pizza (Penna) **9**
Pizza a Taglio **13**
Pizza Al Taglio **72**
Pizza Buona **27**
Pizza Forum **75**
Pizza Re **10**
Pizza Rustica **37**
Sant'Andrea **62**
Sora Lella **39**
Surya Mahal **43**
Taverna del Campo **34**
Tazza d'Oro **23**
Trattoria degli Amici **42**
Vivendo **65**

Ar Montarozzo
$$ Appian Way   ROMAN

This is where we come when we go for a stroll in the Appia Antica Park. We like the old-fashioned atmosphere, which gives a feeling of bygone Rome. The huge restaurant has several rooms and an outdoor area that fills with local families delighting in their traditional weekend lunches. We are partial to the *bucatini all'amatriciana,* and — if you like delicate and juicy roasts — the *petto di vitella alla fornara* (roasted veal).

Via Appia Antica 4. ☎ *06-77208434.* www.armontarozzo.it. *Reservations required. Bus: Archeobus, 118, 218, 360. Secondi: 8€–21€ ($10–$27). AE, DC, MC, V. Open: Tues–Sun 12:45–3 p.m. and 7:45–11 p.m. Closed Jan.*

Bolognese
$$$ Piazza del Popolo   BOLOGNESE

Elegant and hip yet welcoming, this restaurant serves well-prepared food at moderate prices in a nicely appointed dining room or, in good weather, on the outdoor terrace. It is so popular that you'll almost always need a reservation. Even Romans admit that Bologna has produced some good dishes, such the lasagna prepared so well here; *tagliatelle alla Bolognese* (homemade pasta with tomato and meat sauce) and *fritto di verdure e agnello* (tempura of vegetables and lamb tidbits) are mouthwatering. End with something from the unusually large selection of delicious desserts.

See map p. 116. Piazza del Popolo 1. ☎ *06-3611426. Reservations required. Bus: 117, 119. Secondi: 14€–29€ ($18–$38). AE, DC, MC, V. Open: Daily 12:30–3 p.m. and Tues–Sun 8:15 p.m. to midnight. Closed Aug.*

Capricci Siciliani
$$ Navona/Pantheon   SICILIAN/FISH

You'll love the location: In Palazzo Taverna, only steps from Piazza Navona, you'll dine among frescoed walls sitting on modern furnishings. The cuisine relies on seafood and moves easily between tradition and innovation, from *carpaccio di spigola* (seabass carpaccio) to *pasta con le sarde* (pasta with fresh sardines) to *involtini di pesce spada* (swordfish rolls). Do not miss the perfect Sicilian *cannoli* or *cassata* for dessert.

See map p. 116. Via di Panico 83. ☎ *06-6873666. Reservations recommended; required for dinner. Bus: 70, 84, 116. Secondi: 22€–32€ ($29–$42). AE, DC, MC, V. Open: Tues–Sun 12:30–3 p.m. and 8–11 p.m. Closed Aug.*

Checchino dal 1887
$$$ Testaccio   ROMAN

Elegant and lively, Checchino is one of the oldest and best restaurants in Rome. Housed in Monte Testaccio (the ancient Roman pottery dump), it is certainly the most traditional. It serves real Roman specialties such as *lingua con salsa verde* (tongue in a green sauce of garlic, parsley, and olive

Ethnic and non-Italian dining

"When in Rome, do as the Romans do" goes the adage, and indeed, you'll find that Rome's cosmopolitan population has mostly embraced the local culinary culture: Ethnic restaurants are rare and often more expensive than others. The ubiquitous Chinese restaurant — about one per neighborhood, and none to write home about — costs about as much as the local *trattoria* or *pizzeria*. The others are fancy places where Romans go for something special or exotic, with prices to match.

We love Japanese, and some of the city's best is available at **Hasekura** (Via dei Serpenti 27; ☎ 06-483648; Mon–Sat 12:30–3 p.m. and 7:30–11 p.m.) and **Hamasei** (Via della Mercede 35; ☎ 06-6792134; Tues–Sun 12:30–2:30 p.m. and 7:30–11 p.m.). Also serving Japanese, **Doozo** (Via Palermo 51; ☎ 06-4815655; www.doozo.it; Tues–Sun noon to 11 p.m.), is a sushi bar–cum–bookstore and art gallery, with a small Zen garden. The best deal is the prix-fixe lunch for 12€ ($16). Our choices for Indian are the moderately priced **Il Guru** (Via Cimarra 4; ☎ 06-4744110; Mon–Sat 7:30–10:30 p.m.), the north Indian **Jaipur** (Via San Francesco a Ripa 96; ☎ 06-5803992; Tues–Sun 12:30–3 p.m. and daily 7:30–10:30 p.m.), and the more upscale **Surya Mahal** (Piazza Trilussa 50; ☎ 06-5894554; Mon–Sat 7:45–11 p.m.). A few other interesting choices are South American cuisine at **Baires** (Corso Rinascimento 1; ☎ 06-6861293; daily 12:30–2:30 p.m. and 7:30–10:30 p.m.), Caribbean at **Macondo** (Via Marianna Dionigi 37; ☎ 06-3212601; Mon–Sat 7:30–11 p.m.), and French Colonial at **Eau Vive** (Via Monterone 86; ☎ 06-68801095; Mon–Sat 12:30–2:30 p.m. and 7:30–10:30 p.m.). Not a restaurant but a fast-food place is **Oriental Express** (Via Calatafimi 7; ☎ 06-4818791; daily noon to 3:30 p.m.), which serves excellent Arab fare.

You'll find more moderate prices among the Europeans: **Bistrot d'Hubert** (Via Sardegna 135; ☎ 06-42013161; Mon–Fri 12:30–3 p.m. and Mon–Sat 7:30–10:30 p.m.; closed three weeks in Aug) serves really good traditional French. For a taste of "Mittel Europe," try **Birreria Viennese** (Via della Croce 21, off Piazza di Spagna; ☎ 06-6795569; daily 12:30–2:30 p.m. and 7:30–11:30 p.m.), or **Cantina Tirolese** (Via Vitelleschi 23, off Castel Sant'Angelo to the west; ☎ 06-6869994; Tues–Sat). The best Swiss restaurant in Rome, **Charly's Saucière** (Via San Giovanni in Laterano 270; ☎ 06-70495666; Tues–Fri 12:30–2 p.m. and Mon–Sat 8–11 p.m.), offers all the great classics, from steak tartare to fondue. If you fancy Greek, head for **Ouzerie** (Via dei Salumi 2; ☎ 06-5816378; Mon–Sat noon to 2:30 p.m. and 7–11 p.m.; live music Fri and Sat nights). Finally, **Naturist Club CMI** (Via della Vite 14 on the fifth floor; ☎ 06-6792509; Mon–Sat noon to 2 p.m. and 7–10:30 p.m.) isn't an ethnic restaurant but offers organic vegetarian meals, with a menu that changes daily.

oil) and the classic *coda alla vaccinara* (oxtail with pignoli and raisins), as well as excellent pasta dishes, including *penne con broccoletti strascinati al pecorino Romano* (short pasta with broccoli rabe sautéed with pecorino cheese). The large variety of meat and fish choices is prepared following true traditional recipes. On the extensive wine list, you'll also find selections by the glass.

Via di Monte Testaccio 30. ☎ *06-5743816.* www.checchino-dal-1887.com. *Reservations recommended. Metro: Piramide, but taking a cab is best. Secondi: 14€–25€ ($18–$33). AE, DC, MC, V. Open: Tues–Sat 12:30–3 p.m. and 8 p.m. to midnight. Closed Aug and Dec 23–Jan 1.*

Checco er Carettiere
$$ Trastevere   ROMAN

This traditional trattoria is faithful to the old Italian-cuisine values of fresh ingredients and professional service. It even prepares fish at your table. The *bombolotti all'amatriciana* (pasta in spicy tomato sauce with bacon) is excellent, as are *abbacchio scottadito* (grilled lamb chops) and *coda alla vaccinara* (oxtail stew). The restaurant is justly proud of its homemade desserts, which round out the menu nicely.

See map p. 116. Via Benedetta, 10 near Piazza Trilussa. ☎ *06-5800985.* www.checco ercarettiere.it. *Reservations recommended. Bus: 23, 115 to Piazza Trilussa. Secondi: 13€–18€ ($17–$23). AE, DC, MC, V. Open: Daily 12:30–3 p.m. and Mon–Sat 7:30–11 p.m.*

Da Benito e Gilberto
$$ San Pietro   FISH

Don't expect a written menu and a lot of time to make up your mind at this informal restaurant; you'll have to listen to the daily offerings and your waiter's recommendations, and then go for it. Don't worry; you won't regret it: The quality of the ingredients and the preparation of the food are outstanding. The *pasta e fagioli con frutti di mare* (bean and seafood soup) is warm and satisfying; *tagliolini alla pescatora* (homemade pasta with seafood), delicate; and *fritto di paranza* (fried small fish), delicious. Also try the grilled daily catch.

See map p. 116. Via del Falco 19, at Borgo Pio. ☎ *06-6867769.* www.dabenito egilberto.com. *Reservations required several days in advance. Bus: 23 and 81 to Via S. Porcari. Secondi: 12€–18€ ($16–$23). AE, MC, V. Open: Tues–Sat 7:30–11:30 p.m. Closed Aug.*

Da Giggetto
$$ Teatro Marcello   JEWISH ROMAN

This famous restaurant has been a local favorite for decades. Like everybody else, we love going there to savor Jewish-Roman cuisine specialties. Some old salts protests because what was once (decades ago) a cheap joint now charges regular prices, but it is worth it. Nowhere else in Rome will you find *carciofi alla giudia* (crispy fried artichokes) prepared as well, together with other traditional Roman dishes such as *fettuccine all'amatriciana* (pasta with tomato-and-bacon sauce) and *broccoli colle salsicce* (Roman green cauliflower sautéed with sausages).

See map p. 116. Via del Portico d'Ottavia 21. ☎ *06-6861105.* www.giggetto alporticodottavia.it. *Reservations recommended. Bus: 63, 23; then walk* *north behind the synagogue. Secondi: 12€–18€ ($16–$23). AE, DC, MC, V. Open: Tues–Sun noon to 3 p.m. and Tues–Sat 7:30–11 p.m. Closed two weeks in Aug.*

Dante Taberna de' Gracchi
$$ San Pietro   ROMAN

A pillar of Roman culinary tradition, this classic Roman restaurant has served thousands of happy diners over decades. You'll dine in one of several small (and air-conditioned) dining rooms, off a solid menu where the specialties are *sfizi fritti* (fried tidbits), *spaghetti alla vongole* (spaghetti with clams), and *scaloppine al vino bianco* (veal cutlets sautéed in white wine); we also recommend the daily soup.

See map p. 116. Via dei Gracchi 266, between Via M. Colonna and Via Etzio. ☎ 06-3213126. www.tabernagracchi.com. Reservations required. Metro: Line A to Lepanto; walk on Via Colonna for 3 blocks, and turn right. Secondi: 12€–16€ ($16–$21). AE, DC, MC, V. Open: Tues–Sat 12:30–3 p.m. and Mon–Sat 7:30–11 p.m. Closed Christmas and three weeks in Aug.

Ditirambo
$$ Campo de' Fiori   CREATIVE ROMAN

The success of this restaurant rests not only on the perfect location and moderate prices, but on the quality of the food and the courtesy of the always-professional service. We like the seasonal menu, with just the right touch of innovation, which may produce a wild boar as well as fresh seafood. We loved the vegetarian menu and the large choice of reasonably priced wine by the half bottle.

See map p. 116. Piazza della Cancelleria 74. ☎ 06-6871626. www.ristorante ditirambo.it. Reservations required. Bus: 64 to Corso Vittorio Emanuele. Secondi: 8€–18€ ($10–$25). MC, V. Open: Tues–Sun 12:30–3 p.m. and daily 7:30– 11:30 p.m. Closed three weeks in Aug.

Er Faciolaro
$ Navona/Pantheon   ROMAN

We come here, as generations of Romans have before us, for the warmth of the service and the homemade food, which includes some hard-to-find classics. The restaurant is justly famous for beans — hence the name, which translates as "the bean-eater" — prepared *al fiasco* (cooked inside an old-fashioned wine bottle) or as a pasta soup. Our favorite pasta dish is the *spaghetti alla gricia,* but many come for the *carbonara* (spaghetti with egg and Italian bacon), *trippa alla Romana* (tripe), and *coda alla vaccinara* (oxtail stew). We recommend the terrace in the good season.

See map p. 116. Via dei Pastini 123. ☎ 06-6783896. Reservations recommended on weekends. Bus: 64 to Corso Vittorio Emanuele. Secondi: 8€–18€ ($10–$23). MC, V. Open: Tues–Sun 12:30–3 p.m. and daily 7:30 p.m.–1 a.m.

Luxury dining in Rome's top hotels

You may think of hotel dining as a last resort. Well, you may be missing a once-in-a-lifetime experience. As the best hotels in Rome compete for Michelin stars and other culinary titles, their restaurants have reached unprecedented heights and become favorite destinations of gourmets in the know. One great place is **Moscati** in the **Hotel Mövenpick** (Via Moscati 3, ☎ 06-3051216; Mon–Sat 7:30–11 p.m.), where you can enjoy a gourmet meal in luxury at moderate prices (the tasting menu costs 33€/$43); it is particularly pleasant in good weather, when the panoramic terrace is open. The seasonal menu covers surf and turf and may include *spaghetti cacio e pepe con guanciale di cinta senese* (spaghetti with sheep's-milk cheese and Sienese bacon) and *frittura di gamberi e porcini* (deep-fried jumbo shrimp and porcini mushrooms). Do not miss the desserts; we had a fantastic crème brûlée with Calvados. Another excellent, more expensive choice is **Ninfa** in the **Hotel Majestic** (Via Vittorio Veneto 50; ☎ 06-421441; daily 11:30–11 p.m.), where you can enjoy creative Italian cuisine all day long. The changing menu may include salad of Mediterranean lobster with grilled Roman artichokes, or homemade buckwheat tortelli with vegetables and *pecorino di fossa* (sheep cheese aged in a dirt pit), and ricotta and grain soufflé with orange-blossom water for dessert. We also like **La Veranda** in the **Hotel Columbus** (Borgo Santo Spirito 73; ☎ 06-6872973; www.laveranda.net; daily 12:30–3:15 p.m. and 7:30–11:15 p.m.), where you sit in the frescoed 15th-century loggia of the Palazzo della Rovere, while savoring delectable creative Italian cuisine; the loggia opens on the delightful inner garden, where you can dine in fine weather. We enjoyed the *fettuccine alla menta con amatriciana di tonno fresco* (fresh mint pasta with fresh tuna sauce) and *tris di pesce alla griglia con salse* (three different grilled fish filets served with special sauces); you will find more innovative creations on the menu, and simplified versions at lunch. The food is absolutely divine at **Pauline Borghese** in the **Grand Hotel Parco dei Principi** (Via G. Frescobaldi 5; ☎ 06-854421; www.parcodeiprincipi.com; daily 12:30–3 p.m. and 7:15–11 p.m.) where the homemade bread comes hot out of the oven to your table, and the menu may include Parmesan risotto with Parma *prosciutto* and asparagus, and calamari stuffed with *burrata* (a creamy cheese from Campania and Apulia). The vegetarian menu costs 65€ ($85), and the creative desserts are to die for. A close competitor is **Vivendo** at the **St. Regis Grand** (Via Vittorio Emanuele Orlando 3; ☎ 06-47092736; www.tasteinitaly.com; Mon–Fri 12:30–2:30 p.m. and Mon–Sat 7:30–10:30 p.m.; closed Aug), a refuge of subdued elegance and gourmet food at surprisingly moderate prices (tasting menus are 55€/$72 and 65€/$85). You'll find homemade breads and an inventive menu based on Italian ingredients, including such dishes as goose liver escalope with caramelized peaches, and perfectly cooked herbed lamb with reduction of *renetta* apples and eggplant. The desserts are excellent, and the wine list includes numerous selections by the glass. For a fascinating setting, head for **Le Jardin du Russie** at the **Hotel de Russie** (Via del Babuino 9; ☎ 06-328881; www.hotelderussie.it; daily 12:30–3 p.m. and 7:30–11 p.m.), if only to visit the splendid inner garden. The cuisine is very good but overpriced. Another restaurant to visit for its unique setting is **Olympus**, on the rooftop of the **Bernini Bristol** (Piazza Barberini 23; ☎ 06-488931; www.berninibristol.com; daily 12:30–3 p.m. and 7:30–11 p.m.), which served as the background location for many scenes in Dan Brown's novel *Angels and Demons*. You can enjoy a 360-degree view over Rome while having a relatively moderately priced dinner. **Imago,** at the **Hotel Hassler** (Piazza Trinità dei Monti 6; ☎ **06-69934726;** www.hotelhasslerroma. com; daily 7:30–10:30 p.m. and Sept–June 12:30–2:30 p.m.) affords an even better view. It opened just recently, and the food is very promising. The 65€ ($85) Sunday brunch is lovely. **Mirabelle** in the **Hotel Splendide Royal** (Via di Porta Pinciana 14; ☎ **06-42168838;** www.splendideroyal.com; daily noon to 2:30 p.m. and 7:30–11 p.m.) offers the second-best dining with a view in Rome after La Pergola (see later in this chapter) at more affordable prices. The service is perfect and the food excellent: We enjoyed the napoleon of zucchini and eggplant, chickpea-and-seafood soup, and *filetto di pezzogna capperi e olive* (local fish filet with capers and olives). Ask for a table on the terrace.

Gino
$ Navona/Pantheon   ROMAN

The "canteen" of Italian MPs (the Congress is next door), this affordable *trattoria* is hardly a secret, but we like the good food and reasonable prices. When in season, we come for the *fettuccine ai carciofi* (homemade pasta with Roman artichokes); otherwise, we go for the excellent *pasta all'amatriciana,* followed by *abbacchio alla cacciatora* (stewed lamb) and *cicoria ripassata in padella* (sautéed dandelion greens).

See map p. 116. Vicolo Rosini 4. ☎ *06-6873434. Reservation not accepted. Bus: 62, 63, 116. Secondi: 10€–18€ ($13–$23). MC, V. Open: Mon–Sat 12:30–3 p.m. and 7:30–11 p.m. Closed Aug.*

Girarrosto Fiorentino
$$ Via Veneto   TUSCAN

We like this pillar of Tuscan cuisine in the heart of Rome. Only a short distance from Via Veneto, this is where you can find a real *bistecca alla fiorentina* (steak of Chianina cow) served in the traditional style. The menu features many Tuscan specialties, but the steak is why you come here (be prepared to share, because the real thing is about two pounds of meat — a slice of cow, really — serving two hungry people). The nice choice of good Tuscan wines is the perfect complement to the meat.

See map p. 116. Via Sicilia 46. ☎ *06-42880660.* www.girarrostofiorentino. it. *Reservations recommended on weekends. Bus: 62, 63, 492. Secondi: 20€–32€ ($26–$42). AE, DC, MC, V. Open: Daily 12:30–3 p.m. and 7:30–11 p.m. Closed Christmas.*

Grappolo d'Oro Zampanò
$$ Campo de' Fiori   CREATIVE ITALIAN/PIZZA

Across from Ditirambo (see earlier), this is another very successful restaurant serving well-rounded dishes, homemade bread, and (except on Mon) good pizza. The outdoor terrace is a pleasant plus. The seasonal menu may include *ravioli di Parmigiano e scorza di limone con riduzione di basilico e pomodorini* (parmesan and lemon zest ravioli with basil and cherry toma-toes reduction) or *carré d'agnello con spuma di sedano* (rack of lamb with celery mousse). Desserts are simple but tasty.

See map p. 116. Piazza della Cancelleria 80. ☎ *06-6897080.* www.grappolodoro zampano.it. *Reservations recommended. Bus: 64 to Corso Vittorio Emanuele. Secondi: 8€–18€ ($10–$22). AE, DC, MC, V. Open: Sat–Sun 12:30–3 p.m. and daily 7:30–11 p.m. Closed Aug.*

Gusto
$$ Piazza del Popolo CREATIVE ITALIAN/PIZZA

If an establishment can be all things to all people, this is it: a restaurant, an *enoteca* (wine bar), a pizzeria, a cigar club — and a kitchenware store. The pasta dishes are tasty — if it's on the menu, try the *carbonara di mac-cheroncini con fave* (carbonara with homemade pasta and fava beans) or *trancio di tonno alla cajun con finocchi e olio di agrumi* (Cajun tuna steak with fennel and citrus oil). As for the pizzas, we are partial to *cicoria e funghi* (with dandelion greens and mushrooms). The menu also includes couscous, wok-prepared Asian dishes, and Continental recipes. Popular with workers during the day and young people at night, the restaurant keeps late hours. The Osteria in back (Via della Frezza 16) focuses on dishes in the Roman tradition; the atmosphere is quieter than in the main dining room. A great brunch buffet is served on Saturday and Sunday, but service and quality are sometimes uneven.

See map p. 116. Piazza Augusto Imperatore 9. ☎ *06-3226273. Reservations recom-mended for dinner. Bus: 117 or 119 from Piazza del Popolo to Via della Frezza/Piazza Augusto Imperatore. Secondi: 11€–21€ ($14–$27). AE, MC, DC, V. Open: Daily noon to 3 p.m. and 7 p.m. to midnight.*

Hostaria da Nerone
$ Colosseo ROMAN

We love this old family *trattoria,* conveniently located near the ruins of Nero's palace — but you don't need an emperor's budget to enjoy the view from the terrace (or the good food). We like it especially for heartier Roman specialties, such as *osso buco* (stewed veal shank) and even *trippa alla Romana* (tripe, with a light tomato sauce) — an acquired taste.

See map p. 116. Via Terme di Tito 96, off Via Nicola Salvi, uphill from the Colosseum. ☎ *06-4817952. Reservations required Sat only. Metro: Colosseo. Secondi: 9€–14€ ($12–$18). AE, MC, V. Open: Mon–Sat noon to 2:30 p.m. and 7–11 p.m.*

Hostaria L'Archeologia
$$ Appian Way ROMAN

This old *trattoria* is decorated like a country tavern, with beamed ceilings and rustic decorations — the kind of place Romans like to visit on a week-end outing. If you're visiting the nearby catacombs, it's convenient. The hearty fare includes *vitello alla massenzio* (veal with mushrooms, arti-chokes, and olives), *tagliatelle al ragù di scorfano* (homemade pasta with tomato sauce and rockfish), grilled meats, and homemade gnocchi on Thursday — the traditional day for the Roman potato-dumpling dish.

Via Appia Antica 139. ☎ *06-4880828. Reservations recommended on weekends. Bus: 218 to Appia Antica. Secondi: 12€–21€ ($16–$27). AE, DC, MC, V. Open: Wed–Mon 12:30–3 p.m. and 7:30–11 p.m.*

Il Convivio Troiani
$$$$ Navona/Pantheon   **CREATIVE ROMAN**

This is the best restaurant in Rome, provided that what you're after is excellent food and not the superb views La Pergola (see later in this chapter) enjoys. The subdued, classic elegance of the dining rooms is a perfect background to the unforgettable food — and besides, your bill will be about one-third lower here. Chef Angelo Troiani concocts wonderful, innovative combinations of traditional ingredients in his own renditions of great Roman classics. The menu varies; you may find the much-imitated *sorbetto di pomodoro* (tomato savory sherbet) and superb *roast beef di tonno laccato al miele e zenzero con insalata di mele verdi* (ginger-and-honey-glazed tuna with green apple salad). Leave enough room for one of the really good desserts. The wine list is extensive and well priced.

See map p. 116. Vicolo dei Soldati 31, steps from Piazza Navona to the north. ☎ *06-6869432. Reservations recommended. Bus: 116 or 116T to Piazza di Ponte Umberto I. Secondi: 29€–31€ ($38–$40). AE, DC, MC, V. Open: Mon–Sat 1–2:30 p.m. and 8–11 p.m.*

Il Drappo
$ Campo de' Fiori   **SARDINIAN**

The subdued atmosphere makes Il Drappo a perfect setting for serious cuisine at moderate prices. The *malloreddus con vongole pomodorini e basilico* (homemade pasta with clams, cherry tomatoes, and basil) and the *fettuccine con fiori di zucca* (homemade pasta with zucchini flowers) contain wonderful bursts of flavors. Other typical dishes are *maialino al mirto* (suckling pig) and *anatra alle mele* (duck with apples).

See map p. 116. Vicolo del Malpasso 9, off Via Giulia. ☎ *06-6877365. Reservations recommended. Bus: 116, 117 to Lungotevere Sangallo. Secondi: 11€–16€ ($14–$21). AE, DC, MC, V. Open: Mon–Sat 12:30–3 p.m. and 7:30–11 p.m. Closed four weeks in Aug–Sept.*

Il Matriciano
$$ San Pietro   **ROMAN**

This family-run restaurant is a wonderful place to eat outside in summer, but you must have a reservation, because it's well known and popular. The name reflects one of the specialties, *bucatini all'amatriciana* (*bucatini* is a kind of thick spaghetti with a hollow center). You can also find excellent versions of other typical Roman specialties, such as *abbacchio al forno* (roasted lamb).

See map p. 116. Via dei Gracchi 55. ☎ *06-3212327. Reservations required. Metro: Ottaviano/San Pietro. Walk south on Via Ottaviano; the third left is Via dei Gracchi.*

Secondi: 12€–18€ ($16–$23). AE, DC, MC, V. Winter Thurs–Tues noon to 3 p.m. and 7:30–11 p.m.; summer Sun–Fri noon to 3 p.m. and 7:30–11 p.m. Closed three weeks in Aug.

La Pergola
$$$$ Monte Mario   CREATIVE ITALIAN

No doubt about it, this restaurant, in the Rome Cavalieri Hilton on the Monte Mario (a steep hill overlooking Prati), is a hike. It's also one of the best, most magical restaurants in Italy. The site is breathtaking, with the panorama of Rome laid out at your feet, and the elegance of the furnishings and professionalism of the service — both kind and discreet — add to the experience. Chef Heinz Beck, a master of Italian cuisine, is known for concocting unexpected combinations, such as *tortellini verdi con vongole e calamaretti* (green tortellini with clams and squid) and *triglia su ragout di carciofi* (red mullet over a ragout of artichokes). The tasting menu is a perfect way to sample several inventions (there's even a tasting menu of seven desserts). Finding your way here by public transportation would be impressive but laborious; take a taxi.

Via A. Cadlolo 101, up the Monte Mario hill. ☎ 06-35092152. Reservations required. Secondi: 36€–54€ ($47–$70). AE, DC, MC, V. Open: Tues–Sat 7:30–11 p.m. Closed three weeks in Jan and two weeks in Aug.

Matricianella
$ Navona/Pantheon   ROMAN

We love this little restaurant tucked away off Piazza Navona: the food is good and the price is right. The menu centers on dishes in the Roman tradition, including a large choice of deep-fried foods to which we are rather partial (try the fried *ricotta*). We also love the *bucatini all'amatriciana, saltimbocca alla Romana* (savory tidbits of beef escalope rolled with Italian bacon and sage), and *coratella d'abbacchio* (sautéed lamb organ meat). The wine list includes a large selection by the glass.

See map p. 116. Via del Leone 2. ☎ 06-6832100. www.matricianella.it. Reservations recommended. Secondi: 12€–18€ ($16–$23). AE, DC, MC, V. Open: Mon–Sat 12:30–3 p.m. and 7:30–11 p.m. Closed Aug.

Osteria Ponte Sisto
$ Trastevere   ROMAN

Offering traditional Roman fare, this famous *osteria* is a longstanding destination for locals and tourists alike. Try the delicious *risotto al gorgonzola* (Italian rice cooked with Gorgonzola cheese) or, if you dare, some truly Roman specialties such as *trippa alla Romana* (tripe in a light tomato sauce) or beef roasted on a charcoal grill.

See map p. 116. Via Ponte Sisto 80, off Piazza Trilussa. ☎ 06-5883411. Reservations recommended. Bus: 23 or 115 to Piazza Trilussa. Secondi: 9€–16€ ($12–$21). AE, MC, V. Open: Thurs–Tues noon to 3 p.m. and 7–10:30 p.m. Closed Aug.

Sant'Andrea
$$ Piazza di Spagna   ROMAN

We are always surprised to find that this restaurant only a few steps from Piazza di Spagna has not become a tourist trap. Instead, this little place — with a few tables outside in the good season — continues to draw locals who come for the well-rounded menu of traditional Roman cuisine, as we do. We recommend the specialty, *coratella d'abbacchio con cipolla* (sautéed onions and lamb liver and organ meat).

See map p. 116. Via S. Andrea delle Fratte 9. ☎ *06-6793167. Reservations recommended. Metro: Piazza di Spagna. Secondi: 12€–21€ ($16–$27). AE, DC, MC, V. Open: Sun–Fri noon to 3 p.m. and 6–11 p.m. Closed Aug and Dec 25.*

Sora Lella
$$ Trastevere   ROMAN

This family-run restaurant — created by the sister of the famous Roman actor Aldo Fabrizi and operated today by his son and grandsons — was already a Roman institution, but with the recent renovations both in the dining room and on the menu, it has won new admirers. The gnocchi are superb, and complementing the solid traditional menu are many new dishes, such as delicious *polpettine al vino* (small meatballs in a wine sauce). Tasting menus and a vegetarian menu are available, and the traditional Roman *contorni,* such as *cicoria* (dandelion greens) and *carciofi* (Roman artichokes), are exceptional.

See map p. 116. Via di Ponte Quattro Capi 16, on Isola Tiberina, in the river between the center and Trastevere. ☎ *06-6861601. Reservations recommended. Bus: 23, 63, and 115 to Isola Tiberina. Secondi: 14€–20€ ($18–$26). AE, DC, V. Open: Mon–Sat noon to 2 p.m. and 7–11 p.m. Closed two weeks in Jan, two weeks in Aug, and Christmas.*

Trattoria degli Amici
$ Trastevere   ROMAN

Have a good meal and do a good deed at the same time: This restaurant is managed by a local charity organization, the Comunità di Sant'Egidio, to provide a training ground for people with disabilities and facilitate their finding a job. The place will surprise you: The furnishings are tasteful, the food is really good (well prepared, with high-quality ingredients), the service is professional, and you cannot beat the prices. The menu changes regularly with the season and market offerings, but it always includes local traditional dishes, such as *filetto di baccalà* (deep fried codfish filet), *pasta all'amatriciana,* and melt-in-the-mouth pork roast. For dessert, do not miss the homemade *crostate* (fruit tart). The wine list is good, with several choices by the glass.

See map p. 116. Piazza di Sant'Egidio 5. ☎ *06-5806033. Reservations recommended. Bus: 23. Secondi: 8€–12€ ($10–$16). AE, V. Open: Mon–Sat 7:30–11 p.m. Closed Aug.*

Dining and Snacking on the Go

Did you know that fast food was invented in Rome more than 2,000 years ago? Street food was sold at carts and small shops in the Forum, and a quick bite to eat could be had at any *caupona* (the ancient Roman word for *eatery*), standing or perched on a high stool at the counter. You'll see many Romans still doing the same — having a sandwich standing up in a bar or eating a square of pizza from a take-away *rosticceria*. Here is the lowdown on Roman fast food.

Bars

Bars in Rome are sort of cafes that serve alcohol; they rarely have more than a few seats and do most of their business at the counters (note that there is a surcharge for sitting down). During the day, bars are Romans' home away from home: They come for breakfast before work, espresso and *cornetto* (sweet croissant, often filled with cream or jam) being the typical fare; then again for coffee break, for lunch, and finally for *aperitivo* (a predinner drink, with or without alcohol, accompanied by small tidbits to eat) in the evening. For lunch, all bars prepare a large variety of sandwiches, and some operate as small restaurants, offering prepared hot dishes. Sandwiches include the *rosetta* (the typical Roman bread roll), which can be filled with *frittata* (omelet), mozzarella and tomatoes, or cheese and cold cuts; the *tramezzino,* or slices of crustless American-style bread filled with a variety of mayo-based salads; and the *pizza Romana* — our favorite — which is a square of focaccia filled with ham and cheese, eaten cold or warm. Many bars also double as ice cream parlors. For some of the trendiest bars, see Chapter 16, but any bar will provide a basic, good-quality breakfast or lunch.

Wine bars (enoteche)

This typical Italian institution — the *enoteca* — also provides a good alternative to stuffy restaurants for both lunch and dinner. The *enoteca* is more of a wine shop than a bar, and this is why it is open regular shopping hours, from morning to evening (including lunch). They're also popular with the locals during dinner and after-dinner hours. Some strictly sell wine; others also have a few tables and a counter where you can sample the wine together with simple fare ranging from a choice of cheese, cold cuts, and savory tidbits, to full-fledged hot gourmet dishes at the most elegant joints. We review the best of them in Chapter 16.

Picnics

In fine weather, a nice, inexpensive option — and a favorite with children — is to buy sandwiches or pizza and picnic in one of Rome's great public parks, such as Villa Borghese or the Janiculum Hill (see Chapter 11); even smaller neighborhood parks are a good choice.

Keep in mind, however, that sitting on public fountains and monuments to have your lunch is forbidden, and you'll be asked to move. You may even be heavily fined if you're found littering.

For your supplies, try **Fattoria la Parrina** (Largo Toniolo 3, between Piazza Navona and the Pantheon; ☎ **06-68300111**), which offers wonderful organic cheese, wine, and veggies; **L'Antico Forno di Piazza Trevi** (Via delle Muratte 8; ☎ **06-6792866**), where you'll find superb focaccia and bread, as well as a variety of other items; and the bakery — both savory and sweet goods — **Forno Food e Cafè,** with several small shops around the Pantheon (Via della Stelletta 2, ☎ **06-99705346;** Piazza della Rotonda 4, ☎ **06-99705344;** Via della Scrofa 33, ☎ **06-68307505**) and near Via Boncompagni at Via Quintino Sella 8 (☎ **06-47822926**). Any grocer (including the deli counter at a supermarket) will prepare a sandwich with the bread and cheese or cold cuts of your choice, all sold by weight.

Pizza a taglio

Pizza is a very good choice both for a quick and inexpensive meal and to make children happy. The ubiquitous pizza parlors — a typical specimen is a glass counter with ovens in the back — bake pizza all day long (usually Mon–Sat 8 a.m.–8 p.m.) in large, oblong, metal pans. Toppings range from the simple *rossa* (tomato and oregano) and *bianca* (focaccia) to *con i funghi* (mushrooms with tomato sauce or with cheese), *con la mozzarella* (tomato and mozzarella), *con le patate* (with thin slices of crispy potatoes), and *ripiena* (filled with ham and cheese). Some fancier places have a larger variety, but novelty is not necessarily a sign of quality; look instead for steaming-hot pans, which mean constant turnover. (At the best places, you'll see Romans waiting for the next slab of their favorite flavor to roll out.)

The best — and most convenient — are **Pizza** (Via del Leoncino 28; ☎ 06-6867757), **Pizza a Taglio** (Via della Frezza 40; ☎ 06-3227116), **Pizza** (Via della Penna 14; ☎ 06-7234596), **Pizza Rustica** (Via del Portico d'Ottavia, ☎ 06-6879262; and Via dei Pastini 116, ☎ 06-6782468), **Il Tempio del Buongustaio** (Piazza del Risorgimento 50; ☎ 06-6833709), **Pizza Al Taglio** (Via Cavour 307; ☎ 06-6784042), and **PizzaBuona** (Corso Vittorio Emanuele II 165; ☎ 06-6893229). **Pizza Forum** (Via San Giovanni in Laterano 34; ☎ 06-7002515) is a sit-down pizzeria with very fast service.

Pizzerie

For a fast — and cheap — lunch or dinner without giving up on the pleasure of sitting down at a table, Romans choose a *pizzeria.* These are simple restaurants specializing in pizza — strictly individual-size, round pizzas — and range from fancy (with tablecloths and fashionable dining rooms) to more rustic (a piece of paper on a wooden table). They offer pizza with a variety of established toppings, most of which have been defined by name in a longstanding tradition, such as *margherita* (tomato and mozzarella), *napoletana* (tomato, mozzarella, and anchovies), *capricciosa* (tomato, mozzarella, mushrooms, artichoke hearts, olives, ham, and an egg), and *funghi* (mushrooms, tomato, and mozzarella). You'll also find more modern and sometimes original combinations, such as *rugola, bresaola, e parmigiano* (fresh arugula and thin slices of cured beef and Parmesan cheese on simple tomato sauce), *quattro formaggi* (four kinds of cheese), *broccoletti e salsicce* (broccoli rabe and sausage), and so on. In addition, *pizzerie* typically serve a choice of savory and delicious appetizers, such as *bruschetta* (toasted peasant-style bread topped with oil and garlic and, on request, tomatoes, olives, ham, and so on), *supplì* (deep-fried rice balls stuffed with a small piece of mozzarella), *filetti di baccalà* (deep-fried salt cod), *olive ascolane* (deep-fried large green olives stuffed with meat and cheese), and *fiori di zucca* (deep-fried zucchini flowers stuffed with anchovy and mozzarella). If you like *filetti di baccalà,* the best in Rome are at **Filetti di Baccalà** (Largo dei Librari 88, off Via dei Giubbonari at Campo de' Fiori; ☎ **06-6864018;** open Mon–Sat 7:30–11 p.m.), a small restaurant where you can take out or sit down. It also serves a few *contorni* and desserts, but the lines are epic.

For traditional Neapolitan-style pizza that has received the seal of honor from the organization that guards the quality of Neapolitan pizza, try **Al Forno della Soffitta 1** (Via Piave 62; ☎ **06-42011164**) and **Al Forno della Soffitta 2** (Via dei Villini, 1/f; ☎ **06-4404642;** closed Sun) or **Pizza Re** (Via di Ripetta 14; ☎ **06-3211468;** closed Sun). The pizza is also excellent at the elegant **Il Regno di Napoli** (Via Romagna 22; ☎ **06-4745025;** closed Sat–Sun lunch only), which is also a full-scale restaurant and therefore a bit more expensive.

For Roman-style pizza (thinner than the Neapolitan version and less bready, but more savory), try **Baffetto** (Via del Governo Vecchio 114; ☎ **06-6861617**); **Ivo** (Via di San Francesco a Ripa 158; ☎ **06-5817082;** closed Tues); or **Opera** (Via del Leone 23; ☎ **06-68809927**), which offers 30 types of pizza.

Really good coffee

Even if you're on the go, the proper way to finish a meal is with a good coffee — at least that's what Romans believe. Note, however, that many smaller *trattorie* and pizzerias don't make coffee. What better reason to remove yourself to a famous coffee shop after your meal? If you're a coffee aficionado, you should not miss the **Caffè Sant'Eustachio** (Piazza Sant'Eustachio 82, by the Pantheon; ☎ **06-68802048;** Bus: Minibus 116), a traditional bar that has served Rome's best espresso (made with water still carried into the city on the ancient Roman aqueduct) since 1938. Another excellent temple of coffee is **Tazza d'Oro,** also by the Pantheon but on the other side (☎ **06-6789792;** Bus: Minibus 116); you haven't lived until you've tried its *granita di caffè* (a concoction of frozen espresso served with whipped cream).

Note: The coffee lingo in Rome is not what you are used to in the States. The choices are *espresso* (your Italian coffee), *caffe lungo* (*espresso* with a bit more water), *caffe macchiato* (*espresso* with a drop of foamy milk),

caffe latte (a *caffe lungo* with milk; it's what you would call a *latte* in the
U.S.), and *cappuccino* (a foamy *espresso* with milk).

Snack bars, tavola calda, and rosticcerie

These typical Roman fast-food eateries correspond to your local diner or
deli — if not in look and kind of food served, at least in purpose. This is
where you can have a simple lunch at a fraction of the price you would
pay in a restaurant, and where harassed working parents and singles
who don't feel like cooking come for takeout in the evening. These
places present food behind glass counters and sell it by weight or by
the piece. Sometimes they're organized as cafeterias; others have only
standing room at a counter and are mostly takeout. A *snack bar* usually
has fewer offerings than a *tavola calda,* while *rosticcerie* focus on roasted
chickens and pizza, often with an array of side dishes. Some are better
than others: In the simplest snack bar you'll find little more than sandwiches, while in the best *tavola calda* you'll have an ample choice of
tasty and well-prepared hot and cold dishes, including pasta, *secondi,*
and *contorni* — in short, all you need for a full meal. Always look carefully at the food before ordering to be sure it isn't dried out; in mediocre
places, you'll be much worse off than at the local bar, where sandwiches
are usually freshly prepared. The clientele will also help you: Crowds at
mealtime (especially Romans) are an excellent sign.

Midway between a snack bar and a restaurant, **Grillpoint** (Piazzale di
Porta Pia 122; ☎ **06-44236435;** open daily noon to 2:30 p.m.) has an elegant dining room and a wide choice of well-prepared dishes, including
pizza. **Da Maciste al Salario, Pizza, Vino e Cucina** (Via Salaria 179/a, at
Via Metauro; ☎ **06-8848267;** closed Mon dinner and Sun lunch) serves
excellent food cafeteria style and provides ample seating. There is a long
line for lunch; if you arrive late, the best items will be gone. The crowded
Taverna del Campo (Campo de' Fiori 16; ☎ **06-6874402**) serves a large
variety of *crostini, panini,* and beer.

Sweet endings: Gelato

Italian ice cream *(gelato)* is among the best in the world. Serious *gelato*
comes in a variety of flavors and is priced by the size of the cone or cup.
It's served with a special spatula and not by the scoop, so you can have
up to three flavors, even in the smallest size. Romans like to top it with
whipped cream, so you'll be asked if you care for *panna;* our answer is
usually "Yes, plenty!" Flavors are *frutta* (fruit) — *limone* (lemon), *arancio*
(orange), *melone* (melon), *pesca* (peach), *mora* (blackberry), *frutti di
bosco* (mixed wild berries), the list is endless — and *creme* (creams).
Our favorite cream flavors are *zabaglione* (a rum-and-egg combo, reminiscent of eggnog), *bacio* (hazelnut chocolate), and *stracciatella* (vanilla
with chocolate chips), but even plain *crema* (egg cream) and *cioccolato*
(chocolate) can be fabulous when well prepared.

You'll see prepackaged, commercial *gelati* for sale at every bar in town,
but why waste your time — and calories — with industrial ice cream
when you can have handmade gelato? Find a bar that says GELATERIA

outside and look for the sign PRODUZIONE PROPRIA: It means the place makes its own ice cream, and it will be fresh and delicious.

Here are a few of the best (in our not-so-modest opinion) in Rome: **Giolitti** (Via Uffici del Vicario 40; ☎ 06-6991243; Minibus: 116), is the oldest gelato parlor in Rome and is reliably excellent. The superb ice cream at **Il Gelato** (Piazza Sant'Eustachio 47, near the Pantheon; no phone yet), is made by a passion-driven young man who trained at another famous Roman ice cream parlor, **Il Gelatone** (Via dei Serpenti 28, near the Colosseum; ☎ 06-4820187). **Pica** (Via della Seggiola 12; ☎ 06-68803275; Tram: 8), near Campo de' Fiori is another good destination. Near Fontana di Trevi, head for **Gelateria Cecere** (Via del Lavatore 84; ☎ 06-6792060; Bus: 116 or 492). In Trastevere, we love **Gelateria alla Scala** (Via della Scala 5; ☎ 06-5813174; Tram: 8), and in Prati, **Gelateria dei Gracchi** (Via dei Gracchi 272; ☎ 06-3216668; Metro: Lepanto). Happy ice cream!

Index of Establishments by Neighborhood

Appian Way
Ar Montarozzo (Roman, $$)
Hostaria L'Archeologia (Roman, $$)

Campo de' Fiori
Ditirambo (Creative Roman, $$)
Filetti di Baccalà (Roman/Fish, $)
Grappolo d'Oro Zampanò (Creative Italian/Pizza, $$)
Il Drappo (Sardinian, $)
Pica (Gelato, $)
Taverna del Campo (Snacks, $)

Colosseo
Angelino ai Fori (Roman/Fish/Pizza, $$)
Charly's Saucière (Swiss, $)
Hasekura (Japanese, $$)
Hostaria da Nerone (Roman, $)
Il Gelatone (Gelato, $)
Il Guru (Indian, $)
Pizza Al Taglio (Pizza, $)
Pizza Forum (Pizza, $)

Monte Mario
La Pergola (Creative Italian, $$$$)
Moscati (Creative Italian, $$$)

Navona/Pantheon
Baffetto (Pizza, $)
Baires (South American, $$)
Caffè Sant'Eustachio (Coffee, $)
Capricci Siciliani (Sicilian/Fish, $$)
Eau Vive (French Colonial, $)
Er Faciolaro (Roman, $)
Fattoria la Parrina (Snacks, $)
Forno Food e Cafè (Snacks, $)
Gino (Roman, $)
Giolitti (Gelato, $)
Il Convivio Troiani (Creative Roman, $$$$)
Il Gelato (Gelato, $)
Matricianella (Roman, $)
Opera (Pizza, $)
Pizza (Pizza, $)
Pizza (Via della Penna, Pizza, $)
Pizza a Taglio (Pizza, $)
PizzaBuona (Pizza, $)
Tazza d'Oro (Coffee, $)

Parioli
Da Maciste al Salario, Pizza, Vino e Cucina (Roman/Pizza, $)

Piazza del Popolo
Bolognese (Bolognese, $$$)
Gusto (Creative Italian/Pizza, $$)

Le Jardin du Russie (Creative Italian, $$$$)
Pizza (Via della Penna; Pizza, $)
Pizza Re (Pizza, $)

Piazza di Spagna
Birreria Viennese (Mittel Europe, $$)
Hamasei (Japanese, $$)
Imago (Creative Italian, $$$$)
Naturist Club CMI (Vegetarian, $)
Sant'Andrea (Roman, $$)

Porta Pia
Al Forno della Soffitta 2 (Pizza, $)
Grillpoint (Roman/Pizza/Snacks, $)

Prati
Arcangelo (Roman/Creative Italian/Fish, $$$)
Gelateria dei Gracchi (Gelato, $)
Il Tempio del Buongustaio (Pizza, $)
Macondo (Caribbean, $$)

Repubblica
Al Forno della Soffitta 1 (Pizza, $)
Bistrot d'Hubert (French, $$)
Doozo (Japanese, $$)
Oriental Express (Arab, $)
Vivendo (Creative Italian, $$$)

San Pietro
Cantina Tirolese (Mittel Europe, $$)
Da Benito e Gilberto (Fish, $$)
Dante Taberna de' Gracchi (Roman, $$)
Il Matriciano (Roman, $$)
La Veranda (Creative Italian, $$$)

Teatro Marcello
Da Giggetto (Jewish Roman, $$)
Pizza Rustica (Pizza, $)

Testaccio
Checchino dal 1887 (Roman, $$$)

Trastevere
Alberto Ciarla (Roman/Fish, $$$$)
Checco er Carettiere (Roman, $$)
Gelateria alla Scala (Gelato, $)
Ivo (Pizza, $)
Jaipur (Indian, $$)
Osteria Ponte Sisto (Roman, $)
Ouzerie (Greek, $$)
Sora Lella (Roman, $$)
Surya Mahal (Indian, $$)
Trattoria degli Amici (Roman, $)

Trevi
Gelateria Cecere (Gelato, $)
L'Antico Forno di Piazza (Snacks, $)

Via Veneto
Al Forno della Soffitta 1 (Pizza, $)
Girarrosto Fiorentino (Tuscan, $$)
Il Regno di Napoli (Neapolitan/Pizza, $$)
Mirabelle (Creative Italian, $$$)
Ninfa (Creative Italian, $$$)
Olympus (Creative Italian, $$$$)

Villa Borghese
Pauline Borghese (Creative Italian, $$$$)

Index of Establishments by Cuisine

Arab
Oriental Express (Repubblica, $)

Bolognese
Bolognese (Piazza del Popolo, $$$)

Caribbean
Macondo (Prati, $$)

Coffee
Caffè Sant'Eustachio (Navona/Pantheon, $)
Tazza d'Oro (Navona/Pantheon, $)

Creative Italian

Arcangelo (Prati, $$$)
Grappolo d'Oro Zampanò (Campo de'
Fiori, $$)
Gusto (Piazza del Popolo, $$)
Imago (Piazza di Spagna, $$$$)
La Pergola (Monte Mario, $$$$)
La Veranda (San Pietro, $$$)
Le Jardin du Russie (Piazza del
Popolo, $$$$)
Mirabelle (Via Veneto, $$$)
Moscati (Monte Mario, $$$)
Ninfa (Via Veneto, $$$)
Olympus (Via Veneto, $$$$)
Pauline Borghese (Villa Borghese,
$$$$)
Vivendo (Repubblica, $$$)

Creative Roman

Ditirambo (Campo de' Fiori, $$)
Il Convivio Troiani (Navona/Pantheon,
$$$$)

Fish

Alberto Ciarla (Trastevere, $$$$)
Angelino ai Fori (Colosseo, $$)
Arcangelo (Prati, $$$)
Capricci Siciliani (Navona/
Pantheon, $$)
Da Benito e Gilberto (San Pietro, $$)
Filetti di Baccalà (Campo de' Fiori, $)

French

Bistrot d'Hubert (Repubblica, $$)

French Colonial

Eau Vive (Navona/Pantheon, $)

Gelato (Ice cream)

Giolitti (Navona/Pantheon, $)
Il Gelato (Navona/Pantheon, $)
Il Gelatone (Colosseo, $)
Pica (Campo de' Fiori, $)
Gelateria alla Scala (Trastevere, $)
Gelateria Cecere (Trevi, $)
Gelateria dei Gracchi (Prati, $)

Greek

Ouzerie (Trastevere, $$)

Indian

Il Guru (Colosseo, $)
Jaipur (Trastevere, $$)
Surya Mahal (Trastevere, $$)

Japanese

Doozo (Repubblica, $$)
Hamasei (Navona/Pantheon, $$)
Hasekura (Colosseo, $$)

Jewish Roman

Da Giggetto (Teatro Marcello, $$)

Mittel Europe

Birreria Viennese (Piazza di
Spagna, $$)
Cantina Tirolese (Prati, $$)

Pizza

Al Forno della Soffitta 1 (Via Veneto/
Repubblica, $)
Angelino ai Fori (Colosseo, $$)
Baffetto (Navona/Pantheon, $)
Da Maciste al Salario, Pizza, Vino e
Cucina (Parioli, $)
Grappolo d'Oro Zampanò (Campo
de' Fiori, $$)
Grillpoint (Porta Pia, $)
Gusto (Piazza del Popolo, $$)
Il Regno di Napoli (Via Vento, $$)
Il Tempio del Buongustaio (Prati, $)
Ivo (Trastevere, $)
Opera (Navona/Pantheon, $)
Pizza (Navona/Pantheon, $)
Pizza (Via della Penna; Piazza del
Popolo, $)
Pizza a Taglio (Navona/Pantheon, $)
Pizza Al Taglio (Colosseo, $)
PizzaBuona ($, Navona/Pantheon)
Pizza Forum (Colosseo, $)
Pizza Re (Piazza del Popolo, $)
Pizza Rustica (Teatro Marcello, $)

Roman

Alberto Ciarla (Trastevere, $$$$)
Angelino ai Fori (Colosseo, $$)
Arcangelo (Prati, $$$)
Ar Montarozzo (Appian Way, $$)
Checchino dal 1887 (Testaccio, $$$)
Checco er Carettiere (Trastevere, $$)
Da Maciste al Salario, Pizza, Vino e Cucina (Parioli, $)
Dante Taberna de' Gracchi (San Pietro, $$)
Er Faciolaro (Navona/Pantheon, $)
Filetti di Baccalà (Campo de' Fiori, $)
Gino (Navona/Pantheon, $)
Grillpoint (Porta Pia, $)
Hostaria da Nerone (Colosseo, $)
Hostaria L'Archeologia (Appian Way, $$)
Il Matriciano (San Pietro, $$)
Matricianella (Navona/Pantheon, $)
Osteria Ponte Sisto (Trastevere, $)
Sant'Andrea (Piazza di Spagna, $$)
Sora Lella (Trastevere, $$)
Trattoria degli Amici (Trastevere, $)

Sardinian

Il Drappo (Campo de' Fiori, $)

Sicilian

Capricci Siciliani (Navona/Pantheon, $$)

Snacks and picnic meals

Fattoria la Parrina (Navona/Pantheon, $)
Forno Food e Cafè (Navona/Pantheon, $)
Grillpoint (Porta Pia, $)
L'Antico Forno di Piazza Trevi (Trevi, $)
Taverna del Campo (Campo de' Fiori, $)

South American

Baires (Navona/Pantheon, $$)

Swiss

Charly's Saucière (Colosseo, $)

Tuscan

Girarrosto Fiorentino (Via Veneto, $$)

Vegetarian

Naturist Club CMI (Piazza di Spagna, $)

Index of Establishments by Price

Il Tempio del Buongustaio (Pizza, Prati)

Ivo (Pizza, Trastevere)

L'Antico Forno di Piazza Trevi (Snacks, Trevi)

Matricianella (Roman, Navona/Pantheon)

Naturist Club CMI (Vegetarian, Piazza di Spagna)

Opera (Pizza, Navona/Pantheon)

Oriental Express (Arab, Repubblica)

Osteria Ponte Sisto (Roman, Trastevere)

Pica (Gelato, Campo de' Fiori)

Pizza (Pizza, Navona/Pantheon)

Pizza (Via della Penna; Pizza, Piazza del Popolo)

Pizza Al Taglio (Pizza, Colosseo)

Pizza a Taglio (Pizza, Navona/Pantheon)

PizzaBuona (Pizza, Navona/Pantheon)

Pizza Forum (Pizza, Colosseo)

Pizza Re (Pizza, Piazza del Popolo)

Pizza Rustica (Pizza, Teatro Marcello)

Taverna del Campo (Snacks, Campo de' Fiori)

Tazza d'Oro (Coffee, Navona/Pantheon)

Trattoria degli Amici (Roman, Trastevere)

$$

Angelino ai Fori (Roman/Fish/Pizza, Colosseo)

Ar Montarozzo (Roman, Appian Way)

Baires (South American, Navona/Pantheon)

Birreria Viennese (Mittel Europe, Piazza di Spagna)

Bistrot d'Hubert (French, Repubblica)

Cantina Tirolese (Mittel Europe, San Pietro)

Capricci Siciliani (Sicilian/Fish, Navona/Pantheon)

Checco er Carettiere (Roman, Trastevere)

Da Benito e Gilberto (Fish, San Pietro)

Da Giggetto (Jewish Roman, Teatro Marcello)

Dante Taberna de' Gracchi (Roman, San Pietro)

Ditirambo (Creative Roman, Campo de' Fiori)

Doozo (Japanese, Repubblica)

Girarrosto Fiorentino (Tuscan, Via Veneto)

Grappolo d'Oro Zampanò (Creative Italian/Pizza, Campo de' Fiori)

Gusto (Creative Italian/Pizza, Piazza Del Popolo)

Hamasei (Japanese, Navona/Pantheon)

Hasekura (Japanese, Colosseo)

Hostaria L'Archeologia (Roman, Appian Way)

Il Matriciano (Roman, San Pietro)

Il Regno di Napoli (Neapolitan/Pizza, Via Veneto)

Jaipur (Indian, Trastevere)

Macondo (Caribbean, Prati)

Ouzerie (Greek, Trastevere)

Sant'Andrea (Roman, Piazza di Spagna)

Sora Lella (Roman, Trastevere)

Surya Mahal (Indian, Trastevere)

$$$

Arcangelo (Roman/Creative Italian/Fish, Prati)

Bolognese (Bolognese, Piazza del Popolo)

Checchino dal 1887 (Roman, Testaccio)

La Veranda (Creative Italian, San Pietro)

Mirabelle (Creative Italian, Via Veneto)

Moscati (Creative Italian, Monte Mario)

Ninfa (Creative Italian, Via Veneto)

Vivendo (Creative Italian, Repubblica)

$$$$

Alberto Ciarla (Roman/Fish, Trastevere)

Il Convivio Troiani (Creative Roman, Navona/Pantheon)

Imago (Creative Italian, Piazza di Spagna)

La Pergola (Creative Italian, Monte Mario)

Le Jardin du Russie (Creative Italian, Piazza del Popolo)

Olympus (Creative Italian, Via Veneto)

Pauline Borghese (Creative Italian, Villa Borghese)

Part IV
Exploring Rome

The 5th Wave   By Rich Tennant

"It says, children are forbidden from running, touching objects, or appearing bored during the tour."

In this part . . .

Whether you're an architecture buff, an amateur archaeologist, an art aficionado, a devout Catholic, or simply a lover of the world's great cities, you'll be delighted with all that the Eternal City has to offer. In this part, we tell you about Rome's best attractions, both inside and outside the city walls.

Rome is a veritable "who's who" of famous monuments, museums, and ruins, and we cover them all in Chapter 11, along with tips on how best to enjoy them. And although Rome isn't as well known for fashion and shopping as some other Italian cities, it has some fabulous shopping areas specializing in Roman- and Italian-made goods, which we tell you about in Chapter 12. In Chapter 13, we've done some of your planning ahead of time, putting together a choice of the five best itineraries you can take, depending on your interests. And although it has been said that even a lifetime is not enough to visit Rome, in Chapter 14 we suggest five side trips — easy excursions from Rome to unique destinations as absorbing as the great city itself.

Chapter 11

Discovering Rome's Best Attractions

*W*ith over 3,000 years of uninterrupted urban life, Rome boasts a cultural density that's difficult to match. Its historic center displays a unique layering of cultural periods and styles. Century after century, Rome has attracted merchants, politicians, and artists from all over Italy and Europe, starting at the time of the Roman Empire. The Catholic Church, which ruled the city for almost a millennium, also played a crucial role in the cultural shaping of Rome. The resulting melting pot has laid the foundation for a cosmopolitan European culture of which Rome was the heart for centuries, and in which it still plays a central role. Indeed, the Eternal City may have an exalted history, but is no lifeless museum of the past. Almost three million people live and five million work in Rome, where the thoroughfares were designed for chariots instead of cabs.

Moreover, this is an excellent time to be visiting: the Papal Jubilee in 2000 gave impetus to an ongoing stream of much-needed renovations to the entire city, as well as efforts to reduce congestion and pollution. These changes have already had a big impact on the city, and ever-increasing numbers of appreciative tourists are pouring in. Come walking with Romans on ruins from the days of Caesar, turning along the same alleyways trod by Lucrezia Borgia and the masters of the Renaissance, and thrilling to the same lighted fountains that were reflected in the eyes of Fellini's beautiful debauchers, but don't think you can do it all in a day: Set aside several days to do this vibrant city right.

Don't pass up these deals

If you're planning to do a lot of sightseeing in Rome, purchasing one of the discount cards offered by various museums and attractions may just be the ticket.

The new three-day **Roma Pass** (☎ 06-82059127; www.romapass.it) is a worthy bundle. For 20€ ($26) you get admission to two major attractions of your choice, discounts on all others, and public transportation (bus, subway, and trains). Another version also covers attractions outside the city within the province of Rome for 25€ ($33). You can buy either version at any tourist info point and in all participating museums.

If you're planning an extensive visit to the sites of ancient Rome, the best deal is the seven-day **Roma Archeologia Card**. It costs 20€ ($26) and covers the **Colosseum, Palatine Hill,** all the sites of the **National Roman Museum** (Octagonal Hall, Palazzo Altemps, Palazzo Massimo, Terme di Diocleziano, and Cripta Balbi), **Caracalla Baths,** and the two sites at the **Park of the Appian Way** that charge admission (Mausoleum of Cecilia Metella and Villa of the Quintili). You can purchase the card at participating sites (except for the Via Appia locations) and at the main Visitor Center of the Tourist Board of Rome, Via Parigi 5 (☎ **06-36004399**).

The complex of the **Capitoline Museums** also offers a combo ticket; it is valid for seven days and includes admission to the Capitoline Museums and Tabularium, plus the **Centrale Montemartini** (the postmodern annex created in a former power plant), for 8.50€ ($11), a savings of 6.50€ ($8.45).

Finally, the **Appia Antica Card** costs 6€ ($7.80) and gets you into the **Caracalla Baths,** the **Mausoleum of Cecilia Metella,** and the **Villa of the Quintili.** The pass is valid for seven days and available at all three sites.

For a service fee of 1.50€ ($1.95), you can make reservations for a number of attractions — and even buy your tickets online — by contacting **Pierreci** (☎ **06-39967700**; www.pierreci.it), the agency that manages reservations for many Roman attractions. Pierreci e-mails you a voucher, and you pick up your tickets at a special desk at the attraction entrance, skipping the line. Pierreci's hours are Monday through Saturday 9 a.m. to 1:30 p.m. and 2:30 to 5 p.m. The official agent for reservations and tickets for other attractions — such as the Borghese Gallery — is **Ticketeria** (☎ **06-32810;** Fax: 06-32651329; www.ticketeria.it). Like Pierreci, Ticketeria e-mails you a voucher, and you pick up your tickets at a special location at the attraction entrance, thereby avoiding lines.

The **Vatican** is a separate state, with a visitor office that handles reservations for its attractions. In the **Vatican Information Office** (☎ **06-69884466;** Mon–Sat 8:30 a.m.–7 p.m.), located under the colonnade to the left of the entrance to St. Peter's, you can get a small plan of the basilica, make reservations for a tour of the Vatican Gardens, and pick up complimentary tickets for attending the traditional Wednesday papal audience. If your schedule is tight, we recommend you make some reservations by fax before you leave (see listings for specific attractions).

 It is a good idea to check attractions' opening hours, which change often, with the local tourist office before your visit (see Chapter 8 for locations). Attractions' opening hours may be extended, especially during holidays and the summer months, and special night openings are a treat not to be missed (the dramatic Roman ruins by night are just so romantic . . .).

 To fully appreciate the Roman Forum, the Colosseum, and other ruins, pick up a copy of the small book *Rome Past and Present,* sold in bookstores and at stands near the Forum for approximately 10€ ($13). Its plastic overlays show you how Rome looked 2,000 years ago.

Rome's Top Sights

Where do you begin? If you're an archaeology buff, Rome's ancient sights can keep you going for days, weeks, months, and even years. But the city is also loaded with famous museums, impressive monuments, and awe-inspiring churches. In this treasure trove of possibilities, you have to make some decisions. The sights in this section are our roster of the most important Roman attractions. For their locations, see the "Rome Attractions" map on p. 142.

 Rome's attractions tend to be busy at any time of day, crowded with both foreign and local visitors (see Chapter 3 for tips on when to go). If you want to avoid throngs of people, plan your visits for the early morning (before 9:30 a.m.), lunchtime (1–3:30 p.m.), and evening (after 7:30 p.m.); midmorning and midafternoon are the peak visiting hours you should avoid. Remember that as a rule, ticket booths close half an hour to an hour before the stated closing time of a given attraction.

 ### Borghese Gallery (Galleria Borghese)
Parioli

This is a very special gallery, created in 1613 by Cardinal Scipione Borghese inside the Villa Borghese (a large park that's now public; see "Finding More Cool Things to See and Do," later in this chapter). The cardinal wanted the splendid building to house his unique art collection and display it to his special guests. Closed for restoration for 13 years, the building and site are now an attraction in themselves; the art inside is probably the most stunning smaller collection on view in Italy. The ground floor focuses on sculpture, including Canova's sensual reclining ***Paulina Borghese as Venus Victrix*** (Paulina was Napoleon's sister) and breathtaking marble carvings by the young Gian Lorenzo Bernini. His ***David,*** captured in the middle of a slingshot windup, is full of charmingly boyish concentration; ***Apollo and Daphne*** freezes in marble the moment when the nymph turns into a laurel tree, her fingers bursting into leaves and bark

Rome Attractions

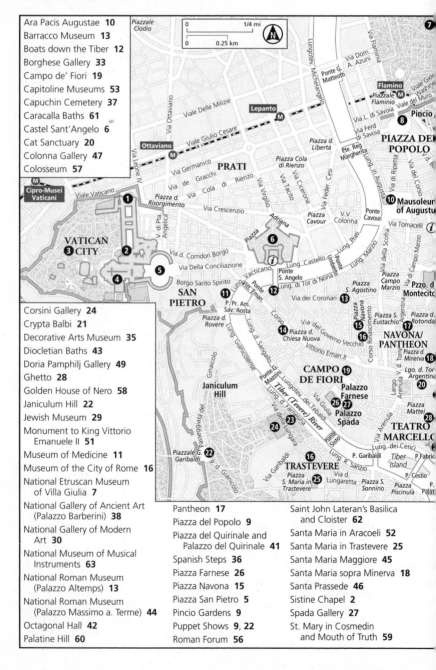

Ara Pacis Augustae **10**
Barracco Museum **13**
Boats down the Tiber **12**
Borghese Gallery **33**
Campo de' Fiori **19**
Capitoline Museums **53**
Capuchin Cemetery **37**
Caracalla Baths **61**
Castel Sant'Angelo **6**
Cat Sanctuary **20**
Colonna Gallery **47**
Colosseum **57**

Corsini Gallery **24**
Crypta Balbi **21**
Decorative Arts Museum **35**
Diocletian Baths **43**
Doria Pamphilj Gallery **49**
Ghetto **28**
Golden House of Nero **58**
Janiculum Hill **22**
Jewish Museum **29**
Monument to King Vittorio
    Emanuele II **51**
Museum of Medicine **11**
Museum of the City of Rome **16**
National Etruscan Museum
    of Villa Giulia **7**
National Gallery of Ancient Art
    (Palazzo Barberini) **38**
National Gallery of Modern
    Art **30**
National Museum of Musical
    Instruments **63**
National Roman Museum
    (Palazzo Altemps) **13**
National Roman Museum
    (Palazzo Massimo a. Terme) **44**
Octagonal Hall **42**
Palatine Hill **60**

Pantheon **17**
Piazza del Popolo **9**
Piazza del Quirinale and
    Palazzo del Quirinale **41**
Spanish Steps **36**
Piazza Farnese **26**
Piazza Navona **15**
Piazza San Pietro **5**
Pincio Gardens **9**
Puppet Shows **9, 22**
Roman Forum **56**

Saint John Lateran's Basilica
    and Cloister **62**
Santa Maria in Aracoeli **52**
Santa Maria in Trastevere **25**
Santa Maria Maggiore **45**
Santa Maria sopra Minerva **18**
Santa Prassede **46**
Sistine Chapel **2**
Spada Gallery **27**
St. Mary in Cosmedin
    and Mouth of Truth **59**

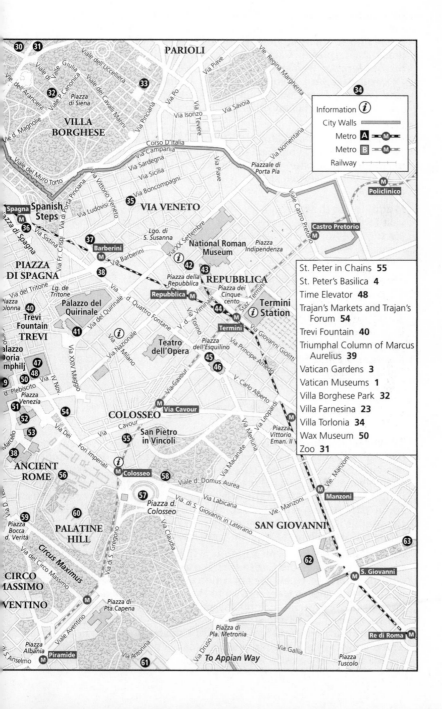

Information (i)

City Walls

Metro A

Metro B

Railway

St. Peter in Chains **55**

St. Peter's Basilica **4**

Time Elevator **48**

Trajan's Markets and Trajan's Forum **54**

Trevi Fountain **40**

Triumphal Column of Marcus Aurelius **39**

Vatican Gardens **3**

Vatican Museums **1**

Villa Borghese Park **32**

Villa Farnesina **23**

Villa Torlonia **34**

Wax Museum **50**

Zoo **31**

enveloping her legs. In the *Rape of Proserpine,* a sculpture Bernini executed in collaboration with his father, the god's fingers uncannily seem to press into her marble flesh. The extensive painting collection contains many masterpieces: Caravaggio's haunting self-portrait as *Bacchus* and his *St. Jerome Writing,* Antonello da Messina's subtle and mysterious *Portrait of a Man,* a young Raphael's *Deposition,* and Tiziano's *Sacred and Profane Love.* Andrea del Sarto, Coreggio, Lucas Cranach, Bronzino, Lorenzo Lotto, and many other artists are also represented in this dazzling display.

The gallery accommodates only 360 people, so reservations are required for admission, and your visit must be limited to two hours. (The astounding number of masterpieces will make you long for a second visit.) Be on time for your reserved slot, or you'll have to pay again for the next available time.

In addition to the main gallery, you can make a reservation for the special visit to the museum storage rooms. Only 18 persons are allowed per day for the one-hour visit (3–4 p.m.); the price is 2€ ($2.60), including the reservation fee, and you don't have to visit the museum to visit the storage rooms. If you are interested, book well in advance.

See map p. 142. Piazzale del Museo Borghese. ☎ 06-8417645. Reservations required: ☎ 06-32810 or www.ticketeria.it. *Bus: 52, 53, or 910 to Via Pinciana, behind the villa; 490 to Viale San Paolo del Brasile, inside the park; or Minibus 116 to the Borghese Gallery. Metro: Line A to Spagna; take the Villa Borghese exit and walk up Viale del Museo Borghese. Admission: Regular 8.50€ ($11), with special exhibit 11€ ($14); prices include 2€ ($2.60) booking fee. Open: Mon 1–7 p.m.; Tues–Thurs and Sun 9 a.m.–7 p.m.; Fri and Sat 9 a.m.–9 p.m. Last admission two hours before closing. Ticket booth closes 30 minutes earlier.*

Capitoline Museums (Musei Capitolini)
Teatro Marcello

The oldest public collection in the world, these museums occupy the two *palazzi* (palaces) that open onto the beautiful **Piazza del Campidoglio,** designed by Michelangelo. They hold a treasury of ancient sculpture and an important collection of European paintings from the 17th and 18th centuries. They also preserve the original second-century bronze **equestrian statue of Marcus Aurelius** (the one in the middle of the piazza is a copy); the statue was saved from destruction only because early Christians thought it was the first Christian emperor, Constantine.

In the Palazzo Nuovo you will find a rich collection of famous ancient sculptures, such as the *Capitoline Venus* and the *Dying Gaul,* a Roman copy of a Greek original. The collection is more accessible since a number of the largest pieces were moved to the Montemartini annex (see listing later in this chapter), making the premises less cramped. Palazzo dei Conservatori houses more sculpture, starting with the dismembered pieces of the ancient 40-foot **statue of Constantine II** in the courtyard, which you may have seen in photographs — the huge head, hands, foot, kneecap, and so on. Also here is the famous *Lupa Capitolina,* the fifth century B.C. bronze that is the symbol of Rome, representing a wolf suckling Romulus and Remus. On the top floor is the **Pinacoteca Capitolina** (picture gallery), a superb collection including such famous paintings as Caravaggio's *Fortune Teller* and *John the Baptist,* Titian's *Baptism of Christ,* and works by Veronese, Rubens, and others.

Between the Palazzo Nuovo and the Palazzo dei Conservatori, enclosing Piazza del Campidoglio to the south, is the **Senatorial Palace (Palazzo Senatorio).** Now home to Rome's municipal offices, it was built in the Middle Ages over the **Tabularium,** an imposing building that housed the public archives of the Roman Republic. The Tabularium itself was built of massive stone blocks, and its facade was decorated with huge Doric columns. You can clearly see its remains from the Forum (3 of the original 11 arcades remain). It's now part of the museum complex, and admission is included in the ticket.

An in-depth visit to these museums can take you about four hours, but you can see the highlights in about two hours.

The museums often schedule special exhibits; the separate admission charge is usually 4.50€ ($5.85), or 1.50€ ($1.95) with museum admission.

See map p. 142. Piazza del Campidoglio 1, off Piazza Venezia. ☎ *06-67102475.* www. museicapitolini.org. *Bus: Minibus 117. Admission: 6.50€ ($8.45). Audio guides: 4€ ($5.20). Open: Tues–Sun 9 a.m.–8 p.m.; Dec 24 and Dec 31 9 a.m.–2 p.m. Ticket booth closes one hour earlier. Closed Jan 1, May 1, and Dec 25.*

Caracalla Baths (Terme di Caracalla)
Aventino

Built by the Roman Emperor Caracalla, these baths were completed in A.D. 216 and operated until 537. They are the best-preserved large thermal baths in Rome, with some of the rich internal decoration still visible, making it possible to imagine what it must have been like: enormous columns, hundreds of statues, colored marble and mosaic floors, marble, stucco, and frescoes on the walls. The baths in Roman times were much more than just places to wash; people also came here to relax and to exercise. After entering the building from the porticos on the northeast side, patrons would use the dressing rooms and then move through the baths. These consisted of deep-cleansing areas, a sort of sauna similar to Turkish baths, starting in the *calidarium* (hot room) and proceeding to the *tepidarium* (first cooling down), the *frigidarium* (complete cooling down), and *natatio* (swimming pool). The baths also housed two gymnasiums (exercise rooms), where trainers used to be on duty, gardens for reading and relaxing, and a library. Plan to spend about an hour here.

See map p 142. Via delle Terme di Caracalla 52. ☎ *06-39967700 (Mon–Sat 9 a.m.– 1:30 p.m. and 2:30–5 p.m.) or* www.pierreci.it *for reservations.* www.archeorm. arti.beniculturali.it. *Metro: Circo Massimo. Bus: 118, 160, 628. Admission: 6€ ($7.80). Includes admission to Mausoleum of Cecilia Metella and Villa of the Quintili. Open: Mon 9 a.m.–2 p.m., Tues–Sun 9 a.m. to one hour before sunset. Ticket booth closes one hour earlier. Closed Jan 1 and Dec 25.*

Castel Sant'Angelo
San Pietro

This "castle" is a perfect example of recycling Roman style: It began as a mausoleum to hold the remains of Emperor Hadrian, became a fortress, and is now a museum. Built in A.D. 123, it may have been incorporated into the city's defenses as early as 403 and was attacked by the Goths (one of the barbarian tribes who pillaged Rome in its decline) in 537. Later, the popes used it as a fortress and hideout and, for convenience, connected it to the Vatican palace by an elevated corridor — the *passetto* — which you can still see near Borgo Pio. Castel Sant'Angelo houses a museum of arms and armor; you can also visit the elegant Renaissance papal apartments, as well as the horrible cells that held political prisoners (among them sculptor Benvenuto Cellini). Count on about two hours for a full visit.

See map p. 142. Lungotevere Castello 50. ☎ 06-6819111. Bus: 62 or 64 to Lungotevere Vaticano. Admission: 5€ ($6.50). Audio guides: 4€ ($5.20). Open: Tues–Sun 9 a.m.–8 p.m. Ticket booth closes one hour earlier. Closed Jan 1 and Dec 25.

Catacombs of Saint Callixtus (Catacombe di San Callisto)
Park of Appia Antica

Rome has several places to visit the catacombs, but the catacombs of St. Callixtus are among the most impressive, with 20km (12½ miles) of tunnels and galleries underground, organized on several levels. The catacombs began as quarries outside ancient Rome where travertine marble and the dirt used in cement were dug. Early Christians hid out, held mass, and buried their dead in the catacombs. The Catacombs of St. Callixtus (Callixtus III was an early pope, elected in 217) have four levels, including a crypt where several early popes are buried and the tomb where St. Cecilia's remains were found. Some of the original paintings and decorations are intact and show that Christian symbolism — doves, anchors, and fish — was already well developed. You can tour the catacombs in about one hour. It's cold down there at 18m/60 ft. under, so bring a sweater. Other catacombs that are open to the public include the **Catacombs of St. Sebastian** (Via Appia Antica 136; ☎ 06-7850350) and the **Catacombs of Ste. Domitilla** (Via delle Sette Chiese 282; ☎ 06-5110342; www.domitilla.it).

See map p. 174. Via Appia Antica 110. ☎ 06-51301580. www.catacombe.roma.it. Metro/Bus: Colli Albani (on Sun to Arco di Travertino); then bus 660 to Via Appia Antica. Admission: 5€ ($6.50). Open: Thurs–Tues 8:30 a.m. to noon and 2:30–5 p.m. (in summer to 5:30 p.m.). Closed Feb.

Colosseum (Colosseo or Anfiteatro Flavio)
Colosseo

The Colosseum and St. Peter's Basilica are Rome's most recognizable monuments. Begun under the Flavian Emperor Vespasian and finished in A.D. 80, the structure we now call the Colosseum was named the Amphiteatrum Flavium. The nickname came from the colossal statue of Nero that was erected nearby in the second century A.D. Estimates are that the Colosseum could accommodate up to 73,000 spectators. The entertainment included fights between gladiators and battles with wild animals. In the labyrinth of chambers beneath the amphitheater's original wooden floor, deadly weapons, vicious beasts, and gladiators were prepared for mortal combat. (Contrary to popular belief, the routine feeding of Christians to lions is a legend.) After the end of the Roman Empire, the Colosseum was damaged by fires and earthquakes, and eventually abandoned; it was then used as a marble quarry for the monuments of Christian Rome until Pope Benedict XV consecrated it in the 18th century. Next to the Colosseum is the **Arch of Constantine,** built in 315 to commemorate the emperor's victory over the pagan Maxentius in 312. Pieces from other monuments were reused, so Constantine's monument includes carvings honoring Marcus Aurelius, Trajan, and Hadrian.

In the summer of 2000, for the first time in centuries, the Colosseum was brought to life again with theater performances under the aegis of the Estate Romana (see Chapters 3 and 15); now it also houses special exhibitions.

We strongly recommend that you reserve tickets to avoid the long lines; you can do so through the number or Web site below. Otherwise, buy your ticket at the nearby Palatine Hill booth, where you'll find only a fraction of the queue (that is, until this hot tip spreads). Plan to spend about an hour for your visit.

See map p. 142. Via dei Fori Imperiali. ☎ *06-39967700 (Mon–Sat 9 a.m.–1:30 p.m. and 2:30–5 p.m.).* www.pierreci.it *for reservations.* www.archeorm.arti. beniculturali.it. *Metro: Colosseo. Bus: Minibus 117. Admission: 9€ ($12) plus 2€ ($2.60) for exhibitions. Advance reservation 1.50€ ($1.95). Ticket price includes admission to the Palatine Hill. Audio guides: 4€ ($5.20). Open: Daily 9 a.m. to one hour before sunset. Ticket booth closes one hour earlier. Closed Jan 1 and Dec 25.*

Golden House of Nero (Domus Aurea)
Colosseo

The complex of the Golden House was the brainchild of the infamous Emperor Nero. Built after the great fire of A.D. 64 (which is traditionally but perhaps incorrectly blamed on him), it once covered more than 200 acres. Buildings dotted a park landscaped to look like romantic countryside, with an artificial lake, pastures, and vineyards. The lavishly decorated main reception building — the Golden House itself — was abandoned after Nero's fall in 68, buried under the thermal baths of the emperors Titus and Trajan, and forgotten. Romans digging in the "hill" across from the Colosseum in the 18th century stumbled upon it when they found caves that turned out to be ceilings of ancient rooms decorated with Roman frescoes. Only since 2000 have tourists been allowed to visit these cavernous spaces, where some of the elegant interior paintings that decorated the walls survive. Often done in red tones, they tend to depict mythological scenes surrounded by fine traceries and flourishes. The site was closed again for restorations in 2006. It is currently "open for restorations": Small groups of visitors (20 maximum) are guided through the site to check out the archeologists and experts at work. We hope the site will be completely

Ancient Rome

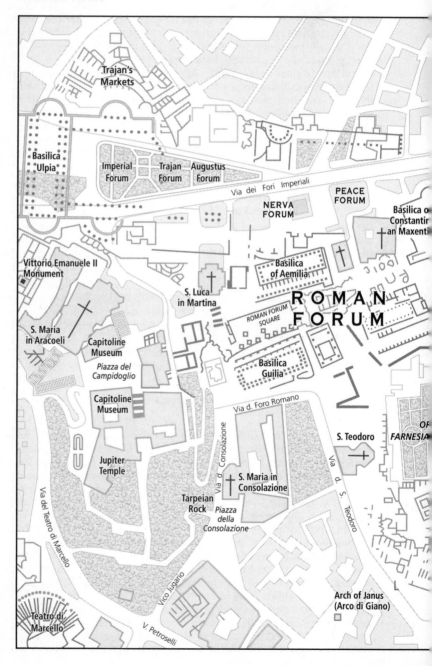

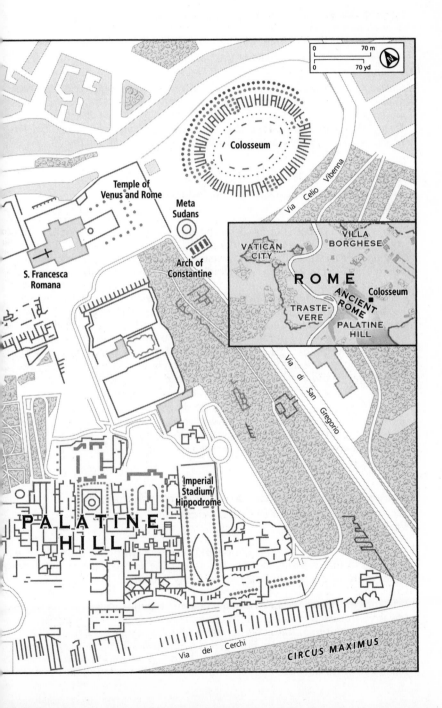

0   70 m
0   70 yd

Colosseum

Temple of
Venus and Rome

Meta
Sudans

S. Francesca
Romana

Arch of
Constantine

Via Celio Vibenna

VILLA
BORGHESE

VATICAN
CITY

ROME

Colosseum

TRASTE-
VERE

ANCIENT
ROME

PALATINE
HILL

Via di San Gregorio

Imperial
Stadium/
Hippodrome

PALATINE
HILL

Via dei Cerchi

CIRCUS MAXIMUS

open by the time of your visit. The restoration visit lasts 40 minutes; book in advance using the number or Web site below, or at the tourist office at Via Parigi 5 or the Palatine Hill ticket booth (Piazza Santa Maria Nova 53). Same-day tickets are for sale at the booking desk of the Colosseum ticket booth.

See map p. 142. Viale della Domus Aurea 1, off Via dei Fori Imperiali. ☎ *06-39967700 (Mon–Sat 9 a.m.–1:30 p.m. and 2:30–5 p.m.).* www.pierreci.it *for reservations.* www.archeorm.arti.beniculturali.it. *Metro: Colosseo. Bus: Minibus 117. Tram: 3. Admission: 4€ ($5.20) with required advance reservation. Open: Tue–Fri 10 a.m.–4 p.m. by guided tour only. Closed Jan 1, May 1, Aug 15, and Dec 25.*

National Etruscan Museum of Villa Giulia (Museo Nazionale Etrusco di Villa Giulia)
Villa Borghese

This splendid papal villa, built by the most prominent architects of the 16th century, houses the world's most important Etruscan collection. Originally from Asia Minor, the Etruscans were a mysterious people who dominated Tuscany and Lazio, including Rome, up to the fifth century B.C. Many of the objects in this museum came from Cerveteri, an important Etruscan site northwest of Rome. One of the most spectacular objects is the **bride-and-bridegroom sarcophagus** from the sixth century B.C., upon which two enigmatic figures recline. You can also see a fairly well-preserved **chariot** and impressive sculptures. Some of the most amazing works are the tiniest: The Etruscans made **intricate decorative objects** from woven gold, employing goldsmithing techniques that remain a mystery today. In the summer, the garden is the site of musical events (see Chapter 15). Block out about three hours for a full visit.

See map p. 142. Piazzale di Villa Giulia 9. ☎ *06-3226571.* www.ticketeria.it. *Tram: 3 or 19 to last stop, then walk down Viale delle Belle Arti to Piazzale di Villa Giulia, or 225 to Via di Villa Giulia. Admission: 4€ ($5.20). Audio guides: 4€ ($5.20). Open: Tues–Sun 8:30 a.m.–7:30 p.m. Ticket booth closes one hour earlier. Closed Jan 1, May 1, and Dec 25.*

National Gallery of Ancient Art in Palazzo Barberini (Galleria Nazionale d'Arte Antica in Palazzo Barberini)
Via Veneto

Completed in 1633, the Palazzo Barberini is a magnificent example of a baroque Roman palace. Bernini decorated the rococo apartments the gallery now occupies, and they're certainly luxurious. Also preserved in the Palazzo Barberini is the wedding chamber of Princess Cornelia Costanza Barberini and Prince Giulio Cesare Colonna di Sciarra, exactly as it was centuries ago. Although the structure itself is an attraction, the collection of paintings that make up the Galleria Nazionale d'Arte Antica is most impressive; it includes Caravaggio's ***Narcissus,*** Tiziano's ***Venus and Adonis,*** and Raphael's ***La Fornarina,*** a loving, informal portrait of the bakery girl who was his mistress (and the model for his Madonnas). Other artists represented are the great Sienese painters Il Sodoma and Simone Martini, as well as Filippo Lippi. The galleria's **decorative-arts collection** contains not only Italian pieces but also fine imported objects, including some from Japan. In addition to the permanent collections, the gallery regularly mounts special exhibits. Allow two and a half hours for a complete visit.

See map p. 142. Via delle Quattro Fontane 13. ☎ *06-4824184. We recommend that you book the visit to the apartments in advance at* ☎ *06-32810 or* www.ticketeria.it. *Metro: Barberini. Admission: 5€ ($6.50) plus 1€ ($1.30) advance reservation. Open: Tues–Sun 8:30 a.m.–7:30 p.m. Ticket booth closes 30 minutes earlier.*

National Gallery of Modern Art (Galleria Nazionale d'Arte Moderna/GNAM)
Villa Borghese

Housed in the beautiful, Liberty-style (Italian Art Nouveau) **Palazzo delle Belle Arti,** this important museum preserves a rich collection of modern art from the 19th and 20th centuries. Italian artists dominate, but the collection includes works by all sorts of great artists. The two sections dedicated to the 19th century hold a great selection of paintings by artists of the *Macchiaioli* movement and a number of works by French modern artists such as **Rodin, Van Gogh,** and **Monet;** but the real riches are in the two sections dedicated to the 20th century, where you can admire a profusion of artwork by **De Chirico, Giorgio Morandi, Marino Marini, Lucio Fontana,** and **Giò Pomodoro,** to name some highlights. The collection also includes international names such as **Pollock, Calder,** and **Tápies,** among others. Schedule about two hours for your visit.

GNAM's new annex, MAXXI (Via Reni 2, off Piazza Apollodoro; ☎ 06-3202438; www.maxximuseo.org) is in the former Barracks Montello nearby; it holds the museum's 21st-century collection. Admission is free; hours are Tuesday to Sunday 11 a.m. to 7 p.m.

See map p. 142. Viale delle Belle Arti 131. (Via Gramsci 71 for visitors with disabilities). ☎ *06-322981; reservations 06-3234000.* www.gnam.arti.beniculturali.it. *Tram: 3, 19. Bus: 88, 95, 490, and 495. Admission: 6.50€ ($8.45), plus 2.50€ ($3.25) special exhibit. Open: Tues–Sun 8:30 a.m.–7:30 p.m. Last admission 40 min. before closing.*

National Roman Museum in Palazzo Altemps (Museo Nazionale Romano Palazzo Altemps)

Navona/Pantheon

Situated behind Piazza Navona, this palazzo was begun sometime before 1477 and finished by Marco Sittico Altemps, who enlarged it at the end of the 1500s. It was restored (revealing the layers of medieval, Renaissance, and later decoration) to house the **Ludovisi Collection.** One of the world's most famous private art collections, it is particularly strong in Greek and Roman sculpture as well as Egyptian works. The single most important piece is a fifth century B.C. Greek masterpiece, the **Trono Ludovisi,** a throne finely carved to depict Aphrodite Urania rising from the waves on one side; a female figure offering incense on another; and a naked female playing a flute on yet another. The remarkable *Dying Gaul,* depicting a man apparently committing suicide with a sword, was commissioned by Julius Caesar and placed in his gardens to commemorate his victories in Gaul. The *Ares Ludovisi,* a statue restored by Bernini in 1622, is believed by art historians to be a Roman copy of an earlier Greek work; it shows a warrior (possibly Achilles) at rest. The colossal head of Hera (also known as Juno) is one of the best-known Greek sculptures; Goethe wrote of it as his "first love" in Rome and said it was like "a canto of Homer." It has been identified as an idealized portrait of Antonia Augusta, mother of Emperor Claudius. Plan to spend at least one hour here.

See map p. 142. Piazza Sant'Apollinare 46. ☎ *06-39967700 (Mon–Sat 9 a.m.–1:30 p.m. and 2:30–5 p.m.), or* www.pierreci.it *for reservations.* www.archeorm.arti. beniculturali.it. *Bus: Minibus 116 to Via dei Coronari; then walk away from Piazza Navona. Admission: 7€ ($9.10), plus 3€ ($3.90) for special exhibitions; includes National Roman Museum of Palazzo Massimo, Cripta Balbi, and Diocletian Baths (use within three days). Audio guides: 4€ ($5.20). Open: Tues–Sun 9 a.m.–7:45 p.m.; Dec 24 and 31 9 a.m.–5 p.m. Ticket office closes one hour earlier. Closed Jan 1 and Dec 25.*

National Roman Museum in Palazzo Massimo alle Terme (Museo Nazionale Romano Palazzo Massimo alle Terme)
Repubblica

This is our favorite museum of antiquity in Rome. The astounding collection of ancient Roman art (from decades of excavations in Rome and its environs) includes — on the upper level — a unique collection of **floor mosaics** and **frescoes.** Entire rooms from the **Villa of Livia** on the Palatine Hill have been reconstructed here, and you can enjoy the frescos as they were meant to be. *Note:* You can visit the fresco collection by guided tour only. You can sign up when you enter, but it is best to make an advance reservation. On the lower floors, you'll find a huge sculpture collection with the striking **satyr pouring wine,** a Roman copy of the original by Greek sculptor Praxiteles; the *Daughter of Niobe,* from the Gardens of Sallust; and an *Apollo* copied from an original by Phidias, one of the greatest ancient Greek sculptors. We also enjoyed the interesting series of sculptures showing how the style of representation changed under various emperors and discussing the family resemblances of the Claudians, Flavians, and other dynasties. Even the basement contains some fascinating things: a well-done **numismatic exhibit,** with coins dating from the 8th century B.C. through the 21st century that explain the economy of ancient Rome and of Renaissance Italy; and the royal house of Savoy's collection of Roman jewelry, including many items from burial sites, such as a **rare Roman mummy** of a child buried with her most precious belongings. The entire visit, including the tour of the fresco collection, will take you a minimum of two hours.

See map p. 142. Largo di Villa Peretti 1. ☎ *06-39967700 (Mon–Sat 9 a.m.–1:30 p.m. and 2:30–5 p.m.), or* www.pierreci.it *for reservations.* www.archeorm.arti. beniculturali.it. *Metro: Line A, B to Termini. Bus: 64 or 70. Admission: 7€*

($9.10), plus 3€ ($3.90) for special exhibitions; includes admission to National Roman Museum of Palazzo Altemps, Cripta Balbi, and Diocletian Baths (use within three days). Audio guides: 4€ ($5.20).Open: Tues–Sun 9 a.m.–7:45 p.m.; Dec 24 and 31 9 a.m.–5 p.m. Ticket booth closes one hour earlier. Closed Jan 1 and Dec 25.

Palatine Hill (Palatino)
Colosseo

This is one of our preferred spots in Rome: Huge blocks of brick surrounded by trees and greenery testify mutely to what was once an enormous residential complex of patrician houses and imperial palaces, built to match the emperors' grandiose ambitions. The throne room of the **Domus Flavia,** for instance, was approximately 30m (100 ft.) wide by 39.3m (131 ft.) long. This hill is also where Romulus drew the original square for the foundation of Rome and the first houses were built; indeed, excavations in the area uncovered remains that date to the eighth century B.C. **Casa di Livia (Livia's House)** is one of the best-preserved homes. During the Middle Ages, the site was used as a fortress, and during the Renaissance it became the play place of the aristocracy: Here Cardinal Alessandro Farnese built the **Horti Palatini,** the first botanical garden in the Western world, in 1625. Built on top of the palaces of Tiberius and Caligula, it was a marvel of architecture, with ramps, terraces, and fountains. Today, after systematic archeological excavations started toward the end of the 19th century, only the aviaries remain, deprived of their pagoda-shaped netting roofs. Housed in the onetime Palace of Caesar — later transformed into a convent — is the **Palatine Museum.** The most precious artwork recovered from the archeological excavations of the Palatino, including frescoes and sculptures, is conserved here. (Admission is included in your ticket.) The ruins on the Palatine Hill are impressive but may be confusing without a guided tour. We definitely recommend taking one; they are cheap and make a world of difference. Depending on your pace and whether you visit the museum, leave one and a half to two and a half hours for your visit. *Note:* At press time, the Casa di Livia and the Casa di Augusto were temporarily closed for restoration, and the Casa dei Grifi was open only on the first Saturday of each month.

See maps p. 142 and p. 155. Via di San Gregorio 30 or Piazza Santa Maria Nova 53, off Piazza del Colosseo. ☎ *06-39967700 (Mon–Sat 9 a.m.–1:30 p.m. and 2:30–5 p.m.), or* www.pierreci.it *for reservations.* www.archeorm.arti.beniculturali. it. *Metro: Colosseo. Bus: Minibus 117. Admission: 9€ ($12), plus 2€ ($2.60) for special exhibitions; includes admission to the Colosseum. Guided tour 3.50€ ($4.55). Open: Daily 9 a.m. to one hour before sunset. Ticket booth closes one hour earlier. Closed Jan 1 and Dec 25.*

Pantheon
Navona/Pantheon

Rome's best-preserved monument of antiquity, the imposing Pantheon was rebuilt by the Emperor Hadrian in A.D. 125 over the smaller original temple constructed by Marcus Agrippa in 27 B.C. to honor all the gods *(pan theon* means "all gods" in ancient Greek). It was eventually saved from destruction by being transformed into a Christian church in A.D. 609. The adjective that all descriptions of the Pantheon should contain is *perfect:* The building is 43m (142 ft.) wide and 43m (142 ft.) tall. The portico is supported by huge granite columns, all but three of which are original, and the bronze doors weigh 20 tons each. Inside, the empty niches surrounding the space once contained marble statues of Roman gods; most of the marble floor is also original. Animals were once sacrificed beneath the beautiful **coffered dome,** whose 5.4m (18-ft.) hole *(oculus)* lets in the light (and sometimes rain) of the Eternal City. An architectural marvel, this dome inspired Michelangelo when he was designing St. Peter's, though he made the basilica's dome 0.6m (2 ft.) smaller. Inside, you'll find the tombs of the painter Raphael and of two of the kings of Italy. Crowds always congregate in the square in front, **Piazza della Rotonda** (Piazza del Pantheon to Romans), one of the nicest squares in Rome; it is graced by a fountain by Giacomo della Porta. Cafes line the square along with a McDonald's, an addition much opposed by the locals. A half-hour should be enough to take in the highlights of the monument; allow another hour to soak in the atmosphere from the terrace of one of the cafes.

See map p. 142. Piazza della Rotonda. ☎ *06-68300230. Bus: Minibus 116. Admission: Free. Open: Mon–Sat 8:30 a.m.–7:30 p.m., Sun 9 a.m.–6 p.m., holidays 9 a.m.–1 p.m.*

Piazza di Spagna and Spanish Steps
Piazza di Spagna

The Piazza and its famous steps are one of the favorite meeting places of Rome. In good weather, you can hardly see the ground when it's covered with wall-to-wall tourists, lovers, backpackers, Roman youth, and so on. The atmosphere is festive and convivial, though, and it's especially romantic in spring, when the steps are decorated with colorful azaleas. The piazza's name dates to the 16th century, when the Spanish ambassador made his residence here. In those days, the piazza was far less hospitable. (People passing through at night sometimes disappeared, because it was technically Spanish territory, and the unwary could be press-ganged into the Spanish army.) In more recent times, the area's most famous resident was English poet John Keats, who lived and died in the house to the right of the steps, which is now the **Keats–Shelley Memorial House** (☎ 06-6784235; Mon–Fri 9 a.m.–1 p.m. and 3–6 p.m., Sat 11 a.m.–2 p.m. and 3–6 p.m.; admission: 3€/$3.60). When you climb the steps, you'll find their real name: Scalinata della Trinità dei Monti, because they lead to the **Trinità dei Monti church,** whose towers loom above. At the foot of the steps, the **boat-shaped fountain** by Pietro Bernini, father of Gian Lorenzo, is one of the most famous in Rome. In May 2007, a drunken vandal damaged the fountain on one side, but he was immediately arrested; restoration was started right after the event and should be completed by the time you read this.

See map p. 142. Via del Babuino and Via dei Condotti. Metro: Line A to Spagna. Bus: Minibus 117 or 119 to Piazza di Spagna.

Palatine Hill

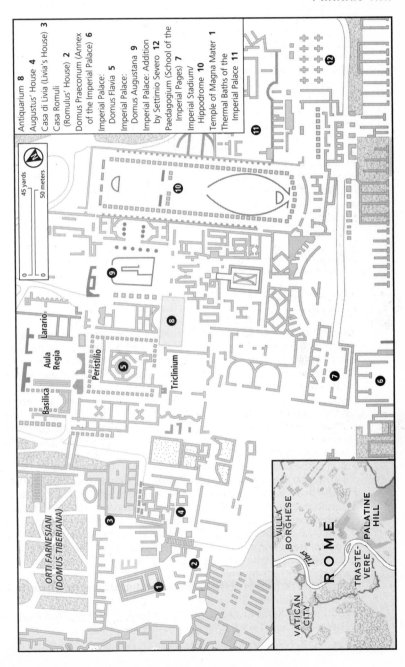

Antiquarium **8**

Augustus' House **4**

Casa di Livia (Livia's House) **3**

Casa Romuli
(Romulus' House) **2**

Domus Praeconum (Annex
of the Imperial Palace) **6**

Imperial Palace:
Domus Flavia **5**

Imperial Palace:
Domus Augustana **9**

Imperial Palace: Addition
by Settimio Severo **12**

Paedagogium (School of the
Imperial Pages) **7**

Imperial Stadium/
Hippodrome **10**

Temple of Magna Mater **1**

Thermal Baths of the
Imperial Palace **11**

45 yards

50 meters

ORTI FARNESIANI
(DOMUS TIBERIANA)

Basilica

Aula
Regia

Larario

Peristilio

Triclinium

VILLA
BORGHESE

ROME

VATICAN
CITY

TRASTE-
VERE

PALATINE
HILL

Tevere

How to attend a papal audience

Papal audiences attract many — Catholics and non — who come to see and hear the pope live as he addresses the crowd gathered in front of him. The audiences are held on Wednesdays, indoors during the winter (Oct–Mar) and outdoors in a gated area in front of the basilica in fair weather (Apr–Sept). Entrance is allowed between 10 and 10:30 a.m., but lines form earlier by the gates, where you pass security (similar to airport screening). Tickets are free but you must reserve them in advance by writing or faxing your request (indicating your language, the dates of your visit, the number of people in your party, and, if possible, the hotel in Rome to which the office should send your tickets the afternoon before the audience) to the **Prefecture of the Papal Household** (00120 Città del Vaticano/Holy See; ☎ **06-69884857**; fax 06-69885863; Mon–Sat 9 a.m.–1 p.m.). You can pick them up the afternoon before the audience at the Prefecture office entrance, near the *porta di bronzo* (bronze door) under St. Peter's right colonnade.

Piazza Navona
Navona/Pantheon

Our favorite piazza in Rome, this is the most beautiful and also one of the most popular hangouts. Built on the ruins of the **Stadium of Domitian** from the first century A.D., where chariot races were held (note the oval track form), it has retained its public role: Between the 17th and 19th centuries, the bottom of the square was flooded for float parades in the summer, and it is now the location of the traditional Epiphany market during the Christmas period. The twin-towered facade of **Santa Agnese in Agone** dominates the piazza. The baroque masterpiece is by Borromini, who renovated and rebuilt the original church, which had been constructed on the site between the 8th and the 12th centuries. The interior was also redecorated in the 17th century, but in the lower level, you'll find vestiges of Domitian's stadium, with an ancient Roman mosaic floor. The square's other great baroque masterpiece is Bernini's **Fountain of the Four Rivers,** with massive figures representing the Nile, Danube, della Plata, and Ganges — the figure with the shrouded head is the Nile, because its source was unknown at the time. Built in 1651, it is crowned by an **obelisk,** a Roman copy from Domitian's time. This fountain came as a monumental addition to the two simple fountains already existing at each end of the square and created in 1576 by Giacomo della Porta. They were decorated with figures only later. Bernini designed the figures of the **Fountain of the Moor** at the piazza's south end (the tritons and other ornaments are 19th-century copies made to replace the originals, which were moved to the Villa Borghese lake garden). The figures of the **Fountain of Neptune,** at the piazza's north end, were added in the 19th century to balance the Fountain of the Moor. On the southeast side of the square is the famous **Palazzo Braschi,** housing the **Museo di Roma** (see listing later in this chapter).

See map p. 142. Just off Corso Rinascimento. Bus: 70 or 116 to Piazza Navona.

St. Peter's Square (Piazza San Pietro)
San Pietro

Bernini designed the piazza, one of the world's greatest public spaces, in the 17th century. As you stand in the huge piazza (no cars allowed), you're in the arms of an ellipse partly enclosed by a majestic Doric-pillared colonnade, atop which stand statues of some 140 saints. Straight ahead is the facade of **St. Peter's Basilica;** the two statues flanking the entrance represent St. Peter, Peter carrying the Keys to the Kingdom, and St. Paul. To the right, above the colonnade, are the ochre buildings of the **papal apartments** and the **Vatican Museums.** In the center of the square is an **Egyptian obelisk,** brought from the ancient city of Heliopolis on the Nile delta. On either side are 17th-century **fountains** — the one on the right by Carlo Maderno, who designed the facade of St. Peter's, was placed here by Bernini himself; the one on the left is by Carlo Fontana. The piazza is particularly magical at night during the Christmas season, when a *presepio* (nativity scene) and a large tree take center stage.

See map p. 142. Bus: 62 or 64. Metro: Ottaviano/San Pietro; take Via di Porta Angelica, and follow it to the end.

Roman Forum (Foro Romano)
Colosseo

This was Rome's original forum, a large public space used as a market and meeting venue. As Rome grew, the structure became too small to accommodate the needs of the imperial capital, and it was gradually expanded by various emperors, who each added an extra bit (creating the Imperial Fori; see listing later in this chapter). The forum remained the heart of public life in ancient Rome for over a thousand years. The ruins lie in the valley between the Capitoline Hill, site of the great Jupiter Temple, and the Palatine Hill, where the royal palace, and later the palaces of other noble families, were located. The forum was built at the end of the seventh century B.C., after the existing marshes were drained by the **Cloaca Massima,** the huge drainage and sewer canal under the forum. The forum is crossed by the **Via Sacra,** the "sacred street," so called because it led to the main temples on the Capitoline Hill (today, Piazza del Campidoglio). A stone discovered under the forum in 1899 bears an inscription from the sixth century B.C., the time of the Roman kings. The forum has many ruins (some, like the sanctuary of the sewer goddess Venus Cloaca, are just a mark on the ground), as well as a few standing buildings. The most important structure is the square **Curia,** where the Senate once met; many of the walls were heavily restored in 1937, but the marble-inlay floor inside is original, from the third century A.D. Also well conserved is the **Temple of Antoninus and Faustina** (the Emperor Antoninus Pius, who succeeded Hadrian in A.D. 138), because it was turned into a church and given a baroque facade (as the Chiesa di San Lorenzo in Miranda).

Near the Curia is the **Arch of Septimius Severus,** built in A.D. 203 to commemorate this emperor's victories. The arch originally mentioned his two sons, Caracalla and Geta, but after Caracalla murdered Geta, Geta's name was removed. At the other end of the forum is the **Arch of Titus.** Titus

The Roman Forum

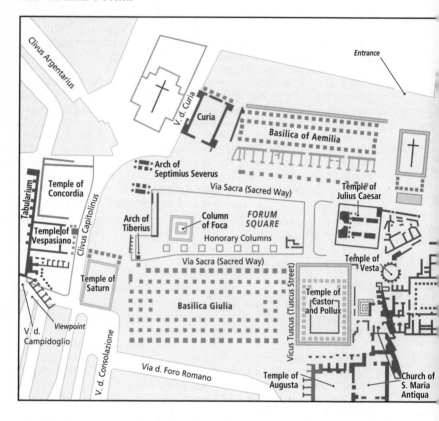

reigned as emperor from A.D. 79 to 81. Nearby is the hulking form of the fourth-century **Basilica of Constantine and Maxentius,** which occupies the site of what was Rome's law courts. The **Temple of the Dioscuri,** dedicated to the twins Castor and Pollux, is immediately recognizable by its three remaining columns joined by a piece of architrave. Against the Capitoline Hill, you see the **Temple of Saturn,** which housed the first treasury of Rome. It was also the site of the feast that was the pagan ancestor of Christmas.

If you buy a map as you enter, you can identify the sometimes faint traces of a host of other structures (also see the map "The Roman Forum," above).

Note: At press time, the **Antiquarium Forense,** which contains materials from the excavations of the forum, was closed for restoration. No date was set for the reopening, but check for updates at the ticket booth or with the tourist office.

As with any archaeological site, things often make much more sense if you take a guided tour. The tour in English is at 10:30 a.m. daily and lasts about an hour. Ask at the ticket booth or, even better, make a reservation.

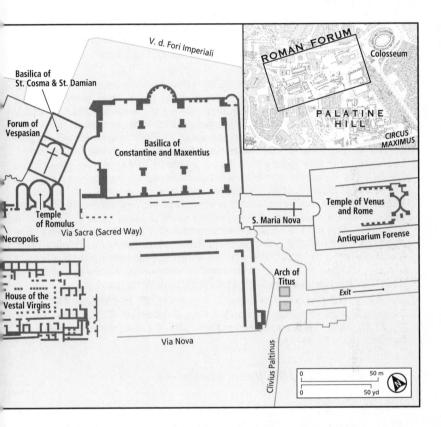

See maps p. 142 and above. Piazza Santa Maria Nova 53, off Piazza del Colosseo; and Largo della Salara Vecchia 5, off Via dei Fori Imperiali. ☎ **06-39967700** (Mon–Sat 9 a.m.–1:30 p.m. and 2:30–5 p.m.), or www.pierreci.it for reservations. www. archeorm.arti.beniculturali.it. Metro: Colosseo. Bus: Minibus 117. Admission: Free. Guided tours: 3.50€ ($4.55). Audio guides: 4€ ($5.20). Open: Daily 9 a.m. to one hour before sunset. Last admission one hour before closing. Closed Jan 1 and Dec 25.

Saint John Lateran's Basilica (Basilica di San Giovanni in Laterano) and Cloister (Chiostro)
Colosseo

Built in A.D. 13 by Constantine, this cathedral of the diocese of Rome (St. Peter's Basilica is in the separate city-state of the Vatican) suffered many indignities, including being sacked by the Vandals (a barbarian tribe), burned, and then damaged in an 896 earthquake. Always faithfully restored, it is quite an impressive sight, chock full of art and religious treasures. The facade, designed and executed by Alessandro Galilei in 1735, is crowned by **15 giant statues** (7m/22 ft. tall) representing Christ, St. John the Baptist, John the Evangelist, and other "doctors" (leading lights) of the Church; they are tall enough to be visible from surprising distant points in Rome. Outside is an **Egyptian obelisk,** the tallest in Rome (32m/105 ft.), consecrated in the fourth century as a symbol of Christianity's victory over pagan cults.

The 17th-century architect **Borromini** redesigned the interior of the basilica as you see it today. Make sure you find the **papal altar,** protected by a beautiful 14th-century **ciborium:** it preserves the wooden altar on which Peter and the other Paleo-Christian popes after him are said to have celebrated mass in ancient Rome's catacombs. Another important relic is preserved by the altar of the **Santissimo Sacramento,** in the left transept: Decorated with four giant gilded-bronze columns salvaged from the original basilica, its ciborium protects what is believed to be the very table of Christ's Last Supper. Attached to the church is the original fourth-century **Baptistery;** built by Constantine, it is the first of the Western world. Restored inside over the centuries, it was redone in its present form by Borromini when he redesigned the rest of the cathedral. Our favorite part in the entire church is the delightful 13th-century **cloister,** accessible through a side door. It was designed by Vassalletto and is a showcase for carvings and other art pieces salvaged from the older basilica, including a number of Paleo-Christian inscriptions. Set aside at least an hour for your visit.

See map p. 142. Piazza di San Giovanni in Laterano. ☎ *06-69886433. Metro: San Giovanni. Bus: 81, 85, 850, or Minibus 117. Tram: 3. Admission: Basilica free; cloister 2€ ($2.60). Open: Basilica and cloister daily 7 a.m.–6 p.m. (in summer to 6:45 p.m.); Baptistery daily 9 a.m.–1 p.m.*

St. Peter's Basilica (Basilica di San Pietro)
San Pietro

In 324, Emperor Constantine commissioned a sanctuary to be built on the site of St. Peter's tomb. The first apostle was thought to have been buried here under a simple stone, and excavation and studies commissioned by the Vatican under the Basilica have confirmed that thesis. The original

Vatican Necropolis and St. Peter's Tomb

If you are 15 or older and interested in religious archeology, you may want to book a visit to the Necropolis and excavations that extend beyond the Grottoes under St. Peter's Basilica. Accessible by guided tour only, they make a fascinating visit. You'll need to make your reservations in advance by fax (06-69873017) or e-mail (scavi@fsp.va) to the Excavation Office specifying desired language, number and names of each person in your party, requested dates, and contact information. You'll receive a proposed time, which you must confirm, again in writing. Admission is 10€ ($13) per person. The Vatican receives more requests for the visit than it can accommodate, so make arrangements well in advance.

The Vatican

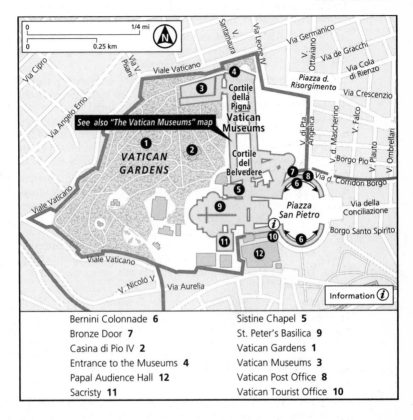

Bernini Colonnade **6**	Sistine Chapel **5**
Bronze Door **7**	St. Peter's Basilica **9**
Casina di Pio IV **2**	Vatican Gardens **1**
Entrance to the Museums **4**	Vatican Museums **3**
Papal Audience Hall **12**	Vatican Post Office **8**
Sacristy **11**	Vatican Tourist Office **10**

basilica stood for about 1,000 years, but with its accrued importance and stability, the Papacy decided it was time for renovations. Work began in 1503 following designs by the architects Sangallo and Bramante. In 1547, Michelangelo was appointed to finish the magnificent dome, but he died in 1564 before seeing its work completed. His disciple Giacomo della Porta finished the job. The inside of the basilica is almost too huge to take in (the best spot to appreciate its huge size is at the central square part); walking from one end to the other is a workout, and the opulence will over-power you. On the right as you enter is Michelangelo's exquisite *Pietà,* created when the master was in his early 20s. (Because of an act of van-dalism in the 1970s, the statue is kept behind reinforced glass.) Dominating the central nave is Bernini's 29m-tall (96-ft.) **baldaquin,** supported by richly decorated twisting columns. Completed in 1633, it was criticized for being excessive and because the bronze was supposedly taken from the Pantheon. The canopy stands over the papal altar, which in turn stands over the symbolic tomb of St. Peter. A **bronze statue of St. Peter** (proba-bly by Arnolfo di Cambio, 13th century) marks the tomb; its right foot has been worn away by the millions of pilgrims kissing it in the traditional devotional gesture to salute the pope. By the apse, above an altar, is the **bronze throne** sculpted by Bernini to house the remains of what is, according to legend, the chair of St. Peter.

At the right-hand side of the Basilica's entrance, under the loggia, you'll find two lines. The one on the right is for **Michelangelo's dome,** and the one on the left is for the **Vatican Grottoes.**

You can visit the dome and marvel at the astounding view. An elevator saves you the first 171 steps of the climb, but you have to book it when you buy your ticket to the dome and pay an additional 3€ ($3.90). Expect a line. The view is already good, but you won't have the full effect (guaranteed to take your breath away) unless you climb the additional 420 steps or so. Make sure that you're ready and willing to climb, however, because after you've started up, you're not allowed to turn around and go back down.

Beneath the basilica are the spaces created during the construction, partly retracing the original Basilica built by Emperor Constantine, and partly going down to the preexisting necropolis over which the emperor built the first St. Peter's. In the main halls you'll find the tombs of the popes and a collection of Paleo-Christian sarcophagi and art fragments salvaged from the original basilica. It is a huge space encompassing two dozen rooms. (*Note:* This is *not* the visit to the Necropolis and archaeological excavations. That is a special affair that needs advance reservation. See sidebar earlier in this chapter.)

From the left nave, you can reach the **Treasury** (Museo del Tesoro di San Pietro). Still very rich in spite of having being pillaged by the Saracens in 846, by Charles V in 1527, and by Napoleon in 1797, it contains several relics and works of art. Look for Donatello's ciborium in hall II, the majestic monument for Sixtus IV by Pollaiolo in hall III, and the splendid Roman sarcophagus in hall IX, depicting scenes from the Old and the New Testament (the prefect buried in it was a convert).

Plan on at least two hours for your visit, and more if you want to see everything. *Note:* Strict security governs public entrance, and you'll have to line up at the right-hand side of the colonnade to pass through the security checkpoint (airport-style procedure, with metal detector). Travelers with disabilities will have to pass security, but then can use a special elevator located at the end of the cloakroom to the right of the steps.

The best time to visit to avoid lines is before 9 a.m. After that, the growing throngs of visitors make for lengthy waits at security.

Consider that at the Vatican, even the men wear ankle-length gowns, and the most popular color is black. Bare shoulders, halter tops, tank tops, shorts, and skirts above the knee will *definitely* result in your being turned away from the basilica, whether you are man or woman.

See maps p. 142 and p. 161. Piazza San Pietro, entrance through security check point on the right-hand side under the colonnade. ☎ *06-69883712. Bus: 62 or 64. Metro: Ottaviano/San Pietro. Take Viale Angelico to the Vatican. Admission: Basilica and grottoes free; dome 4€ ($5.20), 7€ ($9.10) with elevator; treasury 6€ ($7.80). Open: Oct–Mar basilica daily 7 a.m.–6 p.m., dome daily 8 a.m.–4:45 p.m., treasury daily 9 a.m.–5:15 p.m., grottoes daily 7 a.m.–5 p.m.; Apr–Sept basilica Thurs–Tues 7 a.m.–*

7 p.m. and Wed noon to 7 p.m., dome Thurs–Tues 8 a.m.–5:45 p.m. and Wed noon to 5:45 p.m.; treasury Thurs–Tues 9 a.m.–6:15 p.m. and Wed noon to 6:15 p.m., grottoes Thurs–Tues 7 a.m.–6 p.m. and Wed noon to 6 p.m.

Sistine Chapel

See listing under Vatican Museums.

Trajan's Markets and Trajan's Forum (Mercati Traianei and Foro di Traiano)
Colosseo

Julius Caesar was the first to respond to the need for larger public space in the Roman capital, and he created the first of the Imperial Fori between 54 and 46 B.C. As the city continued to grow, the following emperors followed his example, and four more forums were added, each a large open space surrounded by a portico with a temple on one end, and each bearing the name of the emperor who built it. After Augustus, Vespasian, and Nerva, Trajan built the last and most splendid. The luxurious public constructions adjacent to the original Roman Forum (see listing earlier in this chapter) were built between A.D. 107 and 113. They include an elegant open space — **Trajan's Forum** — overlooked by a tall curved building — **Trajan's Markets.** Although maimed by the pillage of marble and decoration during the Middle Ages and the Renaissance (when the marble was used for other construction), the archaeological remains are fascinating. Walking north along the Via dei Fori Imperiali from the Colosseum, you can see the archaeological site from the outside (to your right), but obviously, a visit to the impressive brick complex itself affords an irreplaceable experience. You can walk along stalls and small boutiques — sort of an ancient mall — as well as meeting places. Once inside the compound, it will be easier to imagine what the area must have looked like before the construction in 1920 of Via dei Fori Imperiali, a major transportation artery of modern Rome. Most of the Imperial Fori were covered in that occasion, and today, the entire area is being excavated in the largest Roman archaeological excavation to date, started in 2004. The plan is to exhibit the findings of these excavations in the Trajan Markets. *Note:* To accommodate

Tricky transformers

If you are visiting at the height of summer and have kids in tow, one thing that children (and grown-ups) usually find highly entertaining is watching as tourists try to cover their bare shoulders and knees with flowery scarves and shawls sold by entrepreneurial vendors near the entrance to St. Peter's. Women have to do it, too, but usually men are the most hilarious to watch (no offense meant). We know of people who make it a regular family outing. It can be a good way to entertain the kids while the grown-ups take turns seeing the art inside.

The Holy See

In 1929, the Lateran Treaty between Pope Pius XI and the Italian government recognized the independent state of the Holy See, with its physical seat in Vatican City (St. Peter's Basilica and adjacent buildings). Politically independent from Italy, the Vatican is the world's second-smallest sovereign state, with its own administration, post office, and tourist office. The Vatican comprises St. Peter's Basilica (p. 160), the Vatican Museums (p. 165), and the Vatican Gardens (see below).

the excavation, the visit has temporarily been reduced to Trajan's Forum and part of the semicircular building; the temporary entrance is from Trajan's Column off Piazza Venezia. Count on about 40 minutes for the reduced visit.

Via 4 Novembre 94. ☎ *06-6790048. Metro: Colosseo. Bus: Minibus 117. Admission: 3.20€ ($4.20). Open Tues–Sun 9 a.m.–4:30 p.m. winter, until 6:30 p.m. in summer.*

Trevi Fountain (Fontana di Trevi)
Trevi

Fronting its own little piazza, this massive fountain existed for centuries in relative obscurity before it became one of the must-see sights of Rome, thanks to the 1954 film *Three Coins in the Fountain*. Today, it seems that many of the thousands who clog the space in front of it don't take the time to *really* look at it; instead, they throw coins in it, have their pictures taken in front of it, and go on their way. If you want a tranquil moment to actually appreciate the artwork, you must visit late at night or early in the morning. The fountain was begun by Bernini and Pietro da Cortona, but there was a 100-year lapse in the work, and it wasn't completed until 1751, by Nicola Salvi. The central figure is Neptune, who guides a chariot pulled by plunging sea horses. *Tritons* (mythological sea dwellers) guide the horses, and the surrounding scene is one of wild nature and bare stone.

Of course, you have to toss a coin in the Trevi fountain, something all kids love to do. To do it properly (Romans are superstitious), hold the coin in your right hand, turn your back to the fountain, and toss the coin over your left shoulder. According to tradition, the spirit of the fountain will then see to it that you return to Rome one day.

See map p. 142. Piazza di Trevi. Bus: 62 or Minibus 116 or 119. Take Via Poli to the fountain.

Vatican Gardens (Giardini Vaticani)
San Pietro

People often think that the Vatican is made up of only the basilica and the museums, but behind those walls lies a busy town surrounding a huge — and splendid — park. You can catch a glimpse of the park from the windows of the Vatican Museums, revealing groomed grounds, fountains, and elegant Renaissance buildings. Normally you need a permit to enter the Vatican grounds, but the special guided tours afford a unique opportunity to see what goes on beyond those gates. The two-hour tours take small numbers of visitors to the gardens, partly by bus and partly on foot (some of it on graveled paths). If you forgot to arrange a reservation (by fax or e-mail only; see below), try to sign up directly at the Vatican Information Office (see contact information at the beginning of this chapter) — it may be able to fit you in.

Remember to be clothed in accordance with Vatican rules for your visit (see note at the end of St. Peter's Basilica entry).

See maps p. 142 and p. 161. Piazza San Pietro. ☎ *06-69884676. Fax: 06-69885100.* visiteguidate.musei@scv.va. *Bus: 62 or 64 to Via della Conciliazione. Metro: Ottaviano/San Pietro. Take Viale Angelico to the Vatican. Guided tours: Tues, and Sat 10 a.m. Admission: 12€ ($16).*

Vatican Museums (Musei Vaticani)
San Pietro

This enormous complex of museums could swallow up your entire vacation, with its tons of Egyptian, Etruscan, Greek, Roman, Paleo-Christian, and Renaissance art. Four museums house the art: the **Gregorian Egyptian Museum,** a fantastic collection of Egyptian artifacts; the **Gregorian Etruscan Museum,** a beautiful collection of Etruscan art and jewelry; the **Ethnological Missionary Museum,** a large collection of artifacts from every continent, including superb African, Asian, and Australian art; and the **Pinacoteca (picture gallery),** the most famous of the Vatican Museums, which contains works by medieval and Renaissance masters. In Room 9 of the Pinacoteca is Leonardo da Vinci's *St. Jerome,* which has been pieced back together — one piece had ended up as a stool seat in a shoemaker's shop; the other, as a tabletop in an antiques shop. In Room 2 is Giotto's luminous *Stefaneschi Triptych;* in Room 8, Raphael's *Transfiguration.* Other highlights include works by Beato Angelico, Perugino, Bernini, and Caravaggio (a single but great painting, the *Deposition from the Cross*).

Also part of the museums are the **Stanze di Raffaello.** The name translates as **Raphael's Rooms,** after the artist who frescoed them; they are in fact the private apartments of Pope Julius II. The largest of the four rooms is the room of **Constantine,** painted between 1517 and 1524, which illustrates key moments in the life of the first Christian emperor, including his triumph over Maxentius and his vision of the cross. Along the way, you'll come across the **Appartamento Borgia (Borgia Apartments),** designed for Pope Alexander VI (the infamous Borgia pope), and the **Cappella di Nicola V (Chapel of Nicholas V),** with floor-to-ceiling frescoes by Fra Angelico.

But of course, the **Sistine Chapel (Cappella Sistina),** Michelangelo's masterpiece, is the crowning glory of the museums. Accessible only from the Museums, the chapel is smaller than one would expect. But lift your eyes and you'll be transported into another world: Michelangelo's grandiose frescoes completely cover the ceilings. Years after their restoration (a

20-year affair that started in 1979), conflict continues over whether too much paint was removed, flattening the figures. On the other hand, the brilliant color has been restored. Whether you like the colors of the drapery or not, Michelangelo's modeling of the human form is incredible. *The Creation of Adam* and the temptation and fall of Adam and Eve are the most famous scenes. Michelangelo also painted a terrifying and powerful *Last Judgment* on the end wall. The ceilings' frescoes dwarf the frescoes on the other walls, yet they are by famous 15th-century Tuscan and Umbrian artists: Botticelli, Perugino, Ghirlandaio, and Pinturicchio, among others.

The light is at its best in the morning; try to schedule your visit for that time. Binoculars or even a hand mirror will help you appreciate the Sistine ceiling better; your neck tires long before you can take it all in. Just think how poor Michelangelo must have felt while painting it flat on his back atop a tower of scaffolding!

Note: Visiting the entire museum complex in one day is impossible (do not even think of following it up with a visit to St. Peter's). **Four color-coded itineraries** (A, B, C, or D), take you to the highlights of the museums. They range from one and a half to five hours, and all end at the Sistine Chapel. You can pick and choose according to your personal taste: Perhaps you're fascinated by ancient Egypt and are only marginally interested in paintings; maybe you prefer to view African and Asian art and the frescoed apartments. Whatever you do, we feel that the audio guide is essential (rental: 5.50€/$7.15); it discusses over 300 artworks; select what you want to hear by pressing a work's label number.

The museums charge no admission on the last Sunday of each month, but the crowds are unbelievable, especially in good weather. We recommend paying a visit during a less busy time; after all, you don't know whether you'll have time to come back.

We strongly recommend booking a guided tour, even if you are not the guided-tour type, and particularly if you are visiting during high season. It is the only way to avoid the huge lines to enter the museums (people sometimes line up hours before opening time). The two-hour tour includes Raphael's Rooms and the Sistine Chapel, and it is well worth the money: you'll breeze through the crowds to your desired attraction without further ado. Book in advance (one month to one week), by fax only, at **06-69885100.** You will receive a fax confirmation that grants you access to the "Guided Tour" special ticket booth (main Museums gate, Viale Vaticano, right-hand side line).

Proper attire is required to access the museums; see note at the end of the St. Peter's Basilica entry.

See map p. 167. Viale Vaticano, northeast of St. Peter's Basilica. ☎ *06-69883332. Reservations for guided tours 06-69884676.* www.vatican.va. *Admission: 13€ ($17) adults, 8€ ($10) children under 14; free last Sun of each month. Audio guide: 5.50€ ($7.15). Open: Jan 7 to mid-Mar and Nov 2–Dec 24 Mon–Sat 8:45 a.m.–1:45 p.m.; mid-Mar to Oct and Dec 27–Jan 6 Mon–Fri 8:45 a.m.–4:45 p.m. and Sat 8:45 a.m.–1:45 p.m. Last admission 85 minutes before closing. Closed Catholic holidays (Jan 1 and 6; Feb 11; Mar 19; Easter and Easter Monday; May 1 and Ascension Thursday; Corpus Christi Day in June and June 29; Aug 15 and 16; Nov 1; Dec 8, 25 and 26).*

The Vatican Museums

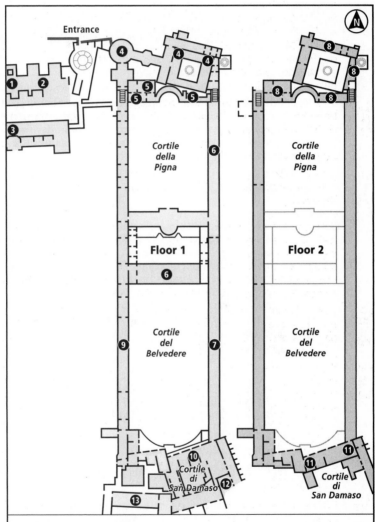

Borgia Apartments **10**
Chapel of Nicholas V **12**
Chiaramonti Museum (Antiquity) **6**
Epigraphy **7**
Ethnological Missionary Museum **1**
Gallery of Candelabra (Antiquity) **9**
Gregorian Egyptian Museum **5**

Gregorian Etruscan Museum **8**
Gregorian Roman
   and Greek collection **2**
Pio-Clementino Museum (Antiquity) **4**
Picture Gallery (Pinacoteca) **3**
Raphael's Rooms (Stanze di Raffaello) **11**
Sistine Chapel **13**

Finding More Cool Things to See and Do

The list of world famous attractions in Rome is so long that hurried tourists often overlook lesser-known sights. Yet so many of them are well worth a visit. Here are a few of our favorites, organized by type.

For art gallery lovers

Painters from all over the world have worked in Rome over the centuries, and their works feature an astounding number of private and public collections around the city. All of the biggies we review in the first part of this chapter have been reorganized and modernized, but not all of the second-tier destinations have yet had the same luck — some remain dusty and old-fashioned.

Colonna Gallery (Galleria Colonna)
Trevi

Reopened after a long closure and completely restored, this is the private gallery of the noble Roman family Colonna, housed in the *palazzo* where some of the family still lives. This is why the gallery is open Saturday only, but seeing it is worth a special effort. The visit includes some of the actual apartments, such as the **Appartamento Principessa Isabelle** in the 15th-century wing, splendidly decorated with frescoes by Pinturicchio (Sala della Fontana) and a collection of paintings by Flemish masters, including such artists as Jan Brueghel the Elder. The 17th-century wing — the actual gallery — is a baroque extravaganza of works of art and precious furnishings, including masterpieces by Lotto, Tiziano, Rubens, and Guercino, among others. *Note:* Travelers with disabilities enter from the main gate.

See map p. 142. Piazza Santi Apostoli 66 (public entrance Via della Pilotta 17). ☎ 06-6784350. www.galleriacolonna.it. Bus: 61, 62, 63, 80 to Piazza San Silvestro. Admission: 7€ ($9.10) adults, 5.50€ ($7.15) children 10 and up, travelers with disabilities, and seniors 60 and older. Open: Sat 9 a.m.–1 p.m. Closed Aug.

Corsini Gallery (Galleria Nazionale d'Arte Antica di Palazzo Corsini)
Trastevere

This lesser-known gallery is a little gem. Located below the Janiculum Hill by Trastevere, it is the only 18th-century picture gallery that has survived intact. Created by Cardinal Neri Maria Corsini, nephew of Pope Clement XII, it was donated, complete with most of the furnishings, to the Italian State in 1883. The painting collection includes works by Italian masters such as Beato Angelico, Andrea del Sarto, and Caravaggio, as well as foreign artists, including some of the best Dutch painters of the period, including Rubens and Van Dyck. Scattered among the rooms you'll also find a number of sculpture masterpieces, of which the most impressive are the first century B.C. *Coppa Corsini* (carved in solid silver), and the

Trono Corsini, an Etruscan-inspired ancient Roman sculpture from the late Republic age.

Via della Lungara 10. ☎ *06-68802323; reservations* ☎ *06-32810. Bus: 23, 44, 56, 60, 65, 75, 170 to Lungotevere. Admission: 4€ ($5.20). Open: Sept–June Tues–Sun 8:30 a.m.– 7:30 p.m.; July–Aug Tues–Sun 8:30 a.m.–2 p.m. Ticket booth closes 30 minutes earlier. Closed Jan 1, May 1, and Dec 25.*

Doria Pamphilj Gallery (Galleria Doria Pamphilj)
Navona/Pantheon

This is the place to come if you want to know what it was like to live in an 18th-century Roman palace. Still the residence of the aristocratic Doria Pamphilj family, it admits the public to the picture gallery and historical apartments. The *palazzo* houses one of Rome's most important private art collections; its lavish apartments abound with tapestries, beautiful furnishings, and art. The gallery holds some superb artwork, including paintings by Filippo Lippi, Raphael, Caravaggio, Tiziano, and our favorite, Velázquez's portrait of Pope Innocent X. The gallery schedules classical music concerts on selected evenings; combine one with a visit to the galleries (check the Web site or with the tourist office for a schedule).

See map p. 142. Piazza del Collegio Romano 1/A, off Via del Corso. ☎ *06-6797323.* www.doriapamphilj.it. *Bus: 62, 116, 117 or 119. Admission: 8€ ($10) including audio guides; 12€ ($16) with the concert. Open: Fri–Wed 10 a.m.–5 p.m. Closed Jan 1, Easter Sunday, May 1, Aug 15, and Dec 25.*

Spada Gallery (Galleria Spada)
Campo de' Fiori

The gorgeous 16th-century **Palazzo Spada** houses Italy's State Council, and for a long time only a small number of the privileged could enjoy the unique art inside. Fortunately for all of us common mortals, it finally partly opened to the public, and we can now admire some of the riches inside. The elegant inner courtyard allows access to the beautiful library, where you can admire the unique **Galleria della Perspettiva** designed by **Borromini** (Borromini's Perspective) — a magnificent corridor in trompe l'oeil style, which appears to be some 35 m (1,050 ft) long but is actually only 8m (24 ft). The rich picture gallery is on the upper floor; its four rooms display a collection of works focusing mostly on 17th-century artists, including **Guido Reni, Guercino,** and **Tiziano.** It is hung in Renaissance style, just as it was when Cardinal Bernadino Spada acquired many of the works: The paintings hang against walls that are richly decorated, gilded, and painted. We find particularly interesting some works by women: **Lavinia Fontana** (1552–1614) and **Artemisia Gentileschi** (1593–1652).

See map p. 142. Piazza Capo di Ferro 13, off Piazza Farnese. ☎ *06-6832409. Bus: 116. Admission: 5€ ($6.50). Open: Tues–Sun 8:30 a.m.–7:30 p.m. Ticket office closes 30 minutes earlier. Closed Jan 1, May 1, and Dec 25.*

For museum buffs

If you love museums, Rome is the perfect destination for you. The problem, if any, is that there are too many to take in on a single visit, unless you're staying for weeks or months. The advantage is that you can find a museum to satisfy everyone's taste and special interests. Here are a few suggestions in addition to the must-see choices in the previous section.

Decorative Arts Museum (Museo delle Arti Decorative)
Via Veneto

Also called the Boncompagni-Ludovisi Museum (after the donors), this museum opened in 1995 in a villa donated by the heirs of Prince Andrea Boncompagni in 1972. The rich collection — mostly from donations by famous artists and collectors — illustrates the evolution of decorative arts in Italy from the end of the 18th century to the present through splendid furnishings and artistic glass windows. Besides a permanent core, the rest of the collection is displayed in rotating thematic exhibitions. One section of the museum is dedicated to haute couture and costumes, based on donations from such famous names as Valentino, Lancetti, and Galitzine.

See map p. 142. Via Boncompagni 18. ☎ *06-42824074.* www.gnam.arti. beniculturali.it. *Bus: 62, 63. Admission: Free. Open: Tues–Sun 9 a.m.–7 p.m. Closed Jan 1, May 1, and Dec 25.*

Jewish Museum and Ghetto (Museo Ebraico)
Teatro Marcello

The Jewish community has played an important role on the shaping of Rome's culture. Many are the traits that exhibit Jewish influence, not least in the cuisine; where would we be without the delicious *carciofi alla giudia* (deep-fried Roman artichokes)! The ruling Catholic Church segregated the Jewish population in the **ghetto** (gated area) in the 16th century, something Romans are not proud of. During the Nazi occupation, many priests and Gentile citizens risked their lives to harbor those targeted by the Germans. Housed in a synagogue, the museum reopened in 2005 after lengthy renovations. It traces the history of the local community. The tour includes a visit to two temples, Tempio Maggiore and Tempio Spagnolo, both housing furnishings from the Ghetto's five original synagogues, which were demolished in 1908. The synagogue is also the meeting point for guided tours of the Ghetto organized by the local cultural association. You can sign up at the museum for the one-hour tour, which costs 8€ ($10) for adults, 5€ ($6.50) for students.

See map p. 142. Tempio Maggiore, Lungotevere Cenci. ☎ *06-68400661.* www.museo ebraico.roma.it. *Tram: 8. Bus: 23, 63, 271, and 630. Admission: 7.50€ ($9.75); children under 10 and visitors with disabilities free. Open: June 16–Sept 15 Sun–Thurs 10 a.m.–7 p.m.; Fri 10 a.m.–4 p.m.; Sept 16–June 15 Sun–Thurs 10 a.m.–5 p.m.; Fri 9 a.m.–2 p.m. Visits by guided tours every hour, included in admission price. Closed Jan 1, Aug 15, and Jewish holidays (see museum's Web site).*

Museum of the City of Rome (Museo di Roma)
Piazza Navona and Trastevere

Housed in the 18th-century Palazzo Braschi, off gorgeous Piazza Navona, this museum reopened in 2002 after being closed for 15 years. Thanks to an $8-million restoration, the *palazzo* and its grand staircase — both justly celebrated for their unique architectural quality — have been returned to their baroque splendor. The collection covers the cultural, social, and artistic life of the city from the Middle Ages to the first half of the 20th century, based on paintings, engravings, sculpture and decorative art. Interesting temporary exhibitions are often on display as well.

A branch of this museum in Trastevere specializes on Roman folklore. It is usually a hit with children, who love the scenes re-creating typical moments of life in bygone Rome. There are only few of those, though, and the rest of the collection is better suited to a more mature audience who will appreciate the collection of drawings, watercolors, and paintings.

See map p. 142. Piazza Navona Branch: Via di San Pantaleo 10; ☎ *06-67108346;* www. museodiroma.comune.roma.it; *open: Tues–Sun 9 a.m.–7 p.m.; admission: 6.20€ ($8); Trastevere branch: Piazza di Sant'Egidio 1/b;* ☎ *06-5899359; open: Tues–Sun 10 a.m.–8 p.m.; admission: 2.60€ ($3.40). Both branches closed Jan 1, May 1, and Dec 25.*

National Museum of Musical Instruments (Museo Nazionale degli Strumenti Musicali)
Colosseo

Even if you aren't a musician, you'll love the incredible variety of instruments — some of them true works of art — in this wonderful museum. Begun with the private collection of the Italian tenor Evan Gorga (he was the first Rodolfo in Puccini's *La Bohème* in 1896), it now consists of more than 3,000 pieces stretching from antiquity to the 19th century. Among the showstoppers is a piano built in 1722 by the inventor of the piano, Bartolomeo Cristofori. Also on display are a beautiful harpsichord built in Leipzig in 1537 by Hans Müller, and a trumpet from 1461. We found most interesting the small ancient Greek and Roman collection including a few actual instruments and a number of objects depicting musical scenes. If you're a fan of musical instruments, schedule at least an hour for your visit.

See map p. 142. Piazza Santa Croce in Gerusalemme 9a, left of the church. ☎ *06-7014796.* www.museostrumentimusicali.it. *Metro: A to San Giovanni. Bus: 87, 117, 186, 360, 649. Tram: 3, 13. Admission 4€ ($5.20); more for special exhibits. Open: Tues–Sun 8:30 a.m.–7:30 p.m. Ticket booth closes 30 minutes earlier. Closed Jan 1, and Dec 25.*

Wax Museum (Museo delle Cere)
Trevi

The third most famous European wax museums (after London's Madame Tussaud's and Paris's Grevin) opened in 1958. The continually growing collection now includes more than 250 life-sized figures, faithful portraits of politicians, artists, and athletes complete with perfectly manufactured clothing (particularly impressive in the historical figures). Some are displayed in perfectly reconstructed situations, including furnishings and audience. In addition to people, the collection includes a section on capital punishment; the best-known instruments of execution have been reproduced with care. Well suited for young visitors is the children's section, where the display includes scale reproductions of dinosaur species, as well as favorite fairy tale characters such as Sleeping Beauty and Snow White.

See map p. 142. Piazza Santi Apostoli 67. ☎ 06-6796482. Bus: 64. Admission: 6€ ($7.80). Open: Daily 9 a.m.–8 p.m.

For serious antiquity lovers

Rome was the cradle of the Roman Empire, and mementoes from the ancient civilization in various levels of repair are everywhere. Ruins are so numerous that you would need months to explore them all. In addition to the "biggies" we list in the first part of this chapter, here are some must-see destinations and personal favorites. If you're interested in archaeology and the ancient world, one good way to get a general overview and to move from one attraction to the other is to use the **Archeobus** (see "Seeing Rome by Guided Tour," later in this chapter).

Appian Way Archaeological Park (Parco Archeologico dell'Appia Antica)

This beautiful park starts beyond the Caracalla Baths, near the Aventino, and stretches for several miles to the south. Here you can walk over an original section of what the ancient Romans called the **Regina Viarum (Queen of Roads).** Started in 312 B.C. as the highway to Capua, this was the first and most important Roman consular road, which was progressively extended to reach Benevento (233km/146 miles to the southeast), then Taranto (an extra 281km/176 miles), and finally Brindisi (another 70km/40 miles), at the tip of the Italian peninsula. It was on this road that St. Peter, in flight from Rome, had his vision of Jesus (a church stands where Peter asked, *"Domine quo vadis?"* or "Lord, where am I going?") and turned back toward his martyrdom. The street is still paved with the original large, flat basalt stones and lined with the remains of villas, tombs, and monuments against the background of the beautiful countryside. Besides the **Catacombs of St. Callixtus** (see listing earlier in this chapter), we think the most interesting attractions in the park are the **Mausoleum of Cecilia Metella** (Via Appia Antica 161), a first century B.C. gentlewoman whose mausoleum was integrated into the fortification of a medieval castle, and the impressive **Villa of the Quintili** (see listing later in this section). Another interesting archaeological attraction is **Maxentius Circus,** where you can see the mausoleum and the ruins of the arena built by the Emperor Maxentius in honor of his son Romulus, as well as the ruins of the emperor's residence (Via Appia Antica 153; ☎ 06-7801324; Tues–Sun winter 9 a.m.–5 p.m., summer 9 a.m.–1 p.m.; admission: 2.60€/$3.40).

It is possible but cumbersome to reach the park by public transportation, and its attractions lay quite a distance from each other. The best way to visit this park and its attractions is on the **Archeobus** (see "Seeing Rome by Guided Tour," later in this chapter) or by renting bicycles at the park visitor center **Cartiera Latina** (Via Appia Antica 42) or at the **Bar Caffe dell'Appia Antica** (Via Appia Antica 175). Bikes rent for 3€ ($3.60) per hour or 10€ ($13) for the day.

See map p. 174. Via Appia Antica. Park: ☎ *06-5130682.* www.parcoappiaantica. org. *Bus: 118, 218. Admission: Free. Open: Daily. Archeological sites:* ☎ *06-39967700 (Mon–Sat 9 a.m.–1:30 p.m. and 2:30–5 p.m.), or* www.pierreci.it *for reservations.* www.archeorm.arti.beniculturali.it. *Metro: A to Colli Albani and then bus 660. Admission: 6€ ($7.80) with the Appia Antica Card, including Caracalla Baths, Villa of the Quintili, and Mausoleum of Cecilia Metella. Open: Tues–Sun 9 a.m. to one hour before sunset. Closed Jan 1, May 1, and Dec 25*

Ara Pacis Augustae
Piazza Navona

This monumental altar (38 ft. × 34.8 ft.) was erected in 9 B.C. to celebrate the Augustan Peace. By securing the frontiers of the empire (particularly in Spain and Gaul), Augustus established a safe environment for commerce and cultural exchange that brought the Roman culture to its highest level of development. The altar is entirely carved in marble, covered with reliefs of great beauty. Long closed to the public, it is finally visible again thanks to the completion of the much-debated new architectural enclosure designed by architect Richard Meier. The result of the expensive, lengthy project is satisfactory insofar as the new enclosure does protect the monument and facilitate its enjoyment by visitors, but we are not sure it was worth the price.

See map p. 142. Lungotevere in Augusta. ☎ *06-82059127.* www.arapacis.it. *Admission: 6.50€ ($8.45). Guided visit 4.50€ ($5.90); available by reservation only. Audio guide 3.50€ ($4.60), or download free podcast from museum's Web site. Open: Tues–Sun 9 a.m.–7 p.m. Dec 24 and 31 9 a.m.–2 p.m. Closed Jan 1, May 1, and Dec 25.*

Barracco Museum (Museo Barracco)
Navona/Pantheon

Housed in a 16th-century *palazzo,* this lesser-known museum displays the private collection of Baron Giovanni Barracco, which he donated to the city at his death in 1904. He conceived his collection as a panoramic history of ancient sculpture, and includes superb examples of Assyro-Babylonian, Egyptian, Greek, and Roman art. It just reopened after several years of restoration and is much improved. You'll need about one and a half hours for a good visit.

See map p. 142. Corso Vittorio Emanuele II 166A. ☎ *06-82059127 or 06-68806848.* www.museobarracco.it. *Bus: 40, 30, 62, 64, 70, 81, 87, 116, and 492. Admission 3€ ($3.90); 2€ ($2.60) extra for special exhibits. Open: Tues–Sun 9 a.m.–7 p.m.; Dec 24 and Dec 31 9 a.m.–2 p.m. Ticket booth closes 30 minutes earlier. Closed Jan 1, May 1, and Dec 25.*

Appian Way Archaeological Park

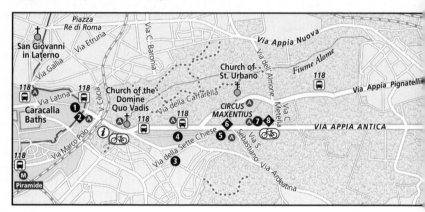

Crypta Balbi
Teatro Marcello

Part of the National Roman Museum, this interesting space shows a slice of Rome's history. The archeological excavations have revealed how a covered portico dating from the first century A.D. was used and changed during the decline of the Roman Empire and the early Middle Ages. The three-floor exhibit displays many findings highlighting everyday life during this period, and you can visit the large archeological area below, walking through the crypt and the adjacent structures, including an ancient water reservoir.

See map p. 142. Via delle Botteghe Oscure 31. ☎ *06-39967700 (Mon–Sat 9 a.m.–1:30 p.m. and 2:30–5 p.m.), or* www.pierreci.it *for reservations.* www.archeorm. arti.beniculturali.it. *Bus: 30, 40, 62, 63, 64, 70, 87, 119, 186, 492, 630. Tram: 8. Admission: 7€/$9.10; admission includes National Roman Museum of Palazzo Altemps, Palazzo Massimo alle Terme, and Diocletian Baths. Open: Tues–Sun 9 a.m.–7:45 p.m.; Dec 24 and 31 9 a.m.–5 p.m. Closed Jan 1 and Dec 25.*

Diocletian Baths (Terme di Diocleziano)
Repubblica

This grandiose complex was built between A.D. 298 and 305 and covered a surface area of almost 1.5 million square feet! If you look at today's Rome map, the baths extended from Via Torino to Via Volturno, and from Piazza dei Cinquecento to Via XX Settembre; this should give you an idea of how enormous they were. Dismembered by the overlaying of newer structures through the centuries, they require you to use your imagination to recreate the grandeur. **Piazza della Repubblica** covers the imprint of what originally was the main *esedra* (semicircular exercise area) at the back of the complex. The church of **Santa Maria degli Angeli** (Piazza della Repubblica; ☎ **06-4880812;** free admission) occupies the central monumental halls and the former *tepidarium* (warming hall). The church, with its attached

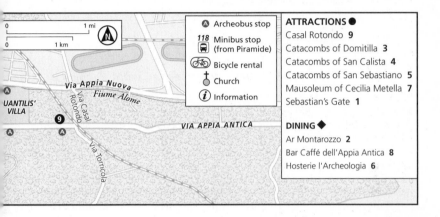

ATTRACTIONS ●
Casal Rotondo **9**
Catacombs of Domitilla **3**
Catacombs of San Calista **4**
Catacombs of San Sebastiano **5**
Mausoleum of Cecilia Metella **7**
Sebastian's Gate **1**

DINING ◆
Ar Montarozzo **2**
Bar Caffé dell'Appia Antica **8**
Hosterie l'Archeologia **6**

Map legend: Ⓐ Archeobus stop; *118* Ⓑ Minibus stop (from Piramide); 🚲 Bicycle rental; ✝ Church; ⓘ Information

monastery and cloisters, was realized in the 16th century by Michelangelo, who made a point of conserving much of the original structures. The church was enlarged and redecorated to its present state by Luigi Vanvitelli in the 18th century. The monastery, with its beautiful main cloister, today houses the **Museum** proper (Viale E. de Nicola 78; ☎ **06-39967700** Mon–Sat 9 a.m.–1:30 p.m. and 2:30–5 p.m.; www.pierreci.it for reservations; www.archeorm.arti.beniculturali.it.; admission: 7€/$9.10, includes National Roman Museum of Palazzo Altemps, Palazzo Massimo alle Terme, and Cripta Balbi; Tues–Sun 9 a.m.–7:45 p.m.; Dec 24 and 31 9 a.m.–5 p.m.; closed Jan 1 and Dec 25). The museum exhibits include sculpture and a rich collection of epigraphy, or inscriptions found in the various archaeological sites in Rome, mostly carved in stone. The Octagonal Hall (see listing later in this section) was probably a *frigidarium* (cooling area). The other surviving structures from the huge bath complex have been integrated in the other buildings around Piazza della Repubblica, and you can still see bits and pieces of their walls.

See map p. 142. Piazza della Repubblica. Metro: Line B to Repubblica, Line A and B to Termini.

Montemartini Annex (Centrale Montemartini)
Testaccio

When the **Capitoline Museums'** Palazzo Nuovo was restored, much of the museums' Greek and Roman sculpture collection moved to this new site, the first electrical plant built in Rome, in 1912. An intriguing, beautiful setting for the art collection, it contains over 400 sculptures; among our favorite pieces are an imposing fifth century B.C. **sculptural ensemble** depicting a battle scene between Greeks and Amazons, the elegant **Esquilin Venus** tying her hair before bathing, and a huge, splendid **mosaic with hunting scenes** (6m × 12m/20 × 40 ft.) recovered from one of the ancient Roman imperial residences. Plan to spend about an hour here.

Via Ostiense 106. ☎ *06-5748042.* www.centralemontemartini.org. *Metro: Line B to Pyramide; walk down Via Ostiense. Bus: 23 to Via Ostiense. Tram: 3 to Piazza di Porta San Paolo (Stazione Ostiense, Piramide). Admission: 4.50€ ($5.80). Open: Tues–Sun 9 a.m.–7 p.m.; Dec 24 and Dec 31 9 a.m.–2 p.m. Ticket booth closes 30 minutes earlier. Closed Jan 1, May 1, and Dec 25.*

Museum of Roman Civilization (Museo della Civiltá Romana)
EUR

Located outside Rome's historic center (but well connected by public transportation), this interesting museum focuses on the history of ancient Rome and the spread of its civilization throughout the world. The big attraction, and a favorite with kids, is an impressive model of Imperial Rome, a perfect reconstruction in 1:250 scale of Rome at the time of Emperor Constantine, measuring 200 sq. m (2,150 sq. ft.), that was 30 years in the making. You'll see all the great buildings intact, which will help you make sense of all the broken columns and holes in the ground elsewhere around the city. Other models display facets of daily life in antiquity — a good complement. You can easily spend two hours here.

Piazza Giovanni Agnelli 10. ☎ *06-5926041.* www.museociviltaromana.it. *Metro: EUR Fermi. Admission: 6.50€ ($8.45). Open: Tues–Sat 9 a.m.–2 p.m. Closed Jan 1, May 1, and Dec 25.*

Octagonal Hall (Aula Ottagona)
Repubblica

Part of the Diocletian Baths (see listing earlier in this section), this is a beautiful example of ancient Roman architecture, completely preserved, including its roof. Adapted into a planetarium in 1928, it is now accessible through a separate entrance from the rest of the complex. Inside is an important sculpture collection originating from several of Rome's bath complexes. Famous statues here include the two **bronzes,** one of a Roman general of the second century and another of a sitting fighter of the first century. A staircase leads to the original level of the floor, under which have been discovered remains of buildings on which the baths were constructed.

See map p. 142. Via G. Romita 8. ☎ *06-39967700.* www.pierreci.it *for reservations.* www.archeorm.arti.beniculturali.it. *Metro: Line A to Repubblica; Bus: 60, 62, or Minibus 116T to Piazza della Repubblica. Admission: Free. Open: Mon–Sat 9 a.m.–1:30 p.m. and 2:30–5 p.m. Closed Jan 1, May 1, and Dec 25.*

Triumphal Column of Marcus Aurelius
(Colonna di Marco Aurelio)
Navona/Pantheon

At the center of beautiful Piazza Colonna, this commemorative column is an imposing sight, 25m (83 ft.) tall and completely decorated with bas-reliefs. The column was erected in honor of Marcus Aurelius, the enlightened emperor who ruled from A.D. 161 to 180, and the reliefs recount his exploits in battles against the German tribes. A statue of the emperor once adorned the top, but in the 16th century, Pope Sixtus V replaced it with the statue of St. Paul that you see today. The **Palazzo Chigi,** on one side of the piazza, is the residence of the Italian prime minister, so don't be surprised if you see intense guys standing around with submachine guns.

See map p. 142. Piazza Colonna, off Via del Corso at Via del Tritone. Bus: 62, 85, or Minibus 116, 117, or 119 to Piazza Colonna.

Villa of the Quintili (Villa dei Quintili)
Park of the Appia Antica

Recently opened after lengthy (and ongoing) excavations, this was the largest private villa in the Roman suburbs. It was the property of the two brothers Quintili, who were consuls in A.D. 151. The structure was enlarged when it became the property of the Emperor Commodus, who loved the quiet and the villa's thermal baths. For centuries, it was a mine of statuary for treasure hunters; many of those works are now on display in the great museums of the world. For its sheer size — it extends between the Appia Antica and the Appia Nuova — the site is quite impressive; it also affords beautiful views of the Roman countryside.

See map p. 174. Via Appia Nuova 1092. ☎ 06-39967700 (Mon–Sat 9 a.m.–1:30 p.m. and 2:30–5 p.m.). www.pierreci.it *for reservations.* www.archeorm.arti. beniculturali.it. *Admission: 6€ ($7.80). Includes admission to Caracalla Baths and Mausoleum of Cecilia Metella. Open: Mon–Sat 9 a.m.–1:30 p.m. and 2:30–5 p.m.*

For families with kids

Kids of all ages love imagining lost civilizations and treasure hunts, and because Rome is essentially one big archaeological site, children will find much to love about the city. Throughout this chapter, we have used the Kid Friendly icon to indicate the best attractions for children. Here, we suggest a few more places and activities that are particularly suited for children or teens. In addition to our suggestions below, **bicycling** can be a great way to enjoy your visit. While riding in Rome's busy streets can be dangerous and unpleasant, we recommend taking the bikes to explore the Tiber banks (see "Boats down the Tiber," below), Villa Borghese Park (see listing later in this section), and the Appian Way Archeological Park (see previous section). The entire family can rent bikes at each of these places. The city has been promoting recreational bicycling (as well as walking and jogging) and claims Rome currently boasts 150 km (90 miles) of bicycle paths. A map of biking and walking trails is available at www.assessoratoambiente.it.

Boats down the Tiber
San Pietro

Sailing down the Tiber is a wonderful way to experience Rome. The **Compagnia di Navigazione Ponte San Angelo** (☎ 06-6789361; www. battellidiroma.it) operates boat service between **Ponte Duca d'Aosta** (right bank) and **Isola Tiberina** (Calata Anguillara on the right bank), with

Parent Savers

If your kids are getting tired of art and churches and you've exhausted our suggestions, here are a few aces in the hole that can be of interest to everybody.

Fire Brigade Museum (Museo dei Vigili del Fuoco): This little-known museum in the Testaccio area is not very big but is extremely interesting. Its ambitious aim is to detail the history of firefighting in Rome from antiquity (about the age of Emperor Augustus) to today. Besides objects and photos, displays include media installations that incorporate videos and special optical and sound effects. (Via Marmorata 15; ☎ 06-5746808; museoromavf@vfdcf.it; Tram: 3; admission: free; Mon–Sat 9–7 p.m.)

Museum of Medicine (Museo Storico dell'Arte Sanitaria): Not far from Castel Sant'Angelo and St. Peter's, this unusual museum provides a good break for older kids and adults. Housed in the working hospital of Santo Spirito, it fills nine separate spaces with historical collections of surgical instruments (some from ancient Roman and medieval times), anatomical tables, and paintings. You'll also visit a typical 17th-century pharmacy and chemist-alchemist lab. Some gruesome objects are on display, including embryos and skeletons illustrating various birth defects. Volunteers lead the mandatory guided tours; make a reservation. Along one of the exterior walls, look for the *rota,* the revolving mechanism where parents could abandon unwanted babies to the care of the sisters in the hospital. (See map p. 142; Lugotevere in Sassia 3; ☎ 06-68352353 or 06-6893051; Fax 06-6833485; admission: 3€/$3.90; Mon, Wed, and Fri 10 a.m.–noon; closed Jan 1, May 1, August, and Dec 25)

Villa Celimontana: On the Celio hill, behind the Golden House of Nero (see listing earlier in this chapter), the grounds of this aristocratic villa have been turned into a public park. A little island of peace in the bustling center of Rome, it has a couple of playgrounds where your tots will be delighted to take a break. It also makes an excellent spot for a quiet family picnic (remember not to litter; you risk heavy fines).

Cat Sanctuary (Torre Argentina): Rome's stray cats, a favorite subject for photographers looking for a special perspective on familiar sights, have taken refuge in these ruins since time immemorial. Here you can meet the furry citizens up close and personal. A short distance from Piazza Navona and the Ghetto, the sanctuary provides a unique insight on Rome's oldest archeological complex, which houses the ruins of four temples dating to 400–300 B.C. Volunteers founded the nonprofit organization that cares for the resident felines. You can visit the shelter and make friends with some of the 250 occupants, and pick up a cat-themed present in the gift shop. (Largo di Torre Argentina, at Via Florida; www.romancats.com.)

Astronomy Museum and Planetarium: In the same building as the Museum of Roman Civilizations (see listing earlier in this chapter), this theater presents an interesting show on the solar system. (Piazza Giovanni Agnelli 10; ☎ 06-82077304; admission: 6.20€ ($8), combo ticket with museum: 8.30€/$10.80; Tues–Fri 9 a.m.–2 p.m. and Sat–Sun 9 a.m.–7 p.m.)

intermediary stops at **Ponte Sant'Angelo** and **Ponte Cavour** (by Piazza Augusto Imperatore). The ride is not only idyllic — far from noise and traffic — and fun, but also a convenient and inexpensive means of transportation, provided that you need to go somewhere along the Tiber. Do not worry if you arrive at a deserted and locked dock. The only staffed location is the Ponte Sant'Angelo, where you'll find the main reservation office; all the other docks are opened by the boat crew when they arrive. Schedules are posted on a board outside and on the Web site.

A recent offering combines the boat ride with a bicycle rental, allowing you to go by boat and bike back along the banks; you can rent the bike at Isola Tiberina and bring it on the boat with you, and then ride back (Bike&Boat; ☎ **06-45495816** or 346-0114697). The best stretch is between Isola Tiberina and Ponte Cavour (a 35-minute ride); while the next leg is a more boring 25-minute ride to Ponte Duca d'Aosta. Ponte Cavour is in the heart of the historic center, but Ponte d'Aosta has little tourist appeal. From there your best bet is to bicycle back, take a bus back, or pay again for the return trip by boat.

The same company also organizes special boat tours (see "Seeing Rome by Guided Tour," later in this chapter), including a wonderful cruise to Ostia Antica, which allows you to get to Rome's ancient seaport in much the same way as the ancient Romans (see Chapter 14).

See map p. 142. Ponte Sant'Angelo, across Castel Sant'Angelo (dock is on the left bank of the Tiber). ☎ *06-6789361 for info and reservations. E-mail:* info@ battellidiroma.it. *Fare: Single trip Mon–Fri 4 p.m. 1€ ($1.30) and Fri–Sun 4 p.m. 3€ ($3.90); single trip plus bicycle rental for the day Mon–Fri 4 p.m. 12€ ($16) and Fri–Sun 4 p.m. 15€ ($20); lower fares for shorter rentals.*

Capuchin Cemetery *(Cimitero dei Cappuccini)*
Via Veneto

In the crypt of the **Chiesa dell'Immacolata Concezione** is a fascinating, if ghoulish, sight. A Capuchin monk used the bones of some 3,700 of his brothers to create a monument that reminds us — literally — that "in the midst of life, we are in the midst of death." Skeletal pieces decorate the ceilings and walls of five underground chapels, creating interesting patterns and designs (for example, rows of spinal vertebrae trace the vaults, while other bones make chandeliers and frame niches displaying robed skeletons). *Note:* This may be a "kid-friendly" sight if you have a teenager, but it would disturb and frighten smaller children.

See map p. 142. Via Veneto 27, before the U.S. embassy. ☎ *06-4871185.* www. cappucciniviaveneto.it. *Metro: Barberini. Bus: 62, 116, and 119 to Largo Tritone. Admission: Recommended donation 4€ ($5.20). Open: Fri–Wed 9 a.m. to noon and 3–6 p.m.*

Luna Park
EUR

Located outside the city center, this huge amusement park (it covers 70,000 sq m/754,000 sq ft) has been attracting visitors of all ages since 1953.

A complete overhaul has taken away the feeling of stepping back into the 1970s, and its 70-plus attractions are all spiffed up. It is famous for its several roller coasters, including one of the largest in the world, and its giant panoramic (Ferris) wheel.

Via delle Tre Fontane. ☎ *06-5914401.* www.luneur.it. *Metro: Eur Magliana, then take a taxi 457m (1,500 ft.). Admission: 22€ ($29) adults, 16€ ($21) children under 1.2m (3.94 ft.) and seniors over 65; admission includes unlimited rides. Open: Oct–May Mon–Fri and Sun 11 a.m.–8 p.m., Sat 11 a.m.–11 p.m.; June–Sept Mon–Fri 3 p.m. to midnight and Sat–Sun 11 a.m. to midnight.*

Puppet Shows
Trastevere and Piazza del Popolo

Only two theaters in Rome still perform this beloved form of entertainment: the traditional Neapolitan puppet show featuring Pulcinella, the white-dressed masked character of the Commedia dell'Arte. Performances are in Italian, but you don't really need to understand the dialogue to laugh at Pulcinella bashing the gendarme on his head or doing other silly tricks. The most traditional show is at the **Teatrino delle Marionette** on the Janiculum Hill. The theater is open-air, with a few folding chairs in front of the wooden theater. Shows are canceled in bad weather, and during the week, reservations are required. If you haven't reserved, the weekend is your best bet. The other shows are presented in the newly renovated **Teatrino dei Burattini San Carlino,** a real theater (with sheltered sitting area) in the Pincio Gardens (see listing later in this chapter), presenting a variety of puppet shows. Reservations are required.

See map p. 142. Janiculum Hill: Teatrino delle Marionette, Piazza Garibaldi. ☎ *06-5827767 or 328-2240129. Admission: 5€ ($6.50). Open: Daily 4–7 p.m., Sat–Sun also 10:30 a.m.–1 p.m. Pincio Gardens: Teatrino dei Burattini San Carlino, Viale dei Bambini (near the Water Orologe).* ☎ *06-3335320 or 329-2967328. Admission: 5€ ($6.50). Shows: Sat 4 and 5:30 p.m.; Sun 11 a.m., noon, and 1 and 4:30 p.m. Closed January and August.*

Time Elevator
Trevi

Here is where you come to experience ancient and Renaissance Rome in 5D (tridimensional images plus multisensory effects and motion simulation). The 45-minute show takes you through virtual reconstructions of historical moments (such as the legend of Romulus and Remus and the assassination of Caesar) and monuments (Colosseum, Caracalla Baths, Sistine Chapel, and so on), some of which are rather well made. Two other shows are offered: *Escape to Bane Manor* is a horror show in a haunted house, and *Ode to Life* takes you back to the big bang and has you running with dinosaurs and primitive men. Shows are offered in six languages (through individual Dolby stereo headsets) and you can ask for a static seat if you are not keen on the full effect or suffer from motion sickness. Children less than 1m (3.28 ft.) tall are not admitted.

See map p. 142. Via Santi Apostoli 20. ☎ **06-97746243**. www.timeelevator.it. Metro: Spagna. Bus: 40, 60, 64, 170, and 175 to Piazza Venezia/Via del Corso. Admission: 11€ ($14) adults; 8€ ($10) children under 12 and seniors over 65. Rome shows daily every hour on the half-hour 10:30 a.m.–7:30 p.m.

Villa Borghese Park
Piazza del Popolo

Just steps from Piazza del Popolo, extending north beyond the city walls, is one of Rome's most beautiful parks. It formerly belonged to the aristocratic Borghese family, who donated it to the city. Famous for the **Borghese Gallery** (see listing earlier in this chapter), it is beloved by Romans, who come here to enjoy the greenery on weekends, especially in summer, when the beautiful Roman pines offer relief from the heat. Inside the park you'll find several attractions, including **Piazza di Siena,** a picturesque oval track surrounded by tall pines, used for horse races and particularly for the **Concorso Ippico Internazionale di Roma** (Rome's official international show-jumping competition), held in May (see Chapter 3). Overlooking Piazza di Siena is **Raphael's Pavillion** (Casino di Raffaello), housing a **children's museum** with playrooms (free of charge) and activities (3€/$3.90; by reservation only at the number below) for visitors ages three to ten (☎ **06-82059127;** www.casinadiraffaello.it; Tues–Sun 9 a.m.–7 p.m.). A short distance to the south, you'll find the **Cinema dei Piccoli,** the smallest movie theater in the world. Features include current movies, for younger children in the early afternoon and teenagers in the late afternoon (Viale della Pineta, off Via San Paolo del Brasile; ☎ **06-8553485;** www.cinemadeipiccoli.it; admission: 5€/$6.50; shows: Wed–Fri 5 p.m. and 6:30 p.m., Sat–Sun 3:30 p.m., 5 p.m. and 6:30 p.m.). Going the opposite direction, to the north, you'll find the romantic **Lake Gardens** (the **Laghetto**) around an artificial lake where you can rent a rowboat (the lake is full of turtles; try to spot one). If you want to take advantage of the long bicycle trails, you can **rent bikes** for the entire family as well as four-seat buggies on Via dell'Uccelliera, near the Borghese Gallery; Piazzale M. Cervantes, near the Zoo; Viale J. W. Goethe, off Viale del Museo Borghese leading to the Borghese Gallery; and in the adjoining Pincio Gardens (see listing later in this chapter). If you prefer to see the park without exertion, you can take a ride on the **Trenino,** the little motor train beloved by younger children (departure point: Viale Goethe, near the bike rental mentioned above; admission: 3€/$3.90; operates daily). Check the Web site for the park's other offerings, including Wi-Fi hotspot locations.

See map p. 142. Enter from Piazzale Flaminio, Pincio Gardens, Piazzale San Paolo del Brasile, Via Pinciana, Via Aldrovandi, Via Raimondi, or Piazzale Cervantes. www.villa borghese.it. Bus: 49, 88, 95, 116, 490, and 495. Metro: Spagna or Flaminio. Admission: Free. Open: Park daily 24 hours.

Zoo (Bioparco)
Villa Borghese

Adjoining Villa Borghese Park (see previous listing) to the north, Rome's zoo is very special. Inaugurated in 1911, it was designed following the revolutionary principles of Karl Hagenbeck, the German expert who advocated the use of natural barriers instead of iron cages to keep animals separated from each other — and from the visitors. Visually more attractive than regular zoos, these zoos are not necessarily less stressful for the animals, because the space allotted to each of them is small. The zoo has been reorganized according to newer concepts, drastically reducing the number of species and changing its focus on scientific observation and teaching. Today about 1,000 animals (72 species of mammals, 92 birds, and 54 reptiles), live on the park's 17 hectares (42 acres), including a few members of protected species. The zoo doubles as a botanical garden; you'll also find a restaurant, bar, and picnic areas inside, and a small motor train for rides.

See map p. 142. Piazzale del Giardino Zoologico 1, to the northwest of the Borghese Gallery. ☎ *06-3608211.* www.bioparco.it. *Tram: 3, 19. Bus: Admission: 8.50€ ($11) adults; 6.50€ ($8.45) children under 13; 2.50€ ($3.25) additional for Reptilarium. Open: Oct–Mar daily 9:30 a.m.–5 p.m.; Apr–Sept daily 9:30 a.m.–6 p.m. Last admission one hour earlier.*

For religious-architecture lovers: More great churches

Rome counts 913 churches just in the historic center, ranging from the 8th to the 18th century (many have even older cores). All are lavishly decorated with masterpieces by the dominant artists of the period, and most deserve a visit. We had room to review only a couple in the previous section, but we feel many more deserve to share the top range. You would need years of dedication to achieve the ambitious task of visiting all of them, but here is our selection of the ones you would really regret not seeing.

St. Mary in Cosmedin and Mouth of Truth (Santa Maria in Cosmedin and Bocca della Verità)
Aventino

This Orthodox church is very pretty inside and outside — it's one of the few Roman churches to have escaped baroque "restoration" — but the real attraction is the famous Roman marble carving lying against a wall under its outer porch. The **Bocca della Verità (Mouth of Truth),** a round marble piece with the relief of a head with an open mouth, in all likelihood was an ancient Roman manhole cover. Associated with it is a legend that has made it famous: It is said that if you put your hand inside the mouth while lying, it will bite it off. (Remember the scene with Gregory Peck and Audrey Hepburn from *Roman Holiday?*) Kids get a kick out of putting their hands in the mouth while naughty parents ask tricky questions. Besides, it is a beautiful piece of carving (I wish manhole covers were still so made), and **Piazza Bocca della Verità,** where the church is located, is one of the nicest squares in town. It's at its best during off hours due to the traffic. Two small Roman temples still stand here: The round one is believed to be dedicated to the goddess Vesta, and the other to the twins of Greek mythology, Castor and Pollux.

See map p. 142. Piazza Bocca della Verità. ☎ 06-6781419. Bus: 81. Admission: Free. Open: Daily 7 a.m.–6:30 p.m.

St. Paul's Basilica (Basilica di San Paolo Fuori Le Mura)
San Paolo

This basilica, second in size and artistic importance only to St. Peter's, was built well outside the city walls in what was then the countryside, along the road that leads from Rome to the ancient Roman seaport of Ostia (Via Ostiense). San Paolo is now a modern neighborhood of Rome, well connected to the city center by public transportation. According to tradition, the body of St. Paul was buried here after his martyrdom. As early as the time of Emperor Constantine in the fourth century A.D., a church was built around St. Paul's tomb (still below the high altar). Consecrated in A.D. 324, the basilica was vastly enlarged over the centuries, but it was almost completely destroyed by fire in 1823. Rebuilt with marble salvaged from the original structure, its apse and triumphal arch are original, while the mosaic in the apse is a faithful copy of the 13th-century work, reconstructed with what was salvaged from the fire. The **ciborium** over the altar — a 1285 masterpiece by Arnolfo di Cambio — miraculously escaped the fire. Under the altar is the **sepulcher of St. Paul,** the tomb containing the saint's remains; it's accessible by a staircase. The basilica's interior is vast and impressive, its naves divided by 80 granite columns; the windows may look like stained glass, but they're actually made of translucent alabaster. Our favorite part is the adjacent original **cloister,** and you'd have to go to Sicily to find such distinctively carved and decorated columns of so many diverse patterns.

Via Ostiense 184. ☎ 06-5410341. Metro: Basilica di San Paolo. Bus: 23. Admission: Free. Open: Church daily 7 a.m.–6:30 p.m.; cloister daily 9 a.m.–1 p.m. and 3–6 p.m.

St. Peter in Chains (San Pietro in Vincoli)
Colosseo

This church is named after the two sets of chains, on display in a bronze urn in the crypt, that held St. Peter in Jerusalem and, later, in Rome. According to Catholic Church legend, the chains were miraculously welded together when they touched each other in this church. The 19th-century makeover hides the actual age of this church, which was built in A.D. 439 over an even older church. The 18th- and 19th-century interior decorations may leave you unmoved, and so might the religious relics, but you should not miss the star of the show. Inside, look for a majestic funeral monument. It was designed by **Michelangelo** for Pope Julius II and is graced by one of his most famous masterpieces, his *Moses.* The monument and the church's charming location are reason enough to visit.

See map p. 142. Piazza San Pietro in Vincoli 4. ☎ 06-4882865. Metro: Colosseo or Cavour. Admission: Free. Open: Daily 8 a.m. to noon and 3:30–6 p.m.

A pocketful of change

In Roman churches, the precious frescoes and fragile paintings are usually kept in semi-obscurity, but you don't need to squint to see them. Look for the light box usually positioned on the wall nearby: When you insert a coin or two, a light pops on to illuminate the painting, fresco, or sculpture for a limited amount of time. Before visiting churches, make sure you have a pocketful of coins; it will make a world of difference.

Santa Maria in Aracoeli
Teatro Marcello

Next to Piazza del Campidoglio and off Piazza Venezia, Santa Maria d'Aracoeli is a scenic church standing at the top of a soaring flight of steps (this is the only drawback to a visit: you'll have to climb). One of few surviving medieval churches in Rome, it dates from 1250 and stands on the site of an ancient Roman temple. Two carved rose windows punctuate the austere exterior; inside you'll be rewarded by several works of art. The floor is an excellent example of **Cosmati marblework** (the Cosmati were a family of Roman master stone artists whose signature mosaic marble floors were imitated all over Italy; they worked during the 12th and 13th centuries). Other masterpieces await you in the **Bufalini Chapel,** lavishly decorated with **Pinturicchio's** frescoes, depicting scenes from the life of St. Bernardino of Siena and St. Francis receiving the stigmata.

See map p. 142. Piazza d'Aracoeli. ☎ *06-6798155. Bus: Minibus 117 to Campidoglio; then walk to the right around the Vittorio Emanuele II Monument. Admission: Free. Open: Daily 7 a.m. to noon and 4–7 p.m.*

Santa Maria in Trastevere
Trastevere

Opening on a square graced by an early baroque fountain, this is believed to be the first church officially opened to the public in Rome, making it the first Roman Catholic church in the world. Its age and the uniqueness of the artwork conserved inside make it one of a kind. Founded by Pope Saint Callixtus in the third century A.D., it was enlarged and given its present look in the 12th century with materials from the Caracalla Baths (see listing earlier in this chapter). The facade is decorated with its original mosaic, while the portico is a later, baroque addition. Inside, take time to admire the **Cosmatesque floor** (see previous listing), as well as the richly decorated wooden ceiling (designed by Domenichino in the 17th century). But then you should dedicate your undivided attention to the unique and beautifully preserved **mosaics** decorating the apse. And let your eyes wander over the main altar: they'll find the *Madonna della Clemenza,* a unique painting from the sixth century.

See map p. 142. Piazza Santa Maria in Trastevere. ☎ *06-5814802. Bus: 23. Tram: 8. Admission: Free. Open: Daily 7:30 a.m.–8 p.m.*

Santa Maria Maggiore
Repubblica

This church's history stretches back 1,600 years, and though it has undergone many changes over the centuries, Santa Maria Maggiore remains one of the city's four great basilicas. Commissioned by Pope Sisto III, it was built as a sanctuary for Mary (mother of Jesus) and was originally referred to as Santa Maria della Neve (St. Mary of the Snow) because its outline was drawn in the snow that had miraculously fallen in the summer of A.D. 352. The baroque facade was designed by Ferdinando Fuga, who sandwiched it between two palaces that had been built in the meantime (one in the 17th and the other in the 18th century). It holds a treasure trove of original masterpieces, starting from the unique mosaics on the apse and side walls. The floors are also original from the 12th century: another of the few existing examples of original **Cosmati marblework** (see Santa Maria d'Aracoeli listing, above). The 15th-century coffered wooden ceiling is richly decorated with gold (said to be the first gold brought back from the New World and donated by the Spanish queen). One of the church's main attractions is in the loggia, shading the **13th-century mosaics** preserved from the old facade. Also, inside, look carefully to the right side of the altar for the **tomb of Gian Lorenzo Bernini,** Italy's most important baroque sculptor-architect. In the crypt are relics of what are said to be pieces of Jesus' crib. Inside the church is a little-known architectural masterpiece by Michelangelo (he designed but did not complete it), the **Cappella Sforza;** the small space is elegantly decorated and artificially enlarged by the clever disposition of its angular columns.

See map p. 142. Piazza di Santa Maria Maggiore. ☎ *06-4881094. Metro: Termini; then walk south on Via Cavour. Bus: 70. Admission: Free. Open: Daily 7 a.m.–7 p.m.*

Santa Maria sopra Minerva
Pantheon

The construction of this church started in the eighth century A.D. on the foundation of an ancient temple to Minerva, goddess of wisdom. The present structure, with its elegant pointed arches and blue starred ceiling, dates from 1280, making it the only Gothic church in Rome. You wouldn't know that from the facade, redone, as were so many other churches in Rome, in the 17th century. Inside are many treasures, including Michelangelo's *Cristo Portacroce* in the presbytery, as well as frescoes by **Filippino Lippi** in the Carafa Chapel. The church also houses a great number of tombs, including the painter **Fra Angelico's.** Under the altar are the **relics of St. Catherine of Siena.** On the square in front of the church is the much-photographed **elephant sculpture** that serves as the base for a sixth-century B.C. Egyptian obelisk; conceived by Bernini, the sculpture was executed by somebody else.

See map p. 142. Piazza della Minerva. ☎ *06-6793926. Bus: 62 or 64 to Largo Argentina, or Minibus 116 to Piazza della Minerva. Admission: Free. Open: Daily 7 a.m.–7 p.m.*

Santa Prassede
Repubblica

Another of Rome's very old churches, Santa Prassede was built before the fifth century A.D. and restored in the Middle Ages. Today's entrance dates to that time. Almost nondescript from the outside, inside it abounds with Byzantine **mosaics,** lining the arch over the main altar, the apse, and the entire chapel of **San Zenone.** This unique chapel is considered Rome's most important Byzantine monument. The church is full of other works of art, including a bust of Bishop G. B. Santoni from 1614, an early work by **Gian Lorenzo Bernini** (located by the third column to the right of the main nave).

See map p. 142. Via Santa Prassede 9, off Piazza Santa Maria Maggiore. ☎ *06-4882456. Metro: Termini. Walk south on Via Cavour. Bus: 70. Admission: 2€ ($2.60). Open: Daily 7:30 a.m.–7:30 p.m.*

For secular-architecture lovers: More delightful Roman piazze and palaces

From the Renaissance onward, master architects worked to redesign the Eternal City to match its looks with its destiny. The results were often spectacular and always unique. Here is our roster of the best architectural jewels in Rome and of some unique monuments, besides those previously listed.

Campo de' Fiori
Campo de' Fiori

Surrounded by cafes, restaurants, and bars, the lovely square of Campo de' Fiori boasts many attractions. Its **fruit-and-vegetable market** is one of the city's best and certainly one of the liveliest. Though popular with working people as a lunch spot, the campo is even hotter with young people (both Romans and foreigners) at night. The **central statue of the hooded Giordano Bruno** hints at the more sinister parts of the campo's history — it was the site of executions in the Middle Ages and the Renaissance, and Bruno was burned at the stake here in 1600. Bruno was a philosopher who championed the ideas of such early scientists as Copernicus and maintained such heretical ideas as that of the Earth revolving around the sun.

See map p. 142. Off Via dei Giubbonari, near Largo Argentina. Bus: 116.

Janiculum Hill (Passeggiata del Gianicolo)
Trastevere

Head up the Janiculum hill rising above Trastevere and St. Peter's for the best **panorama** in Rome: the view is breathtaking at any hour, and you'll also find other entertainment. You can have a break at the kiosk bar and your kids can enjoy the merry-go-round and a traditional Neapolitan puppet show (see listing earlier in this chapter). The promenade deserves its fame as the best overlook on Rome (the other famous one, from the

Pincio Gardens, is considered the most romantic; see listing later in this chapter). On the hill is a park graced by a large fountain, a monument to Giuseppe Garibaldi — perhaps the most beloved figure of the 19th-century Italian struggle for self-determination — and a unique equestrian statue of his wife, Anita, likewise a hard-charging revolutionary. Anita's tomb is under the statue. A small kiosk bar offers refreshments throughout the year. During the summer Estate Romana festival (see Chapters 3 and 16), a cocktail bar offers drinks and seafood dinners (www.fontanonedelgianicolo.it).

See map p. 142. Bus: 119, or take a cab up and stroll down.

Monument to King Vittorio Emanuele II (Vittoriano aka Altare della Patria)
Colosseo

This controversial monument — called "the typewriter" by detractors because of its shape — was built to honor the memory of the first king of Italy, who unified the country. The construction, from 1885 to 1911, employed the most talented Italian artists of the time. Since 1921, it has also housed the **Tomba del Milite Ignoto (Tomb of the Unknown Soldier).** Closed to the public for decades, it has been completely restored, and it is now possible to admire the beautiful decorations. Also, you can climb the stairs and enjoy one of the most beautiful views over Rome, particularly at sunset. The lower floors house excellent art exhibits; check with the tourist office for the current schedule.

See map p. 142. Piazza Venezia. ☎ 06-6991718. Metro: Colosseo. Bus: 64, 62, 63. Admission: Free. Open: Winter 9:30 a.m.–4:30 p.m.; summer 9:30 a.m.–5:30 p.m.

Non-Catholic Cemetery (Cimitero Acattolico)
Testaccio

A pilgrimage site for fans of poets **John Keats** and **Percy Bysshe Shelley,** who are buried here, this is a very pretty small cemetery. Among other famous eternal occupants is the anti-Fascist Antonio Gramsci, who died in 1937 after 11 years in prison. The cemetery has a prestigious next-door neighbor: the **pyramid of Caius Cestius,** a Roman praetor and tribune who died in 12 B.C.

Via Caio Cestio. ☎ 06-5741141. Metro: Line B to Piramide. Bus: 23 or Tram 3 to Via Marmorata. Admission: Free. Open: Tues–Sun 9 a.m.–5 p.m.

Piazza del Popolo
Piazza del Popolo

The "piazza of the people" lives up to its name: Romans like to meet here to talk, have a drink, hang out, and people-watch. You can do the same, though be warned that the two cafes fronting the piazza gouge you unmercifully if you sit at an outdoor table (or even an indoor one) instead of taking your coffee at the counter like a Roman. **Santa Maria del Popolo** (☎ 06-3610836) stands by the gate leading out to busy **Piazzale Flaminio** (where you can catch lots of buses). Founded in 1099, the church contains magnificent Caravaggios as well as a Pinturicchio. The brace of baroque churches directly across the square are the work of Carlo Rainaldi, Bernini, and Carlo Fontana. In the center is an **Egyptian obelisk,** one of Rome's most ancient objects, dating from 1200 B.C. It came from Heliopolis and had been placed there by Ramses II, but was brought to Rome during Augustus's reign (it stood in the Circo Massimo until one of the popes, in their nearly endless reshuffling and meddling with monuments, moved it here). When you leave the piazza, head up the steps into the trees on the east side. This path leads to the Pincio Gardens, one of the best places to see the sun set over Rome (see listing later in this chapter).

See map p. 142. Off Via del Babuino, Via del Corso, and Via de Ripetta. Metro: Flaminio. Bus: 490 to Piazzale Flaminio. Bus: Minibus 117 or 119. Tram: 2.

Piazza del Quirinale and Palazzo del Quirinale
Trevi

Now the home of Italy's president, the Palazzo del Quirinale was the residence of the king up till the end of World War II. Earlier in history, the pope lived here — or hid, in the case of Pius VII, who locked himself in after excommunicating Napoleon (it didn't help: soldiers broke in and carted him off to Fontainebleau). The royal family of Savoy substituted some gaudy, second-rate 19th-century art for earlier decoration, but the palace is still impressive and has some spectacular rooms. The private gardens enclosed by the palace are gorgeous, especially in spring. *Note:* Bring your passport — you'll need to pass through an identity and security check to enter.

On the square, the **fountain (Fontana di Monte Cavallo)** has two giant statues of Castor and Pollux, the twin sons of Leda and Zeus. The **Egyptian obelisk** adorning the square was taken from the Mausoleum of Augustus by Pius VI in 1793. Across from the palace's entrance on the same side of the square are the smaller buildings that were the **Scuderie del Quirinale (Palace Stables),** today the setting of many fine-art exhibits (check with the tourist office for the current schedule).

See map p. 142. Piazza del Quirinale off Via del Quirinale, the continuation of Via XX Settembre. ☎ *06-46991.* www.quirinale.it. *Metro: Barberini. Bus: Minibus 116 or 117 to Via del Quirinale. Admission: 5€ ($6.50). Open: Sun and June 2 8:30 a.m. to noon. Closed July, Aug, and major holidays.*

Piazza Farnese
Campo de' Fiori

This delightful piazza is dominated by the **Palazzo Farnese,** surely one of Rome's most dramatic buildings, designed by Sangallo and Michelangelo. A cleaning completed in 1999 turned its somber gray a startling pale yellow and brought out the delicate decorations. Currently home to the French embassy, it's open to visitors on selected Sundays; call the French embassy at ☎ **06-686011.**

See map p. 142. Off Via dei Baullari, near Campo de' Fiori. Bus: 116.

Pincio Gardens
Piazza del Popolo

Famous for the **terrace** overlooking Piazza del Popolo, which is maybe the most romantic spot in Rome, these gardens offer more than a good panorama (particularly striking at sunset, we warmly recommend it). Wanted by Napoleon during his brief occupation of Rome as a public promenade, the gardens were actually created by the architect Giuseppe Valadier for Pope Pius VII, after Napoleon's demise. Connected to Villa Borghese Park (see later in this chapter) by an overpass over the fourth-century Aurelian city walls, and the embankment, they can also be directly accessed from Piazza del Popolo, through a steep ascent. Statues and fountains adorn the alleys, including the famous 1867 **water clock** (Viale dell'Orologio, on the left of the garden). By the terrace you'll find a merry-go-round, much appreciated by young visitors. You'll also find places, one on Viale Medici and one on Viale dell'Orologio, where you can rent wheels and proceed to Villa Borghese.

See map p. 142. Bus: 49, 88, 95, 116, 490, and 495. Metro: Spagna or Flaminio. Admission: Free. Open: Daily 24 hours.

Villa Farnesina
Trastevere

Not exactly a picture gallery, this gorgeous villa holds a wonderful **collection of frescoes** by Raphael and other artists in a suite of rooms. Built along the Tiber in the early 16th century by the architect Baldassarre Peruzzi — who also decorated part of the interior with frescoes — and surrounded by a pleasant garden, it is a splendid example of Roman architecture. It was unfortunately mutilated in 1884 when the Lungotevere (the riverside road) was built, destroying part of the gardens and a loggia overlooking the river that was probably designed by Raphael. The villa was built for the Chigi family; later it passed to the Farnese, and today it's the seat of the Accademia dei Lincei, a major Italian cultural institute, and of the National Print Gallery, the largest print collection in Italy. The frescoes in the first room — the *Loggia di Psiche* — were done by Raphael's assistants from cartoons by the master, whereas the great fresco of Galatea in the *Sala di Galatea* is by Raphael himself. The *Camera da Letto* on the second floor was frescoed by Sienese artist Il Sodoma.

See map p. 142. Via della Lungara 230. ☎ 06-68027268. www.lincei.it. Bus: 23. Tram: 8. Admission: 5€ ($6.50). Open: Mon–Sat 9 a.m.–1 p.m. Closed holidays.

Villa Torlonia
Porta Pia

The Torlonia were — and are — a noble Roman family (no less than princes), and this was their family residence until the early 20th century, when they donated the entire villa and the surrounding park to the city. The beautiful grounds are a popular place for Romans to exercise, meet, and relax, but the main attraction is the buildings, which have been masterfully restored over the years. The main building is the most recently refurbished (it opened to the public in 2006), the **Casino Nobile.** The elegant villa, which houses a collection of precious objects, is notable for the architecture and decoration created by Giuseppe Valadier in the early 19th century. The luxury and beauty inside will make you long for that bygone era. Nearby is the **Casina delle Civette (Cottage of the Owls),** an Art Nouveau jewel with whimsical architecture and beautiful stained-glass windows. In the 19th century, the prince allowed his artistic son to build this cottage as a bachelor apartment; it now houses an interesting museum of Art Nouveau glasswork. On the other side of the park is the **Casino dei Principi (Cottage of the Princes),** an elegant outbuilding that was the residence of Mussolini when he was in power and that now preserves some of the collected artworks of the Torlonia family. You can make a reservation for a guided tour of the Casina delle Civette, which we recommend.

See map p. 142. Via Nomentana 70; ☎ *06-8207304.* www.museivillatorlonia.it. *Admission: Park free; Casina delle Civette 3€ ($3.90); Casino Nobile 4.50€ ($5.85); combined ticket 6.50€ ($8.45). Open: Park daily. Museums last Sun in Mar–Sept 30 Tues–Sun 9 a.m.–7 p.m.; Oct 1–last Sat in Oct Tues–Sun 9 a.m.–5:30 p.m.; last Sun in Oct–Feb Tues–Sun 9 a.m.–4:30 p.m. Closed Jan 1, May 1, and Dec 25.*

Seeing Rome by Guided Tour

The French author Stendhal once wrote, "As soon as you enter Rome, get in a carriage and ask to be brought to the Coliseum [sic] or to St. Peter's. If you try to get there on foot, you will never arrive: Too many marvelous things will stop you along the way."

Taking a bus tour of this complicated city when you first arrive still is an excellent idea. Doing so helps you get the feel of the place and gives you an idea of what you'd like to see in depth later. If one area in particular appeals to you, take a walking tour, a particularly efficient way to discover most of what there is to know on a specific place.

Bus tours

We like the hop-on/hop-off formula because of its flexibility: You can take a complete tour and get an idea of what's where and what it looks like, and then start again and visit the various stops. The following tours operate daily, year-round.

Rome's public transportation authority, **ATAC,** gives the best bus tours of Rome (☎ **06-46952252** daily 8 a.m.–8 p.m. for reservations and info; www.trambus.com/servizituristici.htm). You can find cheaper operators, but you can't beat the quality or the options. The tours are offered daily, the buses are new (open-deck vehicles progressively being equipped with lifts allowing wheelchair accessibility to the open top deck), and the guides are kind and professional. Tickets can be purchased online, or on the bus with exact change. Each of the three lines covers a two-hour itinerary.

✔ The red tourist **line 110** "open" buses leave from Piazza dei Cinquecento in front of Stazione Termini every 10 minutes from 8:40 a.m. to 7:40 p.m. for an 11-stop loop around Rome's major historic sights (16€/$21 adult; 7€/$9.10 child under 13; children under 6 ride free).

✔ The **Archeobus** tour crosses Rome's historic center and heads for the Appian Way Archeological Park, making 15 stops near historic sites of ancient Rome. The green buses leave from Piazza dei Cinquecento across from Stazione Termini every 40 minutes between 9 a.m. and 4 p.m. (10€/$13, 8€/$10.40 for those with Roma Pass [see beginning of this chapter]).

✔ **Roma Cristiana** is a two-line package offered in cooperation with the Roman Pilgrim Association (OPR) that takes in all the major religious sites in Rome and more. Because churches and other religious sites are scattered throughout Rome, this is an excellent choice. The yellow buses leave every 25 minutes for the St. Peter's loop (19 stops), every 50 minutes for the St. Paul's Basilica loop (22 stops). Both loops start from Via della Conciliazione, across from St. Peter's. They operate between 8:30 a.m. and 7:30 p.m. Tickets cost 15€ ($20) for one day and one line, 20€ ($26) for two and two.

If you prefer a more traditional bus tour, several formulas are available. Tours usually depart around 9 a.m., 3 p.m., and 8 p.m. — with possible pickup from your hotel included — and cost about 28€ ($36) for a three-hour tour. Here are the three best operators: **Appian Line** (Piazza dell'Esquilino 6; ☎ **06-487861**; www.appianline.it), **Green Line** (Via Farini 5/A; ☎ **06-483787**; www.greenlinetours.com), and **Vastours** (Via Piemonte 34; ☎ **06-4814309**; www.vastours.it). They also offer side trips from Rome.

Walking tours

Enjoy Rome (Via Varese 39, 3 blocks north off the side of Stazione Termini; ☎ **06-4451843**; www.enjoyrome.com; Metro: Termini) offers a variety of three-hour walking tours, including a night tour that takes you through the historic center and its sights, and a tour of Trastevere and the Jewish Ghetto. Most tours cost 24€ ($31) adults and 18€ ($23) for those under age 26, including the cost of the tour and admission to sights. The office is open Monday through Friday from 8:30 a.m. to 2 p.m. and 3:30 to 6:30 p.m., and Saturday from 8:30 a.m. to 2 p.m., and you can book on the Web site anytime. Enjoy Rome also organizes a bike tour with English-speaking guides. Reserve at least two weeks in advance, and you can arrange special-interest tours such as "Fascist Rome: The Urban Planning of Mussolini" and "Caravaggio in Rome" (prices quoted upon request).

Boat tours

Besides its regular boat service on the Tiber (see "Finding More Cool Things to See and Do," earlier in this chapter), the **Compagnia di**

Navigazione Ponte San Angelo (☎ **06-6789361;** www.battellidiroma. it) offers a number of **day cruises** on the river. The one-hour tour with audio guide costs 12€ ($16) and leaves from Ponte Sant'Angelo Wednesday through Sunday at 11 a.m., 12:30 p.m., 4 p.m., and 5:30 p.m.; the dinner cruise includes dinner and a two-hour ride for 54€ ($70), with boats leaving from Ponte Sant'Angelo Thursday through Saturday at 9 p.m.

Our personal favorite is the cruise down the river to the Tiber mouth, which includes a two-hour stop at **Ostia Antica** to visit the archaeologi-cal area. Boats leave from the Marconi bridge daily in summer and Friday through Sunday in winter at 10 a.m. and arrive at Ostia at noon; they depart from Ostia at 2 p.m. for scheduled arrival in Rome at 4:30 p.m., but you can take a faster subway ride back if you wish to spend more time at the ruins. Tickets cost 12€ ($16) one-way and 13€ ($17) round-trip.

Air tours

Seeing Rome from a small aircraft is a pricey but unique experience. Daily tours with Cityfly (Aeroporto dell'Urbe, Via Salaria 825; ☎ **06-88333;** www.cityfly.com) cost 70€ ($91) per adult and 49€ ($64) for children under 10. The planes fly at an altitude of about 450m (1,476 ft.) and can take between three and nine passengers for the 20-minute flight. Make reservations at least two days in advance; the minimum is two per-sons. A city train serves the airport (the Monterotondo-Mentana line, departing from Ostinese or Tiburtina stations, to the Salaria-Urbe stop), but a taxi is a lot less cumbersome.

Chapter 12

Shopping the Local Stores

A lot of people say Rome isn't good for shopping, at least not compared with Florence and Italy's fashion capital, Milan. Well, we beg to disagree. You'll find a huge array of goods for sale here in the capital city and a selection of some items — antique prints, for instance — that other Italian cities cannot match. You'll also find bargains here when you know where to look, and you'll have a great time browsing in the process!

Surveying the Scene

Italy's largest city, Rome is full of elegant, fashionable shops where you can find many interesting things at prices that often beat those in Florence and Milan. Some of the best buys include **leather goods** (bags, shoes, and clothing), **apparel** (from moderately elegant to haute couture), and **housewares** — from designer furniture and gadgets to linens. All the big names of Italian **fashion** and design have showrooms here, and you'll find great discounts during the official sales period (see details later in this section). **Children's clothes** deserve special mention: Rome is one of the few places where you can still find delightfully embroidered and handmade items — very special but usually pricey — as well as showrooms of local designers specializing in kids' fashion.

Rome was also once the center of a large artisan community, but here as elsewhere, many historic trades have been lost. In terms of **crafts,** the city isn't as rich as it was in ages past. Alas, very few workshops still practice traditional arts, but those that do produce high-quality work, particularly **gold, plaster and marble work, embroidery, stationery,** and **religious art.** Also, because this is the capital city, you can find showrooms selling high-end items from all the traditional crafts and specialty work from around the country. You can shop for famous products from places that you may not have time to visit, such as **Florentine embroideries and stationery, Venetian glass and Murano chandeliers,** and **Sicilian pottery and ceramic.**

Rome is a center for the arts. If you had a euro for every picture that's been drawn of the Forum, you would be rich enough to buy your own Roman villa. Rome has been a magnet for artists for centuries, and it is a great place to buy **art,** both old and modern. Rome is also the best place in Italy to find both **antique prints** and modern, high-quality prints from antique plates.

Shopping hours are generally 9 or 9:30 a.m. (later for boutiques, which may open as late as 10:30 or 11 a.m.) to about 1 or 1:30 p.m. and then from 3:30 or 4 p.m. to 7:30 or 8 p.m. Shops close Monday morning, except for food and technical shops, which close Thursday afternoon in winter and Saturday afternoon in summer. All close Sunday. In the historical district, however, quite a few shops stay open during the lunchtime break and on Sunday. Most shops observe a **seasonal closing** for two weeks in August (generally around the 15th), and some close for the entire month.

Seasonal sales fall during official dates set by the municipal office. Winter sales last about one month, from the second week of January into February, while summer sales last about one month around July. This is a great time for shopping, but you'll hardly be alone. If you want to attempt the sales, be there early.

Italy's **value-added tax** (known as the IVA) is a steep 19 percent, but you can get a refund for purchases costing more than 155€ ($178). This means that if you spend that much or more with one merchant, regardless of the number of items — three pairs of shoes, or five shirts, or whatever — you can get the rebate. If you buy the three pairs of shoes at three different stores, however, even if they add up to 155€, that doesn't help you, because they're three different purchases.

All quoted prices include value-added tax. Stores displaying a "TAX FREE" insignia can give you an invoice that you can cash at the airport's Customs office as you leave Italy. Otherwise, you have to take the invoice from the store, have it stamped at the airport by Customs, and then mail it back to the store, which will send you a check or credit your charge account.

When shopping for clothes or shoes, keep in mind that Italian sizes are different from those in the United States. Always try things on, because there is quite a bit of variability by brand. Sizes usually tend to run small compared to U.S. sizes, but not always. Use Table 12-1 to find your Italian size.

Table 12-1	Size-Conversion Chart				
Clothes					
Italy	40–42	44–46	48–50	52–54	56–58
U.S. women	S 4–6	M 8–10	L 12–14	XL 16	XXL 18
U.S. men	XS	S	M	L	XL

Men's shirts

Italy	36	37	38	39	41	42	43	44	46
U.S.	14	14½	15	15½	16	16½	17	17½	18

Shoes

Italy	35	35½	36	37	37½	38	38½	39	40	41
U.S. women	5	5½	6	6½	7	7½	8	8½	9	10
U.K. women	2½	3	3½	4	4½	5	5½	6	6½	7½

Italy	40	41	42	43	44	45	46	
U.S. men		7	8	8½	9½	10	11	11½
U.K. men		6½	7½	8	9	9½	10½	11

Italy	26	27	28	29	30	31	32	33	34
U.S. girls	9.5	10.5	11.5	12.5	13	1	2	2.5	3.5
U.S. boys				11.5	12	13	13.5	1	2
U.K.	8	9	10	11	11.5	12.5	13	1	2

Checking Out the Department Stores

Italians are not as big on department stores as Americans are. In Rome, you'll find only three major ones, with a number of locations scattered around the city.

- ✔ **La Rinascente** is an elegant store carrying mainly clothes and accessories, with a larger selection for women and a smaller one for children and men. It also carries a nice cosmetics section on the ground floor and a smallish housewares selection. It has two major locations in Rome: Piazza Fiume 1 (☎ **06-8416081**) and Piazza Colonna (☎ **06-6784209**), both open daily from 9 a.m. to 7:30 p.m.

- ✔ **COIN** is another upscale department store, with a trendier and younger image, carrying a good selection of clothes and accessories for women, men, and children, and some interesting housewares. Its major locations are Via dei Gracchi (☎ **06-36004298**); Piazzale Appio 7, near San Giovanni Basilica (☎ **06-77250177**); and Viale Trastevere 60 (☎ **06-5816036**). It's open daily from 9 a.m. to 7:30 p.m.

- ✔ **UPIM** is a cheaper department store with a good selection of housewares and a rather inexpensive (and sometimes tacky) line of clothes for women, men, and children, as well as a modest selection of toys, stationery, and odds and ends. You'll find it in Via del Tritone 172 (☎ 06-6783336); Piazza di Santa Maria Maggiore (☎ 06-4465579); and Via Giovanni Giolitti 10 (☎ 06-47825909), by Termini station. All are open Monday through Saturday from 9 a.m. to 7:30 p.m.

Going to Market

The most colorful of the **food markets** — and the most famous in Rome — is in the lively and picturesque **Campo de' Fiori** (Bus: 62 or 64 to Largo Argentina), where you'll find fresh fruit and vegetables, fish, meat, cheese, and cured meats, each sold by specialized vendors. It is surprising that the market hasn't become touristy, given the site; the vendors still sell all kinds of great goodies that Romans eat — from artichokes to anchovies — at good prices. Another historic food market, and also a great one, is in **Piazza San Cosimato** in the heart of Trastevere (Tram: 8), with a great variety of vendors and excellent quality and prices; it observes the same hours as Campo de' Fiori. The noisiest and most exuberant food market of them all is in **Piazza Vittorio,** not far from Termini Station, in an area of Rome that has been taken over by Asian and African immigrants, leading to an exotic choice of merchandise. In addition to food, you'll find stands selling cheap clothes and accessories. All food markets operate Monday through Saturday from 7 a.m. (some vendors arrive by 6 a.m.) to 2 p.m.

For a truly uproarious market where you'll see average Romans searching for every conceivable item, visit the most famous **flea market,** at **Porta Portese.** Extending over several streets in Trastevere, this market is organized by type of merchandise: antiques, automotive, clothes, textiles, and so on. You never know what you're going to find, from oil paintings to fur hats. It's a fun place, and you're likely to find something you like, but go early to have a good selection before the mobs have picked over the merchandise. It's open only on Saturday and Sunday from about 6 a.m. to 2 p.m.

Another famous but smaller operation is the flea market in **Via Sannio** (off Piazza San Giovanni in Laterano), with interesting clothes, accessories, and camping equipment. It's open daily from 7 a.m. to 1 p.m. Pickpockets are absolutely dreadful on weekends, when it gets most crowded. At both flea markets, a small amount of dickering over the price is usual, so you can practice your bargaining skills.

One more market worth a mention is the **antiquarian book and print market** on Piazza Fontanella Borghese in the Navona/Pantheon neighborhood (Bus: 81, or Minibus 117 or 119 to the Corso at Via Tomacelli). This historic small market is a great place to browse if you know your stuff, but otherwise, *caveat emptor* (let the buyer beware).

In these bustling markets, particularly the flea markets, be very aware of pickpockets, who take advantage of the crowds.

Discovering the Best Shopping Neighborhoods

Shopping in Rome is great, if only because of the splendid setting of the major shopping areas — right in the heart of the city, among Roman ruins, medieval streets, and Renaissance palaces.

Il Centro

The best shopping area in Rome is in the heart of the historic district, and precisely in the triangle of medieval and Renaissance streets running between **Piazza del Popolo, Piazza San Silvestro** and **Largo del Tritone.** Along **Via del Corso** — the area's main artery, which is partly restricted to pedestrians (except for buses and taxis) — you'll find more affordable stores selling mostly apparel and shoes. Some are fashionable, some touristy, others are just trendy, and a few are rather tacky. If you head for the narrower streets toward **Piazza di Spagna,** such as **Via Frattina, Via dei Condotti,** and **Via Babuino,** you'll find the best designer boutiques and all the stars of Italian fashion. Among the Roman designers are **Laura Biagiotti** (Via Borgognona 43; ☎ 06-6795040), where you can always find greatly discounted items from the previous year's collection; **Renato Balestra** (Via Abbruzzi 3; ☎ 06-4882586); **Roberto Capucci** (Via Gregoriana 56; ☎ 06-6783600); **Raniero Gattinoni** (Via Borgognona 22; ☎ 06-6793786); and **Mila Schon** (Via delle Carrozze 87; ☎ 06-6782408) for women, and **Battistoni** (Via dei Condotti 61/a; ☎ 06-697611); **Testa** (Via Frattina 104, ☎ 06-6791294); and **Brioni** (Via Barberini 79; ☎ 06-484517) for men. Italian designers include **Valentino** (Via dei Condotti 13; ☎ 06-6739420); **Ferragamo** (Via dei Condotti 73; ☎ 06-6798402); **Ferragamo Uomo** (Via dei Condotti 75; ☎ 06-6781130); **Fendi** (Via Borgognona 39; ☎ 06-696661); **Gucci** (Via dei Condotti 8; ☎ 06-6793888); **Armani** (Via dei Condotti 77; ☎ 06-6991460); **Emporio Armani** (Via del Babuino 140; ☎ 06-36002197); **Gianfranco Ferrè** (Piazza di Spagna 70; ☎ 06-6791451); **Versace** (Via Borgogna 24; ☎ 06-6795037 and Via Bocca di Leone; ☎ 06-67800521); **Trussardi** (Via dei Condotti 49; ☎ 06-6780280); **Prada** (Via dei Condotti 88; ☎ 06-6790897; Metro: Line A to Spagna); and **Dominici** (Via del Corso 14; ☎ 06-3610591). Most of the time, prices are so high you may get a nosebleed, but then there are the seasonal sales (see earlier in this chapter). Next door to the big names, you'll find more affordable stores — such the ones selling Italian leather gloves in **Piazza di Spagna** — and young designers' boutiques. For children's clothes, you'll find a branch of **La Cicogna** (Via Frattina 138; ☎ 06-6786959), where Roman mums come for all their needs, and, at the other end of the spectrum, **Pinco Pallino** (Via del Babuino 115; ☎ 06-69190549), the showroom of the famous Italian children's fashion designer who's particularly popular in Europe and Asia. Your girls will enjoy visiting **Pure Gold** (Via del Babuino 150/d; ☎ 06-3235464), specializing in designer eveningwear for kids age 5 to 14: lace, satin, sequins, you name it. More affordable, **Zucca Stregata** (Via Belsiana 70; ☎ 800-503929) sells cute blankets, pajamas, slippers, and accessories with signature prints. Hats are enjoying a comeback, and the historic **Borsalino** (Piazza del Popolo 20; ☎ 06-32650838) is the right address. If you are interested in jewels,

Bulgari (Via dei Condotti 10; ☎ 06-696261) is the star of the show, and a visit to the showroom is a unique experience. Other famous boutiques include **Buccellati** (Via dei Condotti 31; ☎ 06-6786784), the Florentine house whose trademark is designs inspired by Renaissance masters, and **Massoni** (Via Margutta 73; ☎ 06-3216916), maybe the oldest jewelry store in Rome, founded in 1790.

You'll also find shops specializing in items ranging from stylish Italian housewares to antiques. **C.U.C.I.N.A.** (Via Mario de' Fiori 65; ☎ 06-6791275) stocks all kinds of usual and unusual kitchenwares. Also try the small shop attached to the restaurant **Gusto** (Piazza Augusto Imperatore 7; ☎ 06-3236363). **Via del Babuino** and **Via Margutta** are the traditional locations of some of the best — and priciest — antiques shops in town. Among the antiquarian and artwork shops in this area that merit a mention are **Alinari** (Via Alibert 16/a; ☎ 06-6792923) and **Fava** (Via del Babuino 180, ☎ 06-3610807). Both sell artistic prints, the former specializing in Roman and the latter in Neapolitan scenes. At these shops, you can be sure that the antique you're buying is really an antique. If books are what you are after, this is also home to some well-established bookstores carrying titles in English. **Libreria per Ragazzi Mel** (Piazza Santi Apostoli 59; ☎ 06-69941045) has a great selection of children's books, particularly for readers under 6. The best stops for both adults and children are **Anglo-American Book** (Via della Vite 102; ☎ 06-6795222) and the **Lion Bookshop** (Via dei Greci 33; ☎ 06-32654007). If you are looking for paper goods, visit **Fabriano** (Via del Babuino 173; ☎ 06-32600361), the showroom of a paper mill in business since the 13th century. Finally, at **Sermoneta** (Via del Tritone 168; ☎ 06-6795488) and **Frette** (Via del Corso 381; ☎ 06-6786862, and Piazza di Spagna 11; ☎ 06-6790673), you'll find wonderful domestic linens.

Navona/Pantheon

The intricate medieval streets on the west side of the Corso around Piazza Navona and Piazza della Rotonda (Pantheon) hide a great trove of elegant and original boutiques, and some of the oldest establishments in Rome. In these smaller shops, you can buy something that you'd never find at home. Here you'll find unique, high-quality items — from old prints to exclusive fashion, from books to antique furniture and toys — made by small local designers who may be tomorrow's big names. An elegant men's store, **Davide Cenci** (Via Campo Marzio 1–7; ☎ 06-6990681; Bus: Minibus 116 to Pantheon), is popular with locals. Just a stone's throw away is **Tombolini** (Via della Maddalena 31/38; ☎ 06-69200342), which carries handsome clothes and shoes for women and men, with an emphasis on classic style. If you really want to make your friends green with envy, have a pair of shoes custom-made by **Listo** (Via della Croce 76; ☎ 06-6784567). For leather bags and wallets, **Bottega Veneta** (Piazza San Lorenzo in Lucina 9; ☎ 06-68210024; Bus: 81, or Minibus 116 to Piazza San Lorenzo) is famous for its beautiful woven leather designs, often in rich and startling colors. For casual clothes, seek out the showroom of **Replay** (Via della Rotonda 21; ☎ 06-6833073), selling jackets, accessories, and jeans; the children's store is next door. A great place for children's clothes is **Babe** (Via della Palombella 22, ☎ 06-68301975, right behind the Pantheon), offering a choice of colorful garments, plus some shoes and toys for small children. Another good address is **Bonpoint Paris** (Piazza San Lorenzo in Lucina; ☎ 06-6871548), the showroom of the exclusive French boutique carrying haute couture clothes for children up to age 16. Cheaper, but still on the dressy side, is **Kid's Stock** (Via Campo Marzio 37, ☎ 06-6871335), with a large array of outfits for children and teens. But our favorite shops are probably **Marionette** (Piazza del Fico 23, ☎ 06-68210995), near Piazza Navona, where you'll find hip clothes, accessories, and toys, and the French brand **Petit Bateau** (Via di Campo Marzio 10/B; ☎ 06-6792348). It sells great underwear and simple but nice clothing for children up to 8 years old (underwear and pajamas up to age 16).

Local Roman crafts survive here, especially in the medieval area around **Piazza Navona.** You can find *vimini* (basketry) on **Via dei Sediari** and **Via dei Cestari;** ironwork on **Via degli Orsini;** and even reproductions of Roman and Pompeian mosaics at **Studio Cassio** (Via Urbana 98; ☎ 06-4745356) and **Paola Cucchi** (Via Monserrato 49; ☎ 06-6869469). For beautiful ceramic work, try the **Compagnia del Corallo** (Via del Corallo 27; ☎ 06-6833697), and for elegant wrought iron, head to **Nicola Arduini** (Via degli Specchi 12; ☎ 06-68805537). For plasterwork, including reproductions of antique designs (some objects are small enough to take home; others can be shipped), visit the **Laboratorio Marani** (Via Monte Giordano 27; ☎ 06-68307866). For handmade quality jewelry, check out the small **Bottega Mortet** (Via dei Portoghesi 18; ☎ 06-6861629), and the large **Ansuini** (Corso Vittorio Emanuele II 151 ☎ 06-68806909), established in 1860. Stationery is one of the most popular, portable, and affordable gifts for the folks back home. For especially refined stationery and paper, go to **Pineider,** founded in 1774 (Via Fontanella Borghese 22, ☎ 06-6878369, Bus: Minibus 117 or 119 to the Corso at Via Tomacelli; and Via dei Due Macelli 68, ☎ 06-6795884, Bus: Minibus 116, 117, or 119 to Via Due Macelli). You'll find more wonderful paper goods at **Daniela Rosati** (Via della Stelletta 27; ☎ 06-68802053) and **Campo Marzio Design** (Via di Campo Marzio 41; ☎ 06-68807877).

Rome's most special source of intoxicants is **Ai Monasteri** (Corso Rinascimento 72; ☎ 06-68802783; Bus: Minibus 116), off the east side of Piazza Navona. Here, you can find the liqueurs, elixirs, and other alcoholic concoctions that Italian monks have been making since the Middle Ages. Selling herbs and other natural health concoctions, the **Antica Erboristeria Romana** (Via di Torre Argentina 15; ☎ 06-6879493) has been dispensing since 1700, and the original furnishings are still in use.

For books in English, head for the **English Bookstore** (Via di Ripetta 248; ☎ 06-3203301). You'll find a number of other foreign bookstores in this area: German **Herder Librerie** (Piazza Montecitorio 117); French **La**

Procure (Piazza San Luigi dei Francesi 23); Spanish **Sorgente** (Piazza Navona 90); Chinese **Marco Polo** (Via del Seminario 103). Another interesting bookstore is the **Libreria Babele** (Via dei Banchi Vecchi 116; ☎ 06-6876628), Rome's most central gay and lesbian bookstore.

If you're interested in antiques, you'll delight in **Via dei Coronari,** Rome's antiquarian headquarters. This street is lined with antiques dealers, one shop after another on both sides of the street — and it's not short. Whether furniture, glass, lamps, armoires, jewels, or paintings, you'll find it here. If you don't, just continue along adjoining Via Giulia. Even if you aren't planning on lugging home a count's antique bureau or a trestle table from a convent, this area is basically like a museum where you can (if you have the money) buy the exhibits. For high-quality prints, well-known shops are the famous **Nardecchia** (Piazza Navona 25; ☎ 06-6869318; Bus: Minibus 116) and **Antiquarius** (Corso Rinascimento 63; ☎ 06-68802941; Bus: Minibus 116), a nice shop just across the street from the Palazzo Madama. At these shops, you find higher-quality — and somewhat more reliable — articles than at the nearby **antiquarian book and print market** (see earlier in this chapter).

Some shops in this area specialize in religious art and attire, and although you probably don't want to buy a cardinal's outfit, you may be interested in some knee-high red socks. Or explore the huge selection of figurines, bronzes, candleholders, paintings, crèches, and other religious objects. Two good stores are **Ghezzi** (Via de Cestari 32; ☎ 06-6869744) and **Salustri** (Via de Cestai 11; ☎ 06-6791587).

Finally, you should not leave the area without visiting the **Città del Sole** (Via della Scrofa 65; ☎ 06-68803805), where young kids play with the BRIO train table while you can check the high-tech adult toys and beautifully crafted coffee-table entertainment accessories. A great selection, for yourself and the kids in your life.

Cola di Rienzo

Although this area on the San Pietro side of the Tevere doesn't boast the luxury shops of Via dei Condotti and nearby streets, you can still find big-name Italian fashion and, what's more, it may even be affordable. Stores line both sides of **Via Ottaviano** and **Via Cola di Rienzo.** Among the many clothes and shoe stores, with shops catering to every level of price and style, you'll find a branch of **La Cicogna** (Via Cola di Rienzo 268; ☎ 06-6896557) as well as **Iana** (Via Cola di Rienzo 211; ☎ 06-68892668). Both carry cute and affordable children's clothing. At **Kid's Stock** (Via Vittoria 52; ☎ 06-692022289), you'll find a large array of outfits on the dressy side for children and teens. A very special store if you are keen on model-building is **Giorni** (Via dei Gracchi 31; ☎ 06-3217145), which carries everything from model planes to lead soldiers. You'll also find a branch of our favorite toy store for adults and children, **Città del Sole** (Via Marcantonio Colonna 5; ☎ 06-3216507).

Although this is not a traditional area for artistic crafts, a handful of very nice workshops turn out high-quality goods, including jewelry at **Carini** (Piazza dell'Unitá 9; ☎ **06-3210715**) and handmade lace at **Ricami Italia Garipoli** (Borgo Vittorio 91; ☎ **06-68802196**). Proceeding farther toward the Vatican, near St. Peter's Basilica, you'll find one of the largest religious-items shops in the city, **Savelli,** with one location specializing in mosaics (Via Paolo VI 27; ☎ **06-68307437**) and another location right off the square, with a huge variety of other objects (Piazza Pio XII; ☎ **06-68806383**).

Via Nazionale

Off Piazza della Repubblica near Stazione Termini, running down toward Piazza Venezia, Via Nazionale used to be an elegant shopping area, but traffic — the street was a main artery between the train station and the *centro* — drove away many customers. Fortunately, Via Nazionale is now open only to buses and taxis, which has reduced the deafening noise. The shops are varied, some good and others less so. The revived area has attracted some big names (perhaps fleeing the ridiculous rents of the Corso), but it is still frequented more by Italians than by tourists. Known especially for leather goods, this may be the best place to find that sleek number you really want without having to go to Florence.

Trastevere

This is where you go for a dip into romantic medieval Rome and an interesting mix of artists' workshops, craftspeople's showrooms, and a great variety of small shops selling anything from mystic art to traditional food. Some of the shops here have been in business for decades, while others are new ventures. **Via della Scala** is the best, lined almost wall-to-wall with showrooms and workshops. **Massimo Langosco di Langosco** (Via della Scala 77; ☎ **06-5896375**) and **Ferrone** (Via della Scala 76; ☎ **06-5803801**) are excellent goldsmiths; **Scala Magica** (Via della Scala 66; ☎ **06-5894098**) and **Scala 14** (Via della Scala 14; ☎ **06-5883580**) are dressmakers. One interesting shop is **Pandora** (Piazza Santa Maria in Trastevere 6; ☎ **06-5895658**), which carries a great selection of Murano glass and Italian designer goods. **Modi e Materie** (Vicolo del Cinque; ☎ **06-5885280**) stocks ceramics from the island of Sardinia; **Ciliegia** (Via della Scala 5; ☎ **06-5818149**) specializes in fashions from Positano, from handmade sandals and dresses to curios; and **Guaytamelli** (Via del Moro 59; ☎ **06-5880704**) sells sundials and other ancient time-measuring instruments. You'll find woodcarving at **Laboratorio Ilaria Miani** (Via degli Orti di Alibert 13/A; ☎ **06-6861366**), stringed instruments at **Mohesen** (Vicolo del Cedro 33; ☎ **06-5882484**), ceramics at **Ceramica Sarti** (Via Santa Dorotea 21; ☎ **06-5882079**), and jewelry at **Elisabeth Frolet** (Via della Pelliccia 30; ☎ **06-5816614**). **Officina della Carta** (Via Benedetta 26; ☎ **06-5895557**) stocks paper and leather goods in the best Italian tradition. You'll even find a nice English bookstore, the **Corner Bookshop** (Via del Moro 48; ☎ **06-5836942**).

Index of Stores by Merchandise

Accessories

Borsalino (Il Centro)
Bottega Veneta (Navona/Pantheon)
Dominici (Il Centro)
Prada (Il Centro)

Antique Prints and Artworks

Alinari (Il Centro)
Antiquarian book and print market (Navona/Pantheon)
Antiquarius (Navona/Pantheon)
Fava (Il Centro)
Nardecchia (Navona/Pantheon)

Books and Magazines

Anglo-American Book (Il Centro)
The Corner Bookshop (Trastevere)
English Bookstore (Navona/Pantheon)
Herder Librerie (Navona/Pantheon)
La Procure (Navona/Pantheon)
Libreria Babele (Navona/Pantheon)
Libreria per Ragazzi Mel (Il Centro)
The Lion Bookshop (Il Centro)
Marco Polo (Navona/Pantheon)
Sorgente (Navona/Pantheon)

Children's Clothing

Babe (Navona/Pantheon)
Bonpoint Paris (Navona/Pantheon)
Iana (Cola di Rienzo)
Kid's Stock (Navona/Pantheon and Cola di Rienzo)
La Cicogna (Il Centro and Cola di Rienzo)
Marionette (Navona/Pantheon)
Petit Bateau (Navona/Pantheon)
Pinco Pallino (Il Centro)
Pure Gold (Il Centro)
Replay (Navona/Pantheon)
Zucca Stregata (Il Centro)

Crafts

Ceramica Sarti (Trastevere)
Ciliegia (Trastevere)
Compagnia del Corallo (Navona/Pantheon)
Elisabeth Frolet (Trastevere)
Laboratorio Ilaria Miani (Trastevere)
Laboratorio Marani (Navona/Pantheon)
Modi e Materie (Trastevere)
Mohesen (Trastevere)
Nicola Arduini (Navona/Pantheon)
Pandora (Trastevere)

Designer Clothing

Armani (Il Centro)
Battistoni (Il Centro)
Brioni (Il Centro)
Bulgari (Il Centro)
Davide Cenci (Navona/Pantheon)
Emporio Armani (Il Centro)
Fendi (Il Centro)
Ferragamo (Il Centro)
Gianfranco Ferrè (Il Centro)
Gucci (Il Centro)
Laura Biagiotti (Il Centro)
Mila Schon (Il Centro)
Raniero Gattinoni (Il Centro)
Renato Balestra (Il Centro)
Roberto Capucci (Il Centro)
Scala 14 (Trastevere)
Scala Magica (Trastevere)
Testa (Il Centro)
Tombolini (Navona/Pantheon)
Trussardi (Il Centro)
Valentino (Il Centro)
Versace (Il Centro)

Flea Markets

Porta Portese (Trastevere)
Via Sannio (Laterano)

Food Markets

Campo de' Fiori (Campo de' Fiori)
Piazza San Cosimato (Trastevere)
Piazza Vittorio (Termini)

Herbal and Pharmacy
Antica Erboristeria Romana
(Navona/Pantheon)

Houseware
C.U.C.I.N.A. (Il Centro)
Gusto (Il Centro)

Jewelry and Goldsmiths
Ansuini (Piazza Navona/Pantheon)
Bottega Mortet (Piazza
Navona/Pantheon)
Buccellati (Il Centro)
Bulgari (Il Centro)
Carini (Cola di Rienzo)
Elisabeth Frolet (Trastevere)
Ferrone (Trastevere)
Massimo Langosco di Langosco
(Trastevere)
Massoni (Il Centro)

Linen and Lace
Frette (Il Centro)
Ricami Italia Garipoli (Cola di Rienzo)
Sermoneta (Il Centro)

Religious Items
Ghezzi (Navona/Pantheon)
Salustri (Navona/Pantheon)
Savelli (Cola di Rienzo)

Shoes
Ciliegia (Trastevere)
Dominici (Il Centro)
Ferragamo (Il Centro)
Ferragamo Uomo (Il Centro)
Listo (Navona/Pantheon)
Tombolini (Navona/Pantheon)

Stationery and Paper Goods
Campo Marzio Design
(Navona/Pantheon)
Daniela Rosati (Navona/Pantheon)
Fabriano (Il Centro)
Officina della Carta (Trastevere)
Pineider (Navona/Pantheon)

Sundials
Guaytamelli (Trastevere)

Toys and Modeling
Città del Sole (Navona/Pantheon and
Cola di Rienzo)
Giorni (Cola di Rienzo)

Wine and Liquors
Ai Monasteri (Navona/Pantheon)

Chapter 13

Following an Itinerary: Five Great Options

*I*n the following five itineraries, we make recommendations on how best to spend your time in Rome and offer a few possible themes to give your vacation focus. You may have limited time, young traveling companions, or special interests that you'd like to satisfy during your visit. No matter what your time restrictions or desires, we've got you covered in this chapter.

Turn to Chapter 11 for full listings of the attractions described in this chapter.

Rome in Three Days

So much to see, so little time! Here, we put together an itinerary for seeing the best Rome has to offer in the shortest possible time without suffering total exhaustion. This itinerary is a great introduction to a city for which, in the words of the great Italian writer Silvio Negro, a lifetime is not enough to know.

Day 1

Start with an overview of the city to get your bearings and get a sense of the flavor by taking the excellent **ATAC bus tour** (see Chapter 11). This tour will leave you hungry for more, but if you start early, you'll have time to take in a major sight before lunch. Make it the **Colosseum,** for which you'll have made reservations (see Chapter 11), and then continue with the adjacent **Roman Forum.** Have lunch in the area at the **Hostaria da Nerone** or at **Angelino ai Fori** (see Chapter 10).

In the afternoon, cross the Tiber and head for **St. Peter's Basilica.** See as much as you can there, and then, if you have time before dinner, take a shopping break on the **Via Cola di Rienzo** (see Chapter 12). You'll be famished afterward; luckily, the charming traditional tavern **Dante Taberna de' Gracchi** (see Chapter 10) is not far away. Or head for the picturesque and inventive **La Veranda** (see Chapter 10), which will give you the excuse of strolling through **Piazza San Pietro** by night, a very romantic sight.

Day 2

Start your day with a visit to the **Vatican Museums,** for which you'll have booked a tour in advance to avoid the lines, and take in the **Sistine Chapel.** If your legs are not too tired, walk toward **Castel Sant'Angelo,** which you can at least admire from the outside, and stroll across its magnificent bridge to the other side of the Tiber. Have lunch at **Capricci Siciliani** (see Chapter 10).

In the afternoon, relax with a stroll through the heart of Renaissance Rome and maybe even indulge in some shopping. Visit **Piazza Navona** and perhaps pop into the **Museum of the City of Rome** before stopping for an espresso at **Antico Caffè della Pace** (see Chapter 16) or a gelato at **Giolitti** (see Chapter 10), then visiting the **Pantheon.** Crossing Corso Vittorio Emanuele II, you come to one of the most atmospheric squares in Rome, the **Campo de' Fiori** (see Chapter 11). Eat dinner at **Ditirambo** (Chapter 10), or cross over to the nearby Ghetto — the old Jewish quarter of the city — and try something different at **Da Giggetto** (Chapter 10).

Day 3

Start your third day with a visit to the **Palazzo Massimo alle Terme** (make a reservation to see the Roman frescoes), and stroll to the nearby **Diocletian Baths,** popping in **Santa Maria degli Angeli** church. When you're finished, take a bus to Via Veneto and have lunch in the area (see Chapter 10).

After lunch, stroll to nearby **Piazza di Spagna** to see the famous **Spanish Steps** (see Chapter 11). Along the way, check out the shops on Via del Babuino — a street lined with antiques stores — as well as the other shops in the area, including Via Margutta, high-fashion Via Frattina, and Via dei Condotti (see Chapter 12). Then make your way to the **Borghese Gallery** (for which you made reservations; see Chapter 11). After your visit, stroll through **Villa Borghese** to the **Pincio Gardens;** it's a beautiful walk, with a gorgeous panorama of Rome that lights up with gold at sunset. Have an *aperitivo* (predinner drink) — at **La Casina Valadier** (see Chapter 16); then stroll to **Trevi Fountain** (see Chapter 11), which is beautifully lit at night, to toss your coin in the fountain: by now you are sure to want to return to the Eternal City.

Rome in Five Days

If you have five days in Rome, you can spend time absorbing the sights rather than just seeing them and moving on. You also don't have to make as many painful choices. Follow "Rome in Three Days" for **Day 1, Day 2,** and **Day 3.**

Day 4

Start your day with a visit to **Santa Maria Maggiore,** a beautiful church that deserves much attention. You can continue with a visit to **Santa Prassede** and **San Pietro in Vincoli** nearby, and then have lunch at **Angelino ai Fori** or at **Hostaria da Nerone,** both off Via Cavour. Or pick one of the sights that you didn't get to see over the previous three days but are particularly interested in (see Chapter 11), and have lunch in the vicinity (see Chapter 10).

In the afternoon, head for **Trastevere** for the rest of the day. There you find not only excellent restaurants and nightlife (see Chapters 10 and 16, respectively), but also great shopping (see Chapter 12) and a number of attractions. If you have to choose just one, we recommend **Santa Maria in Trastevere,** one of the most charming churches in Rome.

Day 5

Dedicate your day to discovering ancient Rome. Sign up for the **Archeobus** (see Chapter 11) and start your day with a visit to the **Caracalla Baths.** Then head for the **Appia Antica Park** (see Chapter 11) and have lunch at **Ar Montarozzo** or the **Hostaria L'Archeologia** (see Chapter 10), or a lighter snack at the **Bar Caffe dell'Appia Antica** (see Chapter 11), where you can also rent bikes. It is impossible to do everything the park has to offer in one day, but take your pick of visiting catacombs (such as the **Catacombs of Saint Callixtus**), the **Maxentius Circus and Imperial Villas,** the **Mausoleum of Cecilia Metella,** or the **Villa of the Quintili.** Or just take in the pretty views of the countryside and the ruins.

For something even more out of the ordinary, book a cruise down the Tiber to **Ostia Antica** (see Chapter 14). Have lunch in the **medieval village** or the cafeteria inside the archeological area. In the afternoon, return to Rome, and maybe pick one of the attractions you're interested in but didn't have time to visit. Make sure you leave time for some last-minute shopping. For dinner, head to the Testaccio, the most Roman of Roman neighborhoods, and have your goodbye meal at **Checchino dal 1887** (see Chapter 10). If you feel like burning the midnight oil, you can then stop in at **Club Picasso,** one of Testaccio's hottest clubs (see Chapter 16). Or treat yourself to the best and most elegant restaurant in Rome and go to **La Pergola.**

Rome for Architecture Lovers

Rome is architects' and art historians' heaven. Shaped by the Renaissance and baroque eras, which completely changed the face of Byzantine and medieval Rome, the center of Rome is basically nothing but historic sites. Splendid palaces and buildings await you at every corner, while large and tiny squares — sudden openings in the fabric of narrow streets — surprise you with their beauty, and parks provide shade and relaxation. If you love architecture, Rome has more to offer than can be related in a few lines, and here is how to see the best of it in one day: Just make sure you wear comfortable shoes!

Start with the **Janiculum Hill,** for a unique view of Rome's historic center. Walk down to the neighborhood of **Trastevere,** where you'll find the **Villa Farnesina,** a lesser-known architectural marvel. Cross the Tiber over **Ponte Sisto** — an elegant Renaissance bridge rebuilt in the 15th century with part of the ruined preexisting Roman bridge — to reach nearby **Piazza Farnese,** graced by the superb **Palazzo Farnese,** with its serene facade and gorgeous courtyard (visible only through a gate at the back). Nearby, you can visit the **Spada Gallery,** a little-known Renaissance palace, especially famous for housing Borromini's Perspective, a unique architectural trompe l'oeil (see Chapter 11). Have a bite to eat on **Campo de' Fiori** or on **Piazza della Cancelleria** (for example, at **Grappolo d'Oro Zampanò;** see Chapter 10).

After lunch, cross over to **Piazza Navona,** perhaps Rome's most beautiful square, and make your way through the narrow streets to **Ponte Sant'Angelo,** for the scenic view of the statue-adorned bridge leading to **Castel Sant'Angelo.** Push on to **Piazza del Popolo** and **Piazza di Spagna** — two of the most scenic spaces in Rome — for a well-deserved tea or coffee break (see Chapter 10). Next, go for a visit to the **Monument to King Vittorio Emanuele II,** an impressive if not unanimously liked building where you can climb for an unusual view over Rome. End your evening with Michelangelo's masterpiece **Piazza del Campidoglio,** defined by the three palaces that house the **Capitoline Museums** (see Chapter 11) — surely one of the great architectural monuments of Rome.

Rome for Michelangelo's Fans

A splendid sculptor, an exquisite painter, and a masterly architect, Michelangelo was extremely active in Rome, where the pope and wealthy local families employed his many talents.

Start with Michelangelo's crowning achievement and one of the most important works in the history of Western culture: the **Sistine Chapel.** Make reservations way in advance to avoid the lines. He worked on this pictorial masterpiece for several years in a row (between 1508 and 1512 for the ceiling, and between 1535 and 1564 for the wall behind the main altar). Continue to **St. Peter's Basilica** to see the beautiful dome he designed but didn't see finished — he died almost 30 years before its faithful completion by architect Giacomo Della Porta. The basilica also houses the splendid *Pietà,* the sculptural masterpiece of Mary and Christ, which Michelangelo carved between 1498 and 1500. After taking in this awe-inspiring sights, cross the Tiber and head to **Campo de' Fiori** for a bite to eat (see Chapter 10).

After your break, stroll to nearby **Piazza Farnese,** where you can admire the facade of Palazzo Farnese, which Michelangelo finished after the death of the original architect, Sangallo the Younger. You can then proceed to **Piazza del Campidoglio,** the square defined by the three beautiful palaces housing the **Capitoline Museums.** This piazza is a great architectural achievement in large part following Michelangelo's design (the 12-pointed star pattern set in the pavement of the square signifies the 12 apostles). From here, it is only a short bus or taxi ride to **San Pietro in Vincoli,** where you can admire the artist's monument to Pope Julius II, decorated with his famous sculpture of **Moses.** Then stroll up the hill — or take a quick bus ride — to **Santa Maria Maggiore,** where you'll find a little-known architectural marvel, the **Cappella Sforza,** designed and begun by Michelangelo but completed well after his death. You can finish your tour with **Santa Maria degli Angeli,** the church Michelangelo created by reorganizing, with great skill and respect for the original architecture, the well-preserved ruins of the **Terme di Diocleziano,** or Diocletian Baths. (See Chapter 11 for all the preceding attractions.)

Rome for Families

Children usually hate the very idea of spending hours in an enclosed space such as a museum or a church. Don't worry. As it has for centuries, Rome will surprise you.

Start your day bright and early by going to the **Roman Forum.** Proceed to the **Palatino** — ancient Rome's most exclusive residential hill — where you can pick up tickets for the **Colosseum** without waiting in line (unless you have already done so in advance, which we recommend). After these three sites, you should have worked up a hearty appetite; head for **Angelino ai Fori,** where parents can have a real meal and children can go for pizza, or head to **Pizza Forum** for a slice on the go (see Chapter 10).

In the afternoon, tackle Renaissance Rome. Descend to the Tiber, where you can take a **boat ride** (see Chapter 11) and view the heart of Rome from the water. Then head for **Villa Borghese** (see Chapter 11), where parents can take turns seeing the art in the **Borghese Gallery** (for which you'll have made reservations), while the kids enjoy the green expanse of the park, renting bicycles, rowing a boat on the small romantic lake — complete with ruined temple — visiting the children's museum, or going on the rides. Descend through the **Pincio Gardens** to the **Spanish Steps,** and walk down to **Piazza di Spagna.** Have a good dinner at **Sant'Andrea.** After dinner, stroll to the **Trevi Fountain** for ice cream and to toss a coin in the fountain, which is most scenic by night.

Chapter 14

Going Beyond Rome: Five Day Trips

- -

In This Chapter

▶ Traveling back in time to Ostia Antica

▶ Visiting the fountains of Tivoli

▶ Dining with the Romans in the Castelli Romani

▶ Discovering Etruscan marvels in Tarquinia

▶ Taking the waters in medieval Viterbo

- -

*L*azio, the region surrounding Rome, is rich in beautiful and fascinating sites that lie only a short drive from the capital. If you have the time, stay a couple of extra days in Rome and branch out from there for some enjoyable day trips.

Each of the towns listed in this chapter is small enough to explore on foot — be prepared to walk a mile or so — and offers taxi service in addition to the public-transit options mentioned in each section.

Ostia Antica: Rome's Ancient Seaport

Southwest of Rome, toward the sea, is **Ostia Antica,** the archaeological site of ancient Rome's commercial harbor. This is a destination not to miss, especially if you're keen on antiquity. Some say it is better than the more famous Pompeii and Herculaneum; it is certainly extremely interesting, cheaper, and much less crowded. It is also an excellent outing for kids, particularly if you get there on a very pleasant boat cruise along the Tiber (see "Taking a tour," later in this section). The ruins are particularly attractive early in the morning and at sunset, when many Romans like to come for an evening *passeggiata* (stroll). It's popular also on weekends for picnics, but most popular are the shows — music and theater — held in the **Roman Theater** (Teatro Romano) in July.

The ancient city of Ostia served as a shipyard, a gathering place for the fleet, and a distribution center for ancient Rome. Founded in the fourth century B.C. as a military colony for the defense of the river Tevere, Ostia flourished for about eight centuries before being progressively abandoned as a result of the silting up of the river and the spread of malaria in the region (no longer a concern, fortunately).

Keep in mind that the ruins are incredibly hot in summer. They're spread across a flat plain, and shade is hard to come by. If you don't like heat, come early and end your visit just before lunch, or wait for the late afternoon.

Getting there

Ostia Antica is about 28km (16 miles) from Rome and is easy to reach by public transportation (buy a day pass; see Chapter 8). The **metropolitan train** to Ostia Lido departs from Stazione Ostiense (take Metro Line B to the Piramide stop, and follow the signs for Ostia Lido to your platform), with trains departing every half-hour and costing 1€ ($1.30) for the 25-minute trip. Get off at Ostia Antica stop; the archeological area is .8km (½ mile) away on foot, or five minutes by taxi or by bus (C19 from Cimitero for one stop to Via Romagnoli/Castello, every 30 minutes). If you want a taxi and none are waiting outside, you can call a local radio taxi (☎ **06-5601646**) or one from Ostia train station (☎ **06-56320466**).

By far the most interesting way to get to Ostia Antica is a boat cruise with the **Compagnia di Navigazione Ponte San Angelo** (☎ **06-6789361** for reservations; info@battellidiroma.it). They run from the Marconi bridge (daily in summer and Fri–Sun in winter at 10 a.m., with arrival at Ostia Antica at noon), covering the ancient Roman route between the capital and its seaside harbor. If you wish, you can catch the boat back from Ostia at 2 p.m. for a scheduled arrival in Rome at 4:30 p.m., or you can return by subway. Tickets cost 12€ ($16) one-way, 13€ ($17) round-trip.

Taking a tour

We feel that taking a tour is the way to go to understand the ruins, but we do not recommend taking a tour directly from Rome: They are usually overpriced and don't allow for a proper leisurely visit. Rather, sign up for the tour offered by the Archaeological Office of Ostia, led by licensed guides and art historians. You can book a tour by calling or faxing the office at ☎ **06-56352830** Tuesday through Sunday. You'll meet your tour guide at the entrance to the excavations.

If you prefer a commercial excursion, including transportation by bus from Rome and entrance to the sights, **Stop n Go/C.S.R.** (Via Ezio 12; ☎ **06-3217054;** csr@gisec.it) offers one of the best. It organizes half-day tours of Ostia Antica, leaving Tuesday through Sunday at 9:30 a.m. from the Stop n Go Terminal on Via Giolitti in Rome (on the side of Termini train station) for 12€ ($16).

Seeing the sights

Near the archeological area, you'll find the **Medieval Borgo of Ostia Antica,** a romantic hamlet with a curious out-of-place feeling, as if something is missing. What's missing is the river: Pope Gregorius IV built the

Rome and Environs

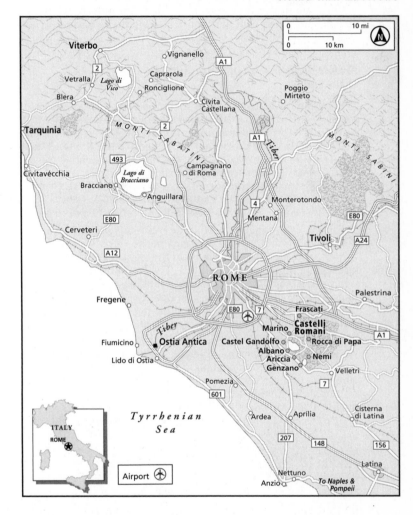

fortified village on the Tiber's banks between A.D. 827 and 844 as an outpost and duty station, and it takes its shape from the river bend. The
outpost gained importance in following centuries, and Pope Julius II
ordered the construction of the **castle** and had it built in 1483. In 1575,
though, a flood dramatically changed the course of the river, moving it
almost 1.6 km (1 mile) to the north. The outpost and castle were abandoned and left virtually untouched until our day. One of the first examples
of modern western military architecture in the world, it is quite interesting to visit. The small church of the Borgo is actually a cathedral —
Sant'Aurea — whose bishop, traditionally, is the dean of the College of

Cardinals. (Piazza della Rocca; ☎ **06-56358024;** fax 06-565150 for reservations; admission free; open by guided tour only; tours Tues–Sun at 10 a.m. and noon; Tues and Thurs also 5 p.m.; closed Jan 1, May 1, and Dec 25.)

Archaeological Area of Ostia Antica
Ostia Antica

The archaeological site covers the impressive excavations of the ancient town of Ostia. The main streets of the town have been unearthed, as have some of the principal monuments. After entering the site, on the right you'll find **Via delle Corporazioni,** leading to the **Roman Theater** (Teatro Romano). Be sure to take note of the mosaics indicating the nature of the businesses that once were housed along this street. The theater is still in use today for performances of works by modern and ancient authors during July as part of the **Estate Romana** festival (www.estateromana. comune.roma.it or ☎ **06-68809505;** Mon–Sat 10 a.m.–5 p.m.).

Returning to the main street and continuing, you'll find on your left the **Forum** and behind it the **thermal baths** *(terme).* Two temples are on the left, and the **Capitolinum** is on the right. The site also includes many interesting houses and buildings. The tourist office in Rome has a relatively good map of the park. Allow a minimum of three hours for the visit, more if you visit the museum. The **Ostiense Museum (Museo Ostiense) —** conserving all the material found during the excavations of the site — exhibits its huge collection in a modern and rational way, making it a pleasure to visit. The entrance to the museum is within the excavations.

We recommend taking an official guided tour (prices on request); you'll learn a lot of interesting details. The site is huge and it is easy to feel overwhelmed. Definitely splurge on the map (2€/$2.60 at the ticket booth) and on the audio guide (4€/$5.20 at the ticket booth). Facilities are by the museum and include a bar cafeteria and a gift shop.

Viale dei Romagnoli 717, off Via Ostiense. ☎ *06-56358099. For guided tours* ☎ *and fax 06-56352830.* www.itnw.roma.it/ostia/scavi. *Admission: 6.50€ ($5) including the museum. Open: Excavations: Jan–Feb and Nov–Dec Tues–Sun 8:30 a.m.–5 p.m.; Mar 1–last Sun in Mar and last Sun in Oct–Oct 31 Tues–Sun 8:30 a.m.–6 p.m.; last Sun in Mar to last Sun in Oct (during daylight saving time) 8:30 a.m.–7:30 p.m. Last admission Nov–Mar one hour before closing; during daylight saving 90 minutes before closing. Museum: Jan–Feb and Nov–Dec Tues–Sun 9 a.m.–4:30 p.m.; Mar 1–last Sun in Mar and last Sun in Oct–Oct 31 Tues–Sun 9 a.m.–5:30 p.m.; during daylight saving Tues–Sun 9 a.m.–1:30 p.m. and 2:15–6:30 p.m. Both closed Jan 1, May 1, and Dec 25.*

Dining locally

The most convenient solution is obviously the **restaurant cafeteria** in the Ostiense Museum, inside the archeological area. There you can get a simple meal (with hot food) at a reasonable price, as well as beverages and ice cream.

Cipriani
$$ Ostia Antica   LATIUM

This classic restaurant is in a medieval house inside the Borgo of Ostia Antica, not far from the castle. The décor is romantic, the cuisine local, with attention paid to the quality of the ingredients. We had excellent *agnolotti* (fresh pasta filled with meat) and *pasta alla gricia* (with Italian bacon and cheese), followed by a delicious platter of grilled meat, including lamb and pork chops and sausages.

Via del Forno 1. ☎ *06-56352956. Reservations recommended on weekends. Secondi: 8€–22€ ($10–$29). AE, DC, MC, V. Open: Thurs–Tues 7:30–11 p.m.*

Spending the night

Rodrigo de Vivar Resorts and Country
$$ Ostia Antica

This is a great place to stay, right inside the medieval hamlet. The guest rooms are in various spaces within a *rocca* (castle), including one in a tower. Furnishings are in elegant country style, and bathrooms are modern and quite spacious. The resort also offers rooms at a farm nearby; they're nicely appointed but not as convenient to the archeological area, and without the medieval charm. The farm offers organic produce and horse rides.

Piazza della Rocca 18. ☎ *06-5651939 or 06-5650114. Fax 06-5652535* www. rodrigodevivar.com. *Rack rates: 163€–265€ ($212–$345) double. Rates include breakfast. AE, DC, MC, V.*

Tivoli and Its Trio of Villas

Tivoli, a small town on a hill 32km (20 miles) northeast of Rome, is our favorite day trip from Rome in the heat of summer. The resort town enjoys a cooler climate during the hot months and has been a traditional getaway from Rome since ancient times. Its three famous villas — one ancient Roman, one baroque, and one from the romantic period — reveal Rome's architectural history as it played out over almost 2,000 years.

Getting there

Trains leave Rome's Stazione Tiburtina for Tivoli about every hour. The ticket costs 2.50€ ($3.25) for the 45-minute trip. The Tivoli train station is outside the town center (which centers on Piazza Giuseppe Garibaldi), about .8km (½ mile) away (take Viale Mazzini, and cross the Aniene River on pedestrian-only Ponte della Pace, or Ponte Gregoriano). You can easily take a **taxi** — available just outside the train station, or call ☎ **0774-317071,** 0774-334233, or 0774-314302 — to get to your destination; the fare to the center of town is about 4€ ($5.25).

COTRAL Busses (☎ 06-4182135 or 06-4181338; www.cotralspa.it) leave Ponte Mammolo station in Rome (on Metro Line B) for Tivoli every

10 or 20 minutes for the 40-minute trip. Tickets cost $6€ ($8). Get off before the last stop, in Piazzale Nazioni Unite in the historic center. It is a good idea to avoid the bus at rush hour (after 4 p.m.), when it tends to be very crowded.

If you are renting a car, Tivoli is a **short drive** away — only 31km (20 miles) — from the capital, at the end of a very busy consular road, the Via Tiburtina, running northeast of Rome, east of the Via Nomentana. Tivoli is a suburb of Rome, and many people commute to and from the city daily, so traffic at peak hours can be horrible. Paid parking is available in Piazza Matteotti but can be difficult to find in the high season.

A shuttle service operates Monday through Saturday in the historic district (2€/$2.60 per ride; departures every 30 minutes), connecting key areas in the historic center with Villa Adriana.

Taking a tour

If you sign up with a tour from Rome, you can avoid both the hassle of driving and the trouble of dealing with transportation in a foreign language. A reliable agency that organizes excursions to Tivoli is **Argiletum Tour Operator** (Via Madonna dei Monti 49, off Via Cavour; ☎ **06-47825706;** www.argiletumtour.com). It runs a four-hour tour Tuesday through Sunday — in the afternoon in summer and in the morning in winter — for 49€ ($64); price includes pickup from centrally located hotels and admission to Villa Adriana, Villa d'Este, and Villa Gregoriana.

Seeing the sights

The **tourist office in Tivoli** is in the central square of Largo Garibaldi (☎ **0774-334522**); summer hours are Monday through Saturday 9 a.m. to 6 p.m. and Sunday 9 a.m. to 2 p.m. (in winter, it closes one hour earlier).

Although visiting the three villas will likely be the focus of your jaunt, be sure to have a look at the town. The highlights are the second century B.C. **Tempio della Sibilla**, on the Roman Acropolis (on the other side of the Aniene River); the 12th-century churches of **San Silvestro** (southwest of the Villa d'Este) and **Santa Maria Maggiore;** and the 1461 **Rocca Pia,** Pope Pius II's castle, which was turned into a prison after 1870.

Villa Adriana

This is the famous ancient Roman villa located about 5km (3½ miles) outside the historic center of town. Hadrian, one of Rome's "good" emperors, had this grandiose villa built between A.D. 118 and 138 as his getaway and retirement home: he spent the last three years of his life here. This villa was built on the site of an older one dating from Republican times. It remains magnificent, though it has lost its marbles, so to speak — many of its sculptures are now in Roman museums. Much of the marble that once covered the structures is gone because the estate was used as a "quarry" during the Renaissance, as were many other Roman buildings, such as the Colosseum. In his villa, Hadrian wanted to be surrounded by the architectural marvels he'd seen during his trips across the Empire: On the 300 acres of this self-contained world for his vast royal entourage, he constructed replicas of famous buildings of antiquity, such as the **Canopus** (the Egyptian round canal ringed with statues) and the **Lyceum** (the school of Aristotle), as well as temples and theaters, monumental thermal baths, fountains and gardens, and a library. Although most of the monuments are in ruins, the effect is still impressive, and the atmosphere Hadrian cultivated mysteriously survives. For a glimpse of what the villa looked like in its heyday, see the reconstruction at the entrance. Kids love both the model and exploring the ruins of the park. Like any ruin in Italy, the villa gets very hot at midday during summer, so the best times to visit are early in the morning or late in the afternoon.

Via di Villa Adriana, 5km (3½ miles) from the center of Tivoli. ☎ *0774-530203. Bus: 4 and 4X from Largo Garibaldi (the main square of Tivoli) to Villa Adriana. Admission: 6.50€ ($8). Open: Daily Nov–Jan 9 a.m.–5 p.m.; Feb 9 a.m.–6 p.m.; Mar and Oct 9 a.m.–6:30 p.m.; Apr and Sept 9 a.m.–7 p.m.; May–Aug 9 a.m.–7:30 p.m. Last admission 90 minutes before closing. Closed Jan 1, May 1, and Dec 25.*

Villa d'Este

Built in 1550 by Cardinal Ippolito d'Este of Ferrara, son of the notorious Lucrezia Borgia and Alfonso I d'Este, this would be just another beautiful 16th-century villa if it weren't for its gardens. Designed by architect Pirro Ligorio, they are graced by a complex system of fountains — a true masterpiece of hydraulic engineering. Using an underground spring and the natural slope of the land, Ligorio managed to have naturally feeding fountains, two of which are *sonorous* (the fountains are a sort of water organ that makes "music"). The magnificent work is enhanced by the sculptural work of the fountains: the **Fontana dell'Organo (Fountain of the Organ),** by Claude Veanard; the **Fontana del'Ovato (Ovato Fountain),** by Ligorio; and the **Fontana del Bicchierone (Fountain of the Big Glass),** by Bernini himself. The **Fontana della Civetta (Fountain of the Owl)** is on at 10 a.m., noon, and 2, 4, and 6 p.m. (in summer) only. With all that water and foliage, the gardens are incredibly refreshing in summer and a perfect spot to be at midday on your visit to Tivoli. You can pick up an audio guide for 4€ ($5.25) at the entrance. *Note:* It is a good idea to check with the ticket office that the fountains will be running during the scheduled time for your visit; they sometimes close for maintenance. If they're not, we recommend you reschedule. The villa and gardens are wheelchair accessible by reservation only.

Piazza Trento, west of Piazza Giuseppe Garibaldi, the main square in the historic center of Tivoli. ☎ *199-766166 within Italy; 0424-600460 from abroad.* www. villadestetivoli.info. *Admission: 6.50€ ($8); 9€ ($12) during special exhibits. Open: Tues–Sat last Sun in Sept–Oct 31 8:30 a.m.–6:30 p.m.; Nov–Jan 8:30 a.m.–5 p.m.; Feb 8:30 a.m.–5:30 p.m.; Mar 1–last Sat in Mar 8:30–6:15 p.m.; last Sun in Mar–Apr 8:30–7:30 p.m.; May–last Sat in Sept 8:30 a.m.–7:45 p.m. Last admission one hour before closing. Closed Jan 1, May 1, and Dec 25.*

Villa Gregoriana

This is a magic place we love. Villa Gregoriana, the latest of the three famous villas of Tivoli, was built in the 19th century — but it isn't a villa at all. In reality, it's a beautiful park created to enhance the natural beauty of the gorges of the Aniene, Rome's second river, where it makes some scenic waterfalls and disappears underground for a short while, creating the **grottoes of Neptune and Sirene** (Grotte di Nettuno e Sirene). Pope Gregory XVI had a path carved all the way down to the bottom of the ravine to allow him to admire the 90m (300-ft.) waterfall, grottoes, and ponds. The deep slopes are covered with vegetation and mighty trees, making it an enchanting spot, especially in summer, when it is a wonderful refuge from the heat. The park was closed for a lengthy restoration, which has brought it back to its original splendor, and is now run by a conservation organization. *Note:* The visit here is a hike in a natural park over picturesque ravines. It is not at all strenuous as the trail goes downhill, but you'll want to wear cross trainers (or even hiking shoes in wet weather) and carry water. Young children need constant supervision as it may get slippery and falls can be dangerous. If you carry young children on a backpack carrier or you are tall, watch your head in galleries and grottoes.

Enter from Piazza Tempio di Vesta, off Largo Sant'Angelo in the historic center of Tivoli (exit on Largo Massimo). ☎ *0774-334522.* www.villagregoriana.it. *Admission: 4€ ($5.25) adult; family of four 10€ ($13). Open: Tues–Sun Oct 16–Nov 30 and Mar 10 a.m.–2:30 p.m.; Apr 1–Oct 15 10:30 a.m.–6:30 p.m. Last admission one hour before closing. Closed Dec–Feb.*

Dining locally

Tivoli has a number of *trattorie* and restaurants that are favorites of Romans on Sunday outings.

Antica Hostaria de' Carrettieri
$$ Villa Gregoriana   ROMAN/SARDINIAN

This old-fashioned restaurant serves excellent, intriguing food. The chef is originally from Sardinia, and the menu features Sardinian specialties side by side with dishes true to the strictest Roman tradition. The *rigatoni all'amatriciana* (pasta in a spicy tomato and bacon sauce) is excellent, and so are *gnocchetti in salsa di formaggio piccante* (little potato dumplings with spicy cheese sauce) and *tortino ai porri* (leek quiche).

Via D. Giuliani 55. ☎ *0774-330159. Reservations recommended on weekends. Secondi: 8€–15€ ($10–$20). AE, DC, MC, V. Open: Thurs–Tues 12:30–3 p.m. and 7:30–10:30 p.m. Closed two weeks in Aug.*

Le Cinque Statue
$$ Villa Gregoriana   ROMAN

Decorated with marble statues — the five statues in the restaurant's name — this reliable family-run restaurant offers typical Roman cuisine, such as *rigatoni all'amatriciana* (pasta in a spicy tomato and bacon sauce) and *agnello alla scottadito* (grilled lamb cutlets), which you can enjoy with a choice of local wines, mostly from the nearby Castelli region. The staff is very welcoming to children and will accommodate their special needs.

Via Quintilio Varo 8, off the entrance to the Villa Gregoriana. ☎ *0774-335366. Reservations recommended on weekends. Secondi: 9€–14€ ($12–$18). AE, DC, MC, V. Open: Sat–Thurs noon to 2:30 p.m. and 7:30–10:30 p.m. Closed second and third weeks in Aug.*

Ristorante Adriano
$$ Villa Adriana   ROMAN

Steps from the ticket booth, this is the best place to eat if you are visiting Villa Adriano. It serves well-prepared Roman specialties, and everything is homemade and delicious. We recommend the fresh pasta, particularly the *cannelloni* and *tortelli,* as well as the mouth-watering *agnello con le patate* (roasted lamb with thyme, rosemary, and new potatoes). The *galletto alla diavola* (spicy charbroiled chicken) was a favorite of the movie director Federico Fellini's. Hadrian's Banquet, a sumptuous brunch, is offered on Sundays (25€/$33). The restaurant is also a hotel (see below) and offers great cooking classes.

Via di Villa Adriana 194, near the Villa Adriana ticket booth. ☎ *0774-382235.* www. hoteladriano.it. *Reservations recommended. Bus: 4 and 4X to Villa Adriana. Secondi: 10€–18€ ($13–$23). AE, DC, MC, V. Open: Daily noon to 3 p.m. and 7–10:30 p.m.*

Spending the night
Although you can visit Tivoli in a day trip from Rome, it's also a nice spot to spend the night.

Hotel Ristorante Adriano
$ Villa Adriana

"Countryside elegance" describes this tree-surrounded villa housing this hotel located by the entrance of Villa Adriana. The few guest rooms are very nicely appointed, with some antiques. Bathrooms are good-size and modern. Suite 14, with a splendid view over Hadrian's Villa, was where the writer Marguerite Yourcenar stayed for a while, perhaps getting ideas for her famous novel *Memoirs of Hadrian.* The restaurant is excellent (see review above).

Via di Villa Adriana 194, near the Villa Adriana ticket booth. ☎ *0774-382235 or 0774 535028. Fax: 0774-535122.* www.hoteladriano.it. *Bus: 4 and 4X to Villa Adriana. Free parking. Rack rates: 120€ ($156) double; 150€–210€ ($195–$273) junior suite. Rates include breakfast. AE, DC, MC, V.*

The Castelli Romani and Their Wines

The hill towns surrounding Rome to the southeast are a favorite destination for locals — including the pope, who enjoys a magnificent villa in

Castel Gandolfo — to escape the summer swelter and enjoy excellent wine and food. Each town is dominated by its own castle (the smallest is called a *rocca*) and is surrounded by fertile countryside, the produce of which is masterfully prepared and served in the many *trattorie*.

Each of the Castelli towns — Albano Laziale, Ariccia, Castel Gandolfo, Frascati, Genzano, Grottaferrata, Lanuvio, Lariano, Marino, Monte Compatri, Monte Porzio Catone, Nemi, Rocca di Papa, Rocca Priora, and Velletri — makes a pleasant day trip. You may also consider taking an overview tour of the area.

Getting there

The best way to visit the Castelli Romani is by **car.** Driving allows you to visit more than one of these attractive small towns. If you decide to rent a car (see the appendix for information), take Via Tuscolana out of Rome and follow it to Frascati. Continue on the local road, which makes a near-loop connecting Frascati with Marino on one side and Rocca di Papa on the other. This route will take you through all the other castelli. You can also reach Marino from the Appia Nuova, taking a 7.2km (4½-mile) detour to the north. From the Appia, you can take another side road for Castel Gandolfo. The Appia then continues to Albano, Ariccia, and Genzano.

If you don't care for driving, a good alternative is taking an **organized tour** (see the following section).

If you want to pick one town, the **train** is a good option. From Rome's Stazione Termini, you can catch a train to Albano Laziale that also stops in Marino and Castel Gandolfo; a train to Frascati; or a train to Velletri that also stops in Lanuvio. They all make several runs per day and cost 3€ ($3.90). The trip from Rome takes about 30 minutes to Lanuvio, Marino, or Frascati; 40 minutes to Castel Gandolfo; 50 minutes to Albano Laziale; and one hour to Velletri. If you prefer not to explore on foot, each town has its own bus system.

You can also take a **COTRAL bus** (☎ 800-431784 toll free within Italy for schedules; www.cotralspa.it). Buses leave from the Subaugusta and Anagnina stops on Metro Line A for Albano every 20 minutes or so. Albano is the hub for service to the other castelli; you can catch COTRAL buses from Albano to Nemi, Ariccia, Genzano, Marino, Grottaferrata, and Frascati. Trip lengths vary, but all are under an hour. The price ranges from 3€ to 6€ ($3.90–$7.80).

Taking a tour

Argiletum Tour Operator (Via Madonna dei Monti 49, off Via Cavour; ☎ 06-47825706; www.argiletumtour.com) organizes four-hour afternoon tours in summer on Tuesday and Saturday for 37€ ($48); the price includes pickup from centrally located hotels.

Seeing the sights

The **central tourist office** for the Castelli Romani is in Albano (Viale Risorgimento 1; ☎ 06-9324081). Another large office is in Frascati (Piazza Marconi 1; ☎ 06-9420331). Both are open Monday through Friday 8 a.m. to 2 p.m. and 3:30 to 6:30 p.m., and Saturday 8 a.m. to 2 p.m. Some of the villages and small towns of the castelli have little more than a charming central square and a few good places to eat. In the rest of this trips section, we describe the most interesting towns.

Albano Laziale

Though it's the most built up of the castelli, Albano maintains its unique charm. It's the center of the area producing the table wine Colli Albani, a pleasant white you often find in *trattorie* around Rome. Albano was the site of an ancient Roman town built along the Appian Way — the *Regina Viarum* (queen of all roads) — around Emperor Domitian's villa. Later, Emperor Septimius Severus housed Roman legions here. The little town remained a village throughout the Middle Ages and the Renaissance, when wealthy Romans again started building elegant villas with beautiful views over the volcanic lake called **Lago di Albano.** During the 19th century, it became a regular stop on the Grand Tour, the extended cultural pilgrimage through Europe that well-to-do young men and women traditionally took. Roman ruins abound — the **Sepolcro degli Orazi e dei Curiazi (Roman tomb),** the **Villa di Pompeo** inside the **Villa Comunale,** and the **Nimpheus** of the Villa di Domitziano — but the great attraction is the volcanic lake formed by two craters, where you can enjoy a variety of watersports.

Ariccia

One of the most ancient towns in Latium, Ariccia was the seat of a sanctuary dedicated to Diana, the hunting goddess, and was already active before Rome became a republic. Ariccia originally lay along the Appian Way, but it was moved to its current location at the top of the rocky cliff during the Middle Ages. Unfortunately, ugly modern buildings have been built around the historic center, but splendid treasures await those who push through.

Ariccia became a key stop on the Grand Tour of Italy in the 18th century, especially for artists drawn to its beauty. Particularly striking is **Locanda Martorelli,** in Piazza di Corte, which is decorated with a cycle of paintings by the Polish painter Taddeo Kuntze. Also on the square is Ariccia's most famous attraction, the 17th-century **Palazzo Chigi.** This grandiose villa belonged to the Chigi family until 1988, when it passed to the town, which started lengthy restorations. Surrounded by a splendid garden, it was transformed into a baroque marvel by Gian Lorenzo Bernini and now houses the **Museum of the Baroque,** which can be visited daily from 10 a.m. to 7 p.m. (Piazza di Corte 14; ☎ 06-9330053; www.palazzo chigiariccia.it; admission: 4€/$5.20). Across from the *palazzo* is the **church of the Assunta,** the last achievement of the great master. Bernini designed and built it with his pupil Carlo Fontana, who was also destined for glory as an architect. Inspired by the Pantheon in Rome, the round church was completed in 1664. The great viaduct over the valley to the historic center was built in 1854, destroyed by the Germans during their retreat in 1944, and rebuilt in 1948.

Another important reason to visit Ariccia is the *fraschette* (small taverns), often with outdoor dining areas, where you can sample local wine and the town's specialty: *porchetta*. Not to be missed, *porchetta* is a whole (deboned) pig carefully roasted with herbs, then sliced and served with peasant bread. A *porchetta* sandwich is one of the best "fast foods" you'll ever have.

Castel Gandolfo

On the slopes of the beautiful Lago di Albano, Castel Gandolfo has a great beach — bring your suit if you want to swim; your kids will love it — and a very pleasant promenade along the lake. The town grew around the 12th-century castle built by the Roman family of the Gandolfi. Since the 17th century, it has been the official summer residence of the pope. The pope's palace and villa (originally Villa Barberini, surrounded by an enormous garden and built atop the villa of the Roman Emperor Domitian), are still part of Vatican territory. The villa also houses the Vatican Observatory, the oldest astronomical research institution in the world. You can't visit the papal villa, but you can enjoy the rest of the town, including Bernini's **San Tommaso di Villanova church** and his **fountain** on the main square, Piazza della Libertà. Just out of town is the **Villa Torlonia,** in neoclassical style and decorated with sculptures by B. Thorvaldsen.

Frascati

Frascati may be the most familiar of the castelli towns because of the famous white wine produced in the surrounding countryside. Romans come here to visit the various *cantine* (cellars), where you can sample the wine and eat simple fare, such as *porchetta* and *pecorino* (sheep's-milk cheese), or a sandwich made with local bread and *salame*. The town is dominated by the imposing 16th-century **Villa Aldobrandini,** set atop a steep slope overlooking the main square. You can visit its gardens daily from 9 a.m. to 1 p.m. by getting a free ticket from the **tourist office,** Piazza Marconi 1 (see "Seeing the sights," earlier in this section).

Genzano

Picturesquely situated above the Lago di Nemi, another crater of an extinct volcano, Genzano is a charming small town surrounded by beautiful countryside. Its famous wine is not the only attraction; among the highlights are the 17th-century **Palazzo Sforza-Cesarini** and the nearby **cathedral.** Genzano's main event is the ***Infiorata*** (literally, "flowering") — held one Sunday in spring when the main street is covered with a carpet of flowers. The wine is good here, and you'll find a few nice *trattorie*.

Marino

The closest of the castelli to Rome (only 24km/15 miles), Marino is a pleasant small town, though the surroundings are modern and bland. The town is most famous for its red wine, particularly enjoyable when it's fresh. On the occasion of the **harvest celebration** in October, the two main baroque fountains in town pour wine instead of water, to the great delight of all. The rest of the time, you can sample it in the various *osterie* and *cantine* in town — just look for the sign VINO!

Nemi

Nemi is a jewel of a small town. It has its own lake, the **Lago di Nemi,** on the slopes of which are cultivated some of the best strawberries in the world, and certainly the best in Italy. Kids will love the opportunity to go for a swim or a boat ride. Nemi also specializes in the production of *salame,* sausage, *pancetta* (Italian bacon), and other mouthwatering items. Alas, you can't bring meat products back into the States, but that's just one more reason to sample them here. They keep quite well, and you can include them in a picnic during your trip.

Rocca di Papa

The town of Rocca di Papa, named after its castle, dominates the Lago di Albano and enjoys breathtaking views of the surrounding hills. It's worth climbing the hill above the town to see the great vista; it's now a park, and all that's left here is the ruin of an old *albergo* (hotel) where people once came to eat and enjoy the pure air. The town below is quite picturesque. The **Chiesa dell'Assunta** is a baroque church that was reconstructed after an 1806 earthquake. Children will love the climb and the ruins, as well as the chance to swim in the lake.

Velletri

This town was an important agricultural center in 63 B.C., when Emperor Augustus was born here, and it remains so today. The historical center of town is very pretty, with many baroque attractions, including the elegant Piazza Cairoli. But the biggest attraction in town is in the cloister of Velletri's Cathedral, which houses the **Diocesan Museum** (Corso della Repubblica 347; ☎ 06-9627217; www.museovelletri.com; admission: 2€/$2.60; daily 10 a.m.–1 p.m. and 3–7 p.m.), a valuable collection that includes precious objects and paintings by Gentile da Fabriano, Antoniazzo Romano, and others.

Dining locally

The castelli contain a procession of *trattorie* and *ristoranti.* They're all quite reliable, but keep in mind the rule of "trust the locals": If it's dinnertime and nobody is eating in a place, there must be a reason. We give you some safe bets in this section, but just follow your nose to find some other great places on your own.

The food in the castelli is typically Roman, including fresh pasta and grilled meats. People come to sample the variety of local *salame* and cheeses, usually served as antipasto. *Porchetta,* a specialty of Ariccia (see "Ariccia," earlier in this chapter), is prepared to some extent everywhere in the castelli. The wine of the castelli is probably the best in Lazio; particularly famous are Frascati and Marino (white and red, respectively).

Antica Abazia
$$ **Albano Laziale   CREATIVE LATIUM**

In the rustic atmosphere of this down-to-earth restaurant, you'll discover the work of an excellent chef serving traditional recipes with a personal twist. The menu changes often, following the seasons, and the service is friendly. Among the best dishes are the *spaghetti con moscardini e pecorino* (pasta with baby squid and pecorino cheese), *fettuccine al ragù di capretto* (homemade fresh pasta with tomato and kid-meat sauce), *stinco di maiale con castagne e mele* (pork shank with apples and chestnuts), and *tagliata di manzo con pomodoretti e finocchio selvatico* (beefsteak with cherry tomatoes and wild fennel). Save room for one of the excellent homemade desserts.

Via San Filippo Neri 19, off via Murialdo, 1 block north of Piazza del Duomo and Piazza Sabatini. ☎ *06-9323187. Reservations recommended on weekends. Secondi: 8€–12€ ($10–$16). AE, DC, MC, V. Open: Tues–Sun noon to 2:30 p.m. and 7:30–10:30 p.m.*

Antico Ristorante Paganelli
$$$$ **Castel Gandolfo   ROMAN/SEAFOOD**

This restaurant, serving a variety of classic Roman food and seafood, has upscale leanings and impeccable service. You can choose from the à la carte menu and the prix-fixe offerings. The menu changes periodically but may include such local specialties as *cannelloni* (oven-cooked, filled tubes of homemade fresh pasta), *agnello arrosto con le patate* (herbed lamb with roasted potatoes), and *fritto misto* (deep-fried small fish, calamari, and shrimp).

Via Gramsci 4. ☎ *06-9360004. Reservations recommended on weekends. Secondi: 14€–25€ ($18–$33). AE, DC, MC, V. Open: Wed–Mon 12:30–3 p.m. and 7:30–10:30 p.m.*

Briciola
$$ **Grottaferrata   ROMAN**

This small restaurant is a real find, offering friendly service and great cuisine in the best Roman Jewish tradition. All the vegetable *contorni* (side dishes) are delicious; if *misticanza con alici al tartufo* (greens sautéed with anchovies and truffle) is on the menu, trust us and order it. Also good are *insalata tiepida di moscardini e fagioli* (warm salad of baby squid and beans), *ravioli ricotta e pecorino con salsa di fave* (ricotta and pecorino cheese ravioli with fava sauce), and *fagottini di vitella alla provola* (veal rolls filled with provola cheese).

Via G. D'Annunzio 12. ☎ *06-9459338. Reservations recommended. Secondi: 9€–13€ ($12–$17). AE, DC, MC, V. Open: Tues–Sun 12:30–3 p.m. and Tues–Sat 7:30–10:30 p.m. Closed three weeks in Aug.*

Cacciani
$$$ Frascati   ROMAN

The renowned Cacciani is family run and serves some of the best food and wine in the area — and that's high praise. The large dining room, divided to afford a feeling of privacy at each table, opens on a beautiful terrace from which you can enjoy a great view over the surrounding hills and where meals are served in the good season. The typical Roman specialties are wonderfully prepared; go for the *rigatoni alla carbonara* (pasta with egg, onion, and bacon sauce) or *fettuccine alle regaglie di pollo* (homemade fresh pasta with chicken-liver and wine sauce). The meat dishes, such as *abbacchio alla cacciatora* (lamb cooked with white wine and rosemary), are also excellent.

Via Armando Diaz 13, off Piazza Roma. ☎ *06-9420378. Reservations required on weekends. Secondi: 12€–21€ ($16–$28). AE, DC, MC, V Open: Tues–Sun noon to 2:30 p.m. and 7:30–10:30 p.m. Closed 10 days in Jan and 10 days in Aug.*

Cantina Comandini
$ Frascati   WINE/TAVERN

Not a restaurant but a "cellar," this family-run business is the outlet of one of Frascati's vineyards. Here you'll be able to sample the famous Frascati wine and accompany it with a sandwich or a choice of local cold cuts and cheese. You can also buy wine to take away, but you'll probably want to drink it before you go home.

Via E. Filiberto 1. ☎ *06-9420915. Reservations recommended. Secondi: 5€–11€ ($7–$14). MC, V. Open: Mon–Sat 7:30–11 p.m.*

Enoteca Frascati
$$ Frascati   WINE/LATIUM

An excellent choice of wines — not just local varieties — accompanied by excellent food; what more can you ask for? This welcoming *enoteca* offers very well-prepared food, including some unusual traditional dishes. The menu is seasonal, but you may find *strozzapreti al sugo di cinghiale* (homemade spaghetti with wild-boar sauce), *fettuccine al nero di seppia con zucchine in fiore e scampi* (homemade fresh pasta with baby zucchini and prawns in squid-ink sauce), or delicious *maialino alla finocchiella con patate speziate al forno* (wild fennel suckling pig with roasted spicy potatoes).

Via A. Diaz 42, off Piazza Roma. ☎ *06-9417449. Reservations recommended on weekends. Secondi: 8€–12€ ($10–$16). MC, V. Open: Mon–Sat 7:30–10:30 p.m. Closed Aug.*

Spending the night

Although the castelli towns make for pleasant day trips from Rome, you may decide to use one of the following hotels as your base from which to explore the countryside.

Castelvecchio
$$ **Castel Gandolfo**

Tucked between the pope's summer residence and the lake, this luxurious hotel offers elegance and beautiful views. Housed in a Liberty-style palace from the end of the 19th century, it has a roof garden with a swimming pool, affording gorgeous views of the surroundings. Guest rooms are tastefully appointed with classic furnishings, fine fabrics, and modern bathrooms.

Viale Pio XI 23. ☎ **06-9360308.** *Fax: 06-9360579.* www.hotelcastelvecchio.com. *Rack rates: 160€ ($210) double; 200€ ($260) junior suite. Rates include buffet breakfast. AE, DC, MC, V.*

Grand Hotel Villa Tuscolo
$$ **Frascati**

Housed in Villa La Rufinella, one of the famous villas built on Mount Tuscolo between the 16th and 17th centuries, this gorgeous hotel is surrounded by a great park with a swimming pool. It offers professional and friendly service. Guest rooms are spacious and bright, with splendid views over the countryside, and are furnished with simple elegance: a few antiques, wooden floors, and plaster walls and moldings. Bathrooms are good-size and modern. The hotel also offers a shuttle to the center of Frascati, and a restaurant with panoramic views over Rome.

Via del Tuscolo at Km 1.5. ☎ **06-942900.** *Fax: 06-9424747.* www.villatusco lana.com. *Rack rates: 180€ ($230) double. Rates include buffet breakfast. AE, DC, MC, V.*

Hotel Culla del Lago
$ **Castel Gandolfo**

This quiet, small hotel sits in the middle of a garden right on the shore of the lake across from the pope's residence. Public spaces are welcoming, and guest rooms are large and bright — many have views of the lake — and simply but tastefully furnished, with good-size bathrooms. The hotel's private beach is a perfect place to enjoy the lake, and the garden is a great spot for relaxing.

Via Spiaggia del Lago 38. ☎ **06-93668231.** *Fax: 06-93668243.* www.culladel lago.com. *Rack rates: 120€ ($160) double. Rates include breakfast. AE, DC, MC, V.*

Hotel Flora
$$ **Frascati**

This splendid hotel is in a picturesque 19th-century palace surrounded by a park, near the historical center of Frascati. Guest rooms are . . . well, palatial — some have frescoed ceilings — furnished with antiques, and decorated with plaster moldings and parquet wooden floors. The marble bathrooms are modern and good-size. The hotel also offers glorious garden terraces, where breakfast is served in the good season, as well as cuisine classes and babysitting.

Via Vittorio Veneto 8. ☎ **06-9416110.** *Fax: 06-9416546.* www.hotel-flora.it. *Rack rates: 180€ ($230) double. Rates include buffet breakfast. AE, DC, MC, V.*

Tarquinia

The mother town of the Etruscan civilization, **Tarquinia** is famous for its Etruscan archaeological remains, including well-preserved frescoes. It also holds a pretty medieval town with a pleasant seaside resort nearby, **Tarquinia Lido.** You can easily visit these attractions in one day, but you won't get bored if you spend the night, especially during the good season, when you can also go to the beach.

Getting there

About 90km (56 miles) north of Rome, Tarquinia is only about 10km (6 miles) north of the town and bustling port of Civitavecchia, near the coast. You can easily reach it by one of the **trains,** which depart every hour, on the hour, from Termini station to Tarquinia; the trip takes one hour and 24 minutes, and costs about 6€ ($8). To order a **taxi,** call ☎ **0766-8560493** or 0766-840835.

You can also reach Tarquinia **by car** from Rome in about 50 minutes on the Via Aurelia, although we do not recommend it: The road is narrow and winding, and people drive like maniacs. (It's a route to Tuscany and points north.)

Taking a tour

The tour operator **Dock&Discover** (☎ **0766-581574;** www.dockdiscover. com) offers guided tours to Tarquinia, starting from Civitavecchia. For a personalized visit of Tarquinia, book a tour with one of the licensed local guides in the town; contact the Tarquinia tourist office for a complete list (**IAT;** Piazza Cavour 23; ☎ **0766-849282;** www.tarquinia.net).

Seeing the sights

Tarquinia was the most important town of the Etruscan kingdom and an important commercial and artistic center that dominated central Italy until the third century B.C., when it was taken over by the Romans. Tarquinia consists of two towns: the original Etruscan settlement and modern-day Tarquinia, which was rebuilt on the neighboring hill to the west of the ancient town in medieval times, leaving the Etruscan archaeological site to await future exploration. The remains of the ancient town are few but monumental, and the necropolis gave an incalculable wealth of material for the understanding of the Etruscan civilization. In the "new" town, the **Castle of Matilde di Canossa** is still in good repair, and the **Duomo** has some nice frescoes from 1508. Lining the main street in the historical center of town, you find artists' and craftsmen's showrooms, particularly fine local goldsmiths and potters who produce jewels and ceramics with an Etruscan flavor and design (excellent gifts or souvenirs). Five kilometers (3 miles) out of town to the west is the beautiful **Lungomare** of Tarquinia Lido, Tarquinia's seaside resort, with pleasant restaurants overlooking the sea, neat little shops, and a good beach.

Archaeological Area of the Civita

First settled around the ninth century B.C., the city was greatly enlarged by the Etruscans, who built the **acropolis** in the seventh century B.C. The Archaeological Area is partially surrounded by the original powerful **city walls** from the fifth century B.C., of which you can still see several miles, including one of the main gates. The acropolis is graced by an important temple from the fourth century B.C.: the **Ara della Regina (Altar of the Queen),** the largest Etruscan temple in Italy. It measures 77m × 35m (253 × 115 ft.) and was built over a temple. The base was decorated with terracotta figures, including the famous **winged horses** that are now preserved in the Tarquinia National Museum.

Pian della Civita, Montarozzi, 7km (3.5 miles) east of Tarquinia on the road to Monte Romano. Free admission. Open: Daily sunrise–sunset.

Tarquinia National Museum (Museo Nazionale Tarquiniense)

One of the most important Etruscan museums in Italy, the National Museum houses not only the extremely rich collection from the thousands of tombs of the nearby necropolis, but also artifacts and remains from more archaic nearby sites, including some Villanovian burial sites that predate the Etruscan period. The museum occupies the elegant Renaissance Palazzo Vitelleschi from the 15th century, which would be worthy of a visit even if it didn't contain Etruscan treasures. Among the huge collection of unique Etruscan objects — artwork, religious and everyday objects, bronze artifacts, sculptures — the jewels and the ceramics are truly outstanding. However, the stars of the show are the four tombs from the nearby necropolis, which have been completely reconstructed with the original frescoes. The freshness of the paintings is extraordinary; you'll find the Tomb of the Olympic Games, the Tomb of the Ship, the Tomb of the Triclynium, and the Tomb of the Racing Chariots, all from between the fifth and fourth centuries B.C.

Palazzo Vitelleschi. ☎ 0766-856036. Admission: 3€ ($3.90). Open: Tues–Sun 8:30 a.m.–7:30 p.m.

Etruscan Necropolis

The necropolis, with its thousands of tombs, is located at the doors of the Etruscan town, the Archaeological Area of the Civita. The tombs, some of which are in outstanding condition and considered quintessential examples of Etruscan tombs, date from between the sixth and first centuries B.C.

Fascinating frescoes, alive with color, decorate the tombs, which are named for the subjects of the paintings; the most famous are the tombs of the Panther, the Bulls, Hunting and Fishing, the Lioness, the Jugglers, and the Ogre. The beautiful portrait of Velia Velcha, an Etruscan woman, is justly considered a great work of Etruscan art.

Montarozzi, 7 km (3.5 miles) east of Tarquinia on the road to Monte Romano. ☎ *0766-856308. Admission: 3€ ($3.90). Open: Tues–Sun 8:30 a.m.–7:30 p.m.*

Dining locally

Don't pass up an opportunity to sample Tarquinian cuisine, which often features wild game and truffles from the countryside, seafood, and excellent goat cheese. Accompany your meal with a bottle of Tarquinian wine.

Chalet del Pescatore
$ Foce del Marta TARQUINIAN/SEAFOOD

Right on the seaside, this is a great place to relax and tuck into some fresh, delicious seafood. The menu includes all kinds of fresh homemade pasta, excellent *risotto alla pescatora* (Italian rice with seafood), and plenty of local fish.

Foce del Marta, Tarquinia Lido. ☎ *0766-864565. Reservations recommended. Secondi: 10€–18€ ($13–$23). AE, DC, MC, V. Open: Tues@ndSun noon to 3 p.m. and 7:30–10:30 p.m.*

La Cantina dell'Etrusco
$$ Tarquinia TARQUINIAN

You can taste local specialties and traditional dishes of the interior at this cantina in the historic center of Tarquinia. Choices include *pappardelle al sugo di cinghiale* (homemade fresh pasta with wild-boar ragout), *ragout di lepre* (hare ragout), and *pollo in salmì* (savory chicken with tomato-and-wine sauce), all of which are very well prepared. The wine list features all the best local vintages, including the famous Est, Est, Est!, as well as Cerveteri, Orvieto Classico, and Vignanello. Do not miss the *tozzetti* (biscotti made with local hazelnuts), with Aleatico di Gradoli (a muscat wine) for dessert.

Via Menotti Garibaldi 13. ☎ *0766-848418. Reservations recommended. Secondi: 11€–18€ ($14–$23). AE, DC, MC, V. Open: Tues–Sun 12:30–3 p.m. and 7:30–11:30 p.m.*

La Cantinetta
$ Tarquinia TARQUINIAN

This pleasant restaurant in the historic center of Tarquinia offers excellent food and a welcoming atmosphere. The seasonal menu may include superb *fettuccine ai ferlenghi* (homemade pasta with local wild mushrooms), *zuppa ceci e castagne* (thick soup with chickpeas and chestnuts), and *lepre in salmì* (savory hare with tomato-and-wine sauce), as well as some fish dishes.

Via XX Settembre 27. ☎ *0766-856810. Reservations recommended. Secondi: 9€–16€ ($12–$21). AE, DC, MC, V. Open: Fri–Wed 12:30–3 p.m. and 7:30–10:30 p.m.*

Spending the night

Be sure to pack your swimsuit if you plan to spend the night in the sea-side resort town of Tarquinia Lido.

Hotel La Torraccia
$ Tarquinia Lido

This family-run hotel, located only steps from the sea, is surrounded by umbrella pines. Guest rooms are well appointed, with quality modern furniture and bright carpeting; most have a private balcony. In good weather, breakfast is served on the pleasant garden terrace.

Viale Mediterraneo 45. ☎ *0766-864375.* *Fax: 0766-864296.* www.torraccia.it. *Rack rates: 120€ ($156) double. Rates include breakfast. AE, DC, MC, V.*

Hotel Ristorante Pizzeria all'Olivo
$ Tarquinia

You'll be pampered at this family-run hotel in the modern part of Tarquinia but near the historic center of town. Accommodations are simple but comfortable and welcoming. Guest rooms are large, with simple modern furnishings, tiled floors, and good-size modern bathrooms. The hotel's restaurant is very good and also serves excellent pizza.

Via Palmiro Togliatti 15. ☎ *0766-857318.* *Fax: 0766-840777.* www.hotel-allolivo.it. *Rack rates: 80€ ($104) double. Rates include breakfast. AE, DC, MC, V.*

Hotel San Marco
$ Tarquinia

This is our choice in town, right across from the Museo Nazionale (see listing earlier in this section) in the historic center. The hotel is in the splendid cloister of the 16th-century convent Agostiniano, which has housed some kind of hostelry since 1876. Guest rooms are large and nicely furnished, with some antiques.

Piazza Cavour 18. ☎ *0766-842234.* *Fax: 0766-842306.* www.san-marco.com. *Rack rates: 70€ ($91) double. Rates include breakfast. AE, DC, MC, V.*

Viterbo

Off the beaten track, yet following in the footsteps of many, from ancient Romans to popes and cardinals, we love taking the day off for a swim at the thermal swimming pool of the **Terme dei Papi,** by the town of **Viterbo.** When we have more time, we like to stroll the streets of the old town as well. Beautifully preserved, the medieval center is a pleasure to the eyes. You will be enchanted with the arched doorways and the many carved details, as well as with the many shopping opportunities. Both attractions are a short trip from Rome.

Getting there

Located 80km (50 miles) north of Rome, Viterbo is well connected to the capital.

If you are going to the thermal baths, the easiest way is to take the dedicated shuttle service from Rome. The spa's bus leaves daily from Piazza Mancini at 8:30 a.m.; for the return, it leaves Terme dei Papi at 1:15 p.m. The public bus leaves daily from the bus station of Via Lepanto (by the Lepanto Metro stop) in Rome at 8:40 a.m. and leaves the Terme dei Papi at 4:20 p.m.

Alternatively, you can ride the **metropolitan trains** (many locals commute daily to Rome) using a day pass that costs 9€ ($12). Take the regional train from Ostiense station (which also stops at Tiburtina station), leaving hourly at 40 minutes past the hour for the one hour, 48 minute ride. Or board the **commuter train** from the Piazzale Flaminio station (off Piazza del Popolo), leaving every 25 minutes during rush hour for the two-and-a-half-hour ride.

Once there, take a **taxi** from the train station or call one (☎ **0761-340777**).

Taking a tour

Contact the tourist office in town (Via Ascenzi 4; ☎ **0761-325992;** fax 0761-308480; infotuscia@libero.it) or at the train station of Porta Romana (☎ **0761-304795;** fax 0761-220957; infoviterbo@apt. viterbo.it) for personalized tours.

Seeing the sights

Famous for its medieval historic district, Viterbo is well worth a stroll. Make the San Pellegrino neighborhood the focus of your visit. An urban area developed along Via San Pellegrino and Via San Gemini in the 12th century, this is one of the world's best-preserved examples of medieval urban architecture. Take the time to stroll along its alleys and charming squares.

National Etruscan Museum in the Rocca Albornoz

Housed in the Albornoz fortress, this interesting museum focuses on the reconstruction of Etruscan daily life. It uses material found in the nearby necropolis, dating from the seventh and sixth centuries B.C. onward. The star of the show is on the third floor, where you can admire the entire "tomb of the Etruscan chariot" *(tomba della biga etrusca)* discovered in Ischia di Castro.

Rocca Albornoz, Piazza della Rocca 21b. ☎ *0761-325929. Admission: 4€ ($5.20). Open: Tues–Sun 8:30 a.m.–7:30 p.m. Closed Jan 1, May 1, and Dec 25.*

St. Lawrence Cathedral (Cattedrale di San Lorenzo)

Originally dating from the 12th century but heavily restored in later times, this church is a beautiful example of eclectic architecture, with its medieval arches, its baroque facade, and its 13th-century Sienese bell tower with black and white stripes. Adjacent to the cathedral is the 13th-century Palazzo dei Papi, which was built as the residence of the pope when the papacy was moved from Rome to Viterbo (a little-known fact) from 1257 to 1281. An elegant medieval building with a unique loggia from which cardinals addressed the populace, it can be visited only by request to the religious administration of the cathedral.

Piazza San Lorenzo. ☎ *0761-341716. Admission: Free. Open: Daily 8 a.m.–12:30 p.m. and 4:30–7 p.m.*

Terme dei Papi

Served by its own shuttle service from Piazza Mancini in Rome, this is a perfect day trip from the capital. The spa complex of Viterbo has ancient origins: The waters were used by the Etruscans and well known to the Romans, who built large thermal baths using the various springs. Most of the waters are hot springs (about 49°C/120°F on average) loaded with sulfur and other minerals, very beneficial to people with skin ailments and arthritis. The hot waters are also a pleasure for everyone, particularly in winter, when it is possible to bathe outside even on colder days. The big outdoor pool is particularly impressive, measuring over 2,000 sq. m. (21,000 sq. ft.). Admission depends on the services requested. For a full day at the spa, including at least one treatment, such as a massage or a facial, budget about 60€ ($78).

Strada Bagni 12. ☎ *0761-3501. Fax: 0761-352451.* www.termedeipapi.it. *Open: Wed–Mon 9 a.m.–7 p.m.; Sat (in July–Aug also Thurs–Fri) 9 p.m.–1 a.m.*

Dining locally

Viterbese cuisine is tasty and hearty; it incorporates local mountain produce, particularly chestnuts and wild mushrooms, which give a unique flavor to soups and stew.

Richiastro
$$ Viterbo   VITERBESE

Taking its name from the local name for the inner garden — delightful in good weather — this is where to come for excellent local fare. We loved everything, from the hot bread served with condiments to the homemade pasta to the grilled meat (try *spiedini di maiale,* or pork skewers with hot pepper and honey). In winter, do not miss the earthy soups.

Via della Marrocca 16. ☎ *0761-228009. Reservations recommended. Secondi: 9€–16€ ($12–$21). AE, DC, MC, V. Open: Fri–Sun 12:30–3 p.m. and Fri–Sat 7:30–10:30 p.m.*

Torre
$$$ Viterbo   CREATIVE VITERBESE/WINE

We love coming to this wine bar doubling as a pleasant restaurant for the excellent choice of local and Italian wines perfectly matched to the delicious food. The creative menu is seasonal: We recommend *lombrichelli con daino e cicerchie* (local fresh pasta with venison and legumes) and the roasted meats. The tasting menus are the way to go: Prices start at 38€ ($49) with a choice of four courses (the price is 55€/$72 including wine); the full menu costs 53€ ($69) without wine and 75€ ($98) with. The *osteria* is open at lunch and serves a more modest menu. Across the street is the shop, where you can buy local wine and foods.

Via della Torre 5. ☎ *0761-226467.* www.enotecalatorrevt.com. *Reservations recommended on weekends. Secondi: 12€–18€ ($16–$23). AE, DC, MC, V. Open: Tues–Sun 12:30–3 p.m. and Tues–Sat 7:30–11 p.m.*

Venezia
$$ Viterbo CREATIVE VITERBESE

Run by the Scarpa brothers, this is the most welcoming restaurant in Viterbo. It's in a palazzo in the historic district. You'll have to trust your hosts for the choice of the food — the menu changes daily depending on market offerings and whims of the chef.

Via delle Maestre 4. ☎ *0761-092069.* www.wbv.it. *Reservations recommended on weekends. Secondi: 8€–15€ ($10–$20). AE, DC, MC, V Open: Tues–Sat 12:30–3 p.m. and 7:30–10:30 p.m.*

Spending the night

Niccolò V Terme dei Papi
$$$ VITERBO

Viterbo's upscale lodging option is particularly convenient if you are interested in the thermal waters (see earlier in this chapter): This is the attached hotel. The few guest rooms are elegantly appointed, with comfortable bathrooms.

Strada dei Bagni 12. ☎ **0761-3501.** *Fax: 0761-352451.* www.termedeipapi.it. *Rack rates: 230€ ($299) double. Rates include buffet breakfast. AE, DC, MC, V.*

Tuscia
$ VITERBO

This modern hotel in the historic district offers good, moderately priced accommodations. Guest rooms are spacious and simply furnished. The tiled bathrooms are new. Book air conditioning in advance; it costs 7€ ($9.10).

Via Cairoli 41, off Piazza san Faustino, near Piazza della Rocca and Porta Fiorentina. ☎ *0761-344400. Fax: 0761-345976.* www.tusciahotel.com. *Rack rates: 74€–82€ ($96–$107) double. Rates include breakfast. AE, DC, MC, V.*

Part V
Living It Up after Dark: Rome's Nightlife

The 5th Wave   By Rich Tennant

"For tonight's modern reinterpretation of Turandot, those in the front row are kindly requested to wear raincoats."

In this part . . .

Still got some energy after a full day of sightseeing? Then this part is for you! Here we offer suggestions for filling those marvelous evenings in Rome, when the air is sweet and soft and everything seems so romantic. Whether you want to attend a performance or show (Chapter 15) or take in the atmosphere at Rome's many bars and discos (Chapter 16), we've got your evening covered.

Chapter 15

Applauding the Cultural Scene

● ●

In This Chapter

▶ Finding out what's going on around town
▶ Reserving tickets
▶ Attending the symphony, opera, and dance performances

● ●

*R*ome offers some splendid opportunities for lovers of the performing arts. All major performers pass through Rome, and the city has traditionally been the hot spot for Italian theater. Of course, a moderate knowledge of Italian is required for theatergoing.

Getting the Inside Scoop

Rome's cultural scene is very hot year-round, with top-notch performers on tour stopping here regularly. The scene positively burgeons in summer, though, when a mind-boggling range of performances go on throughout the city in various indoor and outdoor venues during the famous **Estate Romana (Roman Summer) festival,** discussed later in this section.

The **Parco della Musica** (Viale Coubertin 34; ☎ 06-8082058; www.auditorium.com; Bus: M from Piazza del Popolo) — a daring, modernistic complex — is the principal venue for music in Rome. Designed by the famous architect Renzo Piano, this grand, ambitious project is probably the largest addition to the Roman cultural and architectural landscape in decades. Located 2km (1¼ miles) from **Piazza del Popolo** and connected to the center by a special bus line (Bus M, for music), the entire site takes up 55,000 square meters (13.6 acres). It has three concert halls as well as other structures, including **La Cavea,** a 3,000-seat outdoor concert space reminiscent of a classical amphitheater. In addition to classical, pop, and contemporary music, theater and dance performances take place here. Restaurants, stores, lecture halls, and a host of other activities and services are on site.

Most other performance venues in Rome are in or near the city center. The elegant **Teatro dell'Opera** (Piazza Beniamino Gigli 1, just off Via Nazionale; ☎ 06-48160255; www.operaroma.it; Metro: Line A to Repubblica; Bus: Minibus 116 to Via A. Depretis) — a beautiful venue built at the end of the 19th century — books opera as well as ballet and classical concerts. The **Teatro Olimpico** (Piazza Gentile da Fabriano; ☎ 06-3265991; www.teatroolimpico.it; Tram: 225 from Piazzale Flaminio), another great space, schedules musical performances of all kinds.

From June through September — during many venues' off season — Roman nights come alive with the **Estate Romana (Roman Summer) festival,** a series of musical, theatrical, and other cultural events (also see Chapter 16). These often take place in some of the most picturesque locations and monuments in Rome, lit up especially for the event, which transforms the show into a multidimensional treat.

Among the most impressive settings for the festival is the **Colosseum,** which reopened its doors to the public in 2000 after 15 centuries (don't expect blood sports and severed limbs, however; civilization has changed somewhat in the interim). Also very dramatic is the **Theatre of the Caracalla Baths** (Teatro delle Terme di Caracalla, Viale delle Terme di Caracalla 52; contact the Teatro dell'Opera at ☎ 06-48160255 for information), where the **Teatro dell'Opera** holds some of its summer season. To hear Verdi's *Requiem* resounding at night through the cavernous, massive ruins is a truly remarkable musical experience. Other unique venues for summer events are the **Roman Forum** (Via dei Fori Imperiali; ☎ 06-70393427); **Villa Borghese** (Largo Aqua Felix, entrance at Piazzale delle Ginestre; ☎ 06-82077304 Mon–Thurs 9 a.m.–4 p.m. and Fri 9 a.m.–1 p.m.); the elegant **Chiostro del Bramante** (Via della Pace; ☎ 06-7807695); the **Archeological Park of Teatro Marcello** (Via del Teatro Marcello; ☎ 06-87131590); the mausoleum–cum–fort **Castel Sant'Angelo** (Lungotevere Castello 50; ☎ 06-32869 or 06-32861); and, outside Rome, the **Teatro Romano of Ostia Antica** (Viale dei Romagnoli 717, Ostia Antica; ☎ 06-56352850). You can find details on the festival online at www.estate romana.comune.roma.it (also in English) or get information by calling ☎ 06-68809505 Monday through Saturday from 10 a.m. to 5 p.m.

The opera, classic concerts, and ballet always call for elegant dress, as do the most famous theaters and even the best jazz clubs. More casual attire is okay for other venues and shows.

The curtain is usually right on time, and if you miss it, you'll usually have to wait for the intermission to take your seat. It's customary to give a small tip to your usher.

Shows are usually late enough so that you can have a regular dinner; because most venues are in the center of Rome, you can pick a restaurant in the area (see Chapter 10) and still make it to the show on time. For after-theater restaurants, see the "After-theater dining" sidebar, later in this chapter.

Finding Out What's Playing and Getting Tickets

Rome's tourist office publishes an excellent monthly review called *The Happening City;* you can pick up an English- or Italian-language copy at any of the tourist info points listed in Appendix A and in Chapter 8, or you can request that it be e-mailed to you before you leave (www.roma turismo.it), which is smart if you want to order tickets in advance. Indeed, if you're coming for only a short vacation, you'll do a lot better by ordering your tickets from home, especially for big performances that will be sold out or booked well before your feet touch Italian soil.

We recommend using an Italian ticket service for your bookings; they usually charge less and have access to more shows. A good, comprehensive option is **TicketOne** (☎ 02-392261 for an English-speaking operator; www.ticketone.it). Others we like are **Charta** (www.charta.it) — an Italy-wide Internet-based agent for theater, concerts, and dance — and the user-friendly **Viva Ticket** (www.vivaticket.it). All have English versions and allow you to make reservations and purchase tickets online.

Global Edwards & Edwards (☎ 800-223-6108 in the U.S.; no Web site) is a good ticket agency that's based in England. Many U.S.-based agencies offer advance tickets sales for events in Rome, but none of them is as comprehensive as the Italian services, and they charge steep service fees. Nonetheless, if you want to use a U.S.-based company, a good one is **Culturalitaly.com** (☎ 800-380-0014; fax: 928-639-0388; www.cultural italy.com), a Los Angeles–based company that offers tickets for a nice selection of events.

In Rome, you'll find detailed listings of events in the weekly publication *Roma C'è,* which has a section in English and is available in all newsstands (it comes out on Wed). You can also find information in the **daily newspapers.** Other sources are the fortnightly magazine *Wanted in Rome* (www.wantedinrome.com) and the monthly magazine *The American* (www.theamericanmag.com), which covers all of Italy; both are in English and available in online versions. You'll find them at most newsstands in the historic center of the city. You can also pick up a copy of *The Happening City* or view it online (www.romaturismo.it; click Events in Rome and then Happening in Rome); it's an excellent review of events published by Rome's tourist board. For information about the **Estate Romana** festival, see "Getting the Inside Scoop," earlier in this chapter. Besides the resources listed in this section, your hotel concierge will always be able to help you find out what's on and purchase tickets.

Many venues offer reduced-price tickets and matinees on one day of the week, often Thursday. For last-minute theater tickets at a discount of up to 50 percent, visit the **booth** at Via Bari 20, off Piazza Salerno (☎ 06-44180212; Metro: Line B to Policlinico; Bus: 61, 490, 491, 495; Tues–Sat 2–8 p.m.).

After-theater dining

At least a couple of restaurants near each theater in Rome specialize in after-theater service. Showtime is usually late enough that you can easily have an early dinner anywhere, but if you want to do like the Romans, try to resist until after the show and check out one of these late-night spots.

Among the restaurants we suggest in Chapter 10, those that stay open late are **Bolognese, Checchino dal 1887,** and **Gusto.** You can also try **Il Boscaiolo** (Via degli Artisti; ☎ 06-4884023), a very nice pizzeria behind the Teatro Sistina; **L'Archetto** (Via dell'Archetto; ☎ 06-6789064), a good *spaghetteria* steps from the Teatro Quirino; and the good Roman fare at **Il Cantuccio** (Corso Rinascimento 71; ☎ 06-68802982), not far from the Teatro Valle and the Teatro Argentina.

Raising the Curtain on the Performing Arts

On any given day in Rome, you'll have a large number of shows from which to choose. Here, we highlight the main categories. During the summer, remember to check with the tourist office for the special events of the **Estate Romana** festival.

Symphony

A variety of classical concerts take place in Rome on a daily basis; you can check out programs with the tourist office and in the publications we recommend (see the preceding section) or directly with each of the following organizations. The most important orchestras and associations are the **Accademia Nazionale di Santa Cecilia** (Parco della Musica, Viale Coubertin 34; ☎ 06-8082058; www.santacecilia.it), one of Italy's premier musical groups, which puts on classical concerts and events and holds a summer season during the **Estate Romana** (see earlier in this chapter); the **Opera di Roma** (Teatro dell'Opera, Piazza Beniamino Gigli 1; ☎ 06-48160, or 800-016665 toll free within Italy; www.operaroma.it); and the **Filarmonica di Roma,** also called Accademia Filarmonica Romana (Teatro Olimpico, Piazza Gentile da Fabriano; ☎ 06-3265991; www.teatroolimpico.it).

Other important groups include the **Amici della Musica Sacra** (Via Paolo VI 29; ☎ 06-68301665; www.amicimusicasacra.com), **Il Tempietto** (☎ 06-87201523; www.tempietto.org), the **Orchestra di Roma e del Lazio** (☎ 06-9766711; www.orchestradellazio.it), and the **Fondazione Arts Academy Roma** (☎ 06-44252303; www.artsacademy.it). In addition to regular performance spaces, classical concerts are held in churches and various halls all over the city. One acclaimed series is the concerts scheduled in all of Rome's basilicas for the **International Festival of Sacred Music and Art** (☎ 06-6869187; fax: 06-6873300; www.festivalmusicaeartesacra.net) in October. A particularly pleasant

series is the concerts of the **Musici Veneziani** in the Anglican church of
San Paolo entro le Mura (Via Nazionale 16, at the corner of Via Napoli;
☎ 06-4826296), with a repertoire of operatic arias — Verdi, Puccini, Bizet,
and Mozart, among others — and performers in baroque costumes.
Concerts usually start at 8 p.m., and tickets cost 15€ to 30€ ($20–$40).
Check with the tourist office for a complete schedule of events.

Tickets prices vary according to the performance and, in the largest theaters, the quality of the seat. They range from free to 50€ ($65).

Opera

Opera is pretty much limited to the great national theater of the **Teatro
dell'Opera** (Piazza Beniamino Gigli 1; ☎ 06-48160; www.operaroma.it).
Its season runs from January to June, but it also has a not-to-be-missed
summer season during the famous **Estate Romana** (see earlier in this
chapter), with performances held at the picturesque **Theatre of the
Caracalla Baths** (Teatro delle Terme di Caracalla). Ticket prices run
about 30€ to 120€ ($40–$160), depending on the seat and performance.

Dance

Ballet and dance performances are quite numerous in Rome and are
often of world-class quality. The **Rome Opera Ballet** performs classical
and modern works at the Teatro dell'Opera (see the preceding section);
international performers often stage their shows at the **Teatro Olimpico**
or the **Parco della Musica** (see listings earlier in this chapter).

Ticket prices vary according to the performance, the venue, and — in
large theaters — the quality of the seat. They run from 10€ ($13) for a
performance at the Parco della Musica to 120€ ($160) for the best seat
at the Teatro dell'Opera.

Theater

Rome is famous for theater, and some of the best companies in the country and the world perform here. Italy has produced such playwrights as
Goldoni, Pirandello, and Nobel Prize winner Dario Fo. Of course, if you
don't understand Italian, you won't get much out of Roman theater; but
if you do know the language, you'll be delighted by the number of performances, from classical to contemporary. Fortunately, some shows are
in English, especially in the summer during the **Estate Romana** festival
(see later in this section).

The best theaters in Rome are the **Teatro Argentina** (Largo Argentina
52; ☎ 06-684000345; www.teatrodiroma.net), **Teatro Brancaccio** (Via
Merulana 244, off Piazza Santa Maria Maggiore; ☎ 06-47824893; www.
teatrobrancaccio.net), **Teatro Ghione** (Via delle Fornaci 37; ☎ 06-
6372294; www.ghione.it), **Teatro Quirino** (Via delle Vergini 7, near
Fontana di Trevi; ☎ 06-6794585; www.teatroquirino.it), **Teatro Valle**
(Via del Teatro Valle 21, near Piazza Navona; ☎ 06-68803794; www.teatro
valle.it), and **Teatro Sistina** (Via Sistina 129, off Via del Tritone;

☎ **06-4200711;** www.ilsistina.com). There are a great number of others, all quite good.

During the summer, many theater performances move outdoors for the **Estate Romana** festival. One of the highest rated for tourists is the **Miracle Players** (☎ **06-70393427;** www.miracleplayers.org), an English company that performs in English at the **Roman Forum** (Via dei Fori Imperiali; ☎ **06-70393427**). As the name suggests, the **Toti Globe Theatre** in **Villa Borghese** (Largo Aqua Felix, entrance at Piazzale delle Ginestre; ☎ **06-82077304;** www.globetheatreroma.com) is a replica of the famous Shakespearean theater, where the Toti performs Shakespeare as well as other productions. The **Teatro Romano of Ostia Antica** (Viale dei Romagnoli 717, Ostia Antica; ☎ **06-56358041**), a bit farther afield, is well worth the trip. It always offers a summer season in the highly atmospheric Roman theater in the archaeological site at the ancient sea-port of Ostia.

The **Centrale RistoTheatre** (Via Celsa 6, off Piazza del Gesu; ☎ **06-6780501;** www.centraleristotheatre.com) is an ultramodern restaurant–cabaret–theater presenting musical and theatrical perform-ances that you can enjoy over an *aperitivo* (predinner drink) and a light snack or dinner. The dinner — with a weekly menu based on Tuscan fare — is at 7:30 p.m., and the live show is at 10:30 p.m.

Ticket prices vary according to the performance and venue, but they usually range from 12€ to 26€ ($16–$34).

Chapter 16

Hitting the Clubs and Bars

● ●

In This Chapter

▶ Tuning in to the Roman jazz scene

▶ Getting hip to the city's gay life

▶ Hanging out in the best wine bars, clubs, and pubs

● ●

*R*oman nights keep on being sweet no matter what the season and the set you move in. If you aren't too pooped from sightseeing, come join *la dolce vita* and the ancient and modern pleasures of Rome.

Finding Out What's on Where

The Happening City magazine is an excellent review of events, published by Rome's tourist board and available at www.romaturismo.it (see Appendix A). You can also find extensive listings in the **daily newspapers** and in the weekly publication *Roma C'è,* available at newsstands (it comes out on Wed), with some listings in English. Other sources are *Wanted in Rome,* a fortnightly magazine (Via dei Delfini 17; ☎ 06-6790190; www.wantedinrome.com), and *The American* (www.theamericanmag.com), a 48-page monthly covering all of Italy, with extensive listings for Rome. Both are available at newsstands in the historic center and at selected newsstands elsewhere, and online.

Get details about the **Estate Romana** festival at tourist points and at www.estateromana.comune.roma.it (also in English), or by calling ☎ 06-68809505 Monday through Saturday from 10 a.m. to 5 p.m.

All That Jazz

Romans love jazz, and the city is home to many first-rate venues featuring excellent local musicians as well as all the big international names. Most clubs are in Trastevere and in Prati; doors open around 10 p.m. and close around 3 a.m. Cover charges vary depending on the event and the club, but they usually range between 7€ ($9) for a regular night and 30€ ($39) for special concerts.

The most famous clubs are the **Alexanderplatz** (Via Ostia 9, just off the Musei Vaticani; ☎ 06-39742171; www.alexanderplatz.it; Metro: Line

A to Ottaviano/San Pietro; Bus: 23 to Via Leone IV), where reservations
are recommended; **Big Mama** (Vicolo San Francesco a Ripa 18, Trastevere;
☎ 06-5812551; www.bigmama.it; Metro: Piramide; Tram: 8), which
attracts both small and big names in jazz and blues and is somewhat
more expensive, depending on how bright the star is; and the **Fonclea**
(Via Crescenzio 82/a, behind Castel Sant'Angelo; ☎ 06-6896302; www.
fonclea.it; Bus: 23 to Via Crescenzio), where the emphasis is on jazz,
with excellent ethnic and other concerts. Another great place for jazz,
although a bit out of the city center, is the **La Palma Club** (Via Giuseppe
Mirri 35; ☎ 06-43599029; www.lapalmaclub.it), not far from the
Tiburtina train station; the popular **Fandango Jazz Festival** takes place
here in June and July.

Other seasonal events include the **Rome Jazz Festival** (www.romajazz
festival.it) in November, and concerts during the **Estate Romana festival** (see earlier in this chapter): **Fiesta!** (Ippodromo delle Capannelle,
Via Appia Nuova 1245; ☎ 06-7182139), with Latin American jazz; an
incarnation of the **Rome Jazz Festival** (see above); and **Villa Celimontana
Jazz** (Via della Navicella; ☎ 06-7182139; www.villacelimontanajazz.
com) performances.

In addition to jazz and contemporary music, you may hear traditional
Italian songs at **Arciliuto** (Piazza Montevecchio 5; ☎ 06-6879419; Bus:
62 or 64 to Corso Vittorio Emanuele), in the maze of streets behind
Piazza Navona. Unfortunately, it's closed most of the summer.

Historic Cafes

Rome boasts many famous old cafes that have never lost their glamour.
Although some are protected historical sites, they still operate as regular
bars (Rome-style; see Chapter 10), opening early — usually by 7 a.m. —
and closing around 9 or 9:30 p.m. They are all in the historic center.

Very pleasant, if a little expensive, the **Antico Caffè della Pace** (Via della
Pace 3–7; ☎ 06-6861216; Bus: Minibus 116 to Piazza Navona) is one of
the most popular cafes in the city. You can linger at outdoor tables that
open onto a romantic little square. Another sought-after spot is the
beautifully furnished **Caffè Greco** (Via Condotti 84; ☎ 06-6791700;
Metro: Line A to Spagna); among its customers were such famous writers as Stendhal, Goethe, and Keats. Also noteworthy is the **Caffè Rosati**
(Piazza del Popolo 4–5; ☎ 06-3225859; Bus: Minibus 117 or 119), which
retains its 1920s Art Nouveau décor.

Not a cafe but a historic restaurant, **La Casina Valadier** (Piazza Bucarest,
off the Pincio Gardens; ☎ 06-69922090; Bus: 116 to Piazza del Popolo;
closed Mon) was a hot spot in the era of *La Dolce Vita*. In an early-19th-
century building, with romantic views over Rome from its terraces, it
was closed for decades. You can now enjoy dinner at the expensive
panoramic restaurant or drinks on the lower terrace.

Wine Bars and Pubs

Rome has many a fine *enoteca* (wine shops). Some are regular wine shops that turn into wine bars–cum–restaurants after 8 p.m. (and sometimes also at lunch, between 1 and 3 p.m.). Others are wine bars that open in the evening, usually from 8 p.m. to 1 a.m. or later. Popular hangouts for young and not-so-young Romans, they're scattered everywhere, with some of the most popular in the *centro,* in particular the Navona/Pantheon, Colosseo, Trastevere, and Campo de' Fiori areas.

The granddaddy of Roman wine stores, **Trimani** (Via Goito 20; ☎ **06-4469661;** www.trimani.com; Bus: 60 or 62; closed Sun and Aug) has been run by the same family since 1821 and is in the old residential neighborhood behind the Terme di Diocleziano. In addition to selling thousands of bottles of wine, Trimani is a happening wine bar. Across town, the exceedingly popular, old-fashioned wine bar **Vineria** (Campo de' Fiori 15; no phone) still holds its own amid the nightly crowds swarming the trendy piazza. For something calmer, try the wine bar at **Gusto** (see Chapter 10), which has an intimate, romantic atmosphere.

The best in Rome — if price is not an issue — is the historic **Enoteca Capranica** (Piazza Capranica 99; ☎ 06-69940992), a winery with a wonderful cellar. Considered one of the best restaurants in Rome, it serves delicious creative Italian cuisine. Another famous address is **Ferrara** (Piazza Trilussa 41, at Ponte Sisto, Trastevere; ☎ 06-58333920. www.enotecaferrara.it). It's popular with wine experts and foodies alike; the adjacent store sells wine and specialties.

Not an enoteca but an American-style bar with a DJ, the **Drunken Ship** (Campo de' Fiori 20; ☎ 06-68300535) is often jammed. This is the place where every American student doing his or her year abroad will eventually turn up — be warned or informed, as the case may be.

The European Economic Union has had a definite impact on nightlife: The Italian craze for Irish pubs has hit Rome hard. Among the nicest is **Mad Jack** (Via Arenula 20, off Largo Argentina; ☎ **06-68808223;** Tram: 8), the place for Guinness and light food; it also features live music on Wednesday and Thursday. The **Abbey Theatre Irish Pub** (Via del Governo Vecchio 51–53, near Piazza Navona; ☎ **06-6861341;** Bus: 62 or 64 to Corso Vittorio Emanuele II) is in the oldest part of town and features authentic décor and souvenirs from the famous theater. The **Albert** (Via del Traforo 132, off Via del Tritone, before the tunnel; ☎ **06-4818795;** Bus: Minibus 116, 117, or 119 to Largo del Tritone) is not an Irish pub at all but deserves mention: It offers a real English-pub atmosphere and beer, with everything from the furnishings to the drinks imported from the old country.

Dance Clubs

Romans, especially the younger set, love dancing, and clubs abound. You can hear a mixture of live and recorded music at **Alpheus** (Via del

Commercio 36, near Via Ostiense; ☎ **06-5747826; Bus: 23**, but best to take a cab). Several halls offer different kinds of music, from jazz to Latin to straight-ahead rock, and if you don't want to dance, you can actually find comfortable places to sit and have a drink while listening. **Alien** (Via Velletri 13–19; ☎ **06-8412212;** www.aliendisco.it; Bus: 490 to Piazza Fiume) continues to work at its reputation as Rome's clubbiest club — with mirrors, strobe lights, and a New York–style atmosphere appealing to a frenetic 20-something crowd. Not to be outdone in the club-as-phenom category is **Gilda** (Via Mario de Fiori 97; ☎ **06-6797396;** www.gildadisco club.it; Metro: Line A to Spagna), which caters to an older crowd and plays classic rock as well as some newer stuff.

In **Testaccio,** clubs come and go, but the neighborhood remains one of the preeminent Roman hot spots. **Club Picasso** (Via Monte Testaccio 63; ☎ **06-5742975;** Metro: B to Piramide) plays blasting music — from rock to blues — most of the night.

During the summer, the **Estate Romana** festival (see earlier in this chapter) provides additional dancing venues, including a barge on the Tiber and the terraces and gardens of monuments around town.

Cover charges hover between 10€ and 20€ ($13–$26) for the most elegant and hippest venues. They usually open around 10:30 p.m. and close around 4 a.m.

Gay and Lesbian Bars

Rome's lively gay scene becomes positively sizzling in summer with **Gay Village** (☎ **340-5423008;** www.gayvillage.it), a special section of the **Estate Romana** festival that includes music and theater performances, disco dancing, and other entertainment.

Gay clubs are scattered around the city, although lately, the area between San Giovanni and the Colosseo has been developing into a gay enclave. Hours are the same as at other clubs in town, from around 10 p.m. to around 4 a.m. Cover charge usually runs about 10€ ($13).

Rome's hottest gay club is **Alibi** (Via di Monte Testaccio 40–44; ☎ **06-5743448;** www.alibionline.it; Bus: 23; Tram: 3 to Via Marmorata and then walk down Via Galbani, though a cab is best). It boasts a rotating schedule of DJs and a great summer roof garden. The disco **Angelo Azzurro** (Via Cardinale Merry del Val 13, Trastevere; ☎ **06-5800472;** Tram: 8 to Viale Trastevere at Piazza Mastai) welcomes all ages and offers an eclectic mix of music. Admission is free, and Friday night is ladies only. The **Frequency** (Viale Odoardo Beccari 10; ☎ **06-7851504**) passes as the trendiest cruising bar.

The leading lesbian club is **New Joli Coeur** (Via Sirte 5; ☎ **06-86215827;** Bus: 56 or 88 to Piazza Sant'Emerenziana); it's nonexclusive and welcoming. Saturday night, the club is for women only; all are welcome at other times.

Part VI
The Part of Tens

The 5th Wave   By Rich Tennant

"He had it made after our trip to Italy. I give you Fontana di Clifford."

In this part . . .

Here we add some special details that we hope will make your vacation even more successful and memorable.

Think you can make do in Rome knowing only ten Italian words? Believe it or not, it's possible, and we get you started in Chapter 17. In Chapter 18, we list ten of the greatest Roman artists and point you to where you can find their art and architecture. In Chapter 19, we suggest ten great purchases to serve as beautiful reminders of your visit to the Eternal City.

Chapter 17

Non Capisco: The Top Ten Expressions You Need to Know

In This Chapter

▶ Using salutations

▶ Asking questions

▶ Memorizing some lifesavers

*T*raveling in a country where you don't know the language can be intimidating, but trying to speak the language can be amusing at the very least. Although you can get by in Rome without knowing Italian, locals often appreciate it if you at least make an effort to speak to them in their native tongue. And we think you'll find that Italian is a fun language to speak. If you feel more ambitious, please check out Appendix B, which lists more words and expressions.

Per Favore

Meaning **"please,"** *per favore* (*pehr* fah-*vohr*-ay) is the most important Italian expression you can know. With it, you can make useful phrases such as *Un caffè, per favore* ("A coffee, please") and *Il conto, per favore* ("The bill, please"). There's no need for verbs, and it's perfectly polite!

Grazie

Grazie (*graht*-tzee-ay) means **"thank you";** if you want to go all out, use *grazie mille* (*mee*-lay), meaning "a thousand thanks." Say it clearly and loudly enough to be heard. Saying *grazie* is always right and puts people in a good mood. *Grazie* has other uses as well: Italians often use it to say goodbye or to mark the end of an interaction. It's particularly useful when you don't want to buy something from an insistent street vendor: Say *"Grazie"* and walk away.

Permesso

Meaning **"excuse me"** (to request passage or admittance), *permesso* (pehr-*mehs*-soh) is of fundamental importance on public transportation and in crowded areas. When you're on a bus and need to get off, say loudly and clearly, *"Permesso!"* People will clear out of your path (or feel less irritated as you squeeze through). The same thing applies in supermarkets, trains, museums, and so on. Of course, you may be surrounded by non-Italians, and the effect may be a little lost on them.

Scusi

Scusi (*skoo*-zee) means **"excuse me"** — to say you're sorry after bumping into someone — and is more exactly *mi scusi,* but the shortened form is the one more people use. Again, it's a most useful word in any crowded situation. You'll note that Italians push their way through a narrow passage with a long chain of *"Scusi, permesso, mi scusi, grazie, permesso. . . ."* It's very funny to hear. *Scusi* has another important use: It's the proper beginning to attract somebody's attention before asking a question. Say *"Scusi?",* and the person will turn toward you in benevolent expectation. Then it's up to you.

Buongiorno and Buona Sera

Buongiorno (bwohn-*djor*-noh), meaning **"good day,"** and its sibling *buona sera* (*bwohn*-ah *say*-rah), meaning **"good evening,"** are of the utmost importance in Italian interactions. Italians always salute one another when entering or leaving a public place. Do the same, speaking clearly, when entering a store or restaurant. Occasionally, these words can also be used as forms of goodbye.

Arrivederci

Arrivederci (ahr-ree-veh-*dehr*-chee) is the appropriate way to say **goodbye** in a formal occasion — in a shop, in a bar or restaurant, or to friends. If you can say it properly, people will like it very much: Italians are aware of the difficulties of their language for foreigners.

You'll hear the word *ciao* (chow), the familiar word for goodbye, used among friends (usually of the same age). Note that using the word *ciao* with someone you don't know is considered quite impolite!

Dov'è

Meaning **"where is,"** *dov'è* (doh-*vey*) is useful for asking for directions. Because the verb is included, you just need to add the thing you're looking for: *Dov'è il Colosseo?* ("Where is the Colosseum?") or *Dov'è la stazione?* ("Where is the train station?"). Of course you need to know the names of monuments in Italian, but don't worry! We always give you the Italian names in this book. It makes things much easier.

Quanto Costa?

Knowing how to say **"how much does it cost?"** — *quanto costa? (kwan-*toh *coh*-sta) — is useful all around Italy, for buying anything from a train ticket to a Murano glass chandelier.

Che Cos'è?

Che cos'è? (kay *koss*-ay) means **"what is it?"** and will help you identify something before you buy it. It is particularly useful in restaurants and grocery stores, but it also may come in handy in museums and other places. But then the tricky part begins: understanding the answer. If you don't understand the answer, you can get the person to repeat it by saying the next phrase on our list.

Non Capisco

Non capisco (nohn kah-*peace*-koh) means **"I don't understand."** There's no need to explain this one: Keep repeating it, and Italians will try more and more imaginative ways to explain things to you.

Chapter 18

Ten Great Roman Artists

● ●

In This Chapter

▶ Identifying Rome's great sculptors, painters, and architects
▶ Discovering great women artists
▶ Finding out where to see their work

● ●

*A*lthough hundreds of books have been written about the great figures of Italian art, few have focused specifically on Romans. Rome
and the surrounding territory have given the world a number of important artists, from the Renaissance to modern times. Most interesting,
some of the first professional *women* artists of the Renaissance came
from Rome. Their work is all over the city, decorating some of the most
important monuments you'll see, but their names are often obscure
except to art historians because of the overshadowing reputations of the
male artists who flocked (and flock) to Rome from all over the rest of
Italy and Europe.

We chose ten of the best Roman artists — men and women — who
appear in this chapter in chronological order. We left out many artists
whose names you'll encounter over and over during your visit, such as
Giuseppe Chiari (1654–1727), Giovanni Odazzi (1663–1731), Michelangelo
Cerruti (1663–1748), and Marco Benefial (1684–1764), as well as internationally known modern painters such as Giuseppe Capogrossi (1900–72)
and Toti Scaloja (1914–98).

Pietro Cavallini

Considered the Roman Giotto of medieval painting, the marvelous Pietro
Cavallini (c. 1250–1344) was a very active painter and mosaic designer of
great skill. His documented and extant work includes the splendid mosaic
in the apse of Santa Maria in Trastevere (see Chapter 11). Although
many of his frescoes have been lost — as is the case with Giotto — we
know he decorated the inner facade of St. Peter's Basilica and the main
nave of San Paolo Fuori Le Mura Basilica. At the latter basilica, you can
still admire his mosaic on the facade, as well as the Christ in the main
nave and the crucifix in the Santissimo chapel. Among Cavallini's other
works in Rome, some of the best are the *Giudizio Universale* (Last
Judgment) on the inner facade of Santa Cecilia church in Trastevere,

and the frescoes and decorations in the Savelli chapel in the church of
Santa Maria in Aracoeli, which are unfortunately partially ruined (see
Chapter 11).

Jacopo Torriti

Active at the end of the 13th century, Jacopo Torriti was another mosaic
designer and painter. Although he's considered less innovative than his
colleague Pietro Cavallini (above), his work was outstanding, as you can
judge for yourself when admiring his mosaics in the apse of Santa Maria
Maggiore basilica and the *Enthroned Virgin* in the chapel dedicated to
Santa Rosa in Santa Maria in Aracoeli church (see Chapter 11).

Antoniazzo Romano

Antonio di Benedetto Aquilio degli Aquili (c. 1430–1512) rose to fame in
his native city and soon became the leading painter of the 15th-century
Roman school. He developed a highly refined painting technique, especially for tempera. Indeed, some of his work is exhibited in major international museums, including his *Madonna di Leone IX* in the National
Gallery in Dublin, his *Madonna* at the Detroit Institute of Arts, and his
triptych in the Prado in Madrid. He was very active in Rome, where you
can see his splendid frescoes in the *Camera di Santa Caterina* in the
church of Santa Maria sopra Minerva; his *Nativity* in the National Antique
Art Gallery in Palazzo Barberini; his *Madonna del Tribunale della Sacra
Rota* in the Vatican Picture Gallery inside the Vatican Museums; and his
Madonna in San Paolo Fuori Le Mura basilica (see Chapter 11).

Giulio Pippi

Also known as Giulio Romano (c. 1492–1546) because he was born and
trained in the city, Pippi worked with Raphael in the Vatican. Though
deeply influenced by the greater painter, he quickly developed his own
personal style. He was often called on to finish and complement some of
Raphael's work, such as the frescoes in the Farnesina Villa in Trastevere
and the *Sale di Costantino* in the Vatican. He also worked extensively in
the town of Mantova for the Gonzaga family. His work is all over Rome;
in addition to his frescoes in the Vatican and the Farnesina Villa, you
can see his *Virgin with Child and St. John* in the Borghese Gallery (see
Chapter 11).

Cavalier d'Arpino

Also known as Giuseppe Cesari (1568–1640), this artist may not be a
Roman native — some think he may have been born in Arpino, near

Frosinone, where he spent some of his childhood. In any case, he was back in the city at the age of 14, working as a painter's helper in the Vatican. He was quickly promoted and started getting his own commissions, gaining increasing fame. He worked mostly in Rome but also in Naples, where he frescoed the choir in the Carthusian Monastery of Saint Martin. His elegant Mannerist style modernized with naturalistic elements made him a favorite painter in 16th-century Rome, and Pope Clement VIII often called him in. You can see much of his work around the city, including the frescoes in the Palazzo dei Conservatori of the Capitoline Museums, the transept of San Giovanni in Laterano basilica, the lunettes over the main altar and in the cupola of the Paolina chapel in Santa Maria Maggiore basilica, and the vault of the Olgiati chapel in the church of Santa Prassede. Some of his best paintings are in museums in Rome, such as his *Annunciazione* in the Vatican Picture Gallery inside the Vatican Museums, his *Diana* in the Picture Gallery of the Capitoline Museums, and his frescoes decorating the Borghese Gallery (see Chapter 11).

Artemisia Gentileschi

Born into a life of art — she was the daughter of Orazio, a painter of the Caravaggio school — Artemisia Gentileschi (1593–1652) started in the profession working with her father but soon obtained her own commissions. She worked in Rome, elsewhere in Italy — churches in Naples; paintings in Rome, Florence, and Venice — and even abroad, including in England for King Charles I. She is a great figure both in art and in the history of women. A professional painter at a time when women painters were rare and confined by rigid convention to doing portraits and still lifes, she tackled mythological and religious subjects, producing work that holds its own in comparison with that of other artists of her period. She has been the subject of many books, most recently *Artemisia: A Novel,* by Alexandra La Pierre.

In Rome, you can see her *Cecilia* and a *Madonna and Child* at the Spada Gallery and self-portraits at the National Antique Art Gallery in Palazzo Barberini (see Chapter 11).

Plautilla Bricci

Less well known than Artemisia Gentileschi (above), Plautilla Bricci (1616–90) has her place in history: She was the first woman architect in Rome and in the Western world. She practiced mostly in Rome, in secular and religious architecture. Among her remaining work in the capital is the chapel dedicated to San Luigi in the church of San Luigi dei Francesi, near the Pantheon, where she also painted the great San Luigi IX over the altar.

Pietro Bracci

Considered the greatest sculptor of the 18th century and of the baroque period, Pietro Bracci (1700–73) produced work of powerful expression and grace. He became a master in the use of colored marble, which he used to highlight and provide background for his figures. Among his best works in Rome are Neptune and the Tritons in the Trevi fountain; the monumental tomb of Benedict XIII in the church of Santa Maria sopra Minerva; the statues of angels over the portico of Santa Maria Maggiore basilica; the tomb of Benedict XIV; and the monument to Maria Clementina Sobieski (wife of James Francis Stuart, who would have been James III of England if the Jacobites had had their way) in St. Peter's Basilica (see Chapter 11).

Giuseppe Valadier

A great architect and urbanist, Giuseppe Valadier (1762–1839) made an important contribution to the reshaping of the Eternal City in the early 19th century. He is considered one of the greatest neoclassical architects; he also was an archaeologist and was responsible for the restoration of several monuments in Rome. His greatest work is the transformation of Piazza del Popolo, crowned by the elegant building named after him, La Casina Valadier (now a restaurant; see Chapter 16). Among his other works are the Teatro Valle (see Chapter 15), the reorganization of Piazza San Giovanni in Laterano (see Chapter 11), and the retracing of Via Flaminia.

Duilio Cambellotti

A multifarious artist, Duilio Cambellotti (1876–1960) is one of the greatest figures of the modern style of Art Nouveau. He began his career as an illustrator and in that field produced much work of great expressional intensity, such as his famous illustrations for the Alinari edition of Dante's *La Divina Commedia* in 1901, in perfect Liberty (Italian Art Nouveau) style. He also was a scenographer, a landscape designer, and an interior decorator and designer, and he tackled most other artistic media at one time or another — his glass windows are simply beautiful. We love him most as a sculptor. The majority of his work is in private collections and buildings, but you can admire his frescoes on the vaults of the two small halls in Sant'Angelo Castle off the Sala delle Colonne, and some of his glasswork in the Museum of the Casina delle Civette in Villa Torlonia (see Chapter 11).

Chapter 19

From Antique Prints to Cardinal Socks: The Best Roman Souvenirs

*R*ome is a great shopping destination for high-quality items, from fashion to modern art to century-old traditional crafts and antiques. Whether you plan to spend $10 or $10,000, you'll have no problem finding something that'll remind you of your trip and bring beauty to your home or to the home of a relative or friend (see Chapter 12 for store addresses).

Note: Food and wine specialties make excellent souvenirs, but we left them off this list because of the many Customs exclusions (see the Customs section in Appendix A) and because gourmet specialty stores worldwide sell most packaged edible Italian specialties.

Antique Prints

Rome is known among collectors for its many vendors specializing in antique prints and engravings. Usually representing classic subjects such as monuments, landscapes, and ruins, they are available as valuable — and expensive — original antique prints and as less expensive recent prints from antique engraving plates. Both have their qualities, and you won't have any trouble finding a wide selection. If purchased without a frame, prints can be easily transported and make excellent gifts, not to mention elegant decorations for your home or office walls.

Modern Art

Rome is not only a great city in which to *view* art, but also a great city in which to *buy* art. Numerous young artists and well-established pros have showrooms and studios in Rome, and the numerous galleries welcome visitors to browse — and purchase. Even if you return empty-handed, you'll have a lot of fun just looking.

Fashion

Of course, you can fill your suitcases with designer fashions almost anywhere you go in Italy, but Rome has all the great names of Italian *prêt-à-porter,* as well as lesser-known (and less expensive) designers producing unique and fashionable clothes. And the great thing about Rome's fashion is that it isn't only for girls; a great number of splendid shops are completely devoted to men's needs.

Gold Jewelry

Goldsmiths have an ancient tradition in Rome, and you'll find many skilled artisans who have been at their work for decades — some of them members of age-old goldsmith families. Their work is varied and unique: Some specialize in traditional designs, others follow the inspiration of antiquity and produce Roman- or Etruscan-style jewels, and others explore a modern aesthetic. No matter what your taste, you'll certainly find something to your liking.

High-Quality Stationery

Romans have a true love for stationery, and the city boasts a wonderful selection of sophisticated items, from unique handmade paper to designer fountain pens to elegant leather desk paraphernalia. Even if you use e-mail for most of your correspondence, you may find yourself yearning to put pen to paper when you see thick, cream-colored, handmade stationery or agendas and scrapbooks lined with handmade marbleized paper (a technique, by the way, that was invented either in Florence or Venice). Whether shopping for yourself or someone else, stationery makes a fine souvenir.

Lace and Embroideries

Venice is famous for its lace-making tradition, as Tuscany is for embroidery, and Rome also used to embrace the crafts. Although the tradition has almost disappeared from the city, a few local artisans keep it alive. A number of stores in Rome — well known to connoisseurs — carry a selection of quality merchandise both from local artisans and from other Italian regions. Popular items include exquisite handkerchiefs, tablecloths, bed linens, and children's clothing.

Traditional Art and Crafts

As the country's capital, Rome is also the one-stop shopping destination for Italy's best crafts and artistic items, produced both locally and in other regions. The narrow streets of Rome's historic center have been home to craftsmen for centuries, and although high rents and other factors have greatly reduced the number of local artisans, you can still find some who learned their trades the old-fashioned way: from their fathers. Among the traditional items are wrought iron, basketry, ceramics, and stained glass. If you can't find enough Rome-made specialties to satisfy your needs, a number of showrooms in town showcase the best arts and crafts Italy has to offer. All the greatest specialties are represented, from artistic Venetian glass to brightly colored hand-painted Vietri ceramics to Tuscan marble inlays. What better place than Rome, the heart and marketplace of the Italian peninsula for over 2,000 years, to find an Italian souvenir?

Plaster Reproductions

Because so many artworks, artists, and art schools concentrate in Rome, the traditional art of plaster reproductions has been maintained over the centuries. You can still find a perfect copy of Michelangelo's *Pietà* or of a Roman bust. Smaller reproductions make great gifts and souvenirs, and if you decide you can't live without a copy of the *Pietà* or some other large statue, you can always have it shipped to your home.

Vatican Souvenirs

Rome is a holy city and a pilgrimage destination to millions of Christians around the world. Here you'll find probably the world's largest collection of faith-based souvenirs — from portraits of the pope and his predecessors to signed photographs, religious calendars, scale reproductions of the Vatican, and commemorative teaspoons. This is also where you'll find bookstores carrying the largest collections of Christian books and literature in both Italian and other languages.

Religious Art and Paraphernalia

Even if you're not religious, you may be drawn to the many stores specializing in religious art located near the Vatican and in the city's historic center. The best shops carry work by reputable artists and craftspeople, with prices varying according to the quality, age, and intrinsic value of the object. The choice is enormous, from beautifully bound Bibles to religious paintings, carvings, and figurines — some truly exquisite — by both modern and ancient masters. Also, if you don't feel too blasphemous, religious attire has a quaint attraction: You can purchase beautiful red socks (made for cardinals) and superbly embroidered items in a number of specialty shops.

Appendix A

Quick Concierge

Fast Facts

American Express

The office is at Piazza di Spagna 38 (☎ 06-67641; Metro: Line A to Spagna); it's open Monday to Friday 9 a.m. to 5:30 p.m.; Saturday 9 a.m. to 12:30 p.m.; closed major local holidays.

Area Codes

The area code for Rome and surroundings is 06; the area code for Tivoli and surroundings is 0774; the area code for Civitavecchia and Tarquinia is 0766; the area code for Viterbo and the Lago di Vico area is 0761. Cellphone area codes are all three digits and always begin with a 3. Toll-free numbers start with 800 or 888 (don't add a 1 to them; they won't work). Some pay services use three-digit codes beginning with 9. In addition, some companies have special numbers that don't conform to any of the preceding standards and that are local calls from anywhere in Italy.

ATMs

ATMs are available everywhere in the centers of towns. Most banks are part of the Cirrus network. If you require the PLUS network, your best bet is BNL (Banca Nazionale del Lavoro), but ask your bank for a list of locations before leaving on your trip.

Automobile Club

Contact the Automobile Club d'Italia (ACI) at ☎ 06-4477 for 24-hour information and assistance. For road emergencies in Italy, dial ☎ 116.

Baby Sitters

A number of hotels provide babysitting for guests on request, but they usually don't offer structured activities for children. Rather, they use a professional agency to provide a babysitter who will come to your hotel room. Even if your hotel does not provide babysitting, the concierge should be able to direct you to a reliable provider. If you are stuck, we can recommend Giorgi Tiziana (Via Cavour 295; ☎ 06-4742564).

Business Hours

Shops are usually open Monday through Saturday from 8:30 a.m. to 1 p.m. and again from 4 to 7:30 p.m. Groceries and other food shops traditionally close Thursday afternoon; other shops close Monday morning. A growing number of shops in the historic center stay open during the lunch break and on Sunday. Businesses are usually open Monday through Friday from 8:30 a.m. to 1 p.m. and again from 2:30 to 5:30 p.m., and sometimes also Saturday morning. Banks are open Monday through Friday from 8:30 a.m. to 1:30 p.m. and again from 2:30 to 4 p.m. or 3 to 4:30 p.m. A few banks are open Monday through Friday from 8:30 a.m. straight through to 4 p.m. and Saturday from 8:30 a.m. to 12:30 p.m.

Camera Repair

A good shop is Dear Camera (Via Giuseppe Manno 3; ☎ 06-77073770; www.dearcamera.com; Metro: Furio Camillo).

Credit Cards

If your card is lost or stolen, contact: American Express (☎ 06-72282, 06-72900347, or 1 336 393-1111 collect in the U.S.; www.americanexpress.com); Diners Club (☎ 800-864064 toll-free within Italy; www.dinersclub.com); MasterCard (☎ 800-870866 toll-free within Italy; www.mastercard.com); or Visa (☎ 800-819014 toll-free within Italy; www.visaeu.com).

Currency Exchange

We prefer using our ATM card to get currency at the best rate, but you have many other options. You can find exchange bureaus (marked CAMBIO/CHANGE/WECHSEL) at Fiumicino airport (this location usually offers the best rates in town) and at Termini train station. Most banks provide currency exchange; most hotels also provide this service, at rates that may not be worse than those at other private currency exchange bureaus in town. These are scattered around Rome, with many near Piazza Venezia and Piazza di Spagna.

Customs

Regulations are getting stricter. It is best to carry proof of purchase for your electronics and valuables or register them with Customs before you leave the United States, if you don't want to be charged duty on your way back. U.S. citizens can bring back $800 worth of merchandise duty free. You can mail $200 worth of merchandise per day to yourself and $100 worth of gifts to others — alcohol and tobacco excluded. You can bring 1 liter of alcohol and 200 cigarettes or 100 cigars on the plane. The $800 ceiling doesn't apply to artwork or antiques (antiques must be at least 100 years old). You're charged a flat rate of 10 percent duty on the next $1,000 worth of purchases — for special items, the duty is higher. Make sure you have your receipts handy. Agricultural restrictions are severely

enforced: no fresh products, no meat products, and no dried flowers; other foodstuffs are allowed only if they're canned or in airtight sealed packages. For more information, contact the U.S. Customs Service, 1301 Pennsylvania Ave. NW, Washington, DC 20229 (☎ 877-287-8867), and request the free pamphlet "Know Before You Go," which is also available for download on the Web at www.customs.gov.

Canadian citizens who have been abroad over seven days are allowed a C$750 exemption and can bring back duty free 200 cigarettes, 2.2 pounds of tobacco, 53 imperial ounces of wine or 40 of liquor, and 50 cigars. In addition, you're allowed to mail gifts to Canada from abroad up to the value of C$60 per gift, as long as they're unsolicited and don't contain alcohol or tobacco (write on the package "Unsolicited Gift, Under $60 Value"). Declare all valuables on the Y-38 form before your departure from Canada, including serial numbers of valuables that you already own, such as expensive foreign cameras. You can use the C$750 exemption only once a year and only after an absence of seven days. For more information, contact the Canada Border Services Agency (☎ 800-461-9999 from within Canada, or 204-983-3500 or 506-636-5064 from outside Canada; www.cbsa-asfc.gc.ca).

There's no limit on what U.K. citizens can bring back from an EU country, as long as the items are for personal use (that includes gifts) and the necessary duty and tax have already been paid. However, Customs law sets out guidance levels. If you bring in more than those levels, you may be asked to prove that the goods are for your own use. Guidance levels on goods bought in the EU for your own use are 800 cigarettes, 200 cigars, 1 kilogram of smoking tobacco, 10 liters of spirits, 90 liters of wine (of which not more than 60 liters can be sparkling wine), and 110 liters of beer. For more information, contact HM Customs and Excise, Passenger Enquiry Point, 2nd Floor, Wayfarer House, Great South West Road, Feltham, Middlesex, TW14 8NP (☎ 0845-010-9000; from outside the U.K. ☎ 44-208-929-0152; www.hmce.gov.uk).

Australian citizens are allowed an exemption of A$900 or, for those under 18 years of age, A$450. Personal property mailed back home should be marked "Australian Goods Returned" to avoid payment of duty. On returning to Australia, you can bring in 250 cigarettes or 250 grams of loose tobacco and 2.5 liters of alcohol. If you're returning with valuable goods you already own, such as foreign-made cameras, you should file Form B263. A helpful brochure, available from Australian consulates or Customs offices, is "Know Before You Go." For more information, contact Australian Customs Services, GPO Box 8, Sydney NSW 2001 (☎ 02-9213-2000 or 1300-363-263 within Australia or 612-6275-6666 from outside Australia; www.customs.gov.au).

New Zealand citizens have a duty-free allowance of NZ$700. If you're over 17, you can bring in 200 cigarettes, 50 cigars, or 250 grams of tobacco (or a mix of all three if their combined weight doesn't exceed 250 grams), plus 4.5 liters of wine and beer or 1.125 liters of liquor. New Zealand currency doesn't carry import or export restrictions. Fill out a certificate of export, listing the valuables you're taking out of the country. (That way, you can bring them back without paying duty.) You can find the answers to most of your questions in a free pamphlet available at New Zealand consulates and Customs offices: "New Zealand Customs Guide for Travelers, Notice no. 4." For more information, contact New Zealand Customs, The Custom House, 17–21 Whitmore St. Box 2218, Wellington (☎ 04-473-6099; www.customs.govt.nz).

Doctors

Contact your embassy or consulate to get a list of English-speaking doctors or dentists. You can also ask the concierge at your hotel. For any emergency, go to the emergency room of any nearby hospital (see "Emergencies," later in this appendix).

Electricity

Electricity in Rome is 220 volts. To use your appliances, you need a transformer. Remember that plugs are different, too: The prongs are round, so you need an adapter. You can buy an adapter kit in many electronics stores before you leave.

Embassies and Consulates

Rome is the capital of Italy and the seat of all the embassies and consulates, which maintain 24-hour referral services for emergencies: United States (Via Veneto 119/a; ☎ 06-46741), Canada (Via G.B. de Rossi 27; ☎ 06-445981), Australia (Via Alessandria 215; ☎ 06-852721), New Zealand (Via Zara 28; ☎ 06-4402928), United Kingdom (Via XX Settembre 80/a; ☎ 06-4825441), Ireland (Piazza Campitelli 3; ☎ 06-6979121).

Emergencies

For an ambulance, call ☎ 118; for the fire department, call ☎ 115; for the police, call ☎ 113 or 112; for a road emergency, call ☎ 116.

Hospitals

The major hospitals in the historic center are the Santo Spirito (Lungotevere in Sassia 1; ☎ 06-68351, or 06-68352241 for first aid) and the Fatebenefratelli on the Isola Tiberina (Piazza Fatebenefratelli 2; ☎ 06-68371, or 06-6837299 for first aid).

Hotlines

For drug intoxication, call ☎ 06-3054343 or 06-490663. The Children Hotline (Telefono Azzurro) is ☎ 1-96-96 toll-free for children;

adolescents and adults can call ☎ 199-15-15-15. The tourist information hotline (☎ 06-36004399) provides round-the-clock information on just about anything in four languages, including English.

Information

See "Where to Get More Information," later in this appendix, and the entry above for the tourist hotline.

Internet Access and Cybercafes

Most hotels in Rome will let you check your e-mail, and many have a dedicated internet point free for guests' use. In addition, there are internet cafes everywhere. One good chain is Internet Train (www.internettrain.it), with locations at Via delle Fornaci 22 near San Pietro (Mon–Sat 6:30 a.m.–8:30 p.m. and Sun 6:30 a.m.–1 p.m.), Piazza Sant'Andrea della Valle 3, near Piazza Navona (Mon–Fri 10:30 a.m.–11 p.m. and Sat–Sun 10:30 a.m.–8 p.m.), and Via delle Fratte di Trastevere 44/b (daily 10 a.m.–10 p.m.). Another is Yex, with a perfect location off Corso Vittorio Emanuele II, steps from Piazza Navona (Piazza Sant'Andrea della Valle 1; daily 10 a.m.–10 p.m.). Charges usually run around 5€ ($6.50) for one hour.

Language

Romans speak Italian, and although many know a bit of English, most are far from fluent. Luckily, you can survive in Rome with very little knowledge of the language (see Chapter 17 for a few choice terms), especially because Romans tend to be very friendly and ready to help foreigners in difficulty. However, you'll greatly enhance your experience if you master a dozen or so basic expressions. Good places to start your studies are the glossary in Appendix B and, if you're really serious, the excellent *Italian For Dummies* (Wiley).

Liquor Laws

Italy has no liquor laws, but drinking and driving is forbidden, as is displaying drunken behavior anywhere. Disturbances of the *quiete pubblica* (public quiet) are not tolerated, and you can face stiff fines and police detention for getting drunk and loud in bars, streets, and even private homes. A special wine store is an *enoteca;* supermarkets and grocery stores (see earlier for business hours) sell all kinds of alcohol. Be careful of what you do with your empties: littering laws are strict, and drinking a can of beer while sitting on a bit of ancient Roman wall is considered littering.

Mail

Italian mail has gotten a lot better with the introduction of *Posta Prioritaria* (express/priority). A letter (up to 20gr/0.7 oz.) to Ireland or the U.K. will cost 0.65€ (85¢); to the United States 0.85€ ($1.11), and to Australia and New Zealand 1€ ($1.30). Postcards will be sent slowly — the equivalent of U.S. third-class mail — unless you slip them in an envelope and send them letter rate. Also, make sure you put your mail in the right mailbox, or sorting will take longer: The ones for international mail are blue (the red ones are for domestic mail). For packages, you can choose between the slow regular rate and the faster but expensive priority rate; sometimes, especially for valuables, you may be better off using a private carrier like UPS or DHL, which guarantee delivery.

Maps

You can find free maps at tourist information points (see "Where to Find More Information," later in this appendix). If you want something more detailed, it is a good idea to buy a map with a *stradario* (street directory) at a newsstand or kiosk. One of the best is the somewhat bulky *Tutto Città*, a largish booklet with a full street directory that costs about 8€ ($10).

Pharmacies

Pharmacies are usually open Monday through Friday from 8:30 a.m. to 1 p.m. and again from 4 to 7:30 p.m. A few pharmacies are open all night: Piazza dei Cinquecento 49, at Termini Station (☎ 06-4880019); Via Cola di Rienzo 213 (☎ 06-3244476); Piazza Risorgimento 44 (☎ 06-39738166); Via Arenula 73 (☎ 06-68803278); Corso Rinascimento 50 (☎ 06-68803985); Piazza Barberini 49 (☎ 06-4871195); and Viale Trastevere 229 (☎ 06-5882273).

Police

To call the police, dial ☎ **113** or **112**.

Post Office

The central post office in the historic center is at Piazza San Silvestro 19, the major bus hub near Piazza di Spagna. You'll also find post offices at Via di Porta Angelica 23, near San Pietro, and at Viale Mazzini 101 in the Cola di Rienzo area. They're open Monday through Friday from 8:30 a.m. to 6:30 p.m. and Saturday from 8:30 a.m. to 1 p.m. For information, call ☎ 800-160000 (toll free within Italy).

Many tourists prefer to use the Vatican post office (by the entrance to the Vatican Museums) while they're visiting St. Peter's in Rome; prices are the same as at Italian post offices, but delivery is sometimes faster, and you get special Vatican stamps. Note, though, that you can mail letters with Vatican stamps only from the blue mailboxes in the Vatican.

Restrooms

Public toilets are located at strategic tourist destinations: outside the Colosseum (on the side facing Via Labicana); at Piazza del Popolo (halfway up the steps climbing toward the Pincio and Villa Borghese); in Piazza San Pietro (under the colonnade on both right and left). Make sure you have some change to tip the attendant. Elsewhere, your best bet may be to go to a nice-looking cafe (though you have to buy something, like a cup of coffee or a glass of mineral water, to use the restroom).

Safety

Rome is a very safe city, but petty theft is common. Pickpockets abound in tourist areas, on public transportation, and around crowded open-air markets like the Porta Portese. Observe common big-city caution: Keep your valuables in your hotel's safe, don't be distracted, watch your belongings, don't count your money in public, and avoid displaying valuable jewelry and electronic equipment. Outside the central city are some areas where a wealthy-looking tourist with an expensive camera may be mugged after dark.

If you're a woman traveling alone, chances are you'll attract young men's attention. If you are particularly striking, they may vocalize their admiration and occasionally even approach and try to charm you. However, it's unlikely that they will touch you, let alone harm you, particularly during the day. Still, it's a good idea to ignore and avoid eye contact with anyone who approaches you. Should you feel harassed, immediately speak up; don't hesitate to ask the help of a passerby or enter in a cafe or shop and ask for the attendants' assistance. Rome is a cosmopolitan city, but the dress code in general is stricter than in the United States. Although you'll see a lot of female skin displayed, you'll also notice that the women displaying it always have company; if you are alone, you may want to cover up a bit. Also, it is a good idea not to wander too far from the beaten path at night if you are alone. The area behind Termini train station can be dangerous for lone women, and so can some deserted, dark, and narrow streets in the historic center.

Smoking

In 2005, Italy passed a law outlawing smoking in most public places. Smoking is allowed only where there is a separate, ventilated area for nonsmokers. If you want to smoke at your table, call beforehand to make sure the restaurant or cafe you'll be visiting offers a smoking area.

Taxes

Refer to Chapter 12 for information about Italy's value-added tax, known as IVA.

Taxis

Taxis don't cruise; they wait for a call at a station. If you need a taxi, call ☎ 06-88177, 06-6645, 06-4994, 06-5551, or 06-6545 for radio service. You'll find taxi stations in most neighborhoods; here are some of the most centrally located: Piazza Barberini (at the foot of Via Veneto); Piazza di Spagna; Piazza San Silvestro (near Piazza di Spagna); Piazza Santi Apostoli (not far from the Trevi fountain); Largo Argentina (off Corso Vittorio Emanuele II); Via Veneto; Via Cavour (not far from the Colosseum); Piazza Mazzini; Piazza Risorgimento (near St. Peter's); Piazza Mastai (Trastevere).

Telephone

To call Italy from the United States, dial the international access code, **011**; then Italy's country code, **39**; then the area code for the place you're calling, followed by the telephone number. Area codes for land lines in Italy may have different numbers of digits (**06** for Rome, **0774** for Tivoli, and so on), but they always begin with **0**; cellular lines always have three-digit area codes beginning with **3**. Toll-free numbers have an **800** or **888** area code (don't add a 1). Some pay services use three-digit codes beginning with **9**. Also, some companies' numbers don't conform to any of the preceding standards and are local calls from

anywhere in Italy; one is Trenitalia's railroad info line, ☎ 892021.

To make a call within Italy, always use the area code — including 0 if any — for both local and long distance. To use a public pay phone, buy a *carta telefonica* (telephone card), available at any *tabacchi* (tobacconist, marked by a sign with a white *T* on a black background), bar, or newsstand. The cards can be purchased in denominations from 2€ to 7.50€ ($2.60–$9.75). Tear off the perforated corner, stick the card in the phone, and you're ready to go. A local call in Italy costs 0.10€ (13¢).

To call abroad from Italy, dial the international access code, 00; then the country code (**1** for the U.S. and Canada, **44** for the U.K., **353** for Ireland, **61** for Australia, **64** for New Zealand); and then the phone number. Make sure that you have a high-value *carta telefonica* before you start; your 5€ won't last long when you call San Diego at noon. Lower rates apply after 11 p.m. and before 8 a.m. and on Sunday. The best option for calling home, though, is using your own calling card linked to your home phone. Some calling cards offer a toll-free access number in Italy; others do not, and you must use a *carta telefonica* to dial the access number (you're usually charged only for a local call or not at all). Check with your calling-card provider before leaving on your trip. You can also make collect calls. For AT&T, dial ☎ 800-1724444 and then your U.S. phone number, area code first; for MCI, dial ☎ 800-905825; and for Sprint, dial ☎ 800-172405 or 800-172406. To make a collect call to a country other than the United States, dial ☎ 170. Directory assistance for calls within Italy is a free call: Dial ☎ 12. International directory assistance is a toll call: Dial ☎ 176. Remember that calling from a hotel is convenient but usually very expensive.

Time Zone

Italy is six hours ahead of Eastern standard time in the United States: When it's 6 a.m. in New York, it's noon in Italy. Daylight saving time is in effect from the last Sunday in March to the last Sunday in October.

Tipping

Tipping is customary as a token of appreciation as well as a polite gesture on most occasions. A 10 percent to 15 percent service charge is usually included in your restaurant bill (check the menu when you order — if the service is included, you'll see *servizio incluso*), but it is customary to leave an additional 5 percent to 10 percent if you appreciated the meal; if the service is not included, leave 15 percent to 25 percent. In bars, leave a 5 percent tip at the counter and a 10 percent to 15 percent tip if you sit at a table. Bellhops who carry your bags will expect about 1€ ($1.30) per bag, and you may want to leave a small tip for the hotel housekeeper. Cab drivers will expect 10 percent to 15 percent of the fare.

Transit Info

The local public transportation authority (bus, tram, and subway) is ATAC (☎ 800-431784 or 06-46952027; www.atac.roma.it). For railroad information, call Trenitalia (☎ 892021; www.trenitalia.it).

Weather Updates

Before you go, you can check a local Web site such as http://meteo.it or one of the U.S.–based ones, such as www.cnn.com. When you're in Italy, your best bet is to watch the news on TV (there's no weather telephone number).

Toll-Free Numbers and Web Sites

Airlines that fly to Rome and around Italy

Air France
☎ 800-237-2747
www.airfrance.com

Air New Zealand
☎ 800-737-000
www.airnewzealand.com

Air One
☎ 199-207080 in Italy
☎ 06-488800 from abroad
www.flyairone.it

Alitalia
☎ 1478-65643 toll-free within Italy
or 06-65643
☎ 800-223-5730 in the United States
☎ 800-361-8336 in Canada
☎ 0990-448-259 in the United Kingdom

☎ 020-7602-7111 in London
☎ 1300-653-747 or 1300-653-757
in Australia
www.alitalia.it or
in the United States
www.alitaliausa.com

American Airlines
☎ 800-433-7300
www.aa.com

British Airways
☎ 800-247-9297
☎ 0345-222-111 or 0845-77-333-77
in Britain
www.british-airways.com

Cathay Pacific
☎ 131-747 in Australia
☎ 0508-800454 in New Zealand
www.cathaypacific.com

Continental Airlines
☎ 800-525-0280
www.continental.com

Delta Air Lines
☎ 800-221-1212
www.delta.com

Lufthansa
☎ 800-645-3880 in the United States
www.lufthansa-usa.com

Meridiana
☎ 892928 within Italy
☎ 0789-52682 from abroad
www.meridiana.it

Northwest Airlines
☎ 800-225-2525
www.nwa.com

Qantas
☎ 800-227-4500 in the United States
☎ 612-9691-3636 in Australia
www.qantas.com

United Airlines
☎ 800-241-6522
www.united.com

US Airways
☎ 800-428-4322
www.usairways.com

Major car-rental agencies

AutoEurope
☎ 800-334440 in Italy
☎ 800-223-5555 in the United States
www.autoeurope.com

Avis
☎ 06-41999 in Italy
☎ 800-331-1212 in the United States
www.avis.com

Europe by Car
☎ 800-223-1516 in the United States
www.europebycar.com

Europcar
☎ 800-014410 or 06-65010879 in Italy
www.europcar.it

Hertz
☎ 199-112211 in Italy
☎ 800-654-3001 in the United States
www.hertz.com

Kemwel
☎ 800-678-0678 in the United States
www.kemwel.com

National/Maggiore
☎ 1478-67067 in Italy
☎ 800-227-7368 in the United States
www.maggiore.it

Sixt
☎ 888-749-8227 in the United States
☎ 199-100666 in Italy
www.e-sixt.it and www.sixtusa.com for U.S. citizens

Major hotel chains

Accor
☎ 800-221-4542 in the United States and Canada
☎ 0208-283-4500 in the United Kingdom
www.accor.com

Best Western
☎ 800-780-7234 in the United States and Canada
☎ 0800-39-31-30 in the United Kingdom
☎ 131-779 in Australia
☎ 0800-237-893 in New Zealand
www.bestwestern.com

Hilton Hotels
☎ 800-HILTONS
www.hilton.com

Holiday Inn
☎ 800-HOLIDAY
www.holiday-inn.com

Jolly Hotels
☎ 800-017703 in Italy
☎ 800-221-2626 in the United States
☎ 800-247-1277 in New York state
☎ 800-237-0319 in Canada
☎ 0800-731-0470 in the
United Kingdom
www.jollyhotels.it.

Sofitel
☎ 800-SOFITEL in the United States
and Canada
☎ 020-8283-4570 in the
United Kingdom

☎ 02-29512280 in Italy
☎ 800-642-244 in Australia
☎ 0800-44-44-22 in New Zealand
www.sofitel.com or www.
accorhotels.com/it/home/
index.shtml.

Starwood Hotels
☎ 888-625-5144 for Sheraton, Four
Points, Le Meridien, Westin
☎ 800-325-3589 for St. Regis,
Luxury Collection
www.starwoodhotels.com

Where to Get More Information

As in any other metropolis, getting the proper info is essential in Rome. Here you'll find the best sources around.

Visitor information

The national tourist board, ENIT (www.enit.it), maintains a Web site where you can find all kinds of cultural and practical information — including hotel listings and the mail and Web addresses of local tourist offices. It also maintains the following liaison offices abroad, where you can get brochures and other info (all offices are open Mon–Fri 9 a.m.– 5 p.m. local time):

- **New York** (630 Fifth Ave., Suite 1565, New York, NY 10111; ☎ **212-245-5618** or 212-245-4822; fax 212-586-9249; enitny@ italiantourism.com)

- **Chicago** (500 N. Michigan Ave., Suite 2240, Chicago, IL 60611; ☎ **312-644-0996** or 312-644-0990; fax 312-644-3019; enitch@ italiantourism.com)

- **Los Angeles** (12400 Wilshire Blvd., Suite 550, Los Angeles, CA 90025; ☎ **310-820-9807** or 310-820-1898; fax 310-820-6357; enitla@earthlink.net)

- **London** (1 Princes St., London, WIB 2AY; ☎ **0207-399-3562;** fax 0207-493-6695; italy@italiantouristboard.co.uk)

- **Sydney** (Level 26, 44 Market St. NSW 2000 Sydney; ☎ **02-9262-1666;** fax 02-9262-1677; enitour@ihug.com.au)

- **Toronto** (175 Bloor St., Suite 907, South Tower Toronto M4W3R8 Ontario; ☎ **416-925-4822;** fax 416-925-4799; enit.canada@on. aibn.com)

You can also write to (or visit, after you're there) the separate tourist boards of Rome and the Vatican:

- ✔ **APT Roma** (Via Parigi 11, 00185 Roma; ☎ **06-36004399;** fax 06-4819316; www.romaturismo.it). The walk-in office is at Via Parigi 5 (☎ **06-488991;** Mon–Sat 9 a.m.–7 p.m.).

- ✔ **Vaticano/Holy See — Ufficio Informazioni Turistiche** (Piazza San Pietro, 00163 Roma; ☎ **06-69884466;** Mon–Sat 8:30 a.m.– 6:30 p.m.).

After you arrive in Rome, you can get detailed and up-to-date cultural and practical information, including a calendar of events, and info on special exhibits at the **Fiumicino Airport** (Terminal B; ☎ **06-65956074;** daily 8 a.m.–7 p.m.) and at the many tourist information kiosks about town. They're near major attractions and open daily 9 a.m.–6 p.m.

- ✔ **Castel Sant'Angelo,** Piazza Pia, to the west of the Castel Sant'Angelo (☎ **06-68809707;** Metro: Ottaviano–San Pietro)

- ✔ **Fontana di Trevi,** Via Minghetti, off Via del Corso (☎ **06-6782988;** Bus: Minibus 117 or 119)

- ✔ **Fori Imperiali,** Piazza Tempio della Pace on Via dei Fori Imperiali (☎ **06-69924307;** Metro: Colosseo)

- ✔ **Largo Goldoni,** on Via del Corso at Via Condotti (☎ **06-68136061;** Metro: Piazza di Spagna)

- ✔ **Palazzo delle Esposizioni,** Via Nazionale (☎ **06-47824525;** Bus: 64)

- ✔ **Piazza delle Cinque Lune,** off Piazza Navona to the north (☎ **06-68809240;** Bus: Minibus 116)

- ✔ **San Giovanni,** Piazza San Giovanni in Laterano (☎ **06-77203535;** Metro: San Giovanni)

- ✔ **Santa Maria Maggiore,** Via dell'Olmata, on the southeastern side of the church (☎ **06-4740955;** Metro: Termini)

- ✔ **Stazione Termini,** Piazza dei Cinquecento, in front of the railroad station (☎ **06-47825194;** Metro: Termini)

- ✔ **Stazione Termini,** inside the gallery (☎ **06-48906300;** Metro: Termini)

- ✔ **Trastevere,** Piazza Sonnino (☎ **06-58333457;** Tram: 8)

The 24-hour tourist information hotline (☎ **06-36004399**) provides information in four languages, including English.

Newspapers and magazines

A few periodicals are printed, at least in part, in English.

✔ *The Happening City* (www.romaturismo.it) is an excellent monthly magazine that covers cultural events in the Eternal City. It's published in Italian and in English by the Roman tourist board.

✔ *Roma C'è* (www.romace.it) is a weekly paper with extensive listings of all that is going on in Rome, from markets to art exhibits and concerts. A section of it is in English and lists all the special events that are of particular interest to tourists and expatriates living in Rome. It comes out on Wednesday and costs 1.20€ ($1.60); an online version is also available.

✔ *Wanted in Rome* is an English-language magazine published every two weeks. It's sold at newsstands in the historic center of the city and at selected newsstands elsewhere; the Web site is www.wantedinrome.com.

Other sources of information

For great walking itineraries, check out *Memorable Walks in Rome* (Wiley), a very portable Frommer's title.

The number of Web sites on Italy and Rome is mind-boggling. Here is a small selection.

✔ **Dolce Vita** (www.dolcevita.com) is all about style as it pertains to fashion, cuisine, design, and travel. Dolce Vita is a good place to keep up on trends in modern Italian culture.

✔ **In Italy Online** (www.initaly.com) provides information on all sorts of accommodations (country villas, historic residences, convents, and farmhouses) and includes tips on shopping, dining, driving, and viewing art.

✔ **Roma2000** (www.roma2000.it) was created for the millennium and Papal Jubilee celebrations and never dismantled because it's so full of useful links and info.

✔ **Rome info** (www.rome.info) is a well-made site with plenty of information, from the cultural (monuments and history) to the practical (hotels and restaurants), with some curiosities thrown into the mix.

✔ **Virtual Rome** (www.virtualrome.com) provides information on hotels, other travel-oriented suggestions, and tips on topics from shopping to sightseeing.

✔ **Rome City** (www.romecity.it) provides excellent historical and cultural information, as well as a variety of practical information, including restaurants and hotel listings.

Appendix B

Glossary of Italian Words and Phrases

• •

Although most Romans speak at least some English and will do their best to understand foreigners, knowing even a smidge of Italian will help you enormously. You'll feel freer and more relaxed, and Romans will appreciate your taking an interest in their language. This appendix contains some basic vocabulary to help you get around; if you are interested in learning more, we recommend *Italian For Dummies,* which comes with a CD and is an excellent resource.

Basic Vocabulary

English	Italian	Pronunciation
Thank you	**Grazie**	*graht*-tzee-ay
You're welcome	**Prego**	*prey*-go
Please	**Per favore**	*pehr* fah-*vohr*-ay
Yes	**Si**	see
No	**No**	noh
Good morning or Good day	**Buongiorno**	bwohn-*djor*-noh
Good evening	**Buona sera**	*bwohn*-ah *say*-rah
Good night	**Buona notte**	*bwohn*-ah *noht*-tay
How are you?	**Come sta?**	*koh*-may *stah*
Very well	**Molto bene**	*mohl*-toh *behn*-ney
Goodbye	**Arrivederci**	ahr-ree-veh-*dehr*-chee
Excuse me (to get attention)	**Scusi**	*skoo*-zee
Excuse me (to get past someone)	**Permesso**	pehr-*mehs*-soh
Where is . . . ?	**Dov'è . . . ?**	doh-*vey*
the station	**la stazione**	lah stat-tzee-*oh*-neh
a hotel	**un albergo**	oon ahl-*behr*-goh

a restaurant	un ristorante	oon reest-ohr-*ahnt*-eh
the bathroom	il bagno	eel *bahn*-nyoh
To the right	A destra	ah *dehy*-stra
To the left	A sinistra	ah see-*nees*-tra
Straight ahead	Avanti (*or* sempre dritto)	ahv-*vahn*-tee (*sehm*-pray *dreet*-toh)
How much is it?	Quanto costa?	*kwan*-toh *coh*-sta
The check, please	Il conto, per favore	eel *kon*-toh *pehr* fah-*vohr*-eh
When?	Quando?	*kwan*-doh
Yesterday	Ieri	ee-*yehr*-ree
Today	Oggi	*oh*-jee
Tomorrow	Domani	doh-*mah*-nee
Breakfast	Prima colazione	*pree*-mah coh-laht-tzee-*ohn*-ay
Lunch	Pranzo	*prahn*-zoh
Dinner	Cena	*chay*-nah
What time is it?	Che ore sono?	kay *or*-ay *soh*-noh
Monday	Lunedì	loo-nay-*dee*
Tuesday	Martedì	mart-ay-*dee*
Wednesday	Mercoledì	mehr-cohl-ay-*dee*
Thursday	Giovedì	joh-vay-*dee*
Friday	Venerdì	ven-nehr-*dee*
Saturday	Sabato	*sah*-bah-toh
Sunday	Domenica	doh-*mehn*-nee-kah

Numbers

Number	Italian	Pronunciation
1	uno	*oo*-noh
2	due	*doo*-ay
3	tre	tray
4	quattro	*kwah*-troh
5	cinque	*cheen*-kway
6	sei	say
7	sette	*set*-tay
8	otto	*oh*-toh
9	nove	*noh*-vay

10	**dieci**	dee-*ay*-chee
11	**undici**	*oon*-dee-chee
20	**venti**	*vehn*-tee
21	**ventuno**	vehn-*toon*-oh
22	**venti due**	*vehn*-tee *doo*-ay
30	**trenta**	*trayn*-tah
40	**quaranta**	kwah-*rahn*-tah
50	**cinquanta**	cheen-*kwan*-tah
60	**sessanta**	sehs-*sahn*-tah
70	**settanta**	seht-*tahn*-tah
80	**ottanta**	oht-*tahn*-tah
90	**novanta**	noh-*vahnt*-tah
100	**cento**	*chen*-toh
1,000	**mille**	*mee*-lay
5,000	**cinquemila**	*cheen*-kway *mee*-lah
10,000	**diecimila**	dee-*ay*-chee *mee*-lah

Architectural Terms

abside (apse): The half-rounded extension behind the main altar of a church; Christian tradition dictates that it be placed at the eastern end of an Italian church, the side closest to Jerusalem.

ambone: A pulpit, either serpentine or simple in form, erected in an Italian church.

amorino or **cupido** (cupid): The personification of the mythological god of love as a chubby and winged naked child armed with bow and arrows.

atrio (atrium): A courtyard, open to the sky, in an ancient Roman house; the term also applies to the courtyard nearest the entrance of an early Christian church.

baldacchino or **ciborio** (baldachin, baldaquin, or ciborium): A columned stone canopy, usually placed above the altar of a church.

basilica: Any rectangular public building, usually divided into three aisles by rows of columns. In ancient Rome, this architectural form was frequently used for places of public assembly and law courts; later, Roman Christians adapted the form for many of their early churches.

battistero (baptistery): A separate building or a separate area in a church where the rite of baptism is held.

calidarium: The steam room of a Roman bath.

campanile: A bell tower, often detached, of a church.

capitello (capital): The four-sided stone at the top of a column, often decoratively carved. The Greek classic architectural styles included three orders: Doric, Ionic, and Corinthian.

cariatide (caryatid): A column carved into a standing female figure.

cattedrale (cathedral): The church where a bishop has his chair.

cavea: The curved row of seats in a classical theater; the most prevalent shape was a semicircle.

cella: The sanctuary, or most sacred interior section, of a Roman pagan temple.

chiostro (cloister): A courtyard ringed by a gallery of arches or lintels set atop columns.

cornice: The horizontal flange defining the uppermost part of a building, especially in classical or neoclassical facades.

cortile: An uncovered courtyard enclosed within the walls of a building complex.

cripta (crypt): A church's underground chapel, mostly used as a burial place, usually below the choir.

cupola: A dome.

duomo: A town's most important church, usually also a cathedral.

foro (forum; plural forums or fori): The main square and principal gathering place of any Roman town, usually surrounded by the city's most important temples and civic buildings.

ipogeo (hypogeum): Subterranean structure (such as a temple, a chamber, or a chapel) often used as tomb; also as an adjective (hypogee).

loggia: A covered balcony or gallery.

navata (nave): Each of the longitudinal sections of a church or basilica, divided by walls, pillars, or columns.

palazzo: A large building, usually of majestic architecture; palace.

pergamo: A pulpit.

pietra dura: A semiprecious stone, such as amethyst or lapis lazuli.

portico: A porch with columns on at least one side, usually for decorative purposes.

presbiterio: The area around the main altar of a church, elevated and separated by columns or, in the oldest churches, by a screen *(transenna),* which was traditionally reserved for the bishop and the officiating clergy.

pulvino (pulvin): A typical structure of Byzantine architecture consisting of a four-sided stone, often in the shape of a truncated pyramid and often decorated with carvings of plants and animals, which connected the capital to the above structure.

putto: An artistic representation of a naked small child, especially common in the Renaissance.

stucco: A building material made of sand, powdered marble, lime, and water applied to a surface to make it smooth or used to create a decorative relief.

telamone or **atlante:** A statue of a male figure used as structural support.

terme: Thermal baths or spas, such as the ancient Roman ones.

timpano (tympanum): The triangular wall — sometimes decorated with reliefs — between the cornice and the roof.

transenna: A screen (usually in carved marble) separating the *presbiterio* from the rest of an early Christian church.

travertino (travertine): A type of limestone that is white, pale yellow, or pale reddish and porous, commonly found in central Italy.

Common Menu Terms

agnello or abbacchio: Lamb, usually grilled or baked.

agnello alla scottadito: Thin, charbroiled lamb chops. (*Scottadito* means "burn your fingers"; they are served piping hot, and you're supposed to eat them with your hands.)

amatriciana: Traditional local pasta sauce made with lard, onions, hot red pepper, and tomatoes.

animelle: Intestines of baby veal still filled with milk.

antipasto: Appetizer. The menu may include sliced cured meats such as *prosciutto* and *salame, mozzarella,* sautéed shellfish, *caprese, bruschetta,* and a choice of succulent tidbits and prepared dishes such as *insalata di*

mare, frittata, and cooked and seasoned vegetables. In some restaurants, antipasto is served buffet style.

aragosta: Mediterranean lobster.

baccalà: Dried and salted codfish, usually prepared as a stew.

bistecca: Steak.

bomba alla crema: A deep-fried pastry filled with cream, served for breakfast at bars.

braciola: Chop, usually lamb or pork.

brasato: Beef braised in wine with vegetables.

bruschetta: Toasted peasant-style bread, heavily slathered with olive oil and garlic, and often topped with tomatoes.

bucatini: Thick, hollow spaghetti.

calamari: Squid.

calzone: A filled pocket of pizza dough, usually stuffed with ham and cheese, and sometimes other ingredients. It can be baked or fried.

cannelloni: Tubes of fresh pasta dough stuffed with meat, fish, or vegetables and then baked with cheese, tomato sauce, and sometimes béchamel (creamy white sauce).

caprese: Sliced fresh tomatoes and *mozzarella,* seasoned with fresh basil and olive oil.

carciofi: Artichokes.

carpaccio: Thin slices of raw beef, seasoned with olive oil, lemon, pepper, and slivers of Parmesan. Sometimes raw fish served in the same style but without the cheese.

ciambella: A deep-fried, doughnut-shaped pastry served for breakfast at bars.

coniglio alla cacciatora: Rabbit cooked in wine with olives and herbs.

cornetto: A sort of croissant served for breakfast at bars; it can be plain or filled with a dollop of pastry cream or jam.

cozze: Mussels.

fagioli: Beans.

fegato: Liver; often prepared *alla veneziana,* sautéed with onions.

fiordilatte: A type of cheese mimicking *mozzarella* but made with cow's milk.

fiorentina: Delicious thick T-bone steak from the Chianina cow, a unique and protected species traditionally raised in southern Tuscany; served grilled with a seasoning of olive oil and herbs.

fragaglie: Very small fish, usually served deep fried.

freselle: Whole-wheat rustic croutons served seasoned with fresh tomatoes, fresh basil, salt, and olive oil. Sold in grocery stores, they look like dark, dry, doughnut-shaped flat rounds.

frittata: Italian omelet, thick and often studded with vegetables or potatoes.

fritto misto: A deep-fried medley of seafood, usually calamari and shrimp.

frutti di mare: "Fruits of the sea"; refers to all shellfish.

gelato: Ice cream. The best is sold in bars and parlors that bear the sign **"produzione propria,"** indicating that it is freshly made on the premises in small batches.

gnocchi: Dumplings made from potatoes *(gnocchi alla patate)* and usually served with tomato sauce and grated *Parmigiano;* also *gnocchi alla romana,* semolina rounds baked with a rich seasoning of butter and *Parmigiano.*

granita: Crushed ice made with fresh lemonade or coffee.

insalata di mare: Seafood salad (usually including octopus or squid) seasoned with olive oil and lemon — sometimes vinegar — and fresh herbs.

involtini: Thinly sliced beef, veal, pork, eggplant, or zucchini rolled, stuffed, and sautéed, often served in a tomato sauce.

maritozzo: A sweet bun studded with raisins and little bits of candied citrus fruit served for breakfast at bars; sometimes it is cut in half and filled with whipped cream.

melanzane: Eggplants.

minestrone: A thick and savory soup made of vegetables and beans, served with grated *Parmigiano* and bread.

mozzarella: A nonfermented cheese, typically from Campania, exclusively made from fresh buffalo's milk and served fresh. What is called *mozzarella* in the rest of Italy and abroad is *fiordilatte,* a similar cheese made with cow's milk.

osso buco: Thick slice of beef or veal shank slowly braised in a wine sauce.

pancetta: Italian bacon.

panettone: Rich, sweet, yellow-colored bread studded with raisins

and candied fruit and served traditionally for Christmas.

panna: Heavy cream.

panna montata: Whipped cream.

Parmigiano: Parmesan, a hard and savory yellow cheese usually grated over pastas and soups but also eaten alone; the best is *Parmigiano Reggiano,* followed by *Grana Padano.*

peperoni: Green, yellow, or red sweet peppers (not to be confused with American pepperoni, a kind of *salame* that doesn't exist in Italy).

pesce al cartoccio: Fish baked in a parchment envelope with the chef's choice of seasonings.

pesce spada: Swordfish.

pesto: Fresh basil, garlic, and olive oil, finely chopped into a paste.

piselli: Peas.

pizza: Served as individual rounds in restaurants or by weight from large square pans in take-out joints; varieties include *margherita* (with tomato sauce, cheese, fresh basil, and memories of the first queen of Italy, Marguerite di Savoia, in whose honor it was first made by a Neapolitan chef), *marinara* (with tomatoes and oregano), *napoletana* (tomatoes, cheese, and anchovies; hilariously, these are the same toppings that in Naples make the pizza *romana*).

pizzaiola: A process in which something (usually a slice of beef or a fillet of fish) is cooked in a tomato, garlic, and oregano sauce.

polipetti: Squid.

polpo or **polipo:** Octopus.

prosciutto: Air- and salt-cured pork leg, served thinly sliced.

ragù: Meat-based tomato sauce; the chef's imagination rules.

ricotta: A soft, bland cheese served very fresh and made from sheep's milk or, in lower-quality versions, with cow's milk.

rigatoni: Classic short pasta usually served *all'amatriciana.*

risotto: A typical preparation of Arborio rice. It can be simple or flavored with various ingredients (see below for one example).

risotto alla pescatora: Arborio rice cooked with wine, a little tomato, and lots of fresh seafood.

salame: Seasoned chopped pork formed into a largish air- and salt-cured sausage. It comes in many varieties, somewhat reminiscent of American pepperoni.

semifreddo: A frozen dessert, usually ice cream with sponge cake.

seppia: Cuttlefish (a kind of squid); its black ink is used for flavoring in

certain sauces for pasta and in risotto dishes.

sogliola: Sole.

spaghetti: Long, round, thin pasta, served *al ragù* (with meat sauce), *all'amatriciana* (see earlier entry), *al pomodoro* (with fresh tomatoes), *ai frutti di mare* (with a medley of sautéed seafood), and *alle vongole* (with clam sauce), among others.

spiedini: Pieces of meat grilled on a skewer over an open flame.

tagliatelle: Flat egg noodles.

tonno: Tuna.

trippa: Tripe.

vermicelli: Thin spaghetti.

vongole: Mediterranean clams.

zabaglione/zabaione: Egg yolks whipped into the consistency of custard, flavored with Marsala, and served warm as a dessert; also a flavor of ice cream.

zuccotto: A liqueur-soaked sponge cake molded into a dome and layered with chocolate, nuts, and whipped cream.

zuppa inglese: Sponge cake soaked in custard.

Index

See also separate Accommodations and Restaurant indexes at the end of this index.

General Index

• A •

Accommodations Index

Restaurant Index

Notes

SINESS, CAREERS & PERSONAL FINANCE

7645-5307-0   0-7645-5331-3 *†

Also available:
- Accounting For Dummies †
  0-7645-5314-3
- Business Plans Kit For Dummies †
  0-7645-5365-8
- Cover Letters For Dummies
  0-7645-5224-4
- Frugal Living For Dummies
  0-7645-5403-4
- Leadership For Dummies
  0-7645-5176-0
- Managing For Dummies
  0-7645-1771-6

- Marketing For Dummies
  0-7645-5600-2
- Personal Finance For Dummies *
  0-7645-2590-5
- Project Management
  For Dummies
  0-7645-5283-X
- Resumes For Dummies †
  0-7645-5471-9
- Selling For Dummies
  0-7645-5363-1
- Small Business Kit For Dummies *†
  0-7645-5093-4

ME & BUSINESS COMPUTER BASICS

-7645-4074-2   0-7645-3758-X

Also available:
- ACT! 6 For Dummies
  0-7645-2645-6
- iLife '04 All-in-One Desk Reference
  For Dummies
  0-7645-7347-0
- iPAQ For Dummies
  0-7645-6769-1
- Mac OS X Panther Timesaving
  Techniques For Dummies
  0-7645-5812-9
- Macs For Dummies
  0-7645-5656-8
- Microsoft Money 2004 For Dummies
  0-7645-4195-1

- Office 2003 All-in-One Desk
  Reference For Dummies
  0-7645-3883-7
- Outlook 2003 For Dummies
  0-7645-3759-8
- PCs For Dummies
  0-7645-4074-2
- TiVo For Dummies
  0-7645-6923-6
- Upgrading and Fixing PCs
  For Dummies
  0-7645-1665-5
- Windows XP Timesaving
  Techniques For Dummies
  0-7645-3748-2

OD, HOME, GARDEN, HOBBIES, MUSIC & PETS

-7645-5295-3   0-7645-5232-5

Also available:
- Bass Guitar For Dummies
  0-7645-2487-9
- Diabetes Cookbook For Dummies
  0-7645-5230-9
- Gardening For Dummies *
  0-7645-5130-2
- Guitar For Dummies
  0-7645-5106-X
- Holiday Decorating For Dummies
  0-7645-2570-0
- Home Improvement All-in-One
  For Dummies
  0-7645-5680-0

- Knitting For Dummies
  0-7645-5395-X
- Piano For Dummies
  0-7645-5105-1
- Puppies For Dummies
  0-7645-5255-4
- Scrapbooking For Dummies
  0-7645-7208-3
- Senior Dogs For Dummies
  0-7645-5818-8
- Singing For Dummies
  0-7645-2475-5
- 30-Minute Meals For Dummies
  0-7645-2589-1

TERNET & DIGITAL MEDIA

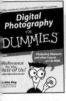

-7645-1664-7   0-7645-6924-4

Also available:
- 2005 Online Shopping Directory
  For Dummies
  0-7645-7495-7
- CD & DVD Recording For Dummies
  0-7645-5956-7
- eBay For Dummies
  0-7645-5654-1
- Fighting Spam For Dummies
  0-7645-5965-6
- Genealogy Online For Dummies
  0-7645-5964-8
- Google For Dummies
  0-7645-4420-9

- Home Recording For Musicians
  For Dummies
  0-7645-1634-5
- The Internet For Dummies
  0-7645-4173-0
- iPod & iTunes For Dummies
  0-7645-7772-7
- Preventing Identity Theft
  For Dummies
  0-7645-7336-5
- Pro Tools All-in-One Desk
  Reference For Dummies
  0-7645-5714-9
- Roxio Easy Media Creator
  For Dummies
  0-7645-7131-1

Separate Canadian edition also available

Separate U.K. edition also available

ailable wherever books are sold. For more information or to order direct: U.S. customers
sit www.dummies.com or call 1-877-762-2974.
K. customers visit www.wileyeurope.com or call 0800 243407. Canadian customers visit
ww.wiley.ca or call 1-800-567-4797.

SPORTS, FITNESS, PARENTING, RELIGION & SPIRITUALITY

0-7645-5146-9

0-7645-5418-2

Also available:
- Adoption For Dummies
  0-7645-5488-3
- Basketball For Dummies
  0-7645-5248-1
- The Bible For Dummies
  0-7645-5296-1
- Buddhism For Dummies
  0-7645-5359-3
- Catholicism For Dummies
  0-7645-5391-7
- Hockey For Dummies
  0-7645-5228-7

- Judaism For Dummies
  0-7645-5299-6
- Martial Arts For Dummies
  0-7645-5358-5
- Pilates For Dummies
  0-7645-5397-6
- Religion For Dummies
  0-7645-5264-3
- Teaching Kids to Read
  For Dummies
  0-7645-4043-2
- Weight Training For Dummies
  0-7645-5168-X
- Yoga For Dummies
  0-7645-5117-5

TRAVEL

0-7645-5438-7

0-7645-5453-0

Also available:
- Alaska For Dummies
  0-7645-1761-9
- Arizona For Dummies
  0-7645-6938-4
- Cancún and the Yucatán
  For Dummies
  0-7645-2437-2
- Cruise Vacations For Dummies
  0-7645-6941-4
- Europe For Dummies
  0-7645-5456-5
- Ireland For Dummies
  0-7645-5455-7

- Las Vegas For Dummies
  0-7645-5448-4
- London For Dummies
  0-7645-4277-X
- New York City For Dummies
  0-7645-6945-7
- Paris For Dummies
  0-7645-5494-8
- RV Vacations For Dummies
  0-7645-5443-3
- Walt Disney World & Orlando
  For Dummies
  0-7645-6943-0

GRAPHICS, DESIGN & WEB DEVELOPMENT

0-7645-4345-8

0-7645-5589-8

Also available:
- Adobe Acrobat 6 PDF
  For Dummies
  0-7645-3760-1
- Building a Web Site For Dummies
  0-7645-7144-3
- Dreamweaver MX 2004
  For Dummies
  0-7645-4342-3
- FrontPage 2003 For Dummies
  0-7645-3882-9
- HTML 4 For Dummies
  0-7645-1995-6
- Illustrator CS For Dummies
  0-7645-4084-X

- Macromedia Flash MX 2004
  For Dummies
  0-7645-4358-X
- Photoshop 7 All-in-One Desk
  Reference For Dummies
  0-7645-1667-1
- Photoshop CS Timesaving
  Techniques For Dummies
  0-7645-6782-9
- PHP 5 For Dummies
  0-7645-4166-8
- PowerPoint 2003 For Dummies
  0-7645-3908-6
- QuarkXPress 6 For Dummies
  0-7645-2593-X

NETWORKING, SECURITY, PROGRAMMING & DATABASES

0-7645-6852-3

0-7645-5784-X

Also available:
- A+ Certification For Dummies
  0-7645-4187-0
- Access 2003 All-in-One Desk
  Reference For Dummies
  0-7645-3988-4
- Beginning Programming
  For Dummies
  0-7645-4997-9
- C For Dummies
  0-7645-7068-4
- Firewalls For Dummies
  0-7645-4048-3
- Home Networking For Dummies
  0-7645-42796

- Network Security For Dummies
  0-7645-1679-5
- Networking For Dummies
  0-7645-1677-9
- TCP/IP For Dummies
  0-7645-1760-0
- VBA For Dummies
  0-7645-3989-2
- Wireless All In-One Desk Reference
  For Dummies
  0-7645-7496-5
- Wireless Home Networking
  For Dummies
  0-7645-3910-8